Natalya Shevchik Ketenci

KAZAKHSTANI ENTERPRISES IN TRANSITION

The Role of Historical Regional Development
in Kazakhstan's Post-Soviet Economic Transformation

ibidem-Verlag
Stuttgart

Bibliografische Information der Deutschen Nationalbibliothek
Die Deutsche Nationalbibliothek verzeichnet diese Publikation in der
Deutschen Nationalbibliografie; detaillierte bibliografische Daten sind im
Internet über http://dnb.d-nb.de abrufbar.

Bibliographic information published by the Deutsche Nationalbibliothek
Die Deutsche Nationalbibliothek lists this publication in the Deutsche Nationalbibliografie;
detailed bibliographic data are available in the Internet at http://dnb.d-nb.de.

Cover picture: Flailing in fall (painted by Idil Uz, 2006), copyright holder: Idil Uz.

∞

Gedruckt auf alterungsbeständigem, säurefreien Papier
Printed on acid-free paper

ISSN: 1614-3515

ISBN-10: 3-89821-831-7
ISBN-13: 978-3-89821-831-3

© *ibidem*-Verlag
Stuttgart 2008

Alle Rechte vorbehalten

Das Werk einschließlich aller seiner Teile ist urheberrechtlich geschützt. Jede Verwertung
außerhalb der engen Grenzen des Urheberrechtsgesetzes ist ohne Zustimmung des Verlages
unzulässig und strafbar. Dies gilt insbesondere für Vervielfältigungen,
Übersetzungen, Mikroverfilmungen und elektronische Speicherformen sowie die
Einspeicherung und Verarbeitung in elektronischen Systemen.

All rights reserved. No part of this publication may be reproduced, stored in or introduced into a retrieval
system, or transmitted, in any form, or by any means (electronical, mechanical, photocopying, recording or
otherwise) without the prior written permission of the publisher. Any person who does any unauthorized act
in relation to this publication may be liable to criminal prosecution and civil claims for damages.

Printed in Germany

Soviet and Post-Soviet Politics and Society (SPPS)   Vol. 83
ISSN 1614-3515

General Editor: Andreas Umland, *Catholic University of Eichstaett-Ingolstadt*, umland@stanfordalumni.org

Editorial Assistant: Olena Sivuda, *Dragomanov Pedagogical University of Kyiv*, sivuda@ukrcognita.com.ua

EDITORIAL COMMITTEE*

DOMESTIC & COMPARATIVE POLITICS
Prof. **Ellen Bos**, *Andrássy University of Budapest*
Dr. **Ingmar Bredies**, *Kyiv-Mohyla Academy*
Dr. **Andrey Kazantsev**, *MGIMO (U) MID RF, Moscow*
Prof. **Heiko Pleines**, *University of Bremen*
Prof. **Richard Sakwa**, *University of Kent at Canterbury*
Dr. **Sarah Whitmore**, *Oxford Brookes University*
Dr. **Harald Wydra**, *University of Cambridge*
SOCIETY, CLASS & ETHNICITY
Col. **David Glantz**, *"Journal of Slavic Military Studies"*
Dr. **Rashid Kaplanov**, *Russian Academy of Sciences*
Dr. **Marlène Laruelle**, *EHESS, Paris*
Dr. **Stephen Shulman**, *Southern Illinois University*
Prof. **Stefan Troebst**, *University of Leipzig*
POLITICAL ECONOMY & PUBLIC POLICY
Prof. em. **Marshall Goldman**, *Wellesley College, Mass.*
Dr. **Andreas Goldthau**, *Stiftung Wissenschaft und Politik*
Dr. **Robert Kravchuk**, *University of North Carolina*
Dr. **David Lane**, *University of Cambridge*
Dr. **Carol Leonard**, *University of Oxford*

Dr. **Maria Popova**, *McGill University, Montreal*
FOREIGN POLICY & INTERNATIONAL AFFAIRS
Dr. **Peter Duncan**, *University College London*
Dr. **Taras Kuzio**, *George Washington University, DC*
Prof. **Gerhard Mangott**, *University of Innsbruck*
Dr. **Diana Schmidt**, *University of Bremen*
Dr. **Lisbeth Tarlow**, *Harvard University, Cambridge*
Dr. **Christian Wipperfürth**, *N-Ost Network, Berlin*
Dr. **William Zimmerman**, *University of Michigan*
HISTORY, CULTURE & THOUGHT
Dr. **Catherine Andreyev**, *University of Oxford*
Prof. **Mark Bassin**, *University of Birmingham*
Dr. **Alexander Etkind**, *University of Cambridge*
Dr. **Gasan Gusejnov**, *University of Bremen*
Prof. em. **Walter Laqueur**, *Georgetown University*
Prof. **Leonid Luks**, *Catholic University of Eichstaett*
Dr. **Olga Malinova**, *Russian Academy of Sciences*
Dr. **Andrei Rogatchevski**, *University of Glasgow*
Dr. **Mark Tauger**, *West Virginia University*
Dr. **Stefan Wiederkehr**, *DHI, Warsaw*

ADVISORY BOARD*

Prof. **Dominique Arel**, *University of Ottawa*
Prof. **Jörg Baberowski**, *Humboldt University of Berlin*
Prof. **Margarita Balmaceda**, *Seton Hall University*
Dr. **John Barber**, *University of Cambridge*
Prof. **Timm Beichelt**, *European University Viadrina*
Prof. em. **Archie Brown**, *University of Oxford*
Dr. **Vyacheslav Bryukhovetsky**, *Kyiv-Mohyla Academy*
Prof. **Timothy Colton**, *Harvard University, Cambridge*
Prof. **Paul D'Anieri**, *University of Kansas, Lawrence*
Dr. **Heike Dörrenbächer**, *DGO, Berlin*
Dr. **John Dunlop**, *Hoover Institution, Stanford, California*
Dr. **Sabine Fischer**, *EU Institute for Security Studies*
Dr. **Geir Flikke**, *NUPI, Oslo*
Dr. **David Galbreath**, *University of Aberdeen*
Prof. **Alexander Galkin**, *Russian Academy of Sciences*
Prof. **Frank Golczewski**, *University of Hamburg*
Dr. **Nikolas Gvosdev**, *Naval War College, Newport, RI*
Prof. **Mark von Hagen**, *Arizona State University*
Dr. **Guido Hausmann**, *Trinity College Dublin*
Prof. **Dale Herspring**, *Kansas State University*
Dr. **Stefani Hoffman**, *Hebrew University of Jerusalem*
Prof. **Mikhail Ilyin**, *MGIMO (U) MID RF, Moscow*
Prof. **Vladimir Kantor**, *Higher School of Economics*
Dr. **Ivan Katchanovski**, *University of Toronto*
Prof. em. **Andrzej Korbonski**, *University of California*
Dr. **Iris Kempe**, *Heinrich Boell Foundation Tiblissi*
Prof. **Herbert Küpper**, *Institut für Ostrecht München*
Dr. **Rainer Lindner**, *Stiftung Wissenschaft und Politik*
Dr. **Vladimir Malakhov**, *Russian Academy of Sciences*
Dr. **Luke March**, *University of Edinburgh*

Prof. **Michael McFaul**, *Stanford University, California*
Prof. **Birgit Menzel**, *University of Mainz-Germersheim*
Prof. **Valery Mikhailenko**, *The Urals State University*
Prof. **Emil Pain**, *Higher School of Economics, Moscow*
Dr. **Oleg Podvintsev**, *Russian Academy of Sciences*
Prof. **Olga Popova**, *St. Petersburg State University*
Dr. **Alex Pravda**, *University of Oxford*
Dr. **Erik van Ree**, *University of Amsterdam*
Dr. **Joachim Rogall**, *Robert Bosch Foundation, Stuttgart*
Prof. **Peter Rutland**, *Wesleyan University, Middletown*
Dr. **Sergei Ryabov**, *Kyiv-Mohyla Academy*
Prof. **Marat Salikov**, *The Urals State Law Academy*
Dr. **Gwendolyn Sasse**, *University of Oxford*
Prof. **Jutta Scherrer**, *EHESS, Paris*
Prof. **Robert Service**, *University of Oxford*
Mr. **James Sherr**, *Defence Academy of the UK, Swindon*
Dr. **Oxana Shevel**, *Tufts University, Medford*
Prof. **Eberhard Schneider**, *University of Siegen*
Prof. **Olexander Shnyrkov**, *Shevchenko University, Kyiv*
Prof. **Hans-Henning Schröder**, *University of Bremen*
Prof. **Yuri Shapoval**, *Ukrainian Academy of Sciences*
Prof. **Viktor Shnirelman**, *Russian Academy of Sciences*
Dr. **Lisa Sundstrom**, *University of British Columbia*
Dr. **Philip Walters**, *"Religion, State and Society," Oxford*
Prof. **Zenon Wasyliw**, *Ithaca College, New York State*
Dr. **Lucan Way**, *University of Toronto*
Dr. **Markus Wehner**, *"Frankfurter Allgemeine Zeitung"*
Dr. **Andrew Wilson**, *University College London*
Prof. **Jan Zielonka**, *University of Oxford*
Prof. **Andrei Zorin**, *University of Oxford*

* While the Editorial Committee and Advisory Board support the General Editor in the choice and improvement of manuscripts for publication, responsibility for remaining errors and misinterpretations in the series' volumes lies with the books' authors.

Soviet and Post-Soviet Politics and Society (SPPS)
ISSN 1614-3515

Founded in 2004 and refereed since 2007, SPPS makes available affordable English-, German- and Russian-language studies on the history of the countries of the former Soviet bloc from the late Tsarist period to today. It publishes approximately 20 volumes per year, and focuses on issues in transitions to and from democracy such as economic crisis, identity formation, civil society development, and constitutional reform in CEE and the NIS. SPPS also aims to highlight so far understudied themes in East European studies such as right-wing radicalism, religious life, higher education, or human rights protection. The authors and titles of previously published and forthcoming manuscripts are listed at the end of this book. For a full description of the series and reviews of its books, see www.ibidem-verlag.de/red/spps.

Note for authors (as of 2007): After successful review, fully formatted and carefully edited electronic master copies of up to 250 pages will be published as b/w A5 paperbacks and marketed in Germany (e.g. vlb.de, buchkatalog.de, amazon.de) and internationally (e.g. amazon. com). For longer books, formatting/editorial assistance, different binding, oversize maps, coloured illustrations and other special arrangements, authors' fees between €100 and €1500 apply. Publication of German doctoral dissertations follows a separate procedure. Authors are asked to provide a high-quality electronic picture on the object of their study for the book's front-cover. Younger authors may add a foreword from an established scholar. Monograph authors and collected volume editors receive two free as well as further copies for a reduced authors' price, and will be asked to contribute to marketing their book as well as finding reviewers and review journals for them. These conditions are subject to yearly review, and to be modified, in the future. Further details at www.ibidem-verlag.de/red/spps-authors.

Editorial correspondence & manuscripts should, until 2011, be sent to: Dr. Andreas Umland, ZIMOS, Ostenstr. 27, 80572 Eichstätt, Germany; e-mail: umland@stanfordalumni.org

Business correspondence & review copy requests should be sent to: *ibidem*-Verlag, Julius-Leber-Weg 11, D-30457 Hannover, Germany; tel.: +49(0)511-2622200; fax: +49(0)511-2622201; spps@ibidem-verlag.de.

Book orders & payments should be made via the publisher's electronic book shop at: www.ibidem-verlag.de/red/SPPS_EN/

Authors, reviewers, referees, and editors for (as well as all other persons sympathetic to) the project "Soviet and Post-Soviet Politics and Society" are invited to join the series' free LinkedIn networking group at: www.linkedin.com/groupInvitation?groupID=103012&sharedKey=449BB20A48F8

Recent Volumes

75 *Heiko Pleines (Hrsg.)*
Corporate Governance in post-sozialistischen Volkswirtschaften
ISBN 978-3-89821-766-8

76 *Stefan Ihrig*
Wer sind die Moldawier?
Rumänismus versus Moldowanismus in Historiographie und Schulbüchern der Republik Moldova, 1991-2006
Mit einem Vorwort von Holm Sundhaussen
ISBN 978-3-89821-466-7

77 *Galina Kozhevnikova in collaboration with Alexander Verkhovsky and Eugene Veklerov*
Ultra-Nationalism and Hate Crimes in Contemporary Russia
The 2004-2006 Annual Reports of Moscow's SOVA Center
With a foreword by Stephen D. Shenfield
ISBN 978-3-89821-868-9

78 *Florian Küchler*
The Role of the European Union in Moldova's Transnistria Conflict
With a foreword by Christopher Hill
ISBN 978-3-89821-850-4

79 *Bernd Rechel*
The Long Way Back to Europe
Minority Protection in Bulgaria
With a foreword by Richard Crampton
ISBN 978-3-89821-863-4

80 *Peter W. Rodgers*
Nation, Region and History in Post-Communist Transitions
Identity Politics in Ukraine, 1991-2006
With a foreword by Vera Tolz
ISBN 978-3-89821-903-7

81 *Stephanie Solywoda*
The Life and Work of Semën L. Frank
A Study of Russian Religious Philosophy
With a foreword by Philip Walters
ISBN 978-3-89821-457-5

82 *Vera Sokolova*
Cultural Politics of Ethnicity
Discourses on Roma in Communist Czechoslovakia
ISBN 978-3-89821-822-1

To my parents

Contents

Acknowledgements

First and foremost this book would not have been undertaken without the kind and generous support of my parents Pyotr and Nina, who have supported me continuously throughout the duration of my studies.

Secondly, I have been fortunate from productive interactions with three supportive supervisors. Especially I am immensely grateful to Dr Yelena Kalyuzhnova, whose outstanding supervision, a decisive contribution, a valued advice and exceptional patience were fundamental to the completion of this book. I wish to thank Dr Philip McCann and Professor Mark Casson for their constructive criticisms and suggestions, which brought consistency and focus to the project.

Many thanks also to Simon Burke and Jean-Yves Pitarakis for their commendable help in areas of econometrics and statistical analysis; to Sandro Leidi who played important role in the creation of the database used in the study; and to Professor Christoph Bluth who provided outstanding contribution to the final result.

During my time at the Centre for Euro-Asian Studies I have benefited from the friendship of the Research students and incredible help of Administrative staff. I would especially like to mention Mrs Sylvia Smelt and Mrs Evelyn McDonald who always supported me, especially during harder times. I am grateful to the supportive School of Business in Reading, special thanks to Jill Turner, Carol Wright and Mrs. Newcombe for their generosity and patience. To the Institute of Economic Research and National Statistical Agency in Kazakhstan, Almaty for providing the data used in this book, without which the data administration would have been much painful.

Among my friends in the School of Business, I would like to thank especially to Rozanna Sarkeyeva and Togzhan Kassenova for their guidance and energy, and, especially, for their friendship forever. I am extremely grateful to Andrej Kalyuzhnov for his valuable advices and support throughout the whole period of studies. I extend my gratitude to Altay, Melis, Andrej, Nigora, Adil, Stefani, Raji and Evangelos. Their invaluable company and friendship enriched my life in Reading.

I am also grateful to reviewers and several academics for valuable comments on the project and during presentations in various academic meetings.

Finally, I thank the people who have been close and supportive all these years: none of this would have been possible without them.

I would never have done such work without the love of my husband Devrim, who constantly supported me.

Abstract

The study analyses data from a survey of Kazakhstani industrial enterprises in order to examine the relationship between industrial performance and the interregional structure of the economy. The study employs a firm-level production function approach, which captures the relationship between the production performance of an enterprise and its industrial and regional characteristics. A transformation of the production function approach allows the employment of a multinomial logit framework. Estimations of the logit model were made on the basis of more than 4000 observations of Kazakhstani industrial enterprises, in total, for the period between 1997 and 2001 on a quarterly basis. The data employed in the research consists of a mixture of secondary data from the national statistics agencies plus questionnaire data from a survey on individual Kazakhstani industrial enterprises. The dependent variable employed in the estimated model is a qualitative measure of the production performance of individual Kazakhstani industrial enterprises, while independent variables include individual, industry-specific and location-specific characteristics of the regional industrial enterprises. Model estimations for 20 quarters of the transition economy in chronological sequence indicate a picture of fluctuations and instability in the recovery of industrial enterprises from the shock effect of the Soviet collapse. The results of the study found support for the argument that the process of economic transition engenders significant spatial industrial restructuring, and that in addition to the characteristics of individual enterprises, the spatial aspects of this restructuring are key determinants of firm performance. Moreover, these effects of spatial restructuring appeared to dominate both industry-specific and location-specific characteristics.

List of Tables

15

List of Figures

List of Maps

Introduction

1.   The significance of the study

The regional development in transition is becoming an increasingly important issue both nationally and internationally, due to the high level of economic potential, which to date is not used in terms of regional co-operation for the efficient development of a country as a whole. The case study of this research is the Kazakhstani economy, which was part of the Soviet economic system until its collapse in 1991. During the Soviet era the study of inter-regional development did not receive a significant academic attention, where the development was concentrated purely on individual regions. Regions of the intensive development were a priority for the growth of the whole Soviet economy and at the same time they increased disparities on the inter-regional level.

Being a part of the Soviet economic system its republics had numerous benefits for their economies, where industrialization and infrastructure played key roles. Created during the Soviet era, industrial enterprises were integrated and linked vertically as well as horizontally across the whole country, where no account was taking of borders between its republics. The infrastructure of the Kazakhstani economy was created in order to facilitate the links between producers and markets of their finished and intermediate goods across the whole Soviet Union. Soviet industrial enterprises of the vertical integrations were connected to enterprises across the borders of republics. However, the build up of the economy infrastructure inside republics was not important enough for the functioning of the whole country. Nevertheless, the structure of the Soviet economy worked adequately and permitted the continuous growth of industrial sectors until 1985.

After the collapse of the Soviet Union, all its republics became newly independent states with no proper internal infrastructure. At the same time industrial links with other newly independent countries of the former Soviet Union were severed. As a result, industrial sectors of the post-Soviet economy had many enterprises in different republics that could no longer function because the links to other industrial enterprises had been vital to enable them to continue production. As a result many industrial enterprises were destroyed because the manufacturing chain of which they constituted one link was no longer viable. Thus, industrial sectors were at the edge of the collapse not only in one particular newly independent state, but in all new transitional countries of the former Soviet Union.

Kazakhstan is the one of few countries in the former Soviet Union, which is well endowed with mineral resources. During the Soviet era, Kazakhstan had a highly developed industry engaged in the extraction of raw materials and in the production of semi-finished goods. The specialisations of the Kazakh SSR in the Soviet industry were oil and gas, metallurgical, machine-building, and agricultural products. The main market for finished and intermediate goods of these sectors was outside the Kazakh SSR. After the collapse of the Soviet Union Kazakhstan was cut off from the main markets for its products, and some industrial enterprises were left without input sources. Production could not be maintained at the same level without sufficient demand and supply of input factors.

After the collapse of the Soviet Union, the socialist system, which was based on the central planning of the economy, has been abandoned in favour of the capitalist system[1]. Formerly Soviet republics followed the planning orders of the central authorities, who had planned all economic activities around the country and were the main decision makers who could not be questioned. However, after the collapse of the Soviet economy, newly independent states had gained independence in political terms, but found themselves literally abandoned in economic terms. The abolition of central planning left new states in a state of uncertainty as they lacked the information necessary to take actions that would permit the independent economies to operate. This

---

1   The Kornai (1998) change of system assumes that the economy shifts from the socialist system changing its specific characteristics towards capitalist system. However it does not mean that all features of the capitalist system immediately were present in the transition economy.

became the starting point for the transition process, which involved the transformation of these countries' economies into new market economies that might take a long time to be stabilised.

In such conditions of uncertainty and the lack of information on how to behave in order to reach desirable results, the main target of transition was the economic stabilisation through the World Bank and IMF package of reforms (International Monetary Fund, 1992). The elaborated regional policy of Kazakhstan did not bring expected results due to the high emphasis on the maintenance of priority regions, such as Western Kazakhstan (hydrocarbon rich regions), Akmola (the region of the new capital) and Almaty (the region of the former capital). Consequently, regions, that were initially better off, started to benefit from the development of the economy, however backward regions could not implement new programmes of development due to the reason of the initial lack of basic economic instruments, such as a developed infrastructure, education and central management, in order to adapt to changes in the economy. Therefore, every year of the transition process the disparities between central and peripheral regions in economic terms widen.

The purpose of this study is a better understanding of causes of the unequal regional development at the industrial level. The answer to the given question would be useful in the design and improvement of a regional policy for economic development and industrial concentration.

Kazakhstan is a valuable producer of oil and gas not only in the Caspian Sea region, but also beyond its borders. Kazakhstani oil extraction amounted to 4.52% of the oil production of the entire Soviet Union in 1990. By 2001 it accounted for 10.55% of oil extraction in the former Soviet Union, while its share of natural gas extraction increased from 0.87% to 1.84% during the same period. The oil and gas production of Kazakhstan as a proportion of world production is of course much lower, but is still a substantial for a single country. Thus, Kazakhstan's share of global oil extraction increased from 0.86% in 1990 to 1.12% in 2001, while its share of the global extraction of natural gas increased from 0.34% to 0.47% for the same period *(Kazakhstan: 1991-2002, 2002; Kazakhstan i strany SNG, 2001)*. However, the concentration on the production of oil and gas damages the whole economy of the country in terms of the lack of the support for the development of other industrial sectors. The higher diversification of the Kazakhstani economy in terms of its industrial sectors would help to the country to be less dependent on such a sensitive sector as the hydrocarbon sector, where success depends not only on internal factors. It also might be affected by external factors, such as world commodity prices. Therefore, the diversification of the economy could promote the development of Kazakhstani regions, which have a high degree of industrial specialisation.

Transition brought many changes to the Kazakhstani economy, which significantly improved the image of Kazakhstan in the world. The share of Kazakhstani exports to countries outside of the former Soviet Union increased from 44% of all exports in 1995 to 70% in 2001. These exports mainly consist of rare mineral resources *(Kazakhstan: 1991-2002,* 2002). However, there is still long way to go to improve that image and to reach a degree of economic stability. In order to design the appropriate policy for the growth of the economy of Kazakhstan, it is necessary to understand the performance of industries and the impact of their location, from the point of view that steady development of regions is the basis for the stable development of the Kazakhstani economy. The industrial economy consists of individual industrial enterprises, while their classification into groups defines the development of particular industrial sectors. Therefore, in order to understand the behaviour of industrial sectors, it is important to study the behaviour of individual industrial firms, where the location can play a crucial role with regard to their performance. Thus, this study will help to provide information on trends of industrial location in Kazakhstan in connection with the characteristics of particular industrial firms, which will play a crucial role in the definition of the regional policy design.

2. Objectives of the Study

The objectives of the present study fall into two parts. The first part examines the *first hypothesis,* which states that the performance of Kazakhstani industrial enterprises in terms of their production growth depends on the set of

specific characteristics of enterprises, such as individual, industrial and location. The second part of the study analyses the *second hypothesis,* which
states that the characteristics of Kazakhstani industrial enterprises were associated with their location, testing to what extent characteristics of industrial
enterprises in transition economies are statistically different for different locations. In addition, the research attempts to identify reasons for regional inequalities in terms of the performance of industrial sectors in Kazakhstan under conditions of transition. The vast territory of Kazakhstan (2.7 million km^2)
requires the fundamental co-operation between regions in order to provide
and to maintain the steady growth of the economy. However, there have been
few studies on regional development and even fewer on the causes of the
unequal regional development of Kazakhstan.

In order to analyse patterns of the behaviour of industrial enterprises by regions, a database on the performance on Kazakhstani industrial enterprises
was created. These enterprises were sampled into groups according to their
industrial sectors, regional location, size of workforce and ownership type and
analyses how the production behaviour of industrial enterprises is related to
their individual, industrial and location characteristics.

3. Organisation of the Study

The plan of this book is to begin with the analysis of location as a factor in the
industrial development of the Kazakh SSR in the Soviet economy. *The first
chapter* underlines trends of the location of particular industries in the Kazakh SSR, where the main reason for the allocation of industrial resources
and infrastructure development was based on the needs of the Soviet economy. The chapter is divided into several sections, which are organised according to the chronological periods of the development of industries in the
Kazakh SSR. The chapter starts from the analysis of the location of industrial
establishments in the Kazakh SSR in the beginning of its creation and during
the war and post-war periods. Then the chapter continues with the exploration of roots of the acceleration of agricultural development in regions adjacent to the Russian border and the industrial growth, which is related to the
growth of agriculture. Then it analyses the development and emergence of

Kazakh SSR industrial clusters on the basis of their location adjacent to borders with other Soviet republics. The next section discusses the period of changes, *perestroika*, where the administrative managerial system, which is analysed in the last chapter, started slowly to move towards giving enterprises greater responsibility for their finances. This had negative effects on the production of industries in the Kazakh SSR, whose causes and consequences are explored in the final section of the chapter. Finally, the last section introduces the administrative managerial system of the Soviet Union, where the planning approach and soft budget constraints played the key role in the production composition.

The second chapter of the study underlines and examines changes of location trends of the industrial performance of Kazakhstan since transition began. The chapter critically evaluates changes in the regional concentration of industrial activities in Kazakhstan caused by transition. Throughout the chapter, the attempt has been made to answer the question: why did the collapse of the Soviet Union negatively affect the industrial growth of Kazakhstan? This chapter begins with the analysis of the impact of the collapse of the Soviet Union on the Kazakhstani economy. It then presents the performance of Kazakhstani industries in the transition process and their reflection of the destabilised economic situation. Furthermore, the chapter highlights the trends of development of Kazakhstani regions and evaluates the need for a regional policy. Finally, the chapter explores the changes in the trends of industrial concentration of each region of Kazakhstan on the basis of the transition process and analyses the effect of the capital transfer on the performance of regional industries.

The third chapter explores the theoretical background of the regional economy applicable to transition economies and their differences in location choices compared to the neoclassical one and two sector models of factor allocation and migration. Neoclassical models are examined in order to investigate possibilities of their application to transition economies with reference to their specific initial conditions. This chapter represents models of interregional factor allocation and growth and attempts to understand how they can be appropriately used for the explanation of location behaviour in transition economies, particularly in ex-Soviet countries. The chapter is laid out as follows: after the short introduction (*3.1*) it presents an analysis of location patterns of industrial development in the Soviet Union on the basis of central planning (section *3.2*). The next section (*3.3*) analyses four models of inter-regional development in order to help to understand the possible outcomes of Kazakhstani regional development during the transition process towards a market economy. However, the free inter-regional mobility of such input factors as labour and capital in the transition economy does not always follow rules of classical regional theories. Therefore, the next section (*3.4*) presents theories and models of regional economics, which might explain the chaotic behaviour of industrial enterprises during transition. This section critically examines models of inter-regional labour migration under the conditions of a transition economy with the specific characteristics of Kazakhstan (e.g. the recent move of the capital). Finally, the chapter presents principles, which could explain the regional economy of Kazakhstan in transition, preparing the background for the next chapter, where the specific model will be applied for the empirical study of the Kazakhstani case.

The final chapter of the book presents the empirical study of the research. The first section presents and analyses the database used in the study and assesses the reliability of its data based on the questionnaire of industrial enterprises. The next section focuses on the model framework for the analysis of the dependence of firms' characteristics on their location followed by the introduction of variables for hypotheses tested in the study. The final section provides and analyses results of the econometric tests of hypotheses within the chosen model framework. Finally, the conclusion summarizes the findings of the study.

1 The Development of the Industrial Sector of the Kazakh SSR on the Basis of the Soviet Economic System

1.1 Introduction

Kazakhstan[2] is in the process of a fundamental transformation of the nature of its economy and radical changes in its industrial structure. This chapter aims to describe and analyse the economic initial conditions of the country by focusing on the industrial development of Kazakh SSR regions on the basis of the Soviet economy. A number of academic studies discuss the overall economic structural changes of Kazakhstan (Peck 2003; Kalyuzhnova 1998; Pomfret 1995, 1996; Kaser 1997; Olcott 1995, 2002; Amrekulov and Masanov 1994; and others), but only few highlight regional industrial perspectives (Massanov 1995; Koshanov, Isaeva and Yesentugelov 1993; Kenzheguzin, Isaeva 1998; and others). A focus on regional issues is important, since development in Kazakhstan was very uneven and industrial activities are concentrated in certain areas. In terms of income, employment, education and other economic opportunities, the disparity between the capital and the rest of the country has persisted over the decade of transition. This raises the question of how to decentralize growth and achieve more balanced development throughout the country.

The Soviet economic system was the basis for the formation of the contemporary Kazakh SSR economy for many years (1917-1991). Industrial devel-

---

2   The following terminology is used in this study: The term *Kazakh SSR* and *Kazakh SSR economy* refer to the country prior to 1991 during the Soviet period. On the other hand, *Kazakhstan* and *Kazakhstani economy* refer to the country prior to 1920 (when it was incorporated in the Soviet Union) and after 1991. Being a part of the Soviet Union, Kazakhstan was called the Kazakh Soviet Socialistic Republic (Kazakh SSR), and after gaining its independence from the Soviet Union in 1991, the country took its current name of Kazakhstan.

opment in the Kazakh SSR was based on the needs of the Soviet Union as a whole, with no consideration of any regional balance. Kazakhstan is a land-locked country, which makes it difficult for it to develop local industries for external trade; however, it is unique by its endowment with a wide variety of mineral resources. Being part of the Soviet Union, the Kazakh SSR happened to be one of the few republics that escaped the German occupation during the Second World War (1941-1945), which played the crucial role in relocation of industrial factories from occupied Soviet republics, such as Russia, Ukraine and Belarus. Factories were moved to distant republics, such as the Kazakh SSR and other Central Asian republics [3] from those occupied by German forces, in order to continue the production of important goods for the population and the war effort. Production facilities were located in regions close to sources of raw material with easy access to republics that remained under control of the USSR. Regions with railway links connecting the Kazakh SSR to republics under Soviet control had mostly benefited from the relocation of factories. The industrial development of the Kazakh SSR increased the inflow of skilled labour to provide the manpower need by the new factories, which significantly increased the skills level of local labour. Industrial enterprises, which moved to the Kazakh SSR not only recovered their production, but also created additional branches in order to satisfy the growing demand of the occupied republics. After the war ended in 1945 many industrial enterprises were left in the Kazakh SSR together with some of the workforce that had moved there. Thus, the Kazakh SSR experienced intensive industrial development not only during the war but also after the war, when industries in the Kazakh SSR were appealed for help with the recovery of destroyed industrial enterprises in occupied republics of the Soviet Union. Thus the development and production level of Kazakh SSR industries was significantly increased.

Thus, the economy of the Kazakh SSR was specifically created on the basis of political decisions, in order to provide for the accelerating needs of the growing Soviet Union and its war effort. It was a response to the wartime cri-

---

3   In terminology of the Soviet Union, Central Asia included the Kyrgyz SSR, the Uzbek SSR, the Turkmen SSR and the Tajik SSR, while the Kazakh SSR was considered separately.

sis and the movement of production activities to the Kazakh SSR. After the war, there was not incentive for industrial enterprises to locate in other regions of the Kazakh SSR as economic decisions were centralised and administratively governed by the Central Government of the Soviet Union. Therefore, the efficient pattern of locating industrial capacity was considered from the point of view of Soviet central planning and not on the basis of the requirements for the efficient development of the Kazakh SSR itself. The underdeveloped infrastructure in regions, which did not have a strategic location and resources for Soviet development, placed a further constraint on the relocation of industry. As a result, the industrial development of the Kazakh SSR is polarised and clustered in few locations, which were determined by the location of important resources for the Soviet Union and easy access to Russia. The development of agricultural regions of the Kazakh SSR at the beginning of the 1950s was based on the growing needs of the Soviet Union as well, however, only northern regions of the Kazakh SSR experienced intensive development due to their proximity to the Russian border. The Russian Federation was one of the main transit territories for the transportation of agricultural output to other Soviet republics, which had other comparative advantages for the total production of the Soviet Union.

At the outset of transition the economy of the Kazakh SSR was the product of the Soviet planned economy based on political decisions with regard to the allocation of industrial capacity, where regions of the Kazakh SSR and its industrial clusters were connected to other Soviet republics, rather than having internal links. Consequently, the system in Kazakhstan was characterised by uneven regional development, which had a very detrimental impact on the whole economy after the collapse of the Soviet Union. Therefore, in order to attempt to explain the unbalanced growth of regional development of Kazakhstan, it is important to analyse the experiences of regional development in the country and examine the role of industrialisation in the country's regional development under the Soviet system, and to assess the gains and losses of regions from centralised management of their industrialisation.

The chapter is divided into several parts, which are organised according to distinct periods of the development of the Soviet economic system. The chapter starts from the analysis of the location of industry in the Kazakh SSR on the basis of Soviet central planning in the beginning of its creation and during the war and post-war periods. Then the chapter continues with the exploration of the roots of agricultural development in regions close to the Russian border and analyses the development of industrial clusters in the Kazakh SSR on the basis of their proximate location to borders with other Soviet republics. The next section discusses the period of changes, *perestroika*, when the administrative managerial system, which is analysed in the last section of the chapter, started slowly to move towards giving enterprises greater responsibility for their financial activities. It is shown that this had a negative effect on industrial production in the Kazakh SSR. The causes and consequences of this are explored in the final part of the chapter. Finally, the last section introduces the administrative managerial system of the Soviet Union, where the approach to planning and soft budget constraints played the key role in determining the organisation of production.

1.2   The establishment of industrial sectors prior and during the Second World War

Historically, Kazakhstan had a nomadic style of life. The majority of the population were migrating livestock farmers and were not engaged in agriculture, except in regions that were located along the rivers Syrdariya, Talas and Chu (the Kzylorda, Zhambyl and Southern Kazakhstan regions, Map 1. Regional division of Kazakhstan, 2003). These three regions compose the Southern part of Kazakhstan with a very warm climate. The presence of rivers makes this part of Kazakhstan very favourable for plant farming. Following the affiliation with Russia in the second part of the 19th century, Kazakhstan significantly developed plant farming and started to create its first industrial firms. Thus, the end of the 19th century was characterised by the mass migration of Russian, Ukrainian, Tatar and Moldavian peasants to Kazakhstan as a result of crop failure and famine in their homeland. Therefore, in order to derive the greatest benefits from farming, migrant-peasants occupied the most suitable lands of Kazakhstan, which did not require artificial irrigation. These regions were located in the north, east and south east of Kazakhstan, i.e. the

Kostanai, Akmola, Pavlodar regions, the Northern and Eastern Kazakhstan regions, and the Almaty region, where migrant-peasants brought a fresh wave of agricultural development, significantly increasing the proportion of Russian people in these regions. However, later in the transition period, the economy of these regions suffered losses as a result of a high percentage of the migration of Russian people from Kazakhstan. Many industries experienced a shortage of labour, including qualified specialists.

The second part of the 19th century is defined as the start of industrial development, led by the mining industry. The central part of Kazakhstan – the Karaganda region became the principal location of newly developed mines. At the end of the 19th and at the beginning of the 20th century[4], the volume of industrial production of Kazakhstan accounted for only 15 % of the total GDP of Kazakhstan (Figure 1.1.) and amounted to a mere 0.7% of the total volume of industrial production of Russia (*Sovetskii Soiuz – Kazakhstan*, 1970). The remaining 85% of Kazakhstani GDP was accounted for by agricultural production.

---

4   Considering period is between 1880 and 1912-13.

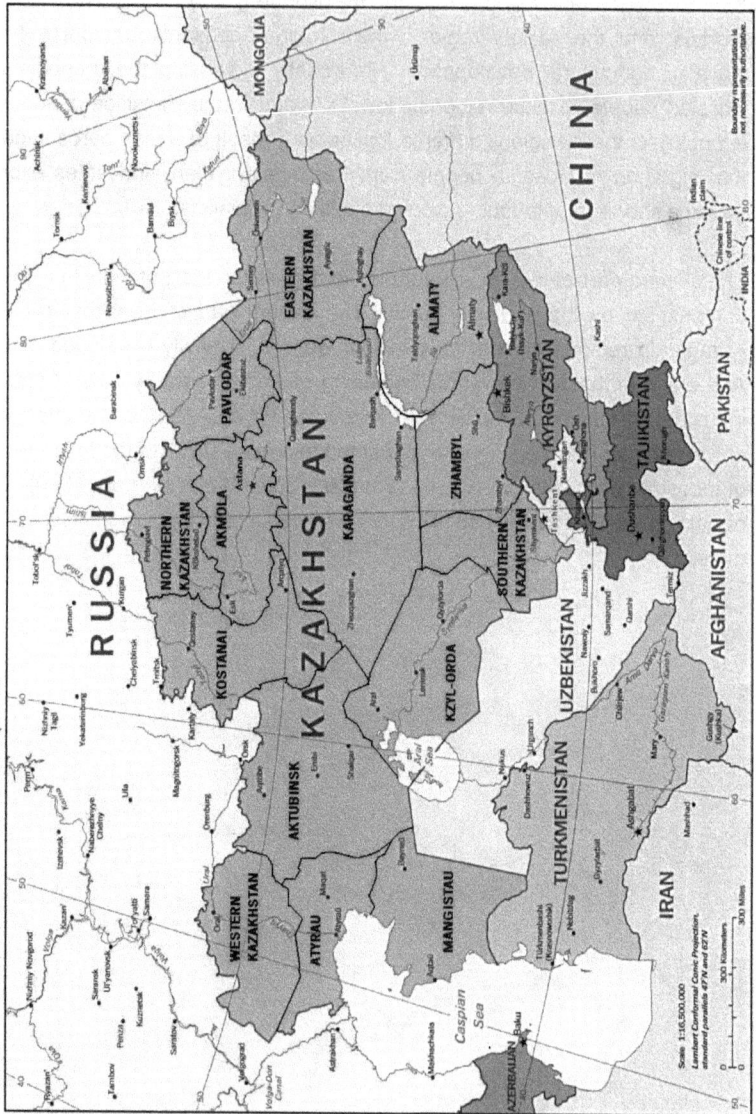

MAP 1   REGIONAL DIVISION OF KAZAKHSTAN, 2003

Food industry accounted for the main share of industrial production (63%), consisting of wheat mills, butcheries, distilleries and breweries. Light industry[5] accounted for 11% of industrial production, mainly the production of cotton, wool and leather. As a result of close cooperation between Russia and Kazakhstan, the factories were located in the northern and eastern regions of Kazakhstan, which share a border with Russia. Intermediate goods manufactured by Kazakhstani light industry were transported to Russia for the production of finished goods. The mining industry was responsible for 20% of the volume of industrial production with factories located throughout the whole of Kazakhstan. Coal mining was concentrated in the Karaganda region, mineral resources, copper and lead mining and manufacture in Eastern and Central Kazakhstan, oil in the Aktubinsk region (on the Emba river) and salt in the Pavlodar and Kzyl-Orda regions.

In 1920, Kazakhstan entered the Soviet Union with its title changed to the Kazakh Soviet Socialist Republic (the Kazakh SSR). The Kazakh SSR was rich with raw materials, however, industry accounted only for 20% of GDP, while the remainder came from agriculture. In order to benefit from the possession of the Kazakh SSR of unique raw mineral materials, the Soviet Union made industrial development in the Kazakh SSR a priority. Entire branches of industry were created, such as chemical, metallurgical, oil and gas industries. New factories for food, light and mining industries were built and old factories were refurbished and modernised. At the same time the railway network was developed with the building of new rail lines to link the central and southern regions of the Kazakh SSR with Russia (Map 2. *Main roads of the Kazakh SSR by 1970*). The industrial development of the Kazakh SSR was directed to the markets of the whole Soviet Union and not specifically those of the Kazakh republic. However, at the beginning of the 1930s the ability of the industries of the Kazakh SSR to sell their products throughout the Soviet Union contributed to industrial growth, which doubled the share of industrial production as a proportion of the GDP of the Kazakh SSR (amounting to 40%).

---

5   The light industry includes the production of goods for consumption such as different types of textile (cotton, wool, silk, linen) leather, fur, clothing, shoes and clothing accessories. (*Ekonomicheskaia enciklopediia-1*, 1962).

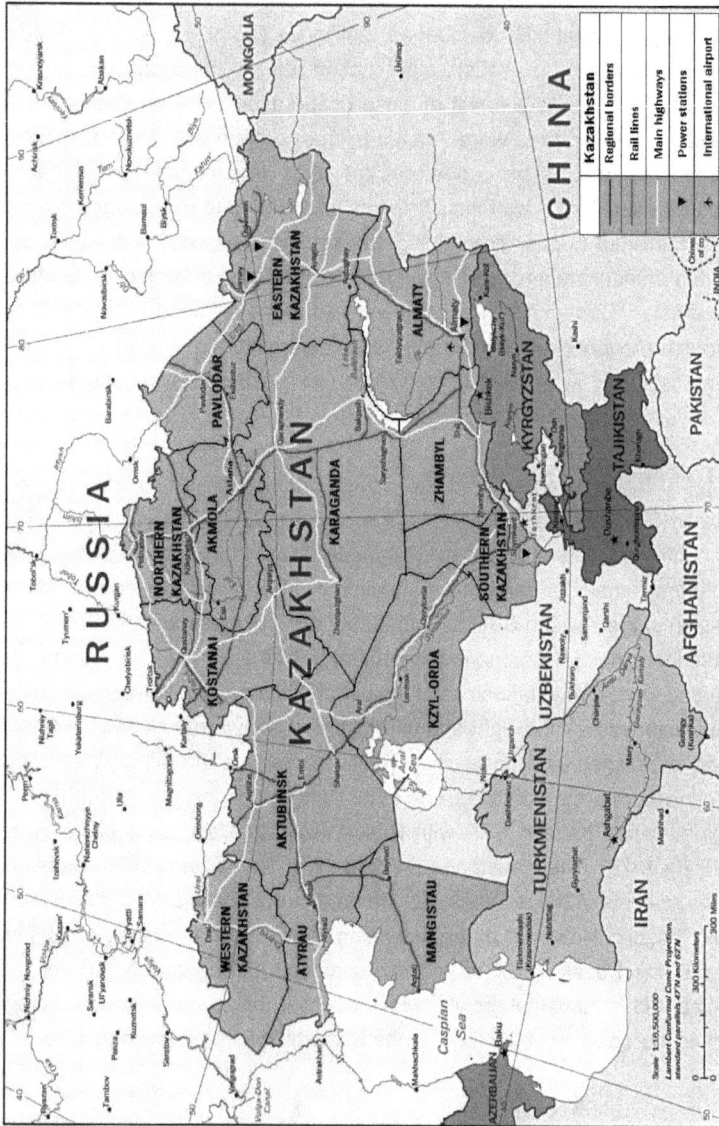

MAP 2 MAIN ROADS OF THE KAZAKH SSR BY 1970

Figure 1.1. Division of GDP in Kazakhstan at the end of the 19th and at the beginning of the 20th century.

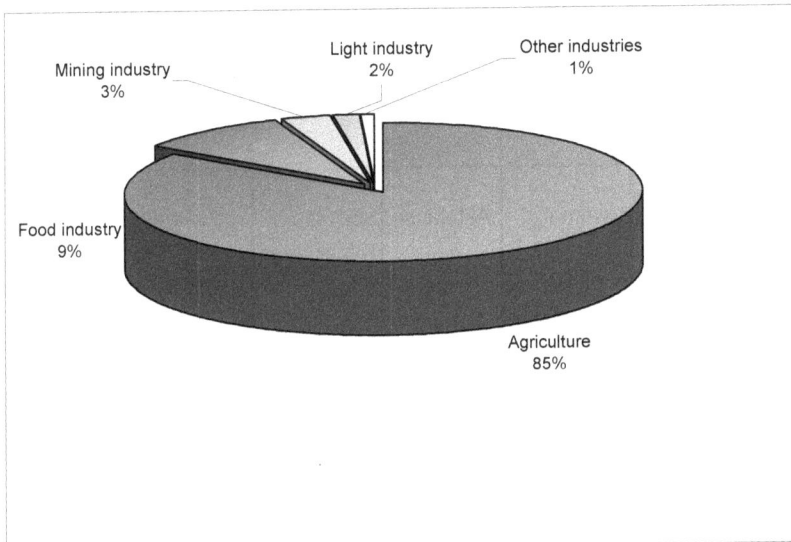

Source: *Sovetskii Soiuz – Kazakhstan*, 1970.

In the mid-1930s Karaganda's coal manufacture became third in the Soviet Union by production volume. The Atyrau and Aktubinsk regions became important regions in the Soviet Union for oil production. Southern and eastern regions of the Kazakh SSR were progressing in the development of metallurgical industry and grew to be the main metallurgical centres of the Soviet Union. By the end of the 1930s the Kazakh SSR had become one of the biggest and most important centres of mineral resources for the Soviet Union after Russia, whose industries became dependent on the raw materials of the Kazakh SSR.

Table 1.1. Specialisation of regions at the end of 19th and beginning of 20th centuries.

Agriculture	Industries				Backward[6] regions
	Light	Mining[7]	Chemical	Food	
Almaty	Almaty	Aktubinsk	Southern Kazakhstan	Almaty	Atyrau
Akmola	Eastern Kazakhstan	Eastern Kazakhstan		Akmola	Mangistau
Eastern Kazakhstan	Northern Kazakhstan	Karaganda		Eastern Kazakhstan	Western Kazakhstan
Kostanai		Kzyl-Orda		Kostanai	
Kzyl-Orda		Pavlodar		Kzyl-Orda	
Northern Kazakhstan				Northern Kazakhstan	
Pavlodar				Pavlodar	
Southern Kazakhstan				Southern Kazakhstan	
Zhambyl				Zhambyl	

Source: Sovetskii Soiuz – Kazakhstan, 1970.

---

6   Backward regions are regions with the low or absent development of any economic sectors and which are not presented in any of the introduced categories of the table.

7   The mining industry includes industries extracting raw materials for the further manufacture. The mining industry includes extraction sectors of chemical industry, fuel, construction, power and metallurgy industries.

By the middle of 1941, the volume of the Kazakh SSR industrial production reached 60% of GDP. The economy of the Kazakh SSR had moved from being dominated by agriculture to one that could be characterized as agro-industrial. However, industrial production in the Kazakh SSR mainly concentrated on the manufacture of semi-finished goods, while the final production was located in Russia and other central republics of the Soviet Union due to their proximity to the principal markets for industrial products in the Soviet Union.

Regional development during World War II

During the Second World War (1941-1945) the Kazakh SSR provided the industrial base for the western occupied regions of the Soviet Union. 142 large industrial factories were moved to the Kazakh SSR, in order to continue production (*Ekonomika Kazakhstana za 60 let: 1917-1977*, 1977). More than 100 of them recovered their previous rate of production, while the remainder were used for the establishment of new manufacturing capacities in the Kazakh SSR, such as machine-building and ferrous metallurgy industries. Despite difficult war times, factories that were brought from other parts of the Soviet Union were located in the Kazakh SSR according to the best access to inputs, such as the provision of raw materials and labour. However, not only factories were moved to the Kazakh SSR, but also a significant number of workers and specialists were evacuated to the Kazakh SSR to maintain work for these factories and to qualify the local labour.

Taking into account that the Kazakh SSR was one of the main mineral resource centres of the Soviet Union, the government developed special wartime programmes for the increase of the financial and material support to aid the development of fuel, energy, metallurgical and machine-building industries. Factories in the Kazakh SSR supplied fighting regions of the Soviet Union with military equipment, arms, fuel and provisions. Therefore non-ferrous metallurgy took the first place in production and importance among all other Soviet republics, while the coal, oil and gas industries of the Kazakh SSR replaced leading industries located in occupied western parts of the Soviet Union during the Second World War. Thus, due to the intensive development[8] of south eastern supportive regions of the Soviet Union, the industrial production volume of the Kazakh SSR, Central Asia and southern regions of Russia[9], increased by a factor of 2.9 in the three years since 1940. As a result, industrial production accounted for 66% of GDP in 1945, compared to 60% in 1940, while other regions of the Soviet Union experienced a significant fall in the whole economy including industrial production (*Ekonomicheskoe razvitie Kazakhskoi SSR*, 1960).

During the war period, many factories of the heavy industry[10] were not only brought from other Soviet Union regions, but additional capacity was created and built in the Kazakh SSR. New metallurgical and ferroalloy factories were built in the *Aktubinsk* region; manganese and nickel ore production started in the *Karaganda* and the Aktubinsk regions, a poly-metallic factory was created in the *Almaty* region, and the ferrous metallurgy of the Kazakh SSR originated from these factories. Due to the acceleration of industrial development in the Kazakh SSR, the republic took the leading position in the production of many important mineral resources. Thus, 2/3 of the entire Soviet molybdenum production took place in the Kazakh SSR. At the same time it produced 80-90% of all the lead and copper in the Soviet Union.

Some factories that produced semi- and finished products of mineral resources were occupied or destroyed during the war as in the case of manganese and wolfram factories in Ukraine and Caucasus, which were the only factories in the Soviet Union for manganese, molybdenum and wolfram. Therefore, as the only source-country left in the Soviet Union for these min-

---

8   Intensive development of the economy implies the productivity growth, decline of production costs and growth of the production on the basis of existing resources. The enhancement of the technology is based on the research and development. (*Ekonomicheskaia enciklopediia-1*, 1962).

9   Central Asia and Southern regions of Russia played the same role during the war as the Kazakh SSR, by supplying the rest of the occupied country with necessary provisions including military equipment.

10 The heavy industry includes the production of goods for the production such as different types of machinery, equipment and raw materials. The heavy industry includes chemical industry, construction, fuel, machine building, metallurgy, power and timber industries. (*Ekonomicheskaia enciklopediia-3*, 1965).

eral resources, the Kazakh SSR had to substitute for the production of lost mineral resources for the whole Soviet Union. As a result, for a very short period, molybdenum mine and refineries were built in the *Almaty* region, and a wolfram factory was built in the *Karaganda* region. Metallurgical and fuel industries saw the most intensive development during the war as their production was the most strategic issue for the armed forces of the Soviet Union. Being the only mineral resource – rich republic in the Soviet Union not occupied by German forces, the Kazakh SSR was supplied with financial, material resources and labour from all over the country to aid the development of the economy of the Kazakh SSR. Russian engineers worked on new projects in industries of the Kazakh SSR, Uzbek factories produced equipment for them, and Ukrainian labour worked in these factories. Thus every single factory in the Kazakh SSR had a intra-Soviet multinational background, while industrial production was growing and diversifying to supply the entire Soviet Union.

The *Karaganda* region developed 20 new coalmines during the war period, increasing the coal production in 1945 to a level 5 times that of 1940 (*Ekonomicheskoe razvitie Kazakhskoi SSR*, 1960). A new oil refinery was built in the *Atyrau* region as three new oil fields came onstream together with 55 kilometres of pipelines, which permitted the extraction of oil to be increased by 26% during the war period. In 1944 and 1945, electricity generation was increased by 50%, while output of industrial power stations was doubled. Twelve new power stations were built including industrial power stations, which supplied electricity to its factories.

Despite the priority accorded the development of fuel and metallurgy industries, light industry increased its production, during the war period by more than 75% (*Ekonomika Kazakhstana za 60 let: 1917-1977*, 1977). About 20 factories for light industry were relocated to the Kazakh SSR from other parts of the Soviet Union and about 10 new factories were built during that time. Light industry factories mainly produced military textiles for soldiers. Thus, during the war years the capacity of light industry increased several times; for example, the manufacture of textiles doubled its capacity, the cloth production increased its capacity threefold, the manufacture of leather products tenfold and that of shoes – twelvefold (*Ocherki ekonomicheskoi istorii Kazahskoi SSR*, 1974).

Due to the urgent need to transport manufactured goods to occupied regions of the Soviet Union, the railway system was developed at the same time as industrial capacity. The length of railway lines increased by 25% by the end of 1945 compared to 1940 (*Ekonomicheskoe razvitie Kazakhskoi SSR*, 1960). As fuel and metallurgical industries were the most strategic for the army, the amount of fuel products transported by railway doubled during the war years and the amount of metallurgical products transported increased by a factor of four. Railways connected remote regions of the Kazakh SSR, which produced essential goods for the Soviet Union, to central regions of Russia. Such a favourable structure of the railway system gave a boost to internal development. The regions of the Kazakh SSR could use the main railway lines connected to Russia or other neighbouring republics, for the improvement of their inter regional industrial relations. However, regions located outside of the main railway network still did not have rail connections to other regions, as the development of railway lines was confined to long-distance links between the republics and not on the creation of effective intra-republican networks (Map 2. *Main roads of the Kazakh SSR by 1970*). This particular way of developing the transport infrastructure increased the degree of crisis for the Kazakh SSR after the collapse of the Soviet system, when the underdevelopment of necessary inter-regional links inside the republic became apparent.

Figure 1.2. Industrial production, 1940 - 1945, (1940 = 100),%.

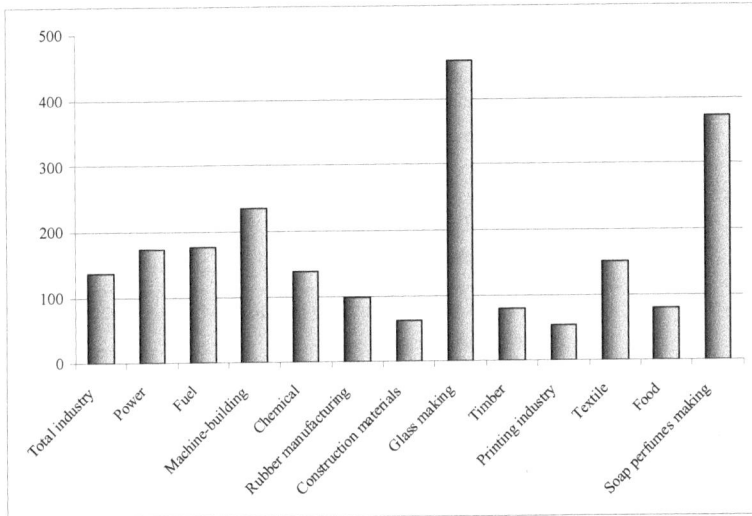

Source: *Ekonomicheskoe razvitie Kazakhskoi SSR*, 1960.

Developing the economy for the needs of the Soviet Union, the whole industry of the Kazakh SSR experienced growth during 5 years of war, which amounted to 36.8% in 1945, when many industries were developing very fast, while newly founded industries were soaring.

44   NATALYA SHEVCHIK KETENCI

Table 1.2.   Main factories created during the war period, 1941-1945.

Regions	Factories
Aktubinsk	Ferroalloy factory, chemical factory, thermo electro station of chemical factory, oil fields
Almaty	Poly metallurgical factory, molybdenum mine and factory, electro and hydro electro stations of industrial factories, machine-building factory, textile factory.
Atyrau	Oil refinery, 55 kilometres oil pipelines, oil fields, thermo electro station of the oil refinery
Eastern Kazakstan	Footwear factory, textile fabric,
Karaganda	Manganese mine, wolfram factory, 20 coal mines,
Southern Kazakstan	Chemical factory, footwear factory, cotton factory

Source: *Ekonomicheskoe razvitie Kazakhskoi SSR*, 1960. *Ekonomika Kazakhstana za 60 let. 1917-1977*, 1977. *Sovetskii Soiuz – Kazakhstan*, 1970.

However, not all industries experienced growth of their production; for example, the construction materials industry faced a decline in production volume by 37% (Figure 1.2.), timber production decreased by 20% and the production of the printing industry fell by 43.3%. Even though the Kazakh SSR was one of the main suppliers of the food industry production to the military and occupied regions of the Soviet Union during the war period, its production declined by 20.5% (Figure 1.2.). The reason for the fall in production of some industries in the same environment in which other industries experienced sharp increases is that these industries were not considered as vital as fuel or metallurgical industries during wartime. Therefore, human capital was to some extent moved to other essential industries and it was not possible to attract financial or any other additional help, as all forces were directed to the industries that were given priority for the war effort.

The overall decline in the production of the food industry during the war was indicated by the fact that the production of some goods, which were not vital such as sugar dropped by 65% during the war period, while spirit production fell by 70%, and the production of such vital goods as meat and milk increased by 30%. At the same time, 35 new factories were built in the Kazakh SSR for different kinds of food production, including sectors new to the Kazakh SSR such as pastry, macaroni, lard and tea. Together with existing factories, they provided the armed forces, the occupied republics and the whole country with food. Despite the overall decline in the food industry, the food production in rural areas increased. The production of vegetables grew threefold, meat production increased by 27%, milk by 10% and wool production grew by 40% (*Narodnoe xoziaistvo Kazakhskoi SSR za 25 let*, 1945). Because of this, agriculture developed significantly in rural areas, however, the main market for these goods was outside the Kazakh SSR.

On the regional level, the *central and southern regions* of the Kazakh SSR experienced the highest level of development during the war period because of the intensive development of fuel and metallurgical industries, which became their areas of specialisation. The *Atyrau* region changed from being classified as one of the backward regions (Table 1.1.) to one with the mining industry as its specialisation, due to the development of oil fields and the new oil refinery. The *Almaty* region achieved the most diversified development during the period 1941-1945 (Table 1.2.), having a competitive advantage with regard to location (distant from occupied parts of the Soviet Union) and resources sufficient for diversified development, so that all economic sectors were significantly boosted.

The progress achieved by the industry of the Kazakh SSR, would not have been possible without the support of a skilled labour force from other parts of the Soviet Union, which manifested itself in the increase of industrial employment in the Kazakh SSR by 38% over five years of war. Qualified human capital was brought to the Kazakh SSR due to evacuation from western and central occupied parts of the Soviet Union together with whole factories, while sharing qualifications and experience with Kazakh SSR labour, which contin-

ued the development and growth of newly created industries, such as machine-building and metallurgy after the war period.

After the war ended, many workers who had been relocated from other parts
of the Soviet Union returned to their homelands. However, a substantial number remained in the Kazakh SSR. In this way the majority of industrial factories that had been relocated during the war period remained in the Kazakh
SSR and supported industrial development in the republic. While many regions of the Soviet Union, which had been occupied during the war, only
reached their pre-war level of development by 1949, the economic development of the Kazakh SSR was ahead of other Soviet Union Republics after the
war period, reaching a more advanced and diversified level. However, the
wartime changes had not only positive consequences. Since a lot of new factories were built and moved from occupied regions, there was a significant
lack of energy and labour for their maintenance, which had to be withdrawn
from other sectors of the economy. As a result, a cut in the production of
goods that were based on imported raw materials occurred, while the production of goods with the use of local raw materials intensified. Some industries
significantly decreased and sometimes ceased the production of some products that were not strategic for the war, but still necessary for living. As a result, the "cards system" was introduced, which limited the acquisition of such
products per person. Because of men being involved in military action, the
percentage of women among industrial workers significantly increased. They
accounted for 47.6% of industrial employment and more than 50% in strategic
industries, such as fuel, metallurgy and light.

At the end and after the war workers in the Kazakh SSR were responsible for
the recovery of the economy of occupied regions of the Soviet Union, where
the skilled labour of the Karaganda region together with appropriate equipment were directed to develop mines and metallurgical factories in Ukraine.
Not only industries demanded help, but agriculture as well. Northern regions
of the Kazakh SSR gave extensive support to the Soviet Union from the agricultural sector as it was not an occupied region and succeeded in development during the wartime, while Eastern Kazakhstan and the Almaty region
were sending textiles, footwear, food provision, agricultural equipment, tools

and qualified agricultural specialists for further development. Regions of the Kazakh SSR were making maximum efforts to advance their specialisations in order to satisfy the needs of the Soviet Union, while no attention was paid to the coherent economic development of the Kazakh SSR as a whole.

1.3 The acceleration of growth, 1945-1953

The Soviet government created a war-recovery development programme, where the Kazakh SSR had targets to continue the development and advance industries that were connected with the production and use of mineral resources. It was important to reschedule the industrial working programme from strategic war production to the recovery and peace style that included the resumption of the production of goods, which were not of strategic importance during the war and whose production therefore had been significantly cut. The war and post-war development of industries in the Kazakh SSR increased their production by 231% between 1940 and 1950. The Kazakh SSR took fourth place in the Soviet Union after Estonian, Latvian and Armenian SSR with growth rates of 342, 303 and 249% respectively.

Heavy industry[11] became the main specialisation of the Kazakh SSR due to the intensive development during and after the war and accounted for 75.8% of total industrial production in 1950. *Light industry*[12] doubled its production between 1940 and 1950, while *heavy industry* raised its production by more than three times. The more progressive expansion of industrial development in the Kazakh SSR compared to the whole Soviet Union can be seen from the growth rates of the fixed capital, which increased by a factor of four between 1940 and 1950, while industrial fixed capital in the Soviet Union as a whole grew only by 54% in the same period. The difference in growth rates increased in 1953, when industrial fixed capital in the Kazakh SSR grew to a level of 6.6 times that of 1940, while that of the whole Soviet Union grew to a level of 2.1 times that of 1940. The reason for such uneven development was

---

11   See the footnote 10
12   See the footnote 5

the wartime occupation of some Soviet Union regions, where fixed capital had been completely destroyed, while the Kazakh SSR was not in the zone of war. The evacuation of plants and factories from other parts of the Soviet Union benefited the economic development of the Kazakh SSR, while the recovery of industrial assets of occupied republics took enormous time and capital. The recovery of regions of the Soviet Union affected by the war depended to some extent on industrial production from the Kazakh SSR, therefore, the transport network was important to supply the markets of the Soviet Union, while internal connections were not developed.

Table 1.3. The dynamics of the post-war development of industries in the Kazakh SSR, 1945-1953, %

Industries	1950 (1945=100)	1953 (1950=100)
Power	281.7	151.5
Fuel	164.4	139.5
Ferrous metallurgy	181.0	200.0
Non-ferrous metallurgy	101.0	160.1
Machine-building	180.0	142.2
Rubber manufacturing	116.1	310.6
Construction materials	479.5	157.5
Chemical	161	161
Timber	203.8	119.4
Textile	139.1	145.2
Food	160.2	120.2
Printing industry	186.7	159.7

Source: *Ekonomicheskoe razvitie Kazahskoj SSR,* 1960.

The majority of industries had increased their production by 1950 compared to 1945, the last year of war (Table 1.3.). This indicates that the intensive development of industries was not a strategic objective during the war and as a result they experienced a decline of their production at that time (Figure 1.2.). Thus the production of *construction materials, timber* and *food* industries had declined during the five years of war by 36.9%, 20.2% and 20.5% respectively, while in the five years after the war the production of these industries rose significantly (by 379.5%, 103.8% and 60.2% respectively). New industries, such as *ferrous metallurgy* and *machine-building*, continued to develop after the war with a high rate of growth (Table 1.3.) as they retained their skilled and experienced labour. One of the main targets of industrial development was the increase in the production of the *power* industry, in order to provide enough energy for intensive growth of different industries. The Kazakh SSR raised the *power* output by 181.7% over the 1945-1950 period. Because of intensive development of the Kazakh SSR economy, the *construction materials* and *power* industries were becoming a strategic priority in the country, in order to maintain the expansion of the rest of the economy.

Figure 1.3. Volume of industrial production in the Kazakh SSR by regions, 1950/1940, %

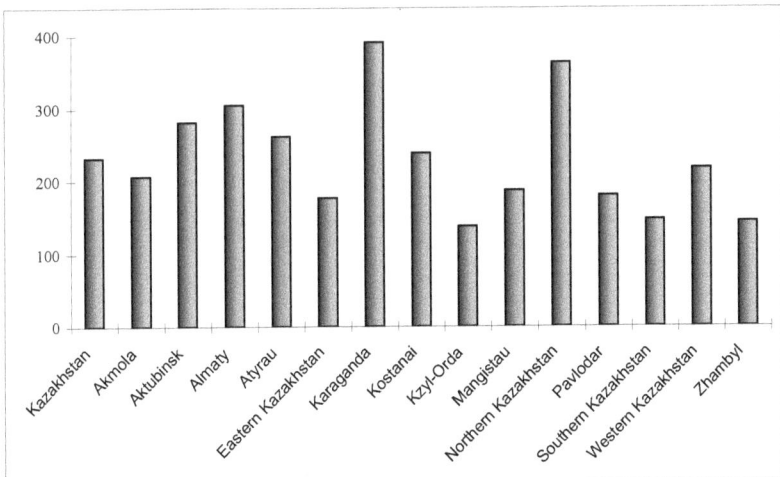

Source: *Promyshlennost' Kazakhstana: 1920-1999 goda*, 2000

The volume of industrial production of the Kazakh SSR increased by 132% between 1940 and 1950. All regions contributed to this growth by significantly increasing their industrial production (Figure 1.3.). The highest growth of industrial production was observed in the *Karaganda* region, where industrial development was diversified with a significant share in the republican output of fuel, mining, metallurgical and construction materials industries (Map 3 Industrial specialisation of the Kazakh SSR region, 1945-1991).

Table[13] 1.4.   Production indices of fuel and mining industries by regions, 1950/1940,%

Regions	Fuel						Mining			
	Coal	Share, 1950	Oil	Share, 1950	Natural Gas	Share, 1950	Copper ore	Share, 1950	Zinc-lead ore	Share, 1950
Kazakh SSR	*249.1*	*100*	*151.9*	*100*	*189.7*	*100*	*241.5*	*100*	*208.8*	*100*
Akmola	105.5	0.4								
Aktubinsk	259.6	0.7	100	24.5	189.7	100				
Almaty									426.9	14.7
Atyrau			182.6	75.5						
Eastern Kazakhstan									186.2	62.8
Karaganda	254.8	94.8					241.5	100		
Kostanai										
Kzyl-Orda										
Mangistau[14]										
Northern Kazakhstan										
Pavlodar	146.9	0.3								
Southern Kazakhstan	187.1	3.76							158.7	22.5
Western Kazakhstan										
Zhambyl										

Source: Data were calculated using: *Promyshlennost' Kazakhstana: 1920-1999 goda*, 2000

---

13   Tables 1.4., 1.5. and 1.6. represent industrial production changes from 1940 to 1950 by regions. The assortment of industrial products is limited in tables, caused by the availability of data by regions for considered years.

14   Mangistau region was a part of Atyrau region until 1973. Some literature gives calculated data separately for Mangistau and Atyrau regions as in Figure 1.3. However, separated data for Tables 1.4., 1.5. and 1.6. are not available.

Table 1.5. Production indices of food, textile and footwear industries by regions, 1950/1940,%

Regions	Food						Textile and footwear					
	Meat	Share, 1950	Sugar	Share, 1950	Groats[15]	Share, 1950	Cotton textile	Share, 1950	Foot-wear	Share, 1950	Shoes	Share, 1950
Kazakh SSR	113.0	100	101.3	100	126.8	100	105	100	5760	100	282.3	100
Akmola	152.9	2.4			126.0	1.2					200	0.6
Aktubinsk	200	3.3			130.2	22.2			3.6	0	177.8	1.0
Almaty	200	0.7	187.0	47.9	106.4	5.7			2258	2.0	128	1.0
Atyrau	141.7	1.6									45.5	0.1
Eastern Kazakhstan	200	3.5			159.7	2.9			14179	35	519.3	28.0
Karaganda	187.8	7.0			145.9	2.8			340	0.1	616.9	14.2
Kostanai	115.8	2.0			108.7	1.2					2135	12.7
Kzyl-Orda	215.4	2.6			153.3	15.1			180	0.2	3300	12.8
Mangistau												
Northern Kazakhstan	80.5	11.3			79.0	0.8			16000	0.1	131.3	1.3
Pavlodar	72.2	1.2			121.7	0.9					112.5	0.8
Southern Kazakhstan	213.0	4.5			86.6	0.5	105	100	9889	62.5	71.9	0.7
Western Kazakhstan	69.0	5.5			121.3	45.2					83.3	1.0
Zhambyl	181.3	2.6	71.2	52.1	110.9	1.5					122.2	0.7

Source: Data were calculated using: *Promyshlennost' Kazakhstana: 1920-1999 goda*, 2000

---

15   The groats production growth is considered for the period 1945 to 1950, as official account of groats production started in 1945.

Table 1.6. Production indices of chemical, machine-building and metallurgy industries by regions, 1950/1940,%

Regions	Chemical		Machine-building[16]		Construction materials		Metallurgy	
	Sulfu-ric acid	Share, 1950	Total	Share, 1950	Total	Share, 1950	Total[17]	Share, 1950
Kazakh SSR	118.5	100	200	100	400	100	3155	100
Akmola			200	100	811.1	5.7		
Aktubinsk	118.5	100			50.8	2.6		
Almaty					153.3	7.2		6.7
Atyrau					63.6	1.6		
Eastern Kazakstan					54.7	7.3		4.3
Karaganda					300.0	41.0		89.0
Kostanai					160.0	2.5		
Kzyl-Orda					150.0	1.0		
Mangistau								
Northern Kazakstan								
Pavlodar					300.0	6.1		
Southern Kazakstan					98.0	23.5		
Western Kazakhtan					93.9	2.4		
Zhambyl					800.0	3.8		

Source: Data were calculated using: *Promyshlennost' Kazakhstana: 1920-1999 goda*, 2000

---

16   Data are available from 1946.
17   Metallurgical industry was introduced in 1943.

Metallurgical industry was highly concentrated in the *Karaganda* region, accounting for 89% of the production in the Kazakh SSR, due to the concentration of resources in the region necessary for the operation and effectiveness of the industry. Metallurgical industry was introduced in the Kazakh SSR during the war and experienced a sharp increase in production, from 3.4 thousand tonnes of ferrous metals production to 107.3 thousand tonnes. At the same time the construction materials industry experienced a 200% increase in production in the region (Table 1.6.), as the only region in the industry producing such important products as cement and lime. Karaganda was one of the few regions with significant fuel production and mining industries. It managed to raise its production by a factor of 2.5 during the 10-year period since 1940. The industrial development of the region was based on its endowment with mineral resources, which were unique in the Kazakh SSR and even the entire Soviet Union. Due to the high importance of regional industrial specialisation in the whole Soviet Union, the region received extra sources for the intensive development of its industries as well as its infrastructure. The mineral rich region, located in the centre of the Kazakh SSR brought benefits to other industries in terms of a convenient location for the transportation of raw materials and intermediate goods. However, in terms of transportation, regions, which were located on railway connections of the Kazakh SSR with other Soviet republics, mostly benefited from access to raw materials from the Karaganda region.

The *Northern Kazakhstan* region experienced a growth of 263% (Figure 1.3.) in its industrial production, taking second position in terms of growth in the Kazakh SSR after the Karaganda region. However, Northern Kazakhstan was one of the least industrially developed regions without heavy industries and with just some light industry. The largest industry of the region was meat production, accounting for 11.3% of meat production in the Kazakh SSR. Even though the share of the food industry was large, its production had declined by 19.5% in 1950 compared to 1940. So the growth of industrial production in the region was entirely due to light industry, which accounted for only 1.3% of the production of light industry in the Kazakh SSR, but its growth was enormous. For example, footwear production in the Northern Kazakhstan region accounted for only 0.1 % of the whole production in the Kazakh SSR in 1950, despite its growth to a level of 15,900% (Table 1.5.) in 1950 compared to production in 1940. The high growth rate reflected the fact that production only started during the war. However, for the entire light industry in the Kazakh SSR these changes were minor without significant effect on total growth. Industrial production in the region was weak despite the high growth, which reflected the low starting point. Nevertheless, despite being the largest meat producer in the Kazakh SSR, the region benefited from its location on the Russian border and close to the transportation links of the Kazakh SSR to the rest of the Soviet Union.

The *Almaty* region is one of the few regions that obtained the highest benefits from the wartime evacuation of the Soviet Union economy sectors to the remote region contained the capital of the Kazakh SSR. In addition, the Almaty region had enough mineral resources to maintain the development of new Kazakh SSR industries such as metallurgy and the production of construction materials. The Almaty region increased its industrial production by 205% over the 10 years from 1940, by dint of growth in the mining, metallurgy, construction materials, food and textile industries. Thus, the extraction of zinc-lead ore (Table 1.4.) grew by 326.9% in 1950 compared to 1940, and accounted for 14.7% of the total national zinc-lead ore extraction, which is in second position after Eastern Kazakhstan out of only two producers in the Kazakh SSR. A metallurgical factory was built in the Almaty region during the war, as one of the first metallurgical factories in the republic, and by 1950, it accounted for 6.7% by volume of the national production in the metallurgical industry after the Karaganda region, where 89% of total production took place. The construction materials industry had increased its production by 53.3% (Table 1.6.), accounting for 7.2% of production in this industry in the Kazakh SSR, following Karaganda, South Kazakhstan regions and reaching the same level as the Eastern Kazakhstan region. The construction materials industry was important during the post war recovery, due to its involvement in every single industrial and non- industrial sector of the economy by constructing new assets. The Almaty region did not hold the leading position in food and light industries as share of the total production, except for sugar, which accounted for 47.9% (Table 1.5.) of republican sugar production. However, Almaty made remarkable progress in developing these industries. Meat production in-

creased by 100%, while footwear production grew by 2158% due to the introduction of new factories, however accounted for only 2% of national share.
The region of the capital city mainly specialised in heavy industry because of
the wartime priorities, while the light and food industries were not strong
points of the region due to the priority assigned to the transfer to heavy industries during the war. The Almaty region played an important role for the Soviet
Union in the recovery of many heavy industries during the war and could not
afford to make greater efforts for the development of the food and light industries, given that it was located in proximity to regions specialising in the food
and light industries, i.e. the southern regions.

The *Aktubinsk* region increased its industrial production by 182%, mainly due
to the growth in fuel, food and chemical production. This region was one of
the main producers of the fuel industry, responsible for 100% of natural gas
production in 1950 with a 89.7% growth over the ten years since 1940 and
24.5% of oil production in 1950 without significant growth over the preceding
decade. 75.5% of oil was extracted in Atyrau region (Table 1.4.). Coal production in the Aktubinsk grew by 159.6% between 1940 and 1950, however, it
constituted a tiny share of the national coal production, as Karaganda produced 94.8% of all coal in the Kazakh SSR. Being the only region with natural
gas extraction, the Aktubinsk region had another unique industry – chemical,
that maintained and increased its production by 18.5% for 10 years (Table
1.6.). Despite its specialisation in heavy industry, the Aktubinsk region was
successful in the food industry, mainly specialising in grain products. All the
heavy industry notwithstanding, the Aktubinsk region experienced a sharp fall
in the production of construction materials and light industries. Thus production of the construction materials industry fell by 49.2% between 1940 and
1950, regardless of the fact that it was a strategic target industry given priority
for development, while textile production declined by 96.4%. Aktubinsk was
the only region extracting natural gas in the Kazakh SSR and one of the two
oil-producing regions. During the war hydrocarbon produced in the region
was supplied not only for the maintenance of strategic industries in the Kazakh SSR but for military needs as well. Therefore, efforts were concentrated
on developing the fuel and chemical industries. Human capital was moved

from other industries in order to fulfil the needs of the Soviet Union. As a result, other industries of the region cut production due to a shortage of labour.

Industries of the *Atyrau* region experienced 162% growth for the ten years from 1940. The main sources of growth were the fuel and food industries, however, their shares of the republican production were significantly different. The Atyrau region was leading in oil extraction, accounting for 75.5% of production in the entire Kazakh SSR. It had increased its production by 82.6% in 1950 since the war.

The food industry of the Atyrau region specialised in meat production, which increased by 41.7% between 1940 and 1950; however, its share of the total meat production of the Kazakh SSR was not significant and amounted to a mere 1.6%. At the beginning of the century, the Atyrau region was a backward region (Table 1.1.) due to the lack of industrial and agricultural development. However, after the discovery of oil and the enormous help it received during the war from the rest of the Kazakh SSR and the Soviet Union due to the strategic priorities in wartime, industry in the region developed significantly with the construction of an oil refinery and oil pipelines. All efforts were directed towards the fuel industry in the Atyrau region to provide for the urgent needs of the Kazakh SSR and the Soviet Union, while others, such as construction materials and light industry, which were weakly developed, experienced steep declines (Table 1.6.) due to the shortage of labour and government support. Thus, the Atyrau region became heavily dependent on the fuel industry, while in turn the fuel industry of the entire Kazakh SSR in terms of oil became highly dependent on the Atyrau region where three quarters of the oil of the Kazakh SSR was produced.

Therefore, the interests of the Kazakh SSR and indeed the entire Soviet Union in the Atyrau region were focussed primarily on oil. This degree of specialisation was to the detriment of other industries of the region.

The *Kostanai* region was classified as an agricultural region in the beginning of the century (Table 1.1.). This had not changed by the middle of the century (Map 3 Industrial specialisation of the Kazakh SSR region, 1945-1991). However, existed industries experienced growth, amounting to 139% between 1940 and 1950. The main industrial growth of the region was occurred in light industry, especially shoe production. Between 1940 and 1950 shoe production grew by 2035% and by 1950 accounted for 12.7% of the total shoe production in the republic. The location of the Kostanai region was favoured agricultural production, which affected the development of food industry in the region. Its total share of food production in the Kazakh SSR remained low, given the high level of food production in the territory of the Kazakh SSR overall. The Kostanai region is adjacent to Northern Kazakhstan and the structure of its economy is very similar, i.e. industrial development is weak and it mainly specialised in agriculture, where the raising of livestock encouraged the steep growth in the production of footwear in these regions. However, their economies remained highly dependent on the food industry.

In *Western Kazakhstan* industrial production increased by 118 %, despite the fact that Western Kazakhstan was classified as a backward region at the beginning of the century (Table 1.1.). The low level of industrial development persisted until the middle of the century, even though there was progress in the food industry. The region accounted for 45.2% of all grain products in the entire Kazakh SSR. Production of other industries in the region, such as construction materials, light industry and food was in decline. The geographical location of Western Kazakhstan was disadvantageous. It was separated from other regions of the Kazakh SSR, due to the absence of railways, which connected the Kazakh SSR with Russia and had no direct links to Western Kazakhstan. By that time the region did not have any resources except favourable conditions for agriculture. Agricultural production could be only used to satisfy local needs. Other industries did not have the opportunity to be developed lacking a transport network. Regions without rail links to other republics were unlikely to be able to develop their industries further.

The *Akmola* region, which mainly specialised in the agricultural sector prior to 1940, progressively developed fuel, machine-building and construction materials industries during the war. Between 1940 and 1950, it increased its total industrial production by 107%. The Akmola region maintained coal production for 10 years after 1940, which accounted for 0.4% of the national level and managed to increase production by 5.5%, despite scarce resources. Akmola became the only region with major machine-building in 1950 and experienced a 100% growth in 5 years. The construction materials industry of the region had the highest growth rate in this sector (Table 1.6.) in the Kazakh SSR, amounting to 711.1% between 1940 and 1950, and accounted 5.7% of the national production. As an agricultural region, Akmola maintained the growth of food and light industries, which were important only for the region, as their production did not exceed 2.5% of the total production of these industries in the Kazakh SSR. The industrial progress of the Akmola region is mainly based on its advantageous location. Being linked to the railway network connecting the adjacent Karaganda region to Russia, the Akmola region could use mineral resources from Karaganda and easily access output markets in both the Kazakh SSR and Russia.

The *Mangistau* region was a part of the Atyrau region until 1973. The territory of today's Mangistau region experienced growth of 87% between 1940 and 1950 principally due to fishing, which accounted for more than half of the national catch. Mangistau does not have favourable conditions for agriculture, but it is rich in oil resources, which were discovered only in 1953. Before the hydrocarbon fields were discovered, Mangistau depended on fishing, which was a seasonal activity. In order to derive maximum benefits during the fishing seasons, the fishing industry in Mangistau did not always follow the rules of rational fishing. Later, because of negligent use, the fish stocks in the Caspian Sea, where the fishermen from Mangistau were operating, started to decline, bringing some rare fish types to the brink of extinction.

Industrial production in *Pavlodar* rose by 80%, mainly due to the coal and construction materials industries, even though the share of these Pavlodar industries in the national production is very small. The production of construction materials increased by 200% (Table 1.6.), accounting for 6.1% of production in the Kazakh SSR. The increase was the result of the location of several construction materials factories in Pavlodar after 1945. The region was a newly developing centre of the coal industry, however, its share of the national production amounted only to 0.3% with 46.9% growth over the five post-war years. Other industries of the region such as light industry and food production accounted for approximately 1% of the national output of these industries with an average growth of 25% in light industry and a 25% decline in the food industry. The Pavlodar region specialised in the construction materials industry, which developed significantly after the war, with the discovery of mineral resources. The development of this industry in Pavlodar was based on the proximity to extremely fast developing metallurgical, fuel and machine-building industries in the neighbouring Akmola and Karaganda regions and the railway pass through Pavlodar, connecting its neighbouring regions to the Russian market.

Industrial production in *Eastern Kazakhstan* increased by 77% due to the growth of mining, light industry and food production. Eastern Kazakhstan is rich in rare mineral resources, where the production of zinc-lead ore accounted for 62.8% of its national production with growth of 86.2% between 1940 and 1950. Construction materials production of the region was third by volume in the Kazakh SSR after Karaganda and Southern Kazakhstan, and accounted for 7.3%. However, the region did not manage to maintain the same level of production as in 1940 and had a decline of 45.3%. Eastern Kazakhstan specialised in light industry as well. Its footwear production accounted for 28% of the total in the Kazakh SSR and grew by 419.3% between 1940 and 1950, while the food industry did not exceed 3.5% of the national output, doubling its production from 1940-1950. Eastern Kazakhstan specialised mainly in heavy and light industries, where the main market for rare mineral resources, extracted in the regions, was located in Russia, which assembled exports from the Kazakh SSR into final products. Therefore, neighbouring metallurgical Russian factories depended on industrial development in Eastern Kazakhstan, while the growth of metallurgical industry of Eastern Kazakhstan was mainly dependent on the level of Russian manufacturing, which would absorb the growing level of mineral resources extracted in the region.

Southern Kazakhstan has one of the most favourable locations for agricultural cultivation and at the same time is generously endowed with mineral resources, making the economy of Southern Kazakhstan widely diversified. Industrial production of the region grew by 47% between 1940 and 1950. Southern Kazakhstan was the second leading region in extraction of the zinc-lead ore after Eastern Kazakhstan and accounted for 22.5% of the national production with 58.7% growth during the ten years since 1940. At the same time, Southern Kazakhstan was second in the country for coal production, accounting for 3.76 % after the leading Karaganda region where 94.8% of all coal was produced. The construction materials industry in Southern Karaganda likewise took second place in the total production in the Kazakh SSR. It accounted for 23.5% and its output remained almost the same level for the 10 years between 1940 and 1950, declining by 2% overall. As in the case of coal production, the construction materials industry in Southern Kazakhstan made second place after the leading Karaganda region with 41% of national share (Table 1.6.). The light industry of the region was dominated by the cultivation of cotton, which could grow only in Southern Kazakhstan. The cotton of the region was supplied not only to other regions in the Kazakh SSR, but other Soviet republics as well for the textile production. Despite the high strategic priority of heavy industries during the war, where labour was being transferred, cotton production in the Southern Kazakhstan region maintained the same level of production with a slight growth of 5% over the ten years since 1940, being the only source for the textile industry in the Kazakh SSR. The food industry of Southern Kazakhstan developed with high growth mainly in meat production, which accounted for 4.5% of the national level, taking fourth position by production volume in the Kazakh SSR. Southern Kazakhstan had widely diversified industrial development, being endowed with rare resources such as zinc-lead and cotton, which were in high demand in other regions and republics of the Soviet Union. As industries in other regions depended on raw materials produced in Southern Kazakhstan, the infrastructure was developed to enable the timely transportation of goods from Kazakhstan to other regions.

.

The *Zhambyl* region is located in the south of the Kazakh SSR on the border with Southern Kazakhstan, however, it did not succeed in cotton cultivation or textile production. Zhambyl achieved 44% growth of industrial production for the ten years from 1940 to 1950 on the basis of chemical, food and construction materials industries. The chemical industry of the Zhambyl region is famous due to its mineral fertilization factories, which supply mineral fertilizers to other regions and Uzbekistan. Using mineral resources from Southern Kazakhstan, Zhambyl had one of the highest growth rates in the construction materials industry, which amounted to 700% between 1940 and1950 even though its share of national production (3.8 % in 1950) was much less than that of the neighbouring Southern Kazakhstan region. The food industry of the Zhambyl region was dominated by sugar production, which accounted for 74% of the national share in 1940, however, as sugar was not one of the strategic goods during the war, the national production level fell by 67.8%. Consequently, the share of sugar in the total production of the Zhambyl region fell to 52.1% by 1950. Given that its major product was not a priority during the war, the Zhambyl region was unable to increase sugar production in 1950 to the pre-war level. The total decline over the whole decade since 1940 amounted to 28.8%. Other goods of the food industry experienced growth, which would be easier, taking into account that their shares in the national production did not exceed 2.6%. Despite the significant drop in sugar production of the region, which was one of its main specialisations, industrial production in the region continued to grow due to the diversity of industries, which kept the economy of the region growing.

The *Kzyl-Orda* region specialised in agriculture and mining, and had (by comparison with other regions of the Kazakh SSR) the lowest growth rate (38%) between 1940 and 1950. However, it still made a significant contribution to the industrial production of the republic. In the 1950s, reserves of mineral resources in the Kzyl-Orda region, which were discovered at the beginning of the 20th century, were significantly declining, depressing production of the heavy industry in the region. Therefore, the region became dependent mainly on agriculture, which grew steadily over the 10 years since 1940. In 1950, grain products accounted for 15.1% of agricultural production. Meat production had the highest growth (115.4% between 1940 and 1950) in the Kazakh SSR and accounted for 2.6% of agricultural production in the republic. After the decline of the mining industry, the region concentrated on the development of other industries. For example, production of shoes accounted for 12.8% of the national share in 1950 with a growth of 3200% over the last decade. Even then, the Kzyl-Orda region did not become fully dependent on agriculture, due to the diversification of industrial development, which mainly was based on the region's endowment with other natural resources. For example, most of the sulphate stocks for glass factories in the Soviet Union were in the Kzyl-Orda region. Production increased eight times over the period between 1940 and 1950, due to the introduction of advanced technology.

Industrial production grew in all regions of the Kazakh SSR during the war and five post war years, where regions endowed with rare mineral resources, such as oil, gas, coal and others had received the maximum level of support from the Soviet government. The reason was the strategic priority of these industries for the requirements of the armed forces during the war and for the recovery of industrial factories destroyed by occupation in other republics in the post-war period. However, in regions with strategic industries the production of other industries inside these regions declined to such an extent that some of them could not recover after the war. Regions close to transport links with Russia or other republics mostly benefited from the development of infrastructure, where they could be connected to other regions, while regions further afield had to rely on their internal production of necessary goods. However, in many cases it was difficult for those regions to meet their requirements due to the lack of resources. The main factor of industrial development was endowment with mineral resources, while the next important factor were transport links to markets for finished products. Thus, the industrial development of such regions without substantial natural resources could benefit from the transport of raw materials for the production of intermediate goods and supply them to markets.

1.4   Industrial development on the basis of boosting the agricultural sector, 1953-1958

The recovery of Soviet industries was proceeding very fast, however, the agricultural sector of the Soviet Union could not provide the country with enough food, particularly bread. As a result a food rationing system was introduced for the even distribution of basic goods, when only a limited amount was available for every person[18]. The Kazakh SSR was the place most suited for the cultivation of wheat, having vast territories with a favourable climate. The period from 1953 to 1958 saw intensive development and transformation of the agricultural sector of the Kazakh SSR to meet the needs of the USSR. Capital investments in the agricultural sector soared significantly, by providing rural areas with new and quality technology and qualified specialist training. In 1953, less than one third of 36 million hectares of land suitable for cultivation was utilized, while in 1955 land used for cultivation increased from 9.7 to 20.6 million hectares. Between 1953 and 1956 the total sown area (area under crops) increased threefold to 27.9 million hectares, while sowing of wheat increased by a factors of four, as the sowing of other principal agricultural crops more than doubled (Table 1.7.).

The development of virgin lands affected all northern, western and eastern regions of the Kazakh SSR, where land for grain cultivation was used mainly for wheat (Figure 1.4.). Indeed, 65.7% of virgin lands were used to cultivate wheat. Regions involved in the development of the agricultural sector had a competitive advantage. They experienced not only the enlargement of the agricultural sector, but also development of the whole regional economy. Cities grew, as the population steeply increased. As such, in 1954-1955, the Kazakh SSR acquired 360 000 new qualified specialists from other Soviet republics for the development of virgin lands (*tselinnye zemli*). The number of new specialists almost doubled during the period 1954-1958, involving 640 000 people including about 5000 managers, which were directed to the Kazakh SSR.

---

18 The food rationing system was based on the limited distribution of consumer basket, mainly bread based goods.

Table 1.7. Sown areas in the Kazakh SSR by regions, th. ha

Regions	1953	1956	1958	1958 to 1953, %
Kazakh SSR	*9716.9*	*27883.1*	*28661.5*	*294.9*
Akmola	2134.8	7938.9	8149.5	381.7
Aktubinsk	491.4	1584.3	1591.8	323.9
Almaty	622.1	1190.4	1263.9	203.1
Atyrau	21.0	37.5	27.9	132.8
Eastern Kazakhstan	1088.4	1736.0	2072.4	190.4
Karaganda	645.6	1508.5	1726.0	267.3
Kostanai	1258.1	5098.0	5223.2	415.1
Kzyl-Orda	75.3	88.5	81.5	108.2
Northern Kazakhstan	945.2	2040.4	1995.2	211.0
Pavlodar	805.7	3366.1	3298.9	409.4
Southern Kazakhstan	545.1	848.8	832.5	152.7
Western Kazakhstan	656.2	1591.0	1510.6	230.2
Zhambyl	428.3	854.7	888.1	207.3

Source: *Ekonomicheskoe razvitie Kazakhskoi SSR*, 1960.

Development of agricultural regions was supported with advanced technology in addition to the inflow of qualified specialists, in order to be able to manage the cultivation of such huge territories in a timely manner. Thus, in 1956 the grain yield had increased to a volume 4.3 times that of 1953. However, due to the seasonal dry weather, the grain yield changed every year. In 1954, the crop yield was 9.1 quintal per ha, in 1955 it was 2.9, in 1956 - grain yield reached the highest level for the developing period, i.e. 10.6 quintal per ha. However, in 1957 it fell to 4.6 again and in 1958 the grain yield rose to 9.4. The agricultural sector was vulnerable to climate conditions due to the lack of agricultural equipment, which mainly was supplied from other republics of the Soviet Union.

Figure 1.4. Grain production in the Kazakh SSR by regions, 1956, mln. quintal.

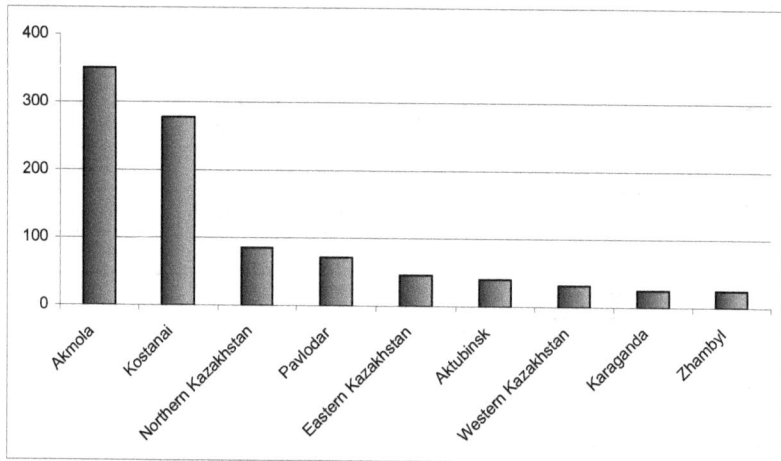

Source: *Ekonomicheskoe razvitie Kazakhskoi SSR, 1960.*

In 1956, 30% of Soviet grain came from the Kazakh SSR compared to a mere 4% in 1952. The Kazakh SSR had become the second largest grain republic in the Soviet Union after Russia and left behind such a major grain producer as Ukraine. In 1956, the Akmola region alone produced almost twice as much more grain as the whole of the Kazakh SSR in 1954. Compared to other Soviet republics, the Kazakh SSR had the highest growth rate in the agricultural sector during the *tselina* lands development period. Despite some bad harvests, the annual grain production of the Kazakh SSR, 1955-1959 increased substantially, reaching a level of 4.5 times the annual production in 1953. At the same time grain stocks in 1959 were 6.5 times higher than in 1953.

Due to the growth of labour productivity and improved mechanisation, grain costs significantly decreased, which substantially improved the economy of the rural areas. Thus, rural areas have made a profit in 1956 for the sold grain, which covered all their debts for the last 20 years. Nevertheless, the development of 'virgin lands' increased not only the production of grain, but that of other crops as well. The cultivation of other crops took place in southern regions, where the growth amounted to 50%, while sugar production almost doubled.

The development of virgin lands and the increase in grain production had a significant impact on livestock. In the period from 1951 to 1953, the level of livestock had declined, and in 1953, it did not reach that of 1928. The explanation lay in the weak development of grain production, which limited the expansion of mixed feed crops. The livestock products of the Kazakh SSR reached the highest growth rate and per capita production of all Soviet republics, increasing the importance of the food industry in the Soviet Union. Thus in 1959, the production of grain per capita in the Kazakh SSR was twice the average in the Soviet Union. Meat production exceeded the Soviet per capita production by 43%, milk production – by 7% and wool production was six times the Soviet per capita production. The biggest growth in the food industry was observed in northern and eastern regions due to the agricultural development of these regions where livestock was mainly allocated. The southern regions of the Kazakh SSR did not have such extremely high growth in the agricultural sector production as northern regions, however, they still played an important role in the agricultural development producing 100% of fruits, grapes, sugar, cotton and tobacco, which were partly supplied to other republics. Thus, the Soviet Union became dependent not only on mineral resources of the Kazakh SSR, but on its agricultural sector as well, providing more modern technologies, organising regional development for better quality and higher production growth.

The industrial infrastructure development

In the early 1950s, the expansion of the agricultural sector and new developments in industry caused the restructuring of the administrative management system of the economy of the Kazakh SSR. In 1954, new ministries were created in the Kazakh SSR as well as in other Soviet republics for the local control and management of fast growing sectors of the economy. The first industries that came under local control were non-ferrous metallurgy, the construction of metallurgical and chemical industries, geology, and bakeries. In 1957, local authorities controlled 98% of enterprises in the Kazakh SSR as opposed to 34% in 1953 (*Ekonomicheskoe razvitie Kazakhskoi SSR*, 1960).

In 1957, the government of the Kazakh SSR established administrative centres on the basis of the regional territorial division[19]. Nine new economic administrative centres were established with the combination of smaller regions under the control of one administrative centre. Every economic administrative centre included the committee *sovnarkhoz*, which was responsible for the management of industries. Local administrative centres together with industrial committees were created in order to achieve the most efficient management of regions and their economies, taking into account the specifics of every region and their industrial identification.

Before creating local administrative centres, the economy of the Kazakh SSR, and especially industry suffered many losses as a result of the centralised management of the Soviet Union. Industrial enterprises were not working in an efficient way by best exploiting their regional location. For instance, the coal energy input source for the Aktubinsk ferroalloy factory was located in the Karaganda region, while the Aktubinsk region produced coal itself, which would be enough to provide for the requirements of its ferroalloy factory. As a result, the Aktubinsk ferroalloy factory was incurred high expenditures for the transport costs of coal, while Aktubinsk coal miners were looking in other regions to market their coal output. Every region had many problems connected with central management, while Soviet authorities were not aware of regional advantages, which could be used with planning based on accurate information and analysis. Capital investments, which were coming from the Soviet government, were equally divided between regions or industries, without paying attention on regional specifics. They were designed to produce benefits for the whole Soviet Union, often in contradiction to the rational regional development of the republic. Electrification was not sufficiently developed, in terms of sectoral diversification. The majority of power stations in the Kazakh

---

19   New administrative centres were established on the basis of the new law, which was introduced by N.Krushev in 1957 "*O dalneishem sovershenstvovanii organizacii upravleniia promyshlennostiu i stroitelstvom*" (The law on restructuring of methods of management in industry and in construction). This law implied the decentralisation of management of industry and construction with the transfer of control to local administrative centres, which became responsible for planning, control and management of industrial enterprises (construction is included). (*Ekonomicheskaia Enciklopediia*, 1965).

SSR were built to supply industry, while other economic sectors and the population had a high demand for electric power. Capital investments were not well allocated for the important industrial construction sites under central management, however, after a management reorganisation, the construction industry became cost-effective. In addition, the centralized management was very bureaucratic and thus retarded the intensive development of the economy[20].

After introducing local administrative centres, the efficiency of production rose significantly, where the local management encouraged industries to search for cooperation with closely located factories, in order to reduce transport costs of raw materials and intermediate goods with the efficient use of regional resources. However, the search for partners depended on their location close to existing transportation links to the rest of the Soviet Union, while in many cases internal links did not exist, which made the interregional cooperation more difficult, while the cooperation between republics was good.

Despite the fast growth of the economy during and after the war (1941-1953), the Kazakh SSR still had a low ratio of industrial production to natural resources. Therefore, during the years of management restructuring and agricultural development (1953-1958), the Soviet Union pushed the Kazakh SSR to increase the development of existing fields of mineral resources and to search for new sources of oil, gas and other ferrous and non-ferrous metals, in order to create new possibilities for the industrial development of the Soviet Union. Capital investments contributed to the growth of the economy of the Kazakh SSR in addition to their efficient management and distribution. Thus, during the period 1946-1950 the Kazakh SSR received 12 billion Soviet roubles from the Soviet government. During the following five years, 1951-1955, the amount increased to 30 billion roubles and for the three years 1956-1958, investments increased by 30% to 39 billion roubles. The government budget of the Kazakh SSR in 1959 was 5.4 times that of 1953, due to the accelerated development of the economy. The high level of investments is explained by the intensive growth of industries, which were important for the whole Soviet

---

20   See the footnote 8.

Union, such as oil, gas, coal, mineral resources and metallurgical industries. Substantial amount of capital investments went to the development of *tselina* lands in the Kazakh SSR, where in 1954-1955 7.5 billion roubles were allocated to the agricultural sector, and this increased to 12 billion roubles during the period 1956-1958. Due to the intensive support from the Soviet Union the industrial production of the Kazakh SSR increased to a level of 2.4 times by 1958 compared to 1950, by 5.6 times compared to1940, and by 44 times compared to 1913, while in the Soviet Union industrial production had increased to a level of 36 times of that in 1913. The distinctive growth was observed over all Kazakh SSR industries compared to the development in the Soviet Union as a whole.

In 1958, the share of capital investments into industry amounted to 53% of total investments of the Kazakh SSR, where the significant part of investments, more than 90%, went to the development of heavy industry. The non-ferrous and ferrous metallurgies and coal production received 56% of total industrial investment, less but still substantial investment went to construction, fuel and power industries (Figure 1.5.). Whereas non-ferrous metallurgy received 21.3% (Figure 1.5.) of total industrial investment, a figure that increased by 29% in 1958 compared to the previous year, investment in ferrous metallurgy rose by 59% in 1958 and accounted for 15.6% of total industrial investment in the Kazakh SSR (*Ekonomicheskoe razvitie Kazakhskoi SSR*, 1960). The coal industry received 19% of total industrial investment in 1958 signifying an increase of 36%. The steep growth (60%) of investment in the construction industry in 1958 can be explained by the extensive[21] development of all economic sectors, however, the share of construction in total industrial investment amounted to 7.8%. The extraction of rare mineral resources played a key role for the Soviet Union, which recovered after the war and increased the level of its industrialisation, while the major percentage of mineral resources was located in the Kazakh SSR, where investments to improve the productivity of industries important for the whole country increased significantly.

---

21   Extensive development of economy implies the attraction of new resources for the production processes, i.e. the development of new deposits of raw materials, the construction of new factories.

Table 1.8. The dynamics of capital investments in regional industrial development.

Regions	1957 to 1956, %	1958 to 1957, %
Almaty	141	120
Aktubinsk	99.5	120
Eastern Kazakhstan	99	120
Atyrau	131	131
Karaganda	128	112
Kostanai	155	119
Northern Kazakhstan	106	159
Semipalatinsk	242	144
Southern Kazakhstan	117	144

Source: *Ekonomicheskoe razvitie Kazakhskoi SSR,* 1960.

Figure 1.5. Share of capital investments in industries, 1958, % (Total industry = 100)

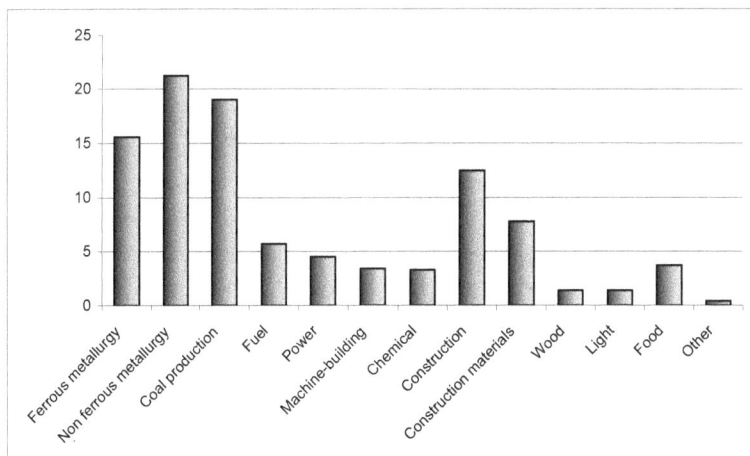

Source: *Ekonomicheskoe razvitie Kazakhskoi SSR.,* 1960.

New industrial committees allocated the major percentage of investments to the completion of the construction of factories, thereby increasing the rate at which new factories began production. Thus, the highest growth rate of investment in 1958 was in Northern Kazakhstan (59%) (Table 1.8.), due to the introduction of new construction materials factories and the enormous construction work connected with development of new *tselina* lands, which were accompanied by the growth and development of new cities around growing developing lands. Investment in Eastern and Southern Kazakhstan grew by 44% between 1957 and 1958, as new high capacity cement factories were built in those regions and a new hydrolysis factory was built in Southern Kazakhstan. These factories were important to maintain the growth of the construction industry. Industrial investment in the Atyrau region grew by 31% due to maintenance work in oil fields. The industrial committees of Kostanai and Karaganda[22] saw a lower growth of investments compared to other regions (19% and 12% respectively). This can be explained by the fact that the level of industries was already advanced compared to other regions, with a high level of productivity for strategically important industries. Examples were the Pavlodar aluminium factory, the Kostanai construction materials factory and Karaganda coalmines, which played a key role in the development of *tselina* lands.

The growth of transportation was important to ensure the development of the Kazakh SSR and *tselina* lands. The railway network expanded by 9% in 1958, most due to the virgin lands development. This development which made access to the market in the Soviet Union easier was beneficial for all sectors of the economy of the Kazakh SSR as transportation costs of raw materials, intermediate goods and final products were significantly reduced. However, only industries located in regions on the railway network to other Soviet republics, benefited from railway expansion. The majority of industrial transport in the absence of rail connections took place by road, or where automobile roads did not exist, by air, which had an enormously negative effect on profitability of production. In 1958, the Kazakh SSR railway management authority was created as a single Kazakh SSR railway controlling com-

---

22   Karaganda industrial committee was responsible for Akmola and Pavlodar regions.

pany, after the integration of a number of independent companies. The creation of a single railway company had a positive effect on the operation of the
railways, eliminating disorganized management, which in the past created difficulties for effective inter regional connections and was an obstacle in further
development due to the diversity of opinion and the difficulties in coming to a
single decision.

Where the railway network had not covered all interregional directions, the
road network was growing very fast. However, the transportation of goods by
road was more time-consuming than by rail and was restricted by weight, reducing the volumes that could be transported and restricting the growth of industries in areas that were not linked to the rail network.

Figure 1.6. The dynamics of the regional industrial productivity, 1958/1957,
%.

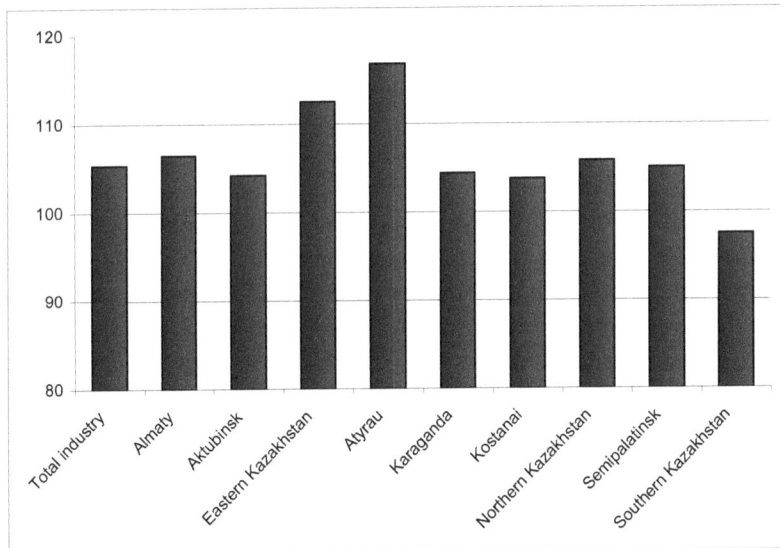

Source: Ekonomicheskoe razvitie Kazakhskoi SSR, 1960.

Together with industrial growth, new technologies and the automation of work were implemented, resulting in a significant increase in productivity after 1950, (to 120% of the 1950 level of productivity in 1953 and 150% in 1958).

The highest annual productivity growth in 1958 was observed in the Atyrau and Eastern Kazakhstan regions with 16.8% and 12.5% respectively (Figure 1.6.), which is explained by the introduction of new technologies for the process automation in the oil extraction industry of the Atyrau region, which had been a highly labour intensive industry. Eastern Kazakhstan had introduced automation innovations for zinc-lead ore extraction, which increased work productivity by 48% between 1957 and 1958. The mining industry made progress all over the country due to new technology, which increased its productivity by 50% between 1956 and 1958. Coal production was an exception. It was a highly labour intensive industry and in 1958, a lot of new technology was introduced. However, productivity did not increase, due to the poor management of this industry. Only Southern Kazakhstan had a slight decline in industrial production (by 2.5%) (Figure 1.6.) due to the low level of investments in the light industry, which was highly concentrated in Southern Kazakhstan and could not advance its technologies. The light industry of Southern Kazakhstan included 100% of the cotton cultivation in the Kazakh SSR, which was completely manual, and the level of its productivity affected the total productivity level of the region. The growth of industrial productivity in the Kazakh SSR was mainly based on industries, which were highly important for the requirements of the entire Soviet Union. Other industries could achieve growth in the case of successful attempts to benefit from the proximate location to important industries for the Soviet Union, such as light industry or food production located in industrial clusters.

The economy of the Kazakh SSR made significant progress in development in 1953-1958, during the years of the *tselina* lands development, when the amount of labour in industrial and agricultural sectors of the economy increased by 56% between 1953 and 1958. The reason was the inflow of specialists from the Soviet Union for the *tselina* development, which brought to the economy significant numbers of skilled workers and increased the level and importance of education in the Kazakh SSR. The economy of the Kazakh

SSR created financial incentives to attract labour, and built modern settlements, which were concentrated in the northern regions of Kazakhstan, as a result of the virgin lands development, and around new industrial concentrations of factories as in the Eastern Kazakhstan and Karaganda regions. The development of the Kazakh SSR economy benefited from the growing demand of the Soviet Union for industrial resources as well as for the development of agriculture. However, a high level of the development of regions, which were rich with resources in high demand, created disparities with the poorer regions, such as Western Kazakhstan, which were cut off from the republic due to the absence of rail links and the low level of development compared to the soaring production of other regions.

1.5 The formation of industrial clusters in the Kazakh SSR and its intensification on the basis of Research and Development, 1970-1985.

Since the establishment of the Soviet Union, there had been an intensive development of its mineral resources in the Kazakh SSR that resulted in the creation and development of new industries. During the first decades of the Soviet Union, the industrial system of the Kazakh SSR consisted of a few factories that specialised in the extraction and manufacture of existing mineral resources in minor volumes. These factories did not have sufficient routes for the connection to output markets, because they were located in empty steppes without any links to inhabited regions. It created many difficulties in the development of new mineral resource fields, which included not only the construction of factories, but also the creation of whole cities with service sectors for the subsistence of the population. As the largest proportion of deposits of mineral resources were separated by some distance from each other, much effort was expended on building new roads, in order to connect neighbouring fields and factories for better efficiency, which could be achieved by combining their input and output markets. In this way, small extraction fields with factories were growing into industrial clusters[23], which or-

---

23   Industrial clusters represented itself a set of closely located industrial productions (i.e. raw material fields, manufactures), which are linked by the field of the speciali-

ganised industrial blocks[24] that played a significant role in the economy of the Kazakh SSR and the Soviet Union economy as well.

Table 1.9. Main Kazakh SSR industrial blocks by its location and specialisation.

#	Industrial blocks	Regions included	Specialisation of blocks by industries	Clusters	Specialisation of clusters by industries
1	Central Kazakstan	Karaganda	Fuel, metallurgy, chemical	1. Karaganda-Temirtau	1. Fuel, metallurgy, chemical
				2. Balhash	2. Metallurgy
				3. Zhezkazgan	3. Metallurgy
2	Eastern Kazakhstan	Eastern Kazakhstan	Non-ferrous metallurgy, power	Ust-Kamenogorsk	Non-ferrous metallurgy, power
3	Pavlodar-Ekibastuz	Pavlodar	Fuel, energy, metallurgy, chemical, machine-building	Pavlodar-Ekibastuz	Fuel, energy, metallurgy, chemical, machine-building
4	Torgai	Kostanai	Mining, construction materials	Kostanai	Mining, construction materials

---

sation (e.g. metallurgy, fuel) and could be connected at the vertical as well as horizontal levels.

24   Industrial blocks were constituted of a set of industrial clusters, which are located on the proximate distance to each other (Adamchuk, V.A., Dvoskin, B.Y., 1968).

# Industrial blocks	Regions included	Specialisation of blocks by industries	Clusters	Specialisation of clusters by industries
5 Southern Kazakhstan	Southern Kazakhstan, Zhambyl	Chemical, metallurgy, light, food, machine-building, construction materials	1. Zhambyl-Karatau 2. Chimkent-Kentau	1. Chemical, light, food 2. Non-ferrous metallurgy, machine-building, construction materials, light, food, chemical
6 Western Kazakhstan	Aktubinsk, Atyrau, Mangistau	Fuel, chemical, metallurgy, construction materials, food	1. Guriev-Emba 2. Mangyshlak 3. Aktubinsk	1. Food, fuel 2. Fuel, construction materials 3. Metallurgy, chemical

Source: Adamchuk and Dvoskin, 1968.

By the end of the 1970s, the Kazakh SSR consisted of six clearly defined main industrial blocks, which were organized according to geographical location, climate, mineral and water resources (Table 1.9., Map 4. Established industrial clusters of the Kazakh SSR by 1970[25].).

---

25   Numbers in circles of the Map 4 correspond to numbers of table 1.9. defining the name of industrial clusters.

MAP 4   ESTABLISHED INDUSTRIAL CLUSTERS OF THE KAZAKH SSR BY 1970

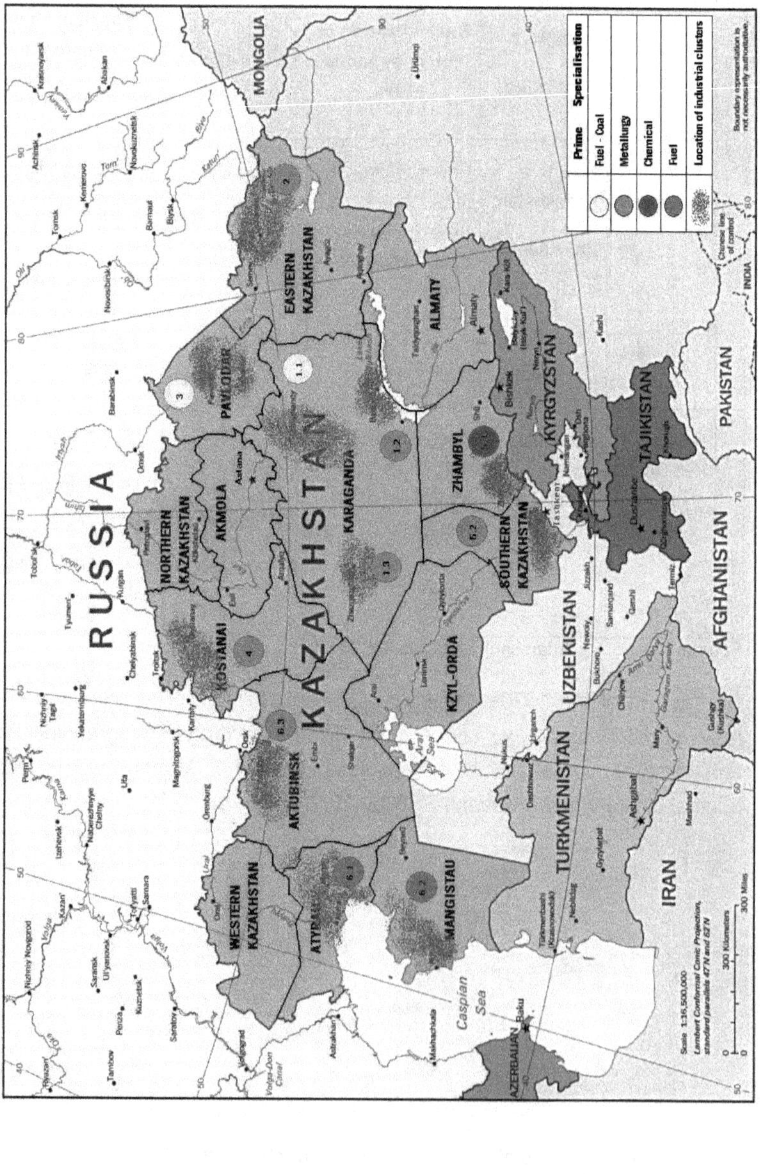

1. The Central Kazakhstan industrial block

Central Kazakhstan is represented by the Karaganda region, which is rich with fuel and mineral resources. At the end of the 1970s, Karaganda was the leading region in industrial production, accounting for 20.8% of the total industrial production in the Kazakh SSR. Clusters of the *Central Kazakhstan block* are unevenly distributed in this region as factories were created according to the location of mineral resources. Thus, three main industrial clusters were distinguished, which are *Karaganda-Temirtau, Balhash and Zhezkazgan*. The *Karaganda-Temirtau cluster* is located in the northeast of the Karaganda region and specialised mainly in coal production. This cluster also has a developed chemical industry, machine-building, metallurgy, construction materials, food and light industries. The cluster was based on coalmines discovered during the first years of the formation of the Soviet Union, producing 14.7 thousand tonnes of coal in 1920, and increasing the production to 38.4 million tonnes in 1970, which accounted for 65% of the total coal production in the Kazakh SSR (*Promyshlennost Kazakhstana: 1920-1999 goda,* 2000). At the beginning of the development of coal production, 95% of the coal was transported to other republics, mainly to Russia, for manufacture, however, later during and after the second world war, the Kazakh SSR created new industries, such as metallurgy, chemical and power, which were highly intensive in coal consumption. Thus, the biggest share of the coal produced started to be manufactured and consumed inside the Kazakh SSR, while the output of industries that used the coal supplied other republics. The metallurgical factory of the Karaganda-Temirtau cluster had a competitive advantage in the proximate location to raw material resources, which manifested itself in lower costs of production, compared to other leading factories of the Soviet Union. The main outputs of the metallurgy industry such as cast iron, ferrous metals and steel in the Karaganda-Temirtau cluster, accounted for more than 95% of their total production in the Kazakh SSR with production growth of over 500% between 1960 and 1970. Specialising in coal production, chemical industry and metallurgy, the Karaganda-Temirtau cluster was the interactive mechanism of the production process, where all factories of the specialisation - coalmines, coal separating factories, chemical factories, metallurgical factories were using each other's products as raw materials or intermediate goods, thereby decreasing their production costs. The chemical factory in the Karaganda-Temirtau cluster, for the production of synthetic rubber, was built to use the output of coalmines and metallurgical production of the cluster; however, the finished goods of the chemical factory were transported to other republics of the Soviet Union, due to the absence of a market for these products in the Kazakh SSR. The development of heavy industries in the region implied the employment of mainly the male population. In order to solve the problem of the high level of unemployment in the female population a number of factories of food and light industries were created in the cluster, which kept the balance in the use of local labour and permitted the reduction of transport costs for the provisions for the local work force.

The *Balhash cluster* was located on the southeast of central Kazakhstan, next to the Balhash Lake and on the border of the Almaty region. The Balhash cluster specialised in the non-ferrous metallurgy. The production of copper ore in the Balhash and Zhezkazgan clusters accounted for 100% of the total production of the Kazakh SSR. The metallurgical factory of the Balhash cluster was built in the middle of the 1930s, using discovered mineral resources as a base. However, by the end of the 1960s copper reserves significantly declined, which forced the metallurgical factories used Balhash copper to search for other raw material sources. At the same time, possible alternatives had significant growth in the neighbouring Zhezkazgan cluster.

The *Zhezkazgan cluster* was located in the centre of the Karaganda region, closer to the southwest part. It specialised in non-ferrous metallurgy, being the second in the Central Kazakhstan block after the Balhash cluster until 1970. The Zhezkazgan cluster was significantly rich with copper resources, which became the basis for the metallurgical factory built in the cluster, whose capacity was not sufficient for the manufacture of all extracted copper. However, this did not create a problem as a significant share of copper concentrate was transported to Russian factories, while another part was used by the metallurgical factory of the neighbouring Balhash cluster after the significant decline in its reserves. The narrow specialisation of the Zhezkazgan cluster in copper extraction had the effect that other mineral resources which were extracted along with the copper could not be used and were wasted because the facilities to process them were not developed. However, the main objective of the Soviet Union was to extract the needed mineral resources in quantity. The processing of other elements would have absorbed significant efforts and therefore reduced the quantity. However, as a result the quality of production was seriously affected.

2. The Eastern Kazakhstan industrial block

The *Eastern Kazakhstan industrial block* is located in the eastern part of the Kazakh SSR in the Eastern Kazakhstan region. This block specialised in non-ferrous metallurgy and had the potential for the development of chemical industry due to its natural resources. The Eastern Kazakhstan block was one of the leaders in the Soviet Union in terms of local mineral resources, and was ahead of other Kazakh SSR regions with regard to the extraction of non-ferrous ores and the production of non-ferrous metals. Zinc, titanium and magnesium were mainly produced in Eastern Kazakhstan, while the generation of electricity in Eastern Kazakhstan was accounted for 21.4% of the total electrical power output in 1970. Due to favourable climate conditions, the timber industry accounted for 11% of the national timber production.

The main industrial cluster of the Eastern Kazakhstan block was *Ust-Kamenogorsk*, which is located in the northeast of the region and was rich in non-ferrous ores, and water resources of the river Irtysh. The mineral resources of the Ust-Kamenogorsk cluster were important for the whole Soviet Union due to their sheer quantity, while its factories, producing zinc and lead concentrates, supplied major zinc-lead factories of the Soviet Union with their output. Extraction of the zinc-lead ore in Eastern Kazakhstan grew immensely after the war, when the first zinc factory was created, amounting to an increase of 70% between 1960 and 1970 and 475% from 1950 to 1970. It accounted for 69% of the entire production in the Kazakh SSR. The Ust-Kamenogorsk cluster was not only important for the Soviet Union for its zinc-lead resources, being the largest producer, but it was also the second largest in the Soviet Union in copper ore resources after the Central Kazakhstan block. However, despite the high level of reserves of mineral resources, the factories of the Ust-Kamenogorsk cluster were not fully provided with local raw materials due to the low level of technology used for mineral resources extraction. Up to 50% of resources were transported from other regions for local factories, increasing their production costs.

Eastern Kazakhstan had favourable conditions for energy intensive indus- tries, due to its high hydro energy potential, which accounted for 38.1% of all hydro energy potentials in the Kazakh SSR in 1970. The generation of elec- tricity from hydro power stations in Eastern Kazakhstan in 1970 amounted to 8 kW per head with 26 times growth between the end of the 1940s and 1965. At the same time the output of hydro power stations in the Kazakh SSR was on average 2 kW per head, compared to 1.7 and 0.63 kW in the Soviet Union and in the USA respectively (Adamchuk and Dvoskin, 1968). However, the dominance of heavy industries in the Eastern Kazakhstan industrial block de- clined due to the involvement of the female population in employment, which accounted for a mere 10% in 1970.

3. The Pavlodar-Ekibastuz industrial block

The *Pavlodar-Ekibastuz* industrial block was based in the Pavlodar region and specialized in fuel, power, metallurgy, chemical industries and machine- building and consisted of one main *Pavlodar-Ekibastuz cluster*. The Pavlodar region was crossed by the railway, which connected the Kazakh SSR with central and eastern parts of Russia, Siberia, and at the same time this region crossed with the Irtysh river, which came from Eastern Kazakhstan to central and southern parts of Russia. Such a favourable location with the transport network created beneficial conditions for the development of any industry.

The *Pavlodar-Ekibastuz industrial cluster* was rich with different types of coal, which is a fuel of better quality, and several times cheaper compared to coal in Karaganda or Russia. However, due to the specific type of Ekibastuz coal, not every factory of the Kazakh SSR could use it, given the different types of technology used for different types of fuel. The majority of heavy industries were based on Karaganda coal, (65% of production in the Kazakh SSR), while Pavlodar-Ekibastuz coal extraction accounted for 37.1% in 1970, grow- ing from 8.2% in 1955. In 1965, only 8% of Ekibastuz coal was consumed inside the Pavlodar-Ekibastuz industrial cluster, while 77.1% of Pavlodar-Ekibastuz went to Russian power plants, where the question of more efficient use of the coal was not an issue. Transportation costs of coal are several times higher than the costs of the transmission of electricity generated by burning the same amount of coal, which could be produced in the Pavlodar-Ekibastuz industrial cluster and then transported to other republics, cutting the cost of the final output. (Map 2. *Main roads of the Kazakh SSR by 1970* illustrates the luck of power stations in the Kazakh SSR, particularly in the proximity to sources of raw materials). However, generating its own electricity from coal could mean the closure of Russian power stations. The priority for the central planning system was to maintain the organised process of cooperation among the factories, even if it would keep costs high.

The Pavlodar-Ekibastuz industrial cluster developed its industries not only on the basis of local resources, but using raw materials of other regions in the Kazakh SSR as well. For example, the Pavlodar oil refinery used oil from Southern Kazakhstan in order to supply its output for the manufacture of finished goods in Russia, while the local chemical factory based its production on waste from the oil refinery. The machine-building industry of the cluster was based on the output of the metallurgical industry of the Karaganda region and on the high demand in northern Kazakhstan where agricultural equipment was manufactured, which had mainly been supplied from Russia until 1970. Thus, the Pavlodar-Ekibastuz industrial cluster was extremely important for production of the heavy industry of the Soviet Union, being well endowed with diversified mineral resources. The industrial cluster mainly specialised in mining, transporting raw materials to other republics of the Soviet Union, while the cost-effectiveness of the production of finished goods declined.

4. The Torgai industrial block

The *Torgai industrial block* was located in the Kostanai region in the north of the Kazakh SSR. The specialisation of the Torgai industrial block was mining, particularly the extraction of iron ore, and the extraction of other mineral resources that are used in the production of construction materials.

One of the main clusters of the Torgai industrial block was *Kostanai*, which was located in the northwest of Kostanai region. The *Kostanai cluster* was the main producer of iron ore in the Kazakh SSR. It was responsible for 89.7% of the production in the Kazakh SSR. In the ten years up to 1970 production grew by 475%, while its reserves amounted to 84% reserves in the Kazakh SSR and 16% of the reserves of the Soviet Union (Adamchuk and Dvoskin, 1968). The high level of other reserves of minerals put the Kostanai cluster ahead of many republics in the Soviet Union, while reserves of asbestos, which is a mineral used in the construction materials industry, constituted 12% of the global reserves of asbestos. The endowment of the cluster with different types of minerals explains the progressive development of the Kostanai region in the construction materials industry, which supplied signifi-cant parts of its output to Russia, being located on its border, while local needs in construction material industries were mainly fulfilled by Eastern Ka-zakhstan.

5. The Southern Kazakhstan industrial block

The *Southern Kazakhstan* industrial block was based on the Southern Ka-zakhstan and Zhambyl regions, where the main specialisation was chemical industry and non-ferrous metallurgy. The main proportion of chemical produc-tion of the Kazakh SSR was based in the Southern Kazakhstan industrial block, while the construction materials industry produced 36.1% of cement in the Kazakh SSR in 1970. The cement output had grown significantly (153.8%) since 1960. The favourable climate of Southern Kazakhstan af-fected the intensive development of light industry and food production. In 1970, the block produced 100% of cotton, 97% of cotton textile, 44% of sugar, 33% of wool and 73.5% of vegetable oil in the Kazakh SSR (Adam-chuk and Dvoskin, 1968).

The Southern Kazakhstan industrial block had two main industrial clusters: *Zhambyl-Karatau* and *Chimkent-Kentau*, which were different by specialisa-tion, but fully complemented each other in the production process. The *Zhambyl-Karatau cluster* specialised in the chemical industry, wool and lather manufacture of light industry, and sugar and spirit production of food industry.

While the *Chimkent-Kentau cluster* had a concentration of non-ferrous metallurgy, machine-building, construction materials, light industry (cotton), vegetable oil production, food industry (wine) and chemical industry. The Southern Kazakhstan industrial block had the most intensive development during and after the war, as many Russian and Ukrainian factories were evacuated to this region, such as a rubber factory, a footwear factory, a garment factory, a machine-building factory and others. The relocation of these factories to the Southern Kazakhstan region helped to create other factories for those industries.

The *Zhambyl-Karatau industrial cluster* was located in the western part of the Zhambyl region, which is richly endowed with raw materials for the chemical industry and with non-ferrous metals. The Zhambyl-Karatau cluster had 40% of all phosphorite reserves of the Soviet Union and its production constituted the entire output in the Kazakh SSR in 1970. The output of the phosphorite factory in Zhambyl mainly supplied local and neighbouring Uzbekistan chemical factories. Apart from the chemical industry, the Zhambyl-Karatau industrial cluster developed light and food industries because of its favourable climate. The wool manufacture factory was the second largest of its type in the Kazakh SSR after Eastern Kazakhstan. Important roles in the Kazakh SSR and in the Soviet Union were played by sugar factories, a spirit factory and other factories in food and light industries.

The *Chimkent-Kentau industrial cluster* of the Southern Kazakhstan industrial block was located in the central part of the Southern Kazakhstan region. The cluster was distinguished by the largest pharmaceutical factory in the Soviet Union, which was located in Chimkent and used medicinal herbs as a source for medical products and toxic chemicals for the agricultural sector, manufacturing 80% of medicinal plants in the Soviet Union in 1970. The Chimkent-Kentau industrial cluster was rich with nonferrous metals, especially zinc and lead, however, its lead factory had a higher capacity compared to the productivity of the Chimkent-Kentau lead mines. As a result, one third of raw materials in the factory were transported from other regions and republics, which made production more expensive and inefficient, taking into account sufficient lead reserves in the region. However, the productivity of the factory grew even faster after being the first factory in the Soviet Union, which introduced new technology for the manufacture of lead using natural gas from the Uzbek SSR, increasing therefore the productivity of lead manufacture by 80%.

The energy supplies of the Chimkent-Kentau cluster were based on the coalmines in the Uzbek SSR, the Kyrgyz SSR and Siberia, while the neighbouring region Karaganda, which was the richest region in the Kazakh SSR in terms of coal, supplied coal to the Uzbek and the Kyrgyz SSR due to the mismanagement of the central authorities. In order to reduce the costs of energy consumption the Chimkent-Kentau industrial cluster had to substitute imported coal by importing natural gas from the Uzbek SSR, becoming de-pendent on the gas supply from the neighbouring republic. However, the de-pendency was not obvious until the collapse of the Soviet Union, when every republic had to ensure its own supply of resources.

6. The Western Kazakhstan industrial block

The *Western Kazakhstan industrial block* included Aktubinsk, Atyrau and Mangistau with specialisation in fuel, chemical and metallurgy industries. The Western Kazakhstan industrial block was divided into 3 main clusters: *Guriev[26]-Emba, Mangyshlak[27]* and *Aktubinsk.*

The *Guriev-Emba industrial cluster* was located in the northern part of the Atyrau region on the side of the Caspian Sea and Emba River. The initial specialisation of the Guriev-Emba industrial cluster was fishing in the Caspian Sea. It was responsible for 55.5% of the total catch of the Kazakh SSR. How-ever, the most important specialisation of the cluster for the Soviet Union was the fuel industry, which had its first refineries built in 1911 and in 1915. Oil ex-traction started after the formation of the Soviet Union and was more inten-sive during the war due to the high priority given to fuel industry to support the military defence of the Soviet Union. Thus, the production of oil increased 20 times between 1913 and 1970, while the share of Guriev-Emba oil in the Ka-

---

26   Guriev was the central city of Atyrau region and later was renamed as Atyrau. In the text, the region is named as Atyrau for simplicity of understanding.
27   Mangyshlak is located in Mangistau region.

zakh SSR oil extraction in 1970 amounted to 18.6%, following a drop from 84% in 1965, as a result of the low level of growth in the Guriev-Emba industrial cluster and the intensive development of the Mangistau oil fields. The latter caused the share of the Kazakh SRR in the total Soviet oil extraction to increase from 0.8% in 1965 to 3.7% in 1970.

The problem of the low growth of Guriev-Emba oil fields resulted from its geographical location, which made oil extraction and the introduction of new technologies to increase productivity and reduce extraction costs difficult. The cost of oil extraction in the Guriev-Emba oil fields was constantly rising and became 4.2 times more expensive than in Russia and 3 times more than the Soviet average, therefore it was not profitable to continue the growth of oil extraction in the region. Before the Second World War, the Guriev-Emba cluster specialised only in oil extraction and was supplied its output to other republics for the needs of industry. During the war the Guriev-Emba industrial cluster introduced a new oil refinery, however, oil extracted in the region continued to be supplied to other republics for refinement, while the Guriev oil refinery processed oil from Russian oil fields, as a result of the chemical composition of local oil, which could not be refined in the local refinery without major reconstruction. Since it relied on oil transported from other regions of the Soviet Union, the Guriev oil refinery had a production cost twice that of refineries in Russia and Azerbaijan. The given example of mismanagement shows ways of irrational and inefficient economy development, which were followed by central authorities. Republics were connected by industrial production, where the allocation of resources and facilities did not take account of the advantages offered by geographical location.

The *Mangyshlak (Mangistau) industrial cluster* had its origin at the end of 1970s as a result of the discovery of large oil and gas fields. The Mangyshlak industrial cluster was located in the Mangistau region, on the eastern part of the Caspian Sea. The Mangyshlak oil fields were found to have good quality oil and were clustered closely together. Their discovery significantly increased the oil reserves of the Kazakh SSR which constituted one of the largest and important oil reserves in the Soviet Union. In 1965, the Mangyshlak fields extracted 16.5% of Kazakh SSR oil. The situation changed significantly in 1970, when the share of Mangyshlak oil increased to 79.2% of the total production in the Kazakh SSR. In only 5 years, from 1965, the Mangyshlak cluster managed to increase its oil extraction 31 times, which increased the total Kazakh SSR oil extraction for these years by 549.6%, while the growth rate of oil extraction in other Kazakh SSR oil fields amounted to only 25.6% from 1960 to 1965. The intensive growth of oil extraction was in part due to its comparative advantage in terms of production costs, which were 2-3 times lower compared to other oil fields in the Soviet Union.

Apart from significant oil reserves, the Mangyshlak region was richly endowed with a diversity of mineral resources, which could be used by the construction materials industry and were considered to have the highest quality in the Soviet Union. The construction materials industry of the Mangyshlak industrial cluster developed significantly and played an important role in the rapid development of the fuel industry.

Apart from the well endowment of the Mangyshlak region with mineral resources, other industries of the region were poor developed due to poor climatic and geographical conditions. The development of industry in such conditions required higher investments than in other regions. Nevertheless, the government allocated investment in the development of regions, whose resources were of high priority for Soviet Union needs. All food provisions for the Mangyshlak industrial cluster were transported from other regions of the Kazakh SSR, Russia and the Caucasus. Mangyshlak was not able to develop agriculture and related industries due to poor soil and the scarcity of water, which put a serious question mark over further development of the industrial cluster and the maintenance of the population and the growth of local industries.

The *Aktubinsk industrial cluster* was based in the Aktubinsk region and specialised in metallurgy and chemical industries, being well endowed with nickel and chromic ores reserves, phosphorite, barite and mineral salts. Aktubinsk's reserves of chrome ore were the largest in the Soviet Union and gave the base for the Aktubinsk factory, which was the biggest in the chemical industry of the Soviet Union, with the highest quality of chrome products, supplied not only to Soviet republics but also to 20 countries outside the Soviet Union.

The Aktubinsk industrial cluster was highly specialised in ferrous metallurgy with many factories relying on local materials, while the location of the cluster was the most advantageous in the Kazakh SSR in terms of access to output markets. The location on the border of Russia on one side and the border with Uzbekistan on the other side opened the way to other Central Asian republics. However, the manufacture and use of local materials was not always sufficient. Thus, the Aktubinsk phosphorite reserves in Aktubinsk constituted 12.6% of Soviet reserves and 34.6% of phosphorite reserves in the Kazakh SSR with much cheaper extraction costs compared to the Soviet Union in 1970. However, the factory based on these reserves mainly used raw materials from other fields in the Kazakh SSR and Russia due to the low level of the development of own fields and mismanagement of the production process.

Although the Aktubinsk cluster produced high quality products, it had significant environmental problems, which were not considered in the Soviet Union as a factor in industrial production. However, apart from environmental damage, factories were not being run efficiently. For example, the Aktubinsk factory of ferroalloys emitted 80 thousand cubic meters of gas from the production of ferrochrome daily, which could replace 42 thousand tonnes of coal. This constituted 8.2% of coal used at the factory annually (Adamchuk and Dvoskin, 1968). The inefficient use of waste was a feature of many factories of the Soviet Union, where central authorities had no reason for investment more in the restructuring of technologies. They allocated resources that were more than sufficient for long-term production.

Between 1960 and 1970, the economy of the Kazakh SSR experienced a rapid growth of its industrial and agricultural production on the basis of natural resources that made the Kazakh SSR one of the attractive and important republics for the Soviet Union from the economic point of view. Thus, the national income of the Kazakh SSR grew by 214% between 1960 and 1970, while the economic assets increased 2.76 times, industrial assets grew by 364% during the same period, agricultural assets increased by 210% and transport assets grew by 247% (*Narodnoe xoziaistvo SSSR v 1970*, 1971). During the period from 1960 to 1970 a large number of powerful and signifi-cant industrial factories were created as part of the overall economic plan of the Soviet Union, such as the Karaganda metallurgical factory, the Almaty cotton factory, the Eastern Kazakhstan titanium-magnesium factory, the Pav-lodar aluminium factory and many others.

The contribution of industry to the GDP of the Kazakh SSR amounted to 48% in 1970, whereas that of agriculture had dropped to 23.7%. This can be com-pared to the beginning of the century when the figures were 15% and 85% respectively.

Figure 1.7. The dynamics of Kazakh SSR industries, 1970/1960, %

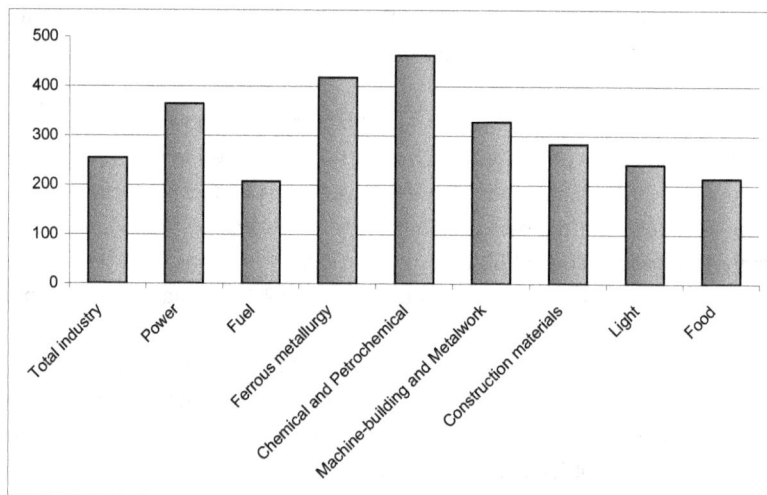

Source: *Ekonomika Kazakhstana za 60 let: 1917-1977*, 1977.

The growth rate of industry in the Kazakh SSR for the period 1960-1970 was 155% (Figure 1.7.), while the average level of industrial growth in the Soviet Union was 127%, whereas Russian industry increased by 115%, Ukrainian by 127%, Uzbek by 103% and Georgian by 116% (*Ekonomika Kazakhstana za 60 let: 1917-1977*, 1977). The chemical and petrochemical industries of the

Kazakh SSR had the highest growth in the period 1960-1970 (263%), reflect-ing the growth of oil production due to the discoveries of new oil fields and the construction of several powerful chemical factories in Southern Kazakhstan. The power industry grew by 265% because of intensive development and construction in this industry in order to maintain the energy supply for newly built factories in all sectors of the economy. Ferrous metallurgy had the sec-ond highest growth rate of 318% between 1960 and 1970 due to numerous discoveries and further development of ferrous metal fields in central and eastern Kazakhstan based on Soviet requirements. Due to the high growth of production, the share of heavy industries in the total volume of industrial pro-duction in the Kazakh SSR increased to 41.6% in 1970 from 37.7% in 1965.

Despite the growth in all sectors of the economy, industries still had prob-lems. For example, there was no proper balance between extraction and manufacturing industries. In many cases manufacturing stagnated because of the discrepancy in manufacturing capacities and mineral resource extraction. As a result, raw materials were supplied to other regions of the Soviet Union for manufacturing and finished products were re-imported. It was also the case that factories in the Kazakh SSR, located in regions endowed with raw materials, imported raw materials from other regions of the Soviet Union, in order continue to use their full capacity. The machine-building industry did not reflect the needs of industries in the Kazakh SSR, as there was no production of any equipment for the light and food industries, while they were undergoing intensive growth. As a result, the potential of these industries could not be completely realised, except with regard to the development of *tselina* lands when the development of agriculture was a priority for the Soviet Union.

The gradual diversification and equalisation of regional industrial develop-ment (except Western Kazakhstan) after the formation of industrial clusters in 1970 can be seen in Table 1.10. In 1940 the most developed group of regions by total industrial production was Eastern Kazakhstan, where the volume of industrial production per square kilometres was 3 times greater than the av-erage in the Kazakh SSR, while in 1975 the figure was only 1.5 times greater than the average industrial production of the Kazakh SSR (Table 1.10.). Other regional groups, (e.g. Western Kazakhstan, Central Kazakhstan and

Northern Kazakhstan) had a level of industrial production, per square km, lower than average figures in the Kazakh SSR. However, in 1975, in the period of intensive development of industrial clusters, the industrial production of those regions exceeded the average level of the Kazakh SSR. Only Western Kazakhstan could not manage to increase the level of diversification, due to very poor geographical and climate conditions for the development of other industries except fuel. The formation of industrial clusters led regions towards a narrow specialisation, but at the same time resulted in the development of a number of other industries related to each other that created an industrial complex.

Table 1.10. Industrial production of regional groups per km^2, (Kazakh SSR industrial production = 100)

Regional groups[28]	1940	1950	1960	1975
Southern Kazakhstan	138	118	112	111
Western Kazakhstan	28	36	29	36
Central Kazakhstan	80	154	144	131
Northern Kazakhstan	52	63	86	116
Eastern Kazakhstan	300	211	209	158

Source: *Ekonomika Kazakhstana za 60 let: 1917-1977*, 1977.

During years of industrial development, regional territories were developed as well that comparatively equalised industrial production volume per square kilometre in 1975 (Table 1.10.), except for the group of regions in Western Kazakhstan. The reason for the low index of Western Kazakhstan is that the only specialisation of the Atyrau and Western Kazakhstan group was oil extraction, and the development of other industries there was very difficult because of the severe climate, which is not suitable for agriculture or the inhabitants. However, the volume of industrial production per square kilometre in

---

28   **Southern Kazakhstan** group includes Almaty, Zhambyl, Kzyl-Orda and Southern Kazakhstan regions; **Western Kazakhstan** group includes Atyrau, Aktubinsk, Mangistau and Western Kazakhstan regions; **Central Kazakhstan** group includes Karaganda region; **Northern Kazakhstan** group includes Kostanai, Akmola, Pavlodar, and Northern Kazakhstan regions; **Eastern Kazakhstan** group consists of Eastern Kazakhstan region.

Western Kazakhstan was 39.6 times higher in 1975 than in 1940. During the same period, the volume of industrial production per square kilometre in Central and Southern Kazakhstan increased to 50.8 and 25.2 times that in 1940. The regional group that achieved the most development during these years was Northern Kazakhstan, which increased its volume of industrial production per square kilometre by 69.5 times in 1975 since 1940, due to the development of *tselina* lands, which were located in Northern Kazakhstan and involved substantial help from other republics of the Soviet Union. By 1975, Northern Kazakhstan had the most developed rail and road network, because of the great need for the rapid transportation of wheat to other parts of the Soviet Union. Therefore, the creation of industrial clusters increased the diversification of regional industrial production at the same time as regional disparities of industrial production were reduced.

All the main industrial blocks of the Kazakh SSR were based on heavy industries with the gradual development of food and light industries for the maintenance of local provisions and the employment of the female population. The development of all industrial blocks was based on the needs of the Soviet economy where the decision of industries allocation was being taken according to the needs of the Soviet Union as a whole, while very often local sources were used inefficiently. The location of factories was based on the deposits of raw materials, however, the manufacture of semi-finished and finished products was based on the proximity to markets, which were outside the Kazakh SSR. The economy of the Kazakh SSR benefited from allocations based on the Soviet economic plan by receiving support in terms of finances, technology and human capital, however, there was a growing gap between resource-rich and resource-poor regions. The latter suffered from a poorly developed infrastructure and had weak links with other regions because of the underdeveloped transport network.

The industrial development of the Soviet economy was based on the utilisation of hitherto unexploited resources, which led to the creation of new industries and the extension of existing ones. By 1970, the growth of production was reaching its limits, and the improvement of technology urgently required to increase production further.

The expansion of Research and Development

The development of the economy of the Kazakh SSR followed the extensive pattern since the formation of the Soviet Union. Its principal objective was the development of new territories and the creation of new industries. However, the development of the economy of the Kazakh SSR was based on the growing demands of the industrial needs of the Soviet Union, so that the Kazakh SSR was well endowed with the necessary resources. Such a route of development increased industrial production in the Kazakh SSR by 125 times from 1913 to 1968, while the whole Soviet Union had increased its industrial production by only 79 times during the same period (*Sovetskii Soiuz – Kazakhstan*, 1970). At the end of the 1970s the potential for increasing the economic capacity of the Kazakh SSR was close to the limit, as 90% of local labour was involved in the economy, and the potential for creating industries on the basis of local raw materials had been well exploited and those industries required further development and improvement. In 1967, the head of the Soviet government L.Brezhnev introduced a new pattern of development in the Soviet Union, which aimed at the intensive development of the economy on the basis of the quality of production due to the advancement of science and technology. New sectors of science were born that created a new generation of machines, such as space exploration, cybernetics, electronics and others. The number of innovations firstly used in the industrial production of the Kazakh SSR increased significantly from 50.8 thousand in 1960 to 108.3 thousand in 1970 and to 144.1 thousand in 1975. Economic effect[29] of use of innovations increased from 38.8 million roubles in 1965 to 123.5 million roubles in 1970 and to 210 million roubles in 1975. In addition to introduction of innovation the government of the Kazakh SSR used many other methods for the efficient production. These methods included employment of new technology, mechanisation and computerisation of production processes, where costs of their introduction increased from 149.6 million roubles in 1970 to 212.7 million roubles in 1975 and to 401.5 million roubles in 1985. The growth of income from the introduction of new methods increased significantly as well from 76.6

---

29   Economic effect in roubles is counted by deduction of income of the planned production from the profit of the production after the introduction of technology innovations. (Smirnickij, 1980)

million roubles in 1970 to 92.2 million roubles in 1975 and to 177.7 million roubles in 1985 (*Narodnoe xoziaistvo Kazakhskoi SSR*, 1987).

Table 1.11. Industrial growth tendency, 1970-1985, %

Industries	1970 (1960=100)	1975 (1970=100)	1980 (1975=100)	1985 (1980=100)
Total industry	*256*	*147*	*115*	*118*
Power	353	161	135	133
Fuel	205	153	130	123
Metallurgy	420	146	137	107
Chemical and Petrochemical	467	182	151	158
Machine-building	321	188	136	132
Timber	202	158	123	130
Construction materials	282	144	110	108
Light	239	147	130	110
Food	219	127	105	110

Source: Data are calculated from: *Ekonomika Kazakhstana za 60 let: 1917-1977*, 1977. *Narodnoe xoziaistvo Kazakhstana za 70 let*, 1990.

The highest growth rates of industrial production were observed in industries, which were involved in research and development, where power, chemical, petrochemical and machine-building industries were ahead of other industries by production growth (Table 1.11.). During the period 1970-1975, the average industrial growth rate was 47%, while machine-building and chemical industries increased their production by 88% and 82% respectively for the same

period. During 1980-1985, the chemical and petrochemical industries increased their production by 58% while the average industrial growth rate was
18%. However, the tendency of growth of industrial production growth was in
decline. Between 1970 and 1975, it amounted to 47%, whereas during the
period 1980-1985 it was 18%. This could mean that high level of resources
used at the current level of technology resulted in the gradual stabilisation of
the production.

Areas of research and development in Kazakh SSR economy included the
electrification of urban and rural areas, the mechanisation of production, the
application of advanced chemicals and the introduction of advanced technology. Thus, by 1975, urban and rural areas were completely electrified and the
generation of electricity per head was 3.2 thousand kW hours, while the Soviet Union as a whole in 1975 generated only 1.6 thousand kW hours per
capita (*Narodnoe xoziaistvo Kazakhstana za 70 let,*1990). By implementing
new technologies, the Kazakh SSR was able to maintain its industrial status
at the level of the Soviet Union as a whole. The Kazakh SSR took third place
in the Soviet Union by industrial production after Russia and Ukraine, first in
the production of non-ferrous metals, second place in the production of oil
and third in other industrial output, such as, coal, iron ore, electricity, cast
iron, steel, agricultural equipment and the production of main agricultural output.

Table 1.12. Shares of industrial assets, %

Industries	Industrial assets			
	1960	1976	1980	1985
Total industry	*100*	*100*	*100*	*100*
Power	13.0	18.8	17.8	16.3
Fuel	16.8	12.2	12.1	13.0
Including: coal	*12.8*	*7.6*	*7.5*	*8.0*
Oil	*4.0*	*4.6*	*4.6*	*5.0*
Metallurgy	33.3	29.1	25.3	23.6
Chemical and Petrochemical	3.2	7.0	9.4	12.4
Machine-building	9.0	11.9	13.9	14.5
Timber manufacture	2.3	1.7	1.4	1.3
Construction materials	9.4	8.4	7.6	6.7
Light	3.4	3.4	3.2	3.1
Food	7.6	6.9	6.2	5.5
Others	2.0	1.7	3.1	3.6

Source: Data are calculated from: *Narodnoe xoziaistvo Kazakhstana za 70 let*, 1990.
Statistical Yearbook of Kazakhstan – 1992, 1993.

The proportion of total Soviet industrial assets in the Kazakh SSR kept changing in line with a change in the intensity of their growth. Research and development intensive industries such as power, chemical, petrochemical and machine building had remarkably increased their assets in 1985 since 1960, accounting for 43.2% of all industrial assets in 1985 compared to 25.2% in 1960 (Table 1.12.). While the assets of metallurgy comprised one third of all industrial assets in 1960, their share had dropped to 23.6% in

1985. Increase in the assets of particular industries signified the higher level of intensity of their development based on research and development.

The share of labour by industries had also changed over time and had reflected the growth pattern of changes in the share of industrial assets. The power industry was an exception whose share of labour declined by 0.9% over the period 1960-1975, while its share of industrial assets increased by 5.8% for the same period, which is the result of the substitution of labour by more advanced technology that increased the labour productivity. The same reason caused a slight decline in the proportion of labour employed in the fuel and non-ferrous metallurgy industries. However, machine-building, metalwork and light industries had significant growth in the share of total labour during 1960-1975, which can be explained by the growth of their industrial capacity that demanded more human capital.

As a result of research and development of industrial production, heavy industry developed new sectors, such as nuclear power, machine-building of new types of equipment that included electrical engineering, the production of reinforced concrete for construction materials, the production of plastic goods in the chemical industry and others that already in 1975 controlled 20% of all industrial assets in the Kazakh SSR. The sitting of industrial capacity was based on the location of raw material deposits. Therefore, the diversity of industries in every region depended on local conditions. At the beginning of industrial development, the exports of the Kazakh SSR consisted only of raw materials, due to the low capacity for the manufacturing factories in the Kazakh SSR. However, in the middle of the 1970s the Kazakh SSR was already an exporter of raw materials and a wide assortment of their final products to 70 countries in the world other than the Soviet Union.

Labour productivity indicates the efficiency of activity in economic sectors, where the trend towards growth in productivity is accompanied by the trend towards lower growth of the workforce. This is due to improved technology in labour intensive industries and due to a higher level of education in the human capital (Table 1.13.). Thus, marginal product grew due to the growth of labour productivity. Growth of the marginal product increased from 44% in

1940/1950 to 76% in 1970/1975, while the growth of labour declined from 74% to 11% respectively. The period 1970-1975 had the highest growth of the marginal product mainly for the reason of research and development growth at the beginning of the 1970s.

Table 1.13.   Labour productivity in Kazakh SSR industry, %.

Years	GDP	Labour size	Labour productivity	Marginal product growth in account of labour productivity growth./1
1940/1950	232	174	127	44
1950/1955	182	140	143	51
1955/1960	174	134	120	54
1960/1965	164	133	123	48
1965/1970	156	122	128	61
1970/1975	146	111	130	76
1975/1980	111	112	108	45
1980/1985	127	108	110	65

Source: Data are calculated from: *Ekonomika Kazakhstana za 60 let: 1917-1977*, 1977. *Narodnoe xoziaistvo Kazakhstana za 70 let*, 1990. *Kazakhstanu 40 let*, 1960. *Narodnoe xoziaistvo SSSR v 1980*, 1981. /1 Data are taken from: *Narodnoe xoziaistvo Kazakhstana za 70 let*, 1990.

However, despite the successful growth of industry in the Kazakh SSR, the regions had not developed evenly, as the aim of the Soviet Union was to derive maximum benefits from the natural resources of republics, therefore the path of least resistance was chosen for the development of industries. Industrial factories were built in regions that were endowed with mineral resources, while further development of the particular industry involved the investment in the infrastructure of a region to provide the necessary transport links. In order to permit the factories to operate efficiently, service centres were created for factories and their equipment, including power stations and the construction materials industry, while cities were growing around factories together with food and light industries so that the subsistence of the employees was provided for and in order to increase the employment level of the female population. In this way, an area rich in mineral resources became one of the largest industrial clusters of the country. Since 1913, the share of industrial production had changed significantly in some regions that were developed on the basis of mineral resources. Thus, industrial production in Southern Kazakhstan accounted for 2.5% of total industrial output in the Kazakh SSR in 1913. By 1939, the proportion had increased to 14.4%, while the proportion of the republican output derived from industrial production in Karaganda grew from 7.9% to 14.6% in the same period. Subsequently the Karaganda region increased its share of republican industrial output to 25.2% in 1950.

All regions of the Kazakh SSR achieved substantial growth in industrial development during the period 1970-1985 (Table 1.14.). The Pavlodar region made the greatest progress of all the regions, increasing its industrial assets by 350.2%. This led to an increase in industrial production by 270% and a 134% growth in productivity. The intensive development of coalfields in Pavlodar resulted in the rise of the region's share of industrial assets from 8.6% in 1970 to 11.2% in 1985, while the construction of new conventional and hydroelectric power stations for maintaining coal mining of the region increased labour productivity due to the high labour-intensity of the coal industry. During the period from 1970 to 1985, industrial production achieved the highest growth in chemical and petrochemical industry and in machine-building by 228% and 221% respectively, while the entire industry of the Kazakh SSR grew only by 100% during this period. As a result, regions, which specialised in these industries, achieved the highest growth of industrial assets. Thus, the industrial assets of the Zhambyl region grew by 394.8% (Table 1.14.), while industrial production in the region increased by 119%. The chemical industry of the Zhambyl region achieved much higher growth (758.9%) in the production of phosphorite in 1970-1985. The Aktubinsk region specialised in chemical industry, and as can be seen from Table 1.14., industrial assets increased in this region by 369.3%, while industrial output increased by 154%, which is higher than the average growth of industrial production in the Kazakh SSR. The industrial assets of the Atyrau region grew by 434% (Table 1.14.), which was the highest growth among other regions due to the high capital-intensity of hydrocarbon extraction, while the industrial production growth amounted only to 99%.

Table 1.14.   Main industrial indicators of regions, 1970-1985, %

Regions	Industrial assets in 1985 (1970=100)	Share in total industrial as-		Industrial produc- tion volume in 1985, (1970=100)	Industrial labour productivity in 1985, (1970=100)	Industries of spe- cialisation
		1970	1985	sets		
Akmola	387.4	5.5	6.2	278	209	Construction materials, machine-building, food
Aktubinsk	469.3	3.0	4.1	254	170	Fuel, machine-building, chemical, light
Almaty	391.3	4.1	4.1	203	140	Construction materials, light, food
Almaty city	273.9	5.1	4.1	187	168	Machine-building, con- struction materials, light, food
Atyrau	534.0	5.4	8.4	199	139	Oil, gas, chemical, food
Eastern Ka- zakhstan	269.0	13.6	10.7	153	132	Chemical, construction materials, light, food
Karaganda	275.0	28.6	23.0	180	143	Coal, metallurgy, chemi- cal, light, food

Regions	Industrial assets in 1985 (1970=100)	Share in total industrial assets		Industrial produc- tion volume in 1985, (1970=100)	Industrial labour productivity in 1985, (1970=100)	Industries of spe- cialisation
		1970	1985			
Kostanai	301.4	9.4	8.3	228	175	Metallurgy, chemical, construction materials, light, food
Kzyl-Orda	355.1	1.3	1.3	240	169	Construction materials, food
Northern Kazakhstan	331.6	2.5	2.4	235	188	Machine-building, con- struction materials, food
Pavlodar	450.2	8.6	11.2	370	234	Coal, metallurgy, ma- chine-building, construc- tion materials, chemical, food
Southern Kazakhstan	375.7	6.9	7.6	177	127	Machine-building, con- struction materials, chemcial, light, food
Western Ka- zakhstan	451.3	1.6	2.1	215	153	Oil, gas, food
Zhambyl	494.8	4.3	6.3	219	150	Chemical, machine- building, light, food

Source: Data are calculated from: *Narodnoe xoziaistvo Kazakhstana za 70 let*, 1990.

The lowest growth of industrial assets was observed in Eastern Kazakhstan and the Karaganda region with increases of 169% and 175% respectively. At the same time, the growth of industrial production was lower compared to other regions. Productions increased by 53% and 80% respectively, which is lower than the average republican level. However, despite having the lowest growth rates in industrial assets and industrial production, these two regions had the most significant shares of industrial assets and industrial production in the Kazakh SSR.

The growth of industrial production was observed in all regions of the Kazakh SSR because of the increasing level of capital investment in regions, which were behind the average industrial development in the Kazakh SSR. However, the equalisation of regional industrial development was carried out artificially by increases of industrial assets, but without the elaboration of an efficient way of industrial development, which could realize certain benefits from the geographical location of industry. The development of some industrial enterprises was subsidised just for the sake of the equalisation of the inter-regional development level. However, such tactics could work only under the conditions of government controlled central planning, but when the transition process began, the location efficiency started to play the key role in further development, because of lower production costs and the comparative advantage compared to other productions, while other industrial factories were on the edge of survival.

1.6   Regional development during the *Perestroika* period

The slowdown in production growth of some industries and in particular the decline in the production of the machine-building industry in the Soviet economy (where the Kazakh SSR was not an exception, see Table 1.15. *Industrial production of the Kazakh SSR*) was characterised by the diminishing returns of the capital accumulation to the technical capital change (Desai, 1986). Let us examine the causes of the economic retardation of the Kazakh SSR, where a shortage phenomena existed for both consumers and producers, where pervasive consequences resulted from the misallocation of resources,

delays in the completion of projects, queuing, hoarding, and rent-seeking behaviour etc. (Qian, 1994). The latter will allow to explain the declining growth
of the Kazakh SSR economy and to provide an analytical understanding of
the impact of the shortage phenomenon on the economic system as a whole.

Kornai related the explanation of shortages in the socialist system with the
soft budget constraint phenomenon (Kornai, 1980), which was one of the
main characteristics of the Soviet socialist economic system. The vast majority of enterprises in the Kazakh SSR (as in the whole USSR) were state-
owned. Their survival and expansion (Kornai, 1992) under the soft budget
constraints did not depend on market behaviour, but on the level of bureaucratic coordination and the success of bargaining with authorities. According
to Kornai, (1992) it is possible to distinguish four main forms of soft budget
constraints: *soft subsidy, soft taxation, soft credit and soft administrative pricing.*

In the Kazakh SSR, *soft subsidies* were the most common, where excessive
expenditures of enterprises could be covered by subsidies from the republican government after some bargaining. However, responsiveness of production activities to prices was very weak, so that a decline in the price of an input substitute did not usually cause the change of the input set. The marginal
utility of output was not taken into account; as a result investments in Kazakh
SSR industrial enterprises grew significantly, while their efficiency fell notably
(Bajmuratov, 2000).

Thus, the shortage and inefficiency of the centrally planned economy were
directly related to the concept of soft budget constraints (Maskin and Xu,
2001). In the case of the market economy with hard budget constraints, enterprises are induced to generate profit from their production process and to
choose efficient and fast projects, as the loan for a project is being negotiated
ex ante, without any chance to extend the loan beyond the final deadline of
the project. Therefore, enterprises, which choose inefficient and slow projects, have low chances of an additional loan for the finishing stage of the incomplete project and a high likelihood of becoming bankrupt, as not many

banks would take a risk for insecure investments. As a result, the efficiency of the production is likely to be high under the hard budget constraints.

The efficiency of state enterprises in the Kazakh SSR economy was directly affected by the expectations of managers with regard to soft budget constraints, as their choice of projects or technology used did not depend on its efficiency or speed, being aware *ex ante* of prospective negotiations of expenses cover *ex post* (Primbetov, 1997). There was no fear of being bankrupt as such a concept of the market economy was replaced by unending government subsidies and *soft credits* in the central planned economy. In the post-Soviet transition period of Kazakhstan the banking system continues to subsidize industrial enterprises, but under stringent market conditions, so that long-term uncertain projects cannot attract government subsidies due to the high risk of failure to achieve completion (Bajtanaeva, 2000). In the Soviet period, the state enterprise itself did not have the possibility of choosing the particular project to undertake, but merely responded to directives (Ericson, 1991) from the administrative hierarchy, which were generally based on outdated information without any serious estimates of likely cost overruns. In addition, the nature of enterprises was determined by the key strategy of the socialist system, where the operation of non-profitable enterprises was planned by the system. The reason for subsidising non-profitable enterprises was explained by the need to provide work for the population, i.e. where the unemployment rate was artificially reduced on a significant scale (Tokbergen, Sulejmenova and Turegeldieva, 1998). For the administrative hierarchy quantitative targets were the priority (Kornai, 1992), which were the plan's indicators. State owned enterprises had incentives to fulfil production targets in time, through wage bonuses. However, there were no incentives for making excessive profits, as the higher profit of enterprises would mean higher targets in the plan for the next period, while excessive profits would be taken away from successive enterprises and absorbed by the budget of the government.

Production losses of state owned enterprises were covered by the central managerial system on the basis of soft budget constraints. In the case of changes in the input substitute costs, enterprises did not have any incentives to change their input set to reduce costs in order to be competitive with other producers of the same product (Qian and Roland, 1998). In fact, state enterprises hold the prior information on external financial support, where the concept of competitiveness, in terms of cost reductions, did not exist in the socialist system due to the "everybody is equal" slogan of Soviet period, which was implemented on the level of enterprises as well. The principle of soft subsidies was directly linked with the principle of *soft taxation* in the Soviet economy, in order to create a balance between production levels. Thus, financial shortfalls of enterprises were made up by subsidies, while excessive profits were taken away for public consumption and the allocations for wage pay-rolls were not increased (Bajmuratov, 2000).

Prices in the socialist economy were centrally administrated by government *soft administrative pricing*, and not by producers themselves, so that market demand and supply was not taken into account in the establishment of prices. Thus, prices were defined on the vertical level with the right of bargaining, while the horizontal establishment of prices did not exist, as it could be expected to operate under the conditions of market economy, where prices are determined by the interaction between buyers and sellers. The detailed information on new ranges of products often reached the top of the hierarchy after long time gaps, which affected the efficiency of setting prices with its elaborate calculations. However, the establishment of prices under the centrally planned economy was not based on a random choice of numbers, but on three main principles: the estimation of social costs, attempts to keep prices for modern technology low in order to make it more attractive and maintain stable prices. The quality of goods and the preferences of consumers were not taken into account.

The economy of the Kazakh SSR was based on the priorities of the Soviet economy, where industrial enterprises were allocated according to the presence of raw material sources and the proximity to markets for intermediate and finished goods in other republics of the Soviet Union. Many industries of the Kazakh SSR were created in order to supply other Soviet republics, while being isolated from internal connections in the Kazakh SSR. The efficiency of industrial allocation was considered from the global point of view of the Soviet Union, whereas the efficient allocation of resources at the inter-regional level of Kazakhstan would reduce production costs and increase productivity. However, industrial enterprises in the socialist system did not heed the lower costs signals under the weak responsiveness of prices, where strong responsiveness could define the best allocation of industries. Thus, the government of the Soviet Union artificially created full employment in the economy. In fact, industrial enterprises did have an incentive for production growth, which was defined by the extra bonus paid to employees. However, there was no threat of enterprise closure, in the event of the non-profitability, because soft budget constraints covered excessive costs. For instance, the ferroalloy factory of the Aktubinsk region used coal from the Karaganda region, while coalmines in Aktubinsk produced enough coal to supply its local factories. However, they supplied their production to Russian factories, while it would have been more efficient if the Aktubinsk factories had used local energy sources (Adamchuk, Dvoskin, 1968). The industrial connections of the Aktubinsk factories with the Karaganda coalmines were established before the Aktubinsk region increased its production of coal, which would have been enough for its local factories. However, the weak responsiveness of prices of the Soviet economic system did not recognise the signals of lower input alternatives.

Thus, production growth slowed down due to the inefficient use of resources. Soft budget constraints did not encourage the search for alternatives to reduce costs.

On top of the problems of the economy of the Kazakh SSR due to central management, there were also problems at the lower level of management (Kalyuzhnova, 1998). This was called the family co-ordination or clan system (Olcott, 1995). It was based on family relations of ethnic Kazakh people and operated inside enterprises. The top managers of state enterprises tried to employ and promote their relatives. As a result, the productivity of such enterprises declined when the quality of labour did not respond to requirements of the priority of relation-links rather than the quality of employees. At the same time, the ethnically Russian population had lower chances to get desirable posts or to be promoted. The family co-ordination in the Kazakh SSR can be considered as a soft employment constraints, which could survive due to the existence of soft budget constraints, where the central planning system provided subsidies for the cover of enterprise losses.

In 1985, Mikhail Gorbachev became General Secretary of the Soviet Union and introduced *perestroika* into the economy of the Soviet Union, which meant reconstruction of a long term planning system for short-term policies. Thus, the programme for 1986-1990 was defined as the acceleration of economic growth. The main target of this programme in the Kazakh SSR was the machine-building industry, which constituted the important basis for the further development of all sectors of the economy. The machine-building industry of the Kazakh SSR consisted principally of factories to provide for the service and repair of industrial equipment, and accounted for 1.8% of production of the machine-building industry in the production of the Soviet Union. Heavy industry and agriculture in the Kazakh SSR played a leading role in the Soviet Union, producing 17% of the coal and 10% of the iron ore of the Soviet Union and in addition, the Kazakh SSR was the second largest producer of grain in the Soviet Union after Russia. The production level of machine-building in the Kazakh SSR in 1985 accounted for 16.3% of the total industrial production of the Kazakh SSR, while Soviet Union machine-building on average produced 30% of its total industrial production (Kalyuzhnova, 1998). The Kazakh SSR had to import 100% of machine-building production for the power industry, oil and gas refining, timber industry, construction materials, food and light industries from other Soviet republics and produced about 25% of necessary machines for other industries including agriculture. The soaring growth of industrial production in the Kazakh SSR for export to the rest of the Soviet Union demanded an increasing quantity of equipment and machines to maintain production.

Despite the fact that investment flow to the machine-building industry had to increase, according to the government plan, its actual amount for the period 1986-1990 had decreased by 25% compared to 1981-1985. The failure to distribute investments in a timely manner became one of the main reasons for structural distortion in the Kazakh SSR. The machine-building industry in the Kazakh SSR faced a decline of production because of the lack of an active governmental policy. Production of machines for metalwork industries declined by 6% between 1980 and 1985, however, after the introduction of a programme for the intensive development of machine-building, the volume of machine production for the metalwork industry had declined even further, going down by 12% between 1985 and 1990. Production of agricultural equipment and machines had declined by 37% and production of some machines had declined by 80% for 5 years of *perestroika*.

In 1987, the government of the Soviet Union introduced a new law on enterprise development. The core of this law was the financial freedom for state enterprises, which at the same time gave them greater responsibility for the quality of production. Enterprises became free to make decisions about the allocation of finance in order to improve and increase the production, however, at the same time the property belonged to the state, such a combination created mistaken understanding that the property does not belong to anybody. As a result of acquiring the financial freedom of income distribution, enterprises were focused on wage increases abandoning investments into technology maintenance and improvement. In order to increase revenue, enterprises targeted the production of more expensive goods, which led to monetary imbalance and hidden inflation. The high supply of more expensive goods did not correspond to the low demand for such goods, while soft budget constraints continued to compensate for the losses of enterprises. Thus, during the period 1986-1990, the money supply increased more than twice, accompanied by lack of goods and services.

Table 1.15.   Industrial production of the Kazakh SSR, %.

Industries	Growth tendency of industrial production		Share of industrial production	
	1985 (1980=100)	1990 (1985=100)	1985	1990
Total industry	120.0	115.6	100	100
Power	133.0	109.2	7.3	6.8
Fuel	118.3	109.0	9.2	8.7
Metallurgy	114.1	108.2	16.7	15.6
Chemical and Petrochemical	158.6	130.4	5.2	5.7
Machine-building	132.4	110.7	16.9	15.9
Timber	130.1	121.7	3.3	3.5
Construction materials	108.0	120.0	5.9	5.6
Light	110.8	116.2	15.8	15.6
Food	113.2	122.7	14.5	15.9

Source: *Kazakhstan v tsifrakh*, 1987. *Statistical Yearbook of Kazakhstan – 1992*, 1993.

During the *perestroika* period, 1985-1991, all industries in the Kazakh SSR exhibited a trend of declining growth, except for construction materials, light industry and food industries. The share of light and food industries in total industrial production in 1991 increased, while that of all other industries declined (Table 1.15.). Because of a failed programme for the machine-building development, which was introduced in 1986, the growth rate of its production declined from 32.4% to 10.7% for 1980/1985 and 1985/1990, while its share in industrial production dropped from 16.9% to 15.9% for the same periods. The decline in production of some industrial machines led to the slowdown in the development of other heavy industries, which were dependent on the new technology and equipment introduction. At the same time of the slowdown of development in the machine-building industry, the economy of the Kazakh SSR entered a period of hidden inflation due to structural mismanagement, which created unfavourable conditions for further development of the remaining industries.

Table 1.16.   Regional industrial development, 1980-1990, %

Regions	Growth of industrial goods[30] production		Growth of consuming goods[31] production		Growth of total industrial production		Industries of specialisation
	1985 (1980=100)	1990 (1985=100)	1985 (1980=100)	1990 (1985=100)	1985 (1980=100)	1990 (1985=100)	
Kazakh SSR	117	111	120	127	120	115	
Akmola	138	121	127	145	135	128	Construction materials, machine-building, food
Aktubinsk	163	124	116	136	147	127	Fuel, machine-building, metallurgy, chemical, light

30   Industrial goods include production of metallurgy, machine-building and construction materials industries and partly production of oil and gas industry (not refined products), partly chemical.
31   Consumer goods include production of power, fuel, chemical (synthetic goods), timber, light and food industries.

Regions	Growth of industrial goods[30] production		Growth of consuming goods[31] production		Growth of total industrial production		Industries of specialisation
	1985 (1980=100)	1990 (1985=100)	1985 (1980=100)	1990 (1985=100)	1985 (1980=100)	1990 (1985=100)	
Almaty	110	130	125	123	114	127	Construction materials, light, food
Almaty city	118	111	116	117	117	114	Machine-building, construction materials, light, food
Atyrau	95	106	99.	103	95	105	Oil, gas, chemical, food
Eastern Kazakhstan	99	108	115	121	103	111	Chemical, construction materials, light, food
Karaganda	103	100	105	125	106	102	Coal, metallurgy, chemical, light, food
Kostanai	114	106	122	145	116	115	Metallurgy, chemical, construction materials, light, food
Kzyl-Orda	111	119	123	135	118	127	Machine-building, construction materials, food
Mangistau	149	99	127	132	152	101	Oil and gas extraction, chemical

Regions	Growth of industrial goods[30] production		Growth of consuming goods[31] production		Growth of total industrial production		Industries of specialisation
	1985 (1980=100)	1990 (1985=100)	1985 (1980=100)	1990 (1985=100)	1985 (1980=100)	1990 (1985=100)	
Northern Kazakh-stan	132	122	120	130	127	124	Machine-building, construction materials, timber, food
Pavlodar	126	102	139	141	128	108	Coal, metallurgy, machine-building, construction materials, chemical, food
Southern Kazakh-stan	114	119	120	147	115	125	Machine-building, construction materials, chemical, light, food
Western Kazakh-stan	127	124	131	127	129	125	Oil, gas, food
Zhambyl	115	110	125	120	117	112	Chemical, machine-building, light, food

Source: Data are calculated from: *Narodnoe khoziaistvo Kazakhstana za 70 let*, 1990. *Regiony Kazakhstana - 1991*, 1992.

The growth of total industrial production in the Kazakh SSR had declined from 20% to 15% during the *perestroika* years compared to the previous five years. The decline was based on the slowdown of the production of industrial goods (Table 1.16.), which accounted for 73% of total industrial production in 1980 and 75% in 1990. The production of consumer goods, i.e. food and light industries, increased by 20% between 1980 and 1985 and by 27% between 1985 and 1990. The relative success of consumer goods production during the *perestroika* years was due the government's aim to improve the supply of consumer goods to industrial enterprises (Kalyuzhnova, 1998). This meant it had to create a farm or any other type of holding, with specialisation in the production of consumer goods, mainly based on foodstuffs, regardless of the principal specialisation of the enterprise. Costs of the production of such holdings were fully imposed on industrial enterprises, which did not have the previous experience either in such products, or in the financial management of their production. The aim of government to satisfy demand in the population for consumer goods was realised, while the quality and efficiency of the main production of industrial enterprises had declined.

Despite the overall slowdown in industrial production, all the regions experienced growth in their industrial production mainly on account of raw materials extraction and the growth in construction materials and food industries.

The *Almaty* region had increased its total industrial production by 27% between 1985 and 1990, while the growth rate for the previous five years was 14%. The progress in the industrial production of the Almaty region was based on the increase in the construction materials industry, whose total production grew by 20% between 1985 and 1990, compared to an 8% increase in 1980-1985. The immense growth in the production of construction materials during the *perestroika* years was the result of another government programme of that period, which sought to increase the funding of accommodation for the population. The programme aimed to eradicate the shortfall in accommodation by 1991 by means of the construction of new housing funded by a higher level of investments. Even though the aim was not achieved, the waiting time for flats which had reached an average of several years was reduced by 70%. The Almaty region was one of the priority areas for the accelerated construction of housing in order to provide good conditions for authorities of the Kazakh SSR, which were concentrated in the capital city. As a result, the construction industry of the Almaty region experienced higher growth which positively affected the level of industrial production.

Almaty city was considered a separate industrial centre from the Almaty region, due to its high concentration of industrial enterprises inside and around the city[32]. The trend of industrial production growth in Almaty city was moving in opposite directions from the growth of the Almaty region (Table 1.16.). Almaty city specialised in industrial goods production as well as in consumer goods production. The growth of industrial production in the city fell from 17% during the period 1980-1985 to 14% growth in 1985-1990, due to the slowdown of the production of industrial goods in Almaty city, which was mainly based on the machine-building and construction materials industries. The production of some construction outputs in Almaty city increased by more than 30%, while the production of key machine-building goods had fallen during the *perestroika* years. The economy of Almaty city as well as the Almaty region was not significantly affected by the decline in machine-building as its output was mainly exported to other regions of the Kazakh SSR or other republics of the Soviet Union with a specialisation in heavy industry and was not used in regional industries, due to the absence of other heavy industries. Almaty city was the largest producer of furniture, food and tobacco and one of the largest producers of textiles in the Kazakh SSR. These sectors experienced continuous growth during the *perestroika* years. Industries of consumer goods production in the Almaty region and especially in Almaty city, as a capital, were under the constant pressure of control from the authorities. Therefore, the location played a more important role given that the Almaty region had a comparative advantage due to the fact that this was where the authorities of the republic were located, and industrial enterprises could solve any emerging problems more easily and speedily. Other regions had to cope with greater time lags exacerbated by the fact that the authorities of the Kazak SSR had to get approval for any changes from the central government of the Soviet Union. Therefore, the proximity of the Almaty region to the seat of the regional authorities, gave local industrial enterprises an advantage.

---

32   Ex-capital Almaty and new capital Astana are considered as separate industrial centres from its regions.

Oil-producing regions comprise all western regions of the republic. During *perestroika* these regions experienced a slowdown of their industrial production except the *Atyrau* region, which managed to increase its industrial production during the *perestroika* years by 5% after the fall by 5% during the previous five years. In that period the output of the Atyrau oil fields had fallen by 51% due to the technical difficulties and the high costs of extraction, compared to the neighbouring Mangistau region. However, during the *perestroika* years the Atyrau region managed to raise oil production by 27%, affecting the increase in the chemical industry production, which was based on refinery waste.

Like Atyrau, the *Mangistau* region is located on the Caspian Sea, where the main specialisation is fuel industry. Its development moved in opposite directions from the neighbouring Atyrau region for the whole decade since 1980. In the first half of the decade, the production of the largest oil producer in the Kazakh SSR was still growing, accounting for 79% of all oil production in the Kazakh SSR. However, during the *perestroika* years production started to decline. In 1990, its share of total oil production was 62%. The decline was due to the gradual depletion of resources in the region. However, the chemical industry of the region, which is based on hydrocarbon waste products, increased its production significantly during the years of *perestroika* as it had done over the previous five years. The production of some chemical goods in the region was accounted for more than 85% of the republican level, with continuous growth over the decade. The growth of the chemical industry was not affected by the decline of oil extraction due to the fact that new factories came on stream, whose capacities sufficient to process a small proportion of hydrocarbon waste. Hence, this industry was not affected by the total industrial decline.

The Caspian Sea regions (Mangistau and Atyrau) had a disadvantage in terms of the geographical and climate conditions for agriculture. Thus their food industry was weakly developed, without a potential for growth. The only sector of the food industry of these regions that was viable was fishing. Due to the neglect of the conservation of stock for future production the fishing industry also went into decline. The prospect of diversified industrial development of the Caspian Sea regions was diminishing, resulting in the dependence of the economy of the regions on the fuel industry. However, during the Soviet period (including the *perestroika* years), the prospect of being dependent on the production of just one industry did not seem problematic, as all industrial enterprises received subsidies from the government if they made a loss. Therefore, there was no incentive to diversify industrial production in order to protect the regional economy, while it was already protected.

Industrial production in *Western Kazakhstan* was previously based on food and light industries, which supplied the region itself because of underdeveloped infrastructure and the lack of interest of the central Soviet authorities in the region. However, in the early 1980s, the region discovered extensive hydrocarbon deposits. Oil production started at the beginning of *perestroika* and reached a level of 15% of oil extraction and 57% of natural gas extraction in the Kazakh SSR by 1990. The status of the region changed from that of a backward region, with weak industrial production, which was based only on local demand, to that of a region with heavy industry. It became a significant exporter of hydrocarbon to other republics of the Soviet Union through pipelines, which connected Atyrau and Mangistau with other parts of the Soviet Union. The immense growth in the production of fuel industry in Western Kazakhstan resulted in the development of its infrastructure and increased employment of its population, which shifted from other industries of the region, such as machine-building. Although Western Kazakhstan did not specialise in agriculture, the machine-building industry of the region produced 1% of agricultural equipment made in the Kazakh SSR mainly for the neighbouring Russian regions, which were the closest market. However, due to the overall decline in the machine-building industry of the Kazakh SSR, the production of the region declined by 60% during the *perestroika* years, while all the attention of authorities including human capital moved to the newly and actively developing fuel industry of the region. Consequently, the production of other industries declined. They accounted only for a small share of republican production, but were important because they made the industrial base of the region slightly more diverse. During the development of hydrocarbon fields in early 1980s, Western Kazakhstan had a high inflow of investments from the

Soviet Union, which kept the region interested in the further development of the fuel industry because it provided a way to escape backwardness.

Aktubinsk was located in the central-western part of the Kazakh SSR and mainly specialised in fuel industry, and unlike the Caspian Sea regions, Aktubinsk had favourable geographic and climate conditions for industrial diversification. Nevertheless, the region increased its concentration on the production of oil and gas, as it attracted the biggest share of investments. In 1985, the Aktubinsk region produced 1.8% of oil in the republic, and had just commenced the gas extraction after a long break since 1970. In 1990 after the significant growth of the hydrocarbon production during perestroika years, the share of oil production of the region was accounted for 10.1% of oil production in the Kazakh SSR, while gas extraction reached 3.3% of the national level.

As well as the fuel industry, Aktubinsk specialised in machine-building and chemical industries, which were the main sources in the Soviet Union of equipment for automation and agricultural machines, and of chemical goods based on mineral resources. The industrial production of the region was based on local and neighbouring sources, and had easy ways of transportation to Russian side markets as well as to Central Asian markets. The share of machine-building output accounted for 31.5% of republican production in 1980 and was worst affected by the machine-building crisis of the *perestroika* years. Its production declined by 67% during the five years of *perestroika*, and its share of the total production in Aktubinsk fell to 10.3% by 1990. Despite of the fact that chemical production in the Kazakh SSR grew by 88% overall during the *perestroika* years, the production of the chemical industry in Aktubinsk declined in the 1980s, while the fuel industry of the region accelerated its production. Even though the production of consumer goods in the Aktubinsk region had increased by 36% during *perestroika* years, (primarily products of the light and chemical industries), its share of the production in the whole of the Kazakh SSR fell, due to the higher growth of these industries in other regions, where new factories had been constructed. Thus, the machine-building crisis during the *perestroika* years significantly reduced the importance of Aktubinsk region in this industry, while the intensified growth and interest in fuel industry in the region affected the decline in the development of other heavy industries of the region. However, even though the production of light and food industries gradually was increased during the *perestroika* period, its share as a proportion of total production in the Kazakh SSR significantly decreased. Consequently, the region became primarily dependent on the fuel industry, despite its potential for the wide diversification.

The endowment of regions with hydrocarbon, which was of great significance for the Soviet Union, became disadvantage for diversified industrial development of regions. Even in those regions, which all had favourable conditions for other industries, the fuel industry suppressed their development due to its high priority for the Soviet Union, creating a regional dependence on fuel production.

The *southern part* of the Kazakh SSR consisted of the Kzyl-Orda, Southern Kazakhstan and Zhambyl regions, which mainly specialised in machine-building, construction materials, and light and food industries.

The industrial production of the *Kzyl-Orda* region was based on machine-building and construction materials industries and was increased by 27% during the *perestroika* years. Despite the overall decline in the production of machine-building in the Kazakh SSR, particularly in the production of agricultural equipment, which suffered a 41% decline between 1985 and 1990, the Kzyl-Orda region had managed to increase the production of agricultural equipment by 12% during the *perestroika* years. This growth is explained by the construction of a new machine-building factory at the end of the 1970s, which used relatively new technology and raised production as a result of increasing returns of scale. The input of the machine-building industry was mainly dependent on supplies from other regions, namely Karaganda and Southern Kazakhstan, while output was mainly supplied to Southern Kazakhstan and Zhambyl, whose agricultural output was dependent on mineral resources from Karaganda. The production of consumer goods in Kzyl-Orda grew by 35% between 1985 and 1990, and by 23% between 1980 and 1985. Food industry was prevalent in all southern regions of the Kazakh SSR due to the climate, which allowed the supply of their production to northern regions and to Russia. The region was developed on the basis of local needs, without significant dependence on other republics of the Soviet Union, and as a result, Kzyl-Orda was less vulnerable to the forthcoming changes of transition.

Southern Kazakhstan was one of the economically developed regions, which increased its industrial production by 25% during 1985-1990. This was mainly based on construction materials, food and light industries. The region specialised in the production of agricultural machinery, however, despite success of the neighbouring Kzyl-Orda region in this sector, production in Southern Kazakhstan was affected by the general crisis of the industry and fell by 36%. While the construction materials industry was progressing to satisfy growing demand for the housing programme, the region produced 30% of cement in the republic and other significant industrial goods. The food programme affected the food industry of the region as well, increasing meat production by 73% during the *perestroika* years and fruit and vegetables by 34%, with a considerably more diversified assortment of food production. The light industry of the region remained at the same level. It consisted principally of textile production, which relied on cotton production that had already reached its limits due to the full use of available land. Southern Kazakhstan had such a high level of diversity in industrial production, that the region could maintain high levels of production. If there was a decline in one industry, resources could always being transferred to other industry. One example is machine-building. During the *perestroika* years, the production of agricultural machines declined significantly, while the production of machines for livestock farming increased by almost 30%.

All regions of the southern part of the Kazakh SSR had accelerated growth of their total industrial production during the years of *perestroika*, except *Zhambyl*, which experienced a slowdown of the production of both industrial and consumer goods. The production of industrial goods of the region was based on chemical industry, the production of equipment for the chemical industry and agricultural machinery. Due to the advantageous location of the Zhambyl region, the chemical industry increased its production by 96% during *perestroika* years. It used raw materials and intermediate goods from the neighbouring Karaganda region, and had a high demand for the output of large chemical factories in the Zhambyl and Southern Kazakhstan regions, however, the production of agricultural machineries declined by 63% for the same period.

The development programme for the improvement of the machine-building industry in the Kazakh SSR during the *perestroika* years, 1985-1991, was directed mainly at branches of industries, which produced the lowest share of the required quantity in the Kazakh SSR, while the rest of the machinery was exported from other republics of the Soviet Union (Table 1.17.). While the machine-building of agricultural equipment achieved the highest level of the required quantity of production in the Kazakh SSR, namely 30-35%, the other 65-70% were exported from other Soviet republics. Such industries as power, oil-processing and gas, timber, construction materials, cotton and food imported 100% of their equipment from other republics of the Soviet Union. Therefore, the development of the production of agricultural machinery production was not the priority of the programme. Its technology was out of date, which contributed to the decline of the production in many regions specialising in the production of agricultural machinery. Even though the whole industry of machine-building experienced a decline during the years of *perestroika*, agricultural machine-building was most severely affected.

Table 1.17.   Dependence of industries of the Kazakh SSR on machine-building production of the Soviet Union, %

Industry	Export of machine-building production from other Soviet republics
Power	100
Oil extraction	90-95
Oil-processing and gas	100
Coal	70-75
Ferrous metallurgy	90-93
Non-ferrous metallurgy	80-85
Chemical and petrochemical	85-90
Machine-building	90-95
Timber	100
Construction materials	100
Cotton	100
Food	100
Agriculture	65-70
Stock-raising	70-75

Source: Kalyuzhnova, 1998.

The food, light and chemical industries of the Zhambyl region experienced a slight slowdown in their production, which did not affect significantly the overall growth of industrial production in the region. The decline in agricultural and other types of machine-building during the *perestroika* years did not have an effect on the agricultural and industrial production of Zhambyl or any other region of the Kazakh SSR during that period. The opposite effect occurred: the volume of production of many industries continued to grow, although the rate of growth was slowed down. However, this was only a short-term effect on the economy, while the long-term negative effect did not take a long time to manifest itself, and was going to affect all industries in transition, when the supply of many goods from other ex-Soviet republics was cut. However, during the *perestroika* period the temporary decline in the machine-building industry did not seem so negative, as it was expected to be temporary, therefore no serious efforts were made on the part of the central government to control and to improve the situation.

Northern regions specialised in both industrial and consumer goods production. The *Kostanai* region experienced a modest slowdown of 1% of its growth rate of industrial production. 1980-1985 industrial production grew by 16.5%, whereas in the following five years growth amounted to 15.5%. This was due to the slight slowdown of agricultural machine-building while industries of the region had substantial growth during the *perestroika* years. Metallurgical and chemical industries of the region were the main exporters of its output, which consisted mainly of raw materials to other Soviet republics, with a gradual growth in production. The construction materials industry of the Kostanai region was one of the main suppliers in the Kazakh SSR for the housing programme, and its production grew by over 20%. The light and food industries in Kostanai experienced a boom during *perestroika* years. A textile factory was opened and as a result the region's share in textile production grew from 0.1% to 13.6% of the total production in the Kazakh SSR in 1990. The food industry also grew substantially mainly to satisfy the high demand of western regions, where development was concentrated on the fuel industry. Regions of the Kazakh SSR provided goods for the whole of the Soviet Union. At the same time, they supplied local regions with necessary goods, and as a result benefited by reaching higher levels of development. However, in this way, regions, mainly those that concentrated on the fuel industry, were becoming highly dependent on provisions from other regions. This became a distinct disadvantage for them at the beginning of the transition period, when every region had to survive on its own, and very often could not afford to support other regions.

The *Akmola* region was the largest producer of agricultural machinery in the Kazakh SSR (55.3% of the national production in 1990), having a comparative advantage due to its location, which was in the centre of *tselina* lands development in the 1950s. However, during the *perestroika* years, production declined by 33.8% as a result of obsolete equipment and the lack of investment in agricultural machine-building. Another specialisation of the region, construction materials, achieved growth of 50% during *perestroika* years because of the housing programme, which was very intensive in the regions of the *tselina* lands, because their population had increased by more than 30% during the virgin lands programme, without being provided with individual accommodation. The growth of the food industry of the Akmola region accelerated during the *perestroika* years, being one of the largest producers of the industry. Being the largest producer of meat, the region increased its production level by 29.8% during *perestroika* years, which was a higher level than the average production of the Kazakh SSR. At the same time, a number of food factories were constructed in the region, which substantially increased the level of food production, a high proportion of which was exported to neighbouring Russia.

Industrial production in *Northern Kazakhstan* slowed down during the *perestroika* years. This was the result of a slowdown in the machine-building industry. Agricultural machine-building slowed down slightly, while the production of automatic machines was stopped in the region during the *perestroika* period after a 70% decline during the previous five years. However, the growth of the production of the main output of construction materials and timber industries accelerated during the *perestroika* period. The average growth of food production in Northern Kazakhstan slowed down slightly, except for meat production, which grew by 58.7% during the *perestroika* years, producing 7.5% of all meat in the Kazakh SSR. The main specialisations of all northern regions of the Kazakh SSR were in machine-building, construction materials and food industries, which were differently affected by the changes brought about by *perestroika*. In the main the production of machine-building was declined, while construction materials and food industries production experienced accelerated growth. Northern regions had diversified economies with a high proportion of agricultural machine-building and food industry. The decline in agricultural machine-building during the *perestroika* period did not have any negative impact on the food industry. However, in the long term crucial changes manifested themselves, which would not be reversed for at least a decade.

The *Pavlodar* region was rich with a diversity of mineral resources, where the coal production of the region had the largest share of coal production in the Kazakh SSR and was the third largest in the Soviet Union, after Russia and Ukraine. The production of coal in the region was maintained at the same level during *perestroika* years, while steel production in the Pavlodar region declined by 14.2% during the *perestroika* years due to high production costs compared to the Karaganda region, which produced 92.9% of steel in the Kazakh SSR. The machine-building industry of the Pavlodar region mainly produced agricultural machines. Production had grown threefold between 1980 and 1985. However, during the *perestroika* years the production level fell by 73.6%, which can be explained by the lack of investments and the decline in the production of regional metallurgy, which was the source of input for machine-building in the region. The production of the chemical industry of the Pavlodar region achieved slower growth than before, mainly due to the absence of improved technology. The construction materials industry was ahead of all other productions in the region; it grew by 30%, due to the housing programme in the whole of the Kazakh SSR. Pavlodar was not the main producer of the food industry, but it was self-sufficient in meat and agricultural crops. The implementation of the food programme resulted in an increase of food production by 37%. The production of canned food was increased by 40% due to the construction of a new factory. Thus, in the highly industrialised regions, production of metallurgy and machine-building industries declined, while food and construction materials grew substantially. However, the main industrial output of the region, coal, had maintained its production at the same level. It was one of the main exports of the Kazakh SSR.

Due to its endowment with mineral resources, *Eastern Kazakhstan* was the main supplier of the construction materials industry, which experienced accelerated growth during the *perestroika* years after a slight decline in previous

years. Other industries, such as chemical, light and food, which were a specialisation of the region, also grew.

Industrial production in *Karaganda* had one of the lowest growth rates in
1980-1985 and 1985-1990, compared to other regions of the Kazakh SSR
(6.7% and 2.8% respectively – see Table 1.16.). The average growth of industrial production in the Kazakh SSR was 20% and 15.6% for the same periods respectively. Karaganda was one of the largest producers of heavy industry in the Kazakh SSR, due to its rich endowment with mineral resources.
Before 1960, Karaganda produced 95% of coal in the Kazakh SSR, being the
third largest producer of coal in the Soviet Union. However, after the Pavlodar-Ekibastuz industrial cluster discovered and developed coal resources, the
share of Karaganda coal production in the total production of the republic fell
to 42.4% in 1980 and to 37.1% in 1990. The growth of coal extraction in
Karaganda was slowed down after new coalfields were discovered in Pavlodar, where extraction costs were lower. Moreover, the Karaganda region
could not maintain the intensive growth of its production due to obsolete
equipment. As a result, during the *perestroika* years coal production in Karaganda started to fall by 2.2%. However, the growth of the extraction of ferrous
metals, where the Karaganda region had a monopoly in the Kazakh SSR, es-
calated due to the high demand of industry throughout the Soviet Union.
However, agricultural machine-building, which accounted for 10% of production in the Kazakh SSR, seemed to suffer a lack of local demand, where decline in investment caused the fall of output by 47.8% during the *perestroika*
years. In reality demand was extremely high, however, the mismanagement
of investment funds resulted in the gradual collapse of the production of machine-building, especially in the agricultural sector. The Karaganda region
was one of the main producers of the construction materials in the Kazakh
SSR, and its output as a proportion of production in the republic reached a
level of 34.7%. However, despite of the general trend of the country to an increase in the production of construction materials for the housing programme,
the main outputs of the industry slowed or declined in Karaganda.

The production of chemical and light industries slowed down during the *perestroika* years. However, the food industry grew significantly, up to 28.7%. The

food industry of the Karaganda region was especially developed in the production of confectionery. Its products were of high quality and constituted the
bulk of production in the Kazakh SSR. As a result of high demand in the Kazakh SSR it steadily increased its production over the years. Industrial production in Karaganda was highly diversified and mainly based on heavy industries, however, there was a trend towards higher growth in the food industry. The food programme was directed to industrial enterprises, but mainly in
regions with a low share of agriculture or food industry production. Therefore
in Karaganda, a larger number of industrial enterprises were involved in the
implementation of the food programme, which successfully reached its target.
However, the main sectors of industry such as construction materials declined, despite high demand for their output in the Kazakh SSR.

On the threshold of transition all Kazakh SSR regions had a minimum of 2-3
industries of specialisation (Map 3. Industrial specialisation of the Kazakh
SSR regions, 1945-1991). However, during the *perestroika* years, many regions, which specialised in mineral resources extraction, experienced a no-
ticeable decline in the production of other alternative industries. Thus, Aktubinsk, Karaganda, Eastern Kazakhstan and Western Kazakhstan were becoming highly dependent on the extraction of mineral resources, which were
exported to other Soviet republics. Finished goods, in whose production mineral resources from the Kazakh SSR had played a part, were to some extent
re-exported to the Kazakh SSR and other republics for consumption. Southern and northern parts of the Kazakh SSR together with the Almaty region
experienced a decline of the machine-building industry, except for the Kzyl-
Orda region, which had operated a relatively new machine-building factory.
Another exception was the production of machinery for the industry and the
raising of live-stock, which was increased during the *perestroika* years. Other
important industries of the specialisation of southern and northern parts were
construction materials and food, where production rose due to government
programmes to increase housing and food production. The economy of the
Kazakh SSR did not show signs of decline, except in machine-building. On
the contrary, such industries as food and construction materials achieved
substantial growth in many regions and on average in the whole of the Kazakh SSR, while other industries experienced a slight slowdown of growth.

However, the continuous decline of machine-building raised the prospect for negative consequences for other industries, whose machines and equipment were out of date and highly dependent on the production of machine-building in other Soviet republics.

1.7 Conclusion

This chapter presented an overview of initial conditions of the economy of the Kazakh SSR in the light of the impact of the Soviet Union on industrial development in the Kazakh SSR. The industrial structure of the regions of the Kazakh SSR was heavily influenced by the priorities set by Soviet central planners in every considered period. Regions rich with rare mineral resources received the maximum industrial development, even though with a narrow specialisation without any attempt of diversification, while the location of many industrial factories was chosen with consideration of easy access to the Soviet market. Regions rich with mineral resources and located far from the Russian border, which played an important role during the evacuation of the war, benefited most from the infrastructure development of the economy due to their intensive industrial growth to supply the needs of the Soviet Union, while other regions were left to fend for themselves. The evacuation of industrial factories from occupied regions of the Soviet Union during the war not only brought much industry to the Kazakh SSR, but skilled labour, which raised the skills level of the local workforce.

By the end of the 1970s, there were six main industrial clusters in the Kazakh SSR, which were dispersed through the whole country with a high level of diversification. However, many of these industrial clusters were directly connected with industrial factories of other republics of the Soviet Union, as their location was determined by sources of raw materials and convenient transport links to Russia. Connections between industrial factories on the regional level were absent in the majority of cases. This meant that local factories were separated from each other, and depended on factories of other Soviet republics. The highly inefficient use of resources was based on the system of central planning and management, which was operated centrally from Mos-

cow. The centre was not able to devise efficient ways of production in all republics of the Soviet Union.

The last five years of the centrally planned system were defined as the *perestroika* period (1985-1990), when the Soviet government attempted to change
the central planning and management of industrial enterprises. They partly
acquired the freedom and responsibility for their production and the management of their finances. However, industrial enterprises were still dependent on
the state, which absorbed any responsibility from enterprises for negative
outcomes. As a result, funds were being distributed on the basis of personal
needs and not the development of production. As a short-term effect, the
economy experienced the slowdown of growth of industrial production, which
was also affected by the decline in machine-building in the Kazakh SSR. The
machine-building industry became the priority for the development of the Kazakh SSR, as the majority of machines required by industry in the Kazakh
SSR were imported from other republics of the Soviet Union. However, due to
government mismanagement of investments in the development of machine-
building, the industry faced a significant decline with a knock-on effect on all
other industries of the Kazakh SSR, whose equipment was obsolete.

The planned economy inherited by the Kazakh SSR was based on the production plans for industries, which were mainly involved in the production of
raw or intermediate goods for the final manufacture in other regions of the
Soviet Union. Thus, on the edge of transition, Kazakh SSR industries were
slowly depreciating due to the changes in management and were highly dependent on the demand and supply of industries in the Soviet Union. The regions themselves had infrastructure designed to enable cooperation with
other republics of the Soviet Union and not internal cooperation within the
Kazakh SSR.

The next chapter examines the patterns of the location of industrial activities
inherited from Soviet planning, which were outlined in this chapter and analyses changes of industrial concentrations in Kazakhstan due to the transition
process. It will attempt to answer the question why and how the collapse of

the Soviet Union affected the patterns and performance of industrial activities on a regional bass.

2 The Effect of Transition on Regional Development

2.1 Introduction

As can be seen from the first chapter, the spatial development of the economy of the Kazakh SSR was based on the organization of the whole economy of the Soviet Union. Industries and industrial clusters in the Kazakh SSR were established on the basis of easy transport access to other Soviet republics, mainly to the Russian Federation, while interregional connections between industrial enterprises of the Kazakh SSR rarely existed. Industrial production in the Kazakh SSR and all republics of the USSR were governed and controlled by the planning system, where 5-year production plans were applied to all industrial establishments. Enterprises competed to overfulfil the plans. Quantity was most frequently given priority over quality and efficiency. One of the basic elements of the socialist system was the soft budget constraint. This phenomenon negatively affected the efficiency of production due to the weak responsiveness to prices and the freedom for enterprises to bargain with central authorities about their plans. The *perestroika* period brought more freedom to industrial enterprises to determine their financial activities. However, due to the lack of knowledge and experience in financial management and the lack of responsibility for efficiency, the production of industrial enterprises slowed down and declined in the machine-building industry. As a result, the economy of the Kazakh SSR entered a slowdown at the end of the existence of the Soviet Union.

This chapter analyses the industrial performance of Kazakhstan after the collapse of the Soviet Union and attempts to comprehensively explore location patterns across industries at the beginning of the transition decade. Moreover, the chapter critically evaluates changes in the regional concentration of industrial activities in Kazakhstan as a result of transition. Throughout the chapter, an attempt has been made to answer a fundamental question on the early development of transition: why and how did the collapse of the Soviet Union affect the regional concentration of Kazakhstani industries? During the period of central planning, the location of industries in the Kazakh SSR remained static without particular attention to the economic interests of the republic. Due to central planning, self-regulating mechanisms were missing, which are important elements of the market economy. As a result, inter-regional development suffered from the manner in which industries had been located in the Soviet period.

Transition brought uncertainty and unpredictability, which affected all spheres of the economic development of the Kazakh SSR. Since transition started, industrial links between former Soviet republics have been broken and the location of Kazakhstani industrial enterprises was discovered to be inefficient for the development of Kazakhstan due to the lack of internal inter-regional industrial links. Consequently, following the fall in demand at the republican level, all industries of Kazakhstan faced a decline in production.

After 74 years of central planning, the governments in charge of the economies of the newly independent states were unfamiliar with this type of self-sustaining economy. The Kazakhstani economy faced enormous structural changes during the transition period, where prices, and as a consequence high inflation, were raised following a fall in industrial production. The whole economy was deteriorating, as indicated by the fact that the share of goods production in Kazakhstani GDP declined from 65.9% in 1991 to 43.3% in 2002. However, the service sector increased from 34.8% to 50.9% of GDP in the same period. Nevertheless, at the end of the first decade of transition the Kazakhstani economy started to develop new internal as well as external markets, where many of them were based on an infrastructure developed by the Soviet system, connecting the Kazakh SSR to other republics. Only industries based on mineral resources had recovered and developed during transition, due to the value of their output in the external market. Manufacturing industries, however, continued to decline due to obsolete equipment and inefficient production, which raised its costs and reduced the quality of its output compared to its competitors. Consequently, during the last ten years the Kazakhstani economy started to become more affected by world prices of commodities due to the low level of industrial diversification.

The regional policy (Academy of Science, Institute of Economics, 1998) implemented in 1996 and based on the principle of even regional development, did not bring the expected results. The industrial production of backward regions continued to decline, while regions with mineral resources continued to recover and significantly grow following the collapse of the Soviet Union. The failure of regional policy was caused by a decline in investment in backward regions, where a weak infrastructure demanded a high level of resources. However, the internal sources of backward regions were directed to financial markets, which could bring higher profits than local industrial production.

In 1997, President Nazarbaev decided for various reasons to move the capital of Kazakhstan to a new location[33]. Astana city, which is located close to the northern border with Russia, was named the new Kazakh capital. The transfer of the capital city became a regional development by proxy. The almost central location made the new capital more accessible for other regions than the former capital Almaty, which is located on the southeastern edge of the country. Therefore, information and new technology may be expected, in the long run, to be circulated with higher speed across regions. This might improve the level of regional development of Kazakhstan.

To date, production and business activities are highly concentrated in three areas of Kazakhstan: the regions of western Kazakhstan, the city Almaty and the city of Astana. The economy of western Kazakhstan is purely based on deposits of mineral resources, which attracted 74.4% of all foreign direct investments in 2001 (*Kazakhstan: 1991-2002*, 2002). However, the concentration of activities in Almaty city is mainly based on highly skilled labour, where the negotiation skills of members of the government, and their easy access to powerful connections with the authorities, turned them and their children into successful businessmen, whilst the city has benefited from the improvement of production activities. The concentration of highly qualified human capital in Almaty can be explained by a historical factor. All intelligentsia and skilled workers were based in the capital in order to increase the returns they could

---

33 The detailed explanation is given in part 2.3 *Changes in regional concentration of industrial activities* in the section *The effect of the transfer of the capital*

get from their education. However, the educational level in Astana was lower than in Almaty and, as a result, in order to preserve the high quality human resources of government institutions, there was a high inflow of highly educated people into the new capital. Generally, high quality of human capital is likely to migrate in order to increase the returns of a high-level of education and entrepreneurial skills. As a result, the inflow of human capital to Astana possesses the necessary skills for successful business activities. Access to highly skilled labour is one of the important elements which attract new businesses to the new capital, gradually increasing their concentration.

This chapter begins with the analysis of the impact of the collapse of the Soviet Union on the Kazakhstani economy. It then presents the performance of Kazakhstani industries during transition and the impact of the destabilised economic situation. Furthermore, the chapter highlights the trends of development of Kazakhstani regions and evaluates the need for the implementation of regional policy. Finally, the chapter explores the changes in the trends of industrial concentration of each region of Kazakhstan on the basis of the transition process and analyses the effect of capital cities on the performance of their regional industries.

2.2 The collapse of the Soviet economic system and its impact on the regional development of the Kazakhstani economy

In 1991, Kazakhstan became an independent state as a consequence of the collapse of the Soviet Union. All republics of the Soviet Union gained political independence, while still being economically dependent on each other and particularly on Russia.

The centralised administration of prices and trade cooperation was liberalised, which affected changes in the pattern of trade between former Soviet republics. As a result, the loss of a market for finished goods was one of the factors that negatively affected the industrial production of Kazakhstan, which fell substantially during the first five years of transition (Figure 2.1.). Links between the former Soviet republics no longer worked because of the difficulty of cooperation on prices and payments between republics. The newly independent states became responsible for the financial governance of their industrial production and also for local economies. Every republic started to work on its survival under the conditions of the new system, with an absence of regulation.

Figure 2.1. The growth of Kazakhstani industrial output from 1985-2001 (1990=100%)

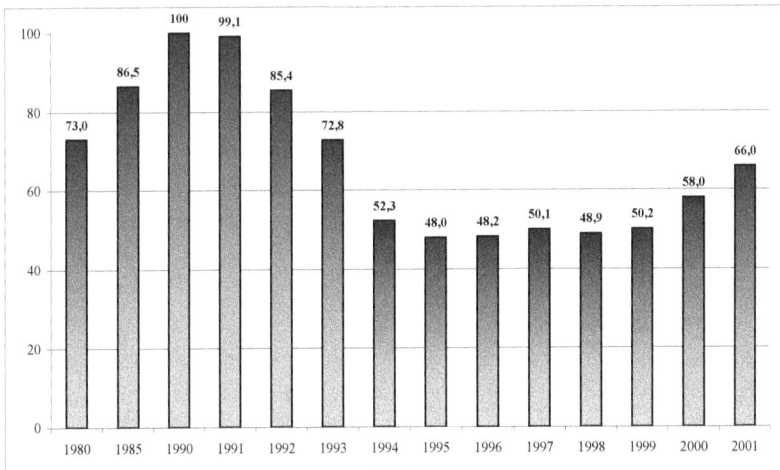

Source: The data are calculated from: *Promyshlennost' Kazakhstana: 1920-1999 goda*, 2000. *Kazakhstan: 1991-2001*, 2001. *Promyshlennost' Kazakhstana i ego regionov: 1998-2001 goda*, 2002

The Kazakh SSR was a source of raw materials for the Soviet economy, where a large portion of goods was consumed and manufactured outside the Kazakh SSR, whilst some of them were transported as intermediate or finished goods back to the Kazakh SSR. Therefore, without the maintenance of the cooperation between industrial enterprises of former Soviet republics, the production of raw materials in Kazakhstan fell sharply during the first five years of transition and created an additional shortage in the economy. Intermediate and finished goods could not be imported from the republics as before the Soviet collapse due to economic disagreements and debts between enterprises and businesses. Thus, the independence gained did not solve the problems of shortage in the economy, which were present before the collapse of the Soviet Union. On the contrary, a substantial number of new problems arose. One of the main problems was the ability of Kazakhstan to survive on its own after being one of the economic regions that played a specific role in the Soviet economy. The independence gained by Kazakhstan required the establishment of a diversified and interregionally connected economic system, which would be sufficient for the whole Kazakhstani economy.

At the beginning of transition, the Kazakhstani economy could be considered to be in the same position as any region of the former Kazakh SSR, albeit on a larger scale, that its links with the larger Soviet economy were broken, while it remained for a time in the rouble zone and therefore could not control its own money supply. The economic miracle of the Kazakhstani economy did not happen after it gained independence. The liberalisation of prices and increasing inflation, the fall of industrial production and the decline of investments, and the further loss of trade and production partners from other Soviet republics negatively affected the growth of the Kazakhstani economy. The Kazakhstani government tried to explain its problems as being due to the legacy of the former Soviet system and the fact that it shared the monetary system with the former Soviet republics and thereby imported inflation, price growth, unemployment and other industrial problems not of the Kazakhstani's government making. The rouble zone was governed by the Russian authorities, while a Kazakhstani currency did not yet exist. As a result, since transition began, the money supply in Kazakhstan was not controlled by the country itself, when information on the volume of money circulation was not available (Bajmuratov, 2000). Therefore, until 1993, the Kazakhstani economy followed Russian monetary policy with all its consequences of inflation (Table 2.1.).

Table 2.1.   Inflation of consuming and industrial goods prices, %[34]

Type of goods	Rouble zone			Tenge	
	1991/1990	1992/1991	1993/1992	1994/1993	1995/1994
Consumer goods	194.6	1117.3	1179.4	2276.4	160.3
Industrial goods	193	2469	1142.8	3020.4	239.8

Source: *Regiony Kazakhstana- 1995*, 1996.

After the introduction of the new currency, the Tenge, in November 1993, in-flation in Kazakhstan increased at higher rate. Thus, the economic problems were not immediately solved. As a result of the non-convertibility of the new currency, trade partners outside Kazakhstan demanded payments in hard currency. In 1994, inflation and inter-enterprises arrears continued to grow, and the inflation growth of prices on industrial and consumer goods even ac-celerated (Table 2.1.). The persistence of inter-enterprises arrears allowed enterprises to continue weak connections on a republican level. At the same time, such trade relations were obstacles in the shift of transition economies towards a market economy, where managers often use arrears for the redi-rection of enterprise profits and for the postponement of the restructuring of enterprises (Andreff, 2003). However, high level of inflation in Kazakhstan did not induce producers to shift from inter-enterprises arrears towards market relations on the monetary basis. The high level of inflation negatively influ-enced conditions of crediting, where credits were mainly available only for short-terms, while the interest rate was incredibly high, 240% in 1993 and 300% in 1994 (National Bank of Kazakhstan)[35], which was almost impossible to pay off. Therefore, inter-enterprises arrears provided the only way of main-

---

34   1990-1993 are defined by the circulation of Soviet roubles. At the end of 1993 the Kazakhstani currency, Tenge, was introduced.
35   Average weighted interest rate for six-month credits of the National Bank of Ka-zakhstan.

taining production on the basis of cooperation with other enterprises, on the background of low reliability to existing financial institutions and to anti-crisis course of actions of government.

Nevertheless, due to a strict anti-inflationary policy,[36] the growth of the inflation of prices for consumer goods slowed down. The anti-inflationary policy consisted of tough monetary and budget policies. The National Bank of Kazakhstan reduced the inflation growth by regulating the distribution of direct government credits in 1994. Thus, inflation grew by only 60.3% in 1995. However, in 1995, the inflation rate of producers' prices for industrial goods was higher and grew by 139.8%. Nevertheless, it was a significant fall from 2920.4% inflation increase in the previous year (Table 2.1.).

The rupture of economic links between the former Soviet republics, falling industrial production, non-competitive production and rising prices became negative characteristics of the transition period. The rouble zone no longer existed and no country of the former-Soviet Union wanted to accept the currency of another for trade transactions due to the weaknesses and uncertainty of their behaviour. As a result, trade links were weakened without any certainty of their future reestablishment.

The rate of decline of GDP reached 20% by the middle of the 1990s, while proportion of GDP by industrial, agricultural and construction production fell from 53% in 1992 to 40% in 1995. However, trade and services increased as a proportion of GDP from 47% to 54% over the same period[37]. Industrial as-

---

36   In 1994 the Kazakhstani government issued a new anti-crisis programme that was directed to strengthening and speeding up the anti-inflationary policy, prevention of the production decline of industrial and consumer goods and the design of conditions for economic growth. (Bajmuratov, 2000).

37   The growth of the service sector during the transition period in Kazakhstan was caused by the dramatic decline in the production of the industrial sector, where the level of redundancy increased significantly and at the same time many enterprises were closed down as bankrupts. Therefore, the big portion of newly unemployed moved to the developing service sector, which mainly constituted of trade and did not require the high level of the qualification. The further growth of the service sector cannot improve the Kazakhstani economy without the growth of the industrial production. Kazakhstan is the landlocked country with the main income coming

KAZAKHSTANI ENTERPRISES IN TRANSITION 139

sets were outdate with no financial opportunities for their modernisation, where production of key export goods in Kazakhstan consumed power at a level that exceeded that of other countries by 5 – 8 times, due to use of old technology. Because production costs were so high compared to those of competitors, production of some mineral resources in Kazakhstan fell even more steeply.

Following the disruption of trade connections between ex-Soviet economic regions, industrial enterprises that managed to survive[38] started to search for internal links. However, it was difficult to find partners, as industrial enterprises were state-owned and contact was not easy due to the lack of financial support from the management and the lack of inter-regional infrastructure.

From 1992 (Kalyuzhnova, 1998), the privatisation process began in Kazakhstan and had three phases (Esirkepov, 1999). The *first phase* (1992-1993) of the Kazakhstani privatisation implied the restructuring of state enterprises and their conversion into Joint-Stock companies for further transfer of the state property to private owners. The *second phase* (1993-1995) of the privatisation was directed on a mass privatisation, where the government issued privatisation coupons and distributed among the public. The public could use these coupons for participating in privatisation of Joint Stock enterprises. In order to avoid high demand for shares in particular enterprises, Investment Privatisation Funds (IPF) were created, where public had to allocate their coupons in exchange for IPF's shares. IPFs used privatisation coupons to buy shares of a portfolio of Joint Stock enterprises in order to maintain their own shares. The *third phase* (1996-1998) of the privatisation was mainly focussed on individual projects of large state enterprises.

---

from natural resources, which production is extremely underdeveloped for the market economy.

38   Many industrial enterprises were close to shut down after the collapse of the Soviet Union, especially enterprises that were highly dependent on demand and supply of goods of other Soviet Union republics. Enterprises that relied on soft budget constraints over a long period without making profits caused immediate break down after the loss of feeding sources in terms of central government authorities of the Soviet Union.

Newly privatised enterprises became more financially responsible for their production moving towards a hard budget constraint, a concept which is equivalent to "profit maximisation" (Kornai, 1992). Privatised enterprises still had support from the government, however, costs were high and subsidies were cut in order to encourage enterprises to develop a more efficient management of production at lower costs (Maskin, Xu, 2001). Under conditions of hard budget constraint profit maximisation, or at least total costs minimisation, became the objective of the new owners of industrial enterprises.

The main purpose of Kazakhstani privatisation was to increase the level of competitiveness of industrial enterprises in order to increase the efficiency of the economy. The majority of service companies were sold through open and closed auctions, but the main proportion of industrial, transport, communication and construction companies were converted to companies of the Joint Stock ownership. Privatisation did not bring the expected results for improvement in the efficiency of industry. On the contrary, the efficiency of privatised enterprise production declined after restructuring. There were many reasons for the failure of privatisation including the mismanagement of the sometimes unfair privatisation procedure. It is possible to discern three elements of Kazakhstani privatisation (Kalyuzhnova, 2003), which led to the failure: changed rules, employment of incompetent staff and corruption with misconduct.

Property was sold at a discount value to groups of managers on the basis of corruption (Atamkulov, Isenov, 1998), where new owners of the property created their own rules of personal interest, whilst not being specialists in the management of privatised enterprises. The enrichment of managers in transition economies during the privatisation process was not based on the efficiency of newly privatised enterprises, but on the intentional and semi-legal extraction of the capital (Andreff, 2003). Apart from the managers of the companies, the remainder of the new owners of privatised companies did not possess any interests or rights in the privatised property even when they controlled a majority of the shares (Kalyuzhnova, 1999). Newly established Investment Privatisation Funds were expected to create portfolios on the basis of investment privatisation coupons from the public. However, Investment Privatisation Funds (IPF) did not bring the expected results due to the lack of a strategy and the lack of qualified employees (Kalyuzhnova, 2003). Funds were not always able to provide financial support for newly privatised enterprises and to supervise their production activities. This created additional difficulties in the operation of enterprises. As a result, IPFs had difficulties in managing to increase the value of invested resources. Unsuccessful privatisation, in numerous cases, did not bring about improvements in the economic system.

Privatisation was mainly undertaken in regions which were rich with mineral resources, such as Eastern Kazakhstan, Kostanai, Karaganda, Southern Kazakhstan and Zhambyl. For the period 1996-2000, the number of privatised industrial enterprises in these regions accounted for 49% of the total Kazakhstani level (Regional Statistical Yearbook of Kazakhstan, 2001). However, the number of privatised enterprises in regions with hydrocarbon deposits, Atyrau, Mangistau and Western Kazakhstan, accounted for only 5% of the total Kazakhstani level, where large scale enterprises were involved. In the majority of cases, the privatisation of enterprises decreased their productivity. Newly privatised companies were unable to afford input factors, such as raw materials and electricity and, as a result, the capacity utilisation was decreased together with its financial conditions. Some companies could not continue the work after a change in ownership because of the lack of financial resources, while other companies could not increase their income because of the low level of productivity.

Becoming responsible for the production process, the management of industrial enterprises cooperated with other enterprises by means of bargaining. Prices that were centrally controlled in the socialist system now had become the product of negotiations between enterprises on the producers level and the product of the supply and demand on the consumer level. Consumer preferences were not considered in the central planning system, as producers knew that there was the support of soft subsidies in case of losses. However, the competitive environment of the transition process made consumer preferences play a crucial role, so that only producers with lower costs and a higher quality of output could survive. Under the pressure of the market, enterprises had to learn how to play by the rules of the new game where the economy was driven by supply and demand.

All determinants of the economy, such as prices, management, supply and demand changed in Kazakhstan after the transition process started and conditions of uncertainty and unpredictability prevailed. Economic policy is based on the assumption that the economy is being transformed into a capitalist market economy type, but the rules of western market economies may not be applicable to transition countries due to the different state of initial conditions and stages of development. At the beginning of transition, it was uncertain how supply and demand would behave under this set of conditions and the behaviour of prices was unpredictable. There was no knowledge of how the economy would operate and what the consequences would be.

Industrial development under transition, 1991-2001
After transition began, the pattern of industrial activity in Kazakhstan shifted heavily towards mineral resources (Map 5. Regional division by groups of specialisation, 1991-2003). During the Soviet period, Kazakhstani industrial production was focused on raw materials such as coal, oil and gas extractions, metallurgy, chemical industry, power, grain, meat and wool production, which were mainly exported to other Soviet republics for final use and manufacture. Thus, after the collapse of the Soviet Union, Kazakhstan was left with a lack of internal industrial connections. Rich hydrocarbon western regions of Kazakhstan were not connected by pipelines to the central and eastern regions of Kazakhstan. The latter regions had their own refineries, the Pavlodar and Shymkentnefteorgsyntez, which processed crude oil, during the Soviet period, from Western Siberia through the pipeline Omsk-Pavlodar-Shymkent-Chardzou, with the final point located in Turkmenistan (Kalyuzhnova, Jaffe, Lynch, Sickles, 2002).

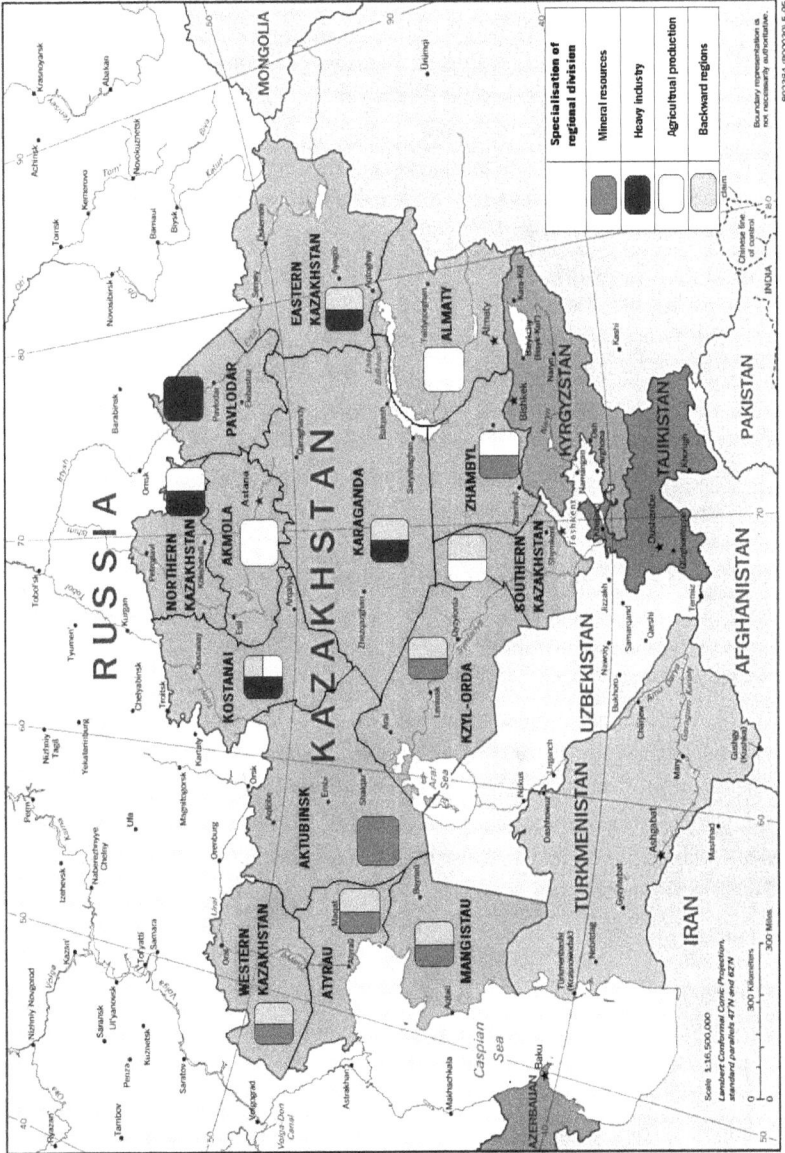

MAP 5 REGIONAL DIVISION BY GROUPS OF SPECIALISATION, 1991–2003

During the time of the Soviet economy, such industrial cooperation was economically efficient and designed to facilitate the centrally controlled Soviet fuel industry. However, after the collapse of the Soviet Union inter-republican relations did not function as before. In order to maintain the same volume of production inside Kazakhstan, it was necessary to build new refineries in western Kazakhstan or to send extracted oil and gas to refineries in eastern and central regions. However, the problem was not only in the absence of pipelines to these regions, but also in the difference of crude oil types from Western Siberia and from the Kazakh oil fields. The Pavlodar and Shymkent refineries were built for the processing of Western Siberian oil. The latter required a different type of technology than the oil from Kazakh fields, which is characterised by its sulphur content. Therefore, the industrial links created for the Soviet economy can not operate efficiently for the transition economies, where the establishment of internal links on the basis of existing factories requires substantial level of investment.

The whole economy of Kazakhstan suffered from the sharp fall in investment amounting to 68% from 1990 to 1993, while the investment in industrial production declined by two thirds over the same period (Kalyuzhnova, 1998). Investment in the construction of industries increased by 0.5% in 1991 compared to the previous year. However, in 1992, construction investment declined by 46.9% and in 1993 by 39%, which amounts to a fall of 68% between 1991 and 1993. Machine-building, chemical and petrochemical industries and the fuel industry were most severely affected by the decline of investment in construction. Thus, from 1990 to 1993, investment in machine-building fell by 280%, while investment in the fuel industry declined by 240% over the same period.

Prior to 1990, the growth of industrial production gradually increased (Figure 2.1.) even during the overall slowdown in the growth of heavy industrial production. In 1990, industrial production in Kazakhstan reached the highest level in its history and after the transition period started, in 1991, industrial production fell substantially until 1995. The fall was the result of the breakdown of industrial and trade connections to other former Soviet republics, hyper inflation and the mismanagement of the privatisation process. Thus, in 1995 the level of industrial production reached just 48% of the 1990 level, the lowest level for the first decade of transition. In 1996, industrial production gradually started to recover, when the inflation started to fall and amounted to 28.7% and 20% for industrial and consumer goods respectively. However, since 1996, despite the gradual growth industrial production has not reached the level at the start of transition, even in 2001, when industrial production amounted to only 66% of the output in 1990 (Figure 2.1.).

Figure 2.2. Changes in the production of Kazakhstani industries in 1990-2001 (1990=100%)

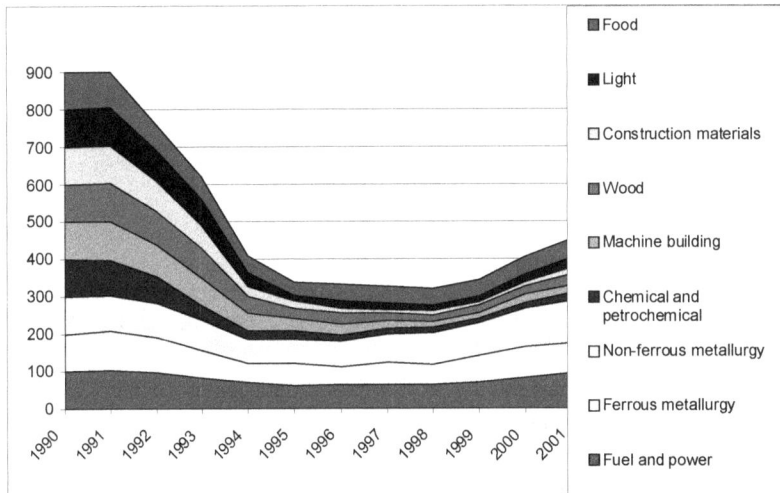

Source: The data are calculated from: *Promyshlennost' Kazakhstana: 1920-1999 goda*, 2000. *Promyshlennost' Kazakhstana i ego regionov: 1998-1999 goda*, 2000. *Promyshlennost' Kazakhstana i ego regionov: 1998-2001 goda*, 2002. *Sotsial'no-ekonomicheskoe polozhenie Kazakhstana - 2000*, 2001.

Figure 2.3. The growth rates of Kazakhstani industries on a year-by-year comparison, %.

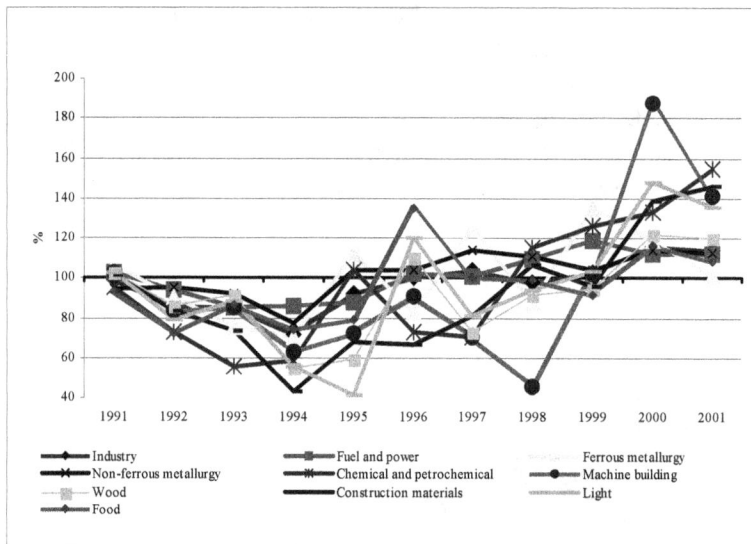

Source: The figure is constructed from information taken from: *Promyshlennost' Kazakhstana: 1920-1999 goda*, 2000. *Regiony Kazakhstana: 1997-2000*, 2001. *Promyshlennost' Kazakhstana i ego regionov: 1998-2001 goda*, 2002.

Figure 2.2. shows shares in the level of total production of industries over the first decade of transition, where each layer denotes the individual industry with 100% of production in 1990, and its changes over the considered period in relation to the base year 1990. The most significant drop in production over the 10 years of transition occurred in the construction materials industry, whose output in 2001 was 19.7% of that in 1990. However, the lowest level of production in the construction materials industry was observed in 1998, where the industry produced 9.7% of the 1990 level. Due to the significant drop in production in the construction materials industry, its share of total production dropped from 5% in 1991 to 0.6% in 2001 (Figure 2.4.).

Figure 2.4. Changes in the structure of industrial production over the years of transition

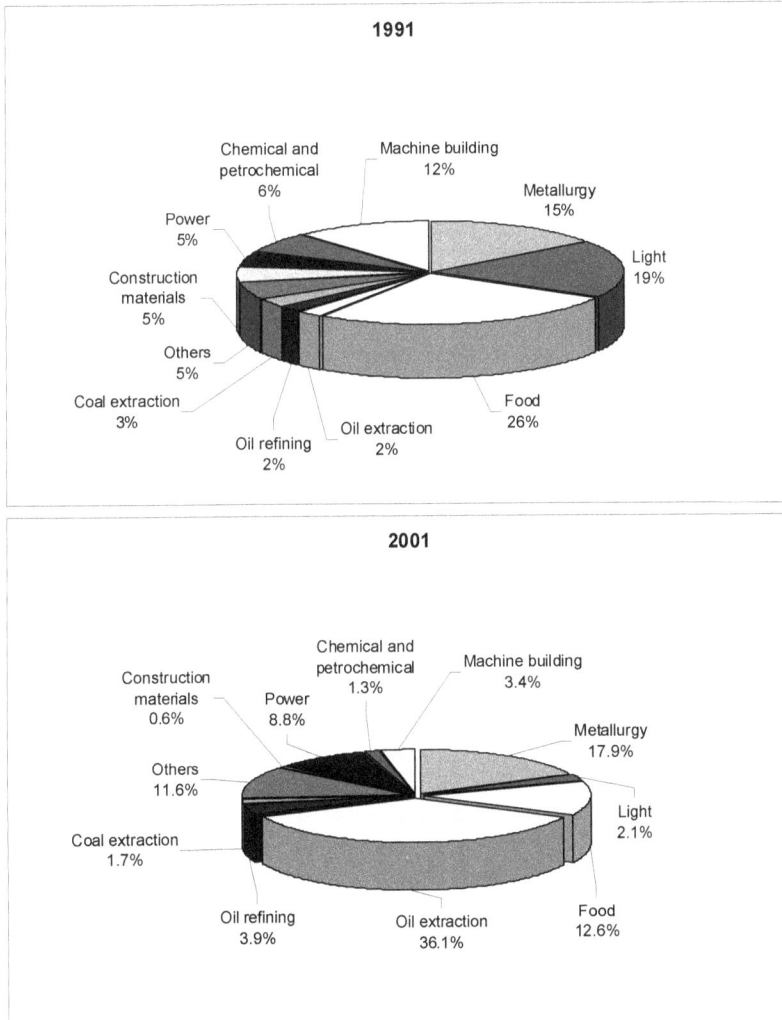

1991

Machine building 12%
Chemical and petrochemical 6%
Metallurgy 15%
Power 5%
Light 19%
Construction materials 5%
Others 5%
Coal extraction 3%
Food 26%
Oil refining 2%
Oil extraction 2%

2001

Chemical and petrochemical 1.3%
Construction materials 0.6%
Machine building 3.4%
Power 8.8%
Metallurgy 17.9%
Others 11.6%
Light 2.1%
Coal extraction 1.7%
Oil refining 3.9%
Oil extraction 36.1%
Food 12.6%

Source: *Kazakhstan: 1991-2001*, 2001. *Kazakhstan: 1991-2002*, 2002.

Even though production in the construction materials industry had soared in 2000 (Figure 2.3.), total output was still very low compared to the beginning of transition. The decline in industrial activity of Kazakhstan significantly reduced the need for the construction of new assets, given the low level of use of existing industrial assets and the fall in investments. The only industry that reached the production level of 1990 in 2001 was non-ferrous metallurgy with an increase of 12.5% between 1990 and 2001 and with a slight increase of its share in the total industry from 15% in 1991 to 17.9% in 2001 (Figure 2.4.). The fuel and power industries, together with ferrous metallurgy, suffered the least decline in their production over the transition decade compared to other industries. The performance of mineral resource based industries started to improve in the second half of the transition decade after the privatisation of numerous deposits of mineral resources. New owners, often foreign shareholders, understood the key importance of mineral resources on the world market and their profitability, which yield significant returns on investments in new technology and would enable a recovery of production. Thus, oil extraction increased its share of the total industrial production from 2% in 1991 to 36.1% in 2001. However, the share of coal extraction in the total industrial production fell from 3% in 1991 to 1.7% in 2001 as a result of low interest in coal mining due the decline in demand, and a gradual move to substitute gas for coal.

Significant falls in production occurred in the light, chemical and petrochemical industries. The persistent decline of the economy in transition caused the production of light industry in 1999 to fall to 14.8% of the output in 1990. The output of the chemical and petrochemical industries was only 12.8% of that in 1990. However, in 2001, both industries increased their production and reached 24.9% (light industry) and 21% (chemical and petrochemical industry) of the 1990 level of output. The share of GDP of the chemical and petrochemical industry declined from 6% to 1.3% over the transition decade, while the share of GDP of light industry fell from 19% in 1991 to 2.1% in 2001. Prior to 1991, the output of the chemical and petrochemical industry of the Kazakh SSR was mainly used by industries in other republics of the Soviet Union for the manufacture of finished goods. However, due to the fact that connections between republics at the beginning of transition were severed, the demand

for the output of chemical and petrochemical industries of Kazakhstan significantly fell. It was unable to recover its level of production during the first decade of transition. The light industry of Kazakhstan was maintained by local
raw materials and local demand. Thus, during the first two years of transition
the industry had declined by only 15-20%, mainly as a result of the mismanagement of the privatisation process, which resulted in financial instability in
the industry. In 1994 production fell by 45% and later the decline became
steeper, due to the low demand for the output, which could not compete with
the number of imported goods from outside the country. Since the beginning
of transition, many employees lost their jobs because of the significant fall in
industrial production. Therefore, in order to survive, many of them entered a
business based on the transportation of consumer goods from outside Kazakhstan that were cheaper and of better quality compared to local goods. As
a result, the business became profitable and involved a growing proportion of
the population, who were not satisfied with their current jobs. Nonetheless,
such businesses caused the production level of light industry in Kazakhstan
to fall considerably.

The output of the food industry of Kazakhstan declined significantly in the first
half of the transition decade due to dramatic falls in agricultural production, as
many farms were transferred from state ownership to private owners. Thus,
poor management in private farms significantly reduced agricultural production. Livestock was especially affected. The number of sheep almost halved
between 1990 and 1995, as private owners were interested in the maximum
current profit growth that could be immediately generated without investing in
the preservation of livestock and land for the future. Since 1995 however,
production in the food industry has gradually increased, but the level of production in 2001 amounted to just 51.7% of the production level in 1991.

The machine-building industry declined significantly during the period of
perestroika, and it was impossible to halt the continuing decline during the
transition period. The production of raw materials needed for machine-
building was in significant decline, while industries which required new
equipment and machines did not have sufficient funds for modernisation.
Therefore, until 1999, the machine-building industry gradually decreased,

when its output was a mere 14.1% of the production level in 1990. Later growth brought the industry to 22.5% of the 1990 production level, while its share of total industrial production declined from 12% in 1991 to 3.4% in 2001.

Despite the total fall in industrial production by 2001 to 66% of the 1990 level and the collapse of production in many industries in Kazakhstan, the proportion of Kazakhstan's GDP contributed by industry increased from 27.1% in 1991 to 30.7% in 2001. This was due to the overall decline of the economy over the years of transition[39], when agricultural production as a proportion of GDP declined dramatically, from 29.5% in 1991 to 8.7% in 2001. At the beginning of the century, when the industrial development of the country had just begun, the agricultural production accounted for 85% of GDP[40]. Despite the overall decline, the new Kazakhstani economy service sector was developing in the opposite direction to the remainder of the economy. Thus, in 1991, services accounted for 34.8% of the Kazakhstani GDP, a proportion that increased to 57.3% by 1996. However, in 2001, after industrial growth, this figure fell to 48.1%.

1998 was particularly difficult for the Kazakhstani economy. In 1997, the capital of Kazakhstan was moved from Almaty (in the southeast of Kazakhstan) to the northern part of Kazakhstan – Astana city (Akmola region). This consumed a significant amount of investment that was redirected from other regions of Kazakhstan to the construction of the new capital. In 1998, world prices of oil and metal fell. These were key export goods of Kazakhstan. In

---

39   The value of GDP accounted for 78.8% in 2001 compared to 1990. (*Kazakhstan: 1991-2002*, 2002).

40   The dramatic fall of the agricultural production in the share of GDP during operation of the Soviet system was caused by the substantial development and growth of industrial production, while the actual volume and assortment of agricultural production increased significantly as well, but with the lower speed. However, the decline of the agricultural production in the share of GDP in the transition period followed the dramatic fall of the actual production in agricultural sector, which was a cause of the mismanagement of the privatisation. The lack of central control in the beginning of the transition process caused the lack of responsibility of administrators of privatisation process and new managers, who were interested only in private profits and not in the production growth. (Kaliev, 2003).

August of the same year neighbouring Russia experienced a financial crisis which affected Kazakhstan and all Central Asian economies and this was followed by the devaluation of the Tenge (the Kazakhstani currency) which lost almost half of its value in April of 1999. Thus, in 1996 and 1997, after the collapse of the former Soviet Union, GDP and industrial production increased for the first time. GDP increased by 0.5% in 1996 and by 1.7% in 1997; the increase in industrial production amounted to 0.3% and 4% respectively. However, in 1998, GDP fell by 1.9% and industrial production by 2.4%. Nevertheless, the Kazakhstani economy recovered relatively quickly from the sudden crisis and by 1999, industrial production increased by 2.2% and GDP increased by 2.7% because of a bumper grain harvest and the recovery of world oil prices that increased Kazakhstani oil revenues. In 2000, the growth in the economy accelerated as indicated by an increase in GDP of 9.6% and in industrial production of 15.5% compared to the previous year due to the industry's strong export performance. However, in 2000, levels of GDP and industrial production were still a long way away from the level of 1990. Thus, in 2000, industrial output was 58% of the 1990 level (Figure 2.1.), while the level of GDP was 69.3% of that of 1990 (Figure 2.5.).

Figure 2.5. Changes in GDP growth 1991-2001, %

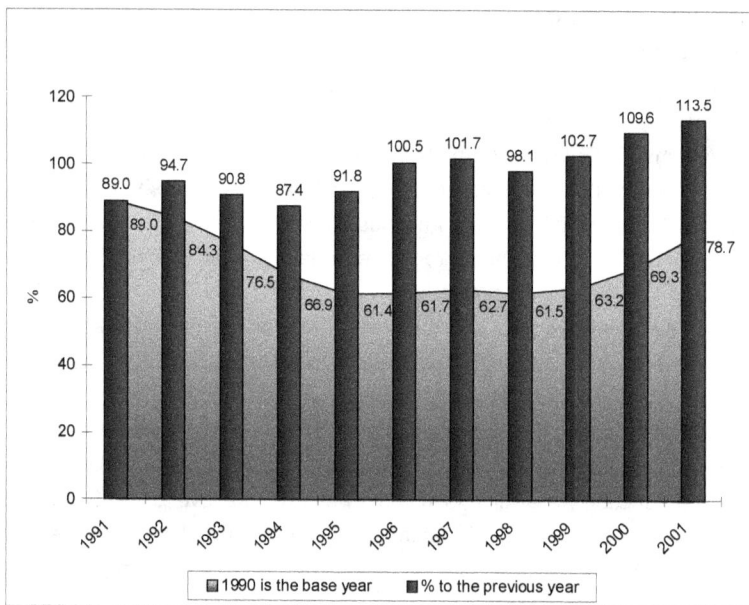

Source: *Kazakhstan: 1991-2001*, 2001.*Kazakhstan: 1991-2002*, 2002

By 2001, the production of all industries in Kazakhstan had fallen substantially, but the industries based on the exploitation of mineral resources had declined the least compared to other industries, and managed to restore their level of production to the approximate level of 1990. Other industries in 2001 could not reach even 30% of the base level of 1990, except in the food industry which reached 51.7% of the 1990 production level. The food industry in Kazakhstan faced a high level of competition from neighbouring countries (i.e. former Soviet republics). However, in 2000, the Kazakhstani government introduced a 200% tax for one year on the import of some consumer goods from neighbouring Kyrgyzstan and Russia. This helped Kazakhstani producers to increase their production without any pressure from outside competitors, whose output was of higher quality at lower prices. However, the remaining industries increased output modestly in 2000-2001. The industrial production of Kazakhstan moved from the diversification of production to one that was strictly orientated towards the exploitation of mineral resources, becoming strongly dependent on commodity price fluctuations (Kalyuzhnova, 2000).

The industrial performance of Kazakhstan in the first decade of transition was directly connected with the location of enterprises. Industrial enterprises that had been linked only to enterprises in other former Soviet republics, but not to other industrial clusters in Kazakhstan, operated in an environment characterised by a severe recession during transition. In order to analyse the performance of industrial enterprises, it is necessary to evaluate the patterns of their location and examine the effect of the collapse of the Soviet system on the performance of industrial enterprises in relation to regional locations.

Regional development under transition
The economic development of the different regions in Kazakhstan reflected the performance of the industries of their specialisation. Two regions of Kazakhstan experienced significant growth during the period of transition (Figure 2.6.). These are the Atyrau and Mangistau regions. Their specialisation is oil extraction, whose share in the Kazakhstani industrial production increased from 2% to 38% over the decade (Figure 2.4.). As a result, these regions had increased their share in total GDP from 5.1% and 1.8% in 1990 to 9.7% and 4.8% in 2001 for the Atyrau and Mangistau regions respectively, while other regions also faced significant changes (Table 2.2.).

Figure 2.6. Change in the structure of Kazakhstani GDP by regions in 1990-2001, %

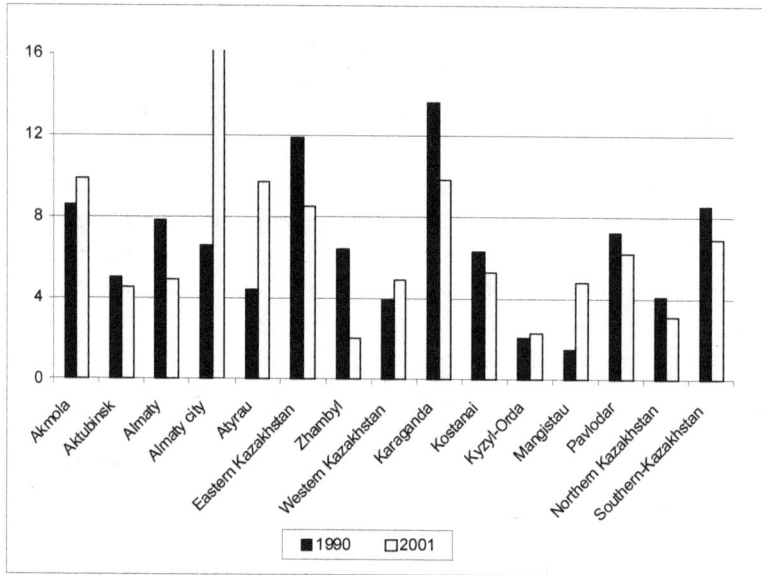

Source: *Regiony Kazakhstana - 1991*, 1992. *Kazakhstan: 1991-2002*, 2002.

Since the beginning of the transition period, the development of the regions has proceeded in an unbalanced way. This had the consequence to increase the gap in development between the regions. Those specialising in mineral resource extraction became highly attractive for investment. This difference in the ability to attract investments reflected total regional growth. Until 1996 other regions fought for survival and attempted to maintain, the same level of production, where growth was not possible due to the lack of financial resources. In 1990, the highest average salary of industrial workers was in the Mangistau region at a level of 128.9% of the average industrial salary in Kazakhstan, while the lowest average industrial salary was in the Kzyl-Orda region at 74.1% of the average in the country as a whole. By 1995, the gap between industrial salaries in the regions increased, where regions specialising in mineral resource extraction had significant growth, while industrial salaries in other regions faced a continuous decline due to cuts in production.

Table 2.2. The structure of Kazakhstani GDP by regions, 1990-2001, %

Regions	GDP			GDP per head		
	1990	1995	2001	1990	1995	2001
Kazakhstan	*100*	*100*	*100*	*100*	*100*	*100*
Akmola	7.8	6.1	3.3	84.1	106.7	61.6
Astana city[41]			6.6			141.1
Aktubinsk	5.6	5.0	4.5	124.3	109.0	106.2
Almaty	7.8	5.1	4.9	76.6	49.8	47.5
Almaty city	6.6	8.1	17.2	112.7	121.7	200.9
Atyrau	5.1	6.1	9.7	195.5	214.5	395.0
Eastern Kazakhstan	11	11.8	8.5	102.1	112.2	81.8
Zhambyl	6.8	2.2	2	107.7	34.8	33.2
Western Kazakhstan	4.3	2.7	4.9	113.1	66.0	125.4
Karaganda	13.4	16.3	9.8	123.3	164.3	108.6
Kostanai	7.5	7.2	5.3	124.7	97.3	78.9
Kzyl-Orda	2.4	2.2	2.3	59.6	52.8	70.8
Mangistau	1.8	5.1	4.8	90.5	249.1	263.0
Pavlodar	7.2	10.7	6.2	111.5	189.1	117.2
Northern Kazakhstan	4.1	7.0	3.1	97.4	93.2	70.7
Southern-Kazakhstan	8.9	4.4	6.9	80.6	35.7	43.5

Source: Data are calculated from: *Regiony Kazakhstana: 1991-1997*, 1998. *Kazakh-stan: 1991-2002*, 2002.

In order to reduce disparities of regional development the Kazakhstani government classified its regions into four main groups for regional development

---

41   Collection and representation of data for Astana city (the new capital of Kazakhstan) began in 1998, after its introduction.

policy implementation[42] (Table 2.3.). The classification of regions was based on the principle of specialisation and economic-geographical conditions of regions.

Different groups of regions demanded a different set of measures for the implementation of the regional development policy depending on initial conditions. Main policy was principally directed at the expansion of regional infrastructure for the development of Kazakhstani markets on a regional basis, in order to improve even regional development. The development of regions during the first decade of transition and the effect of regional policy will be analysed in the following sections.

---

42   Section 2.3 *Changes in regional concentration of industrial activities*, part *Regional development policy.*

Table 2.3. Division of regions into four groups, 1996

Groups	Regions	Specifications
First group	Atyrau, Aktubinsk, Mangistau, Western Kazakhstan, part of Kzyl-Orda and Zhambyl	Mineral resources endowment, mainly oil and gas
Second group	Eastern Kazakhstan, Pavlodar, Karaganda, Kostanai and Northern Kazakhstan	Heavy industry
Third group	Northern Kazakhstan, Akmola, Kostanai, Zhambyl, Southern Kazakhstan, Western Kazakhstan and Almaty	Agricultural production
Fourth group	Southern part of Kostanai region (Torgai area), Kzyl-Orda, North-Western part of Eastern Kazakhstan region (Semipalatinsk area), agricultural areas of Atyrau, Mangistau, Southern Kazakhstan and agricultural areas of the Western part of Karaganda region (Zhezkazgan agricultural area).	Backward regions

Source: This table is created using information from: *Issledovatel'skii otchet*, 1995.

Table 2.4. Industrial production growth rates by regions,%, year by year basis.

Regions	1991	1992	1993	1994	1995	1996	1997	1998	1999	2000	2001
Kazakhstan	*99*	*86*	*85*	*71*	*91*	*100*	*104*	*97*	*102*	*115*	*113*
Akmola	104	85	90	75	84	91	98	94	94	112	116
Aktubinsk	99	91	93	83	99	67	125	99	106	117	115
Almaty	100	86	91	67	74	87	92	108	108	108	107
Atyrau	113	103	92	94	93	122	117	99	103	110	114
Eastern Kazakhstan	98	80	85	71	95	91	104	101	100	119	116
Zhambyl	91	74	81	71	103	98	98	104	100	105	121
Western Kazakhstan	102	83	83	65	92	98	105	100	123	131	107
Karaganda	96	95	86	78	79	92	111	100	113	115	108
Kostanai	104	85	88	70	103	85	107	76	101	125	102
Kzyl-Orda	97	99	92	76	87	121	103	117	121	132	116
Mangistau	93	73	85	70	86	104	98	79	106	107	117
Pavlodar	100	88	84	70	100	93	84	102	92	118	113
Northern Kazakhstan	100	79	87	66	74	76	75	104	99	115	110
Southern-Kazakhstan	100	86	77	61	72	96	93	97	102	105	111
Astana city	-	-	-	-	-	-	102	100	95	112	118
Almaty city	97	86	90	71	70	102	105	105	105	127	122

Source: Data are taken from: *Regiony Kazakhstana: 1996-1999*, 2000. *Regiony Kazakhstana: 1997-2000*, 2001. *Kazakhstan: 1991-2002*, 2002. *Regiony Kazakhstana- 1997*, 1998. *Issledovatel'skii otchet*, 1995.

Figure 2.7. Industrial production of Kazakhstan by regions, 1991-2001%.

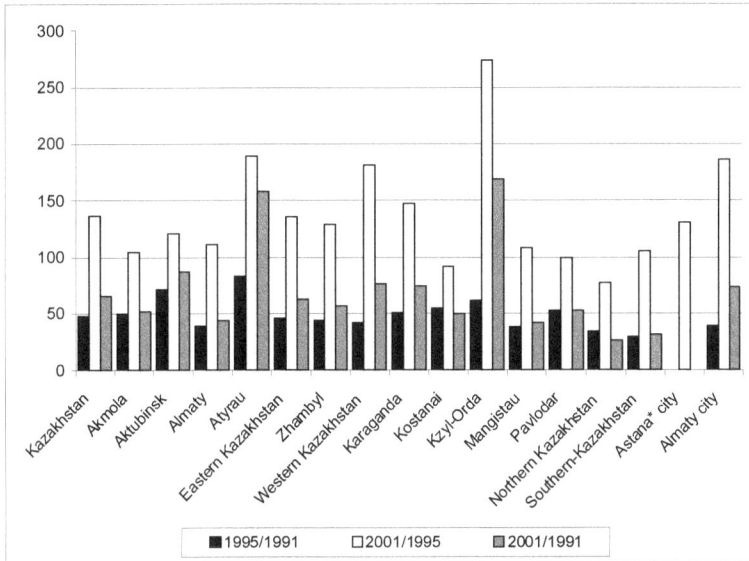

Source: Figure is created on the basis of Table 2.4.
          * Separation of statistical information on Akmola region and Astana city
          started in 1997 after introduction of Astana city as the Kazakhstani capital.

2.3 Changes in the regional concentration of industrial activities

Since 1996, after the initial collapse (1991-1996) in all sectors of the Kazakhstani economy, industrial development of particular regions has shown signs
of recovery (Table 2.4.). This recovery became possible as a result of specific
governmental regional policy. The latter was based on a government strategy
of working with foreign investors in certain (mainly oil and gas) regions. This
was based on the partial implementation of the regional policy through the investment of foreign companies.[43] The government itself lacked financial resources and the government (state) investments drastically declined in all

---

43   The detailed analysis of the regional policy is given in the section *Regional devel-
     opment policy*   (p. 188)

economic sectors. Thus, fixed capital investments in 1996 accounted for 10.9% of investments in 1991 (Central Asia 2010: Prospects for Human development, 1999).

The most significant growth over the transition decade occurred in the *Kzyl-Orda* region (Figure 2.7.), which was considered to be a backward region in 1995 (Table 2.3.). Industrial production in the Kzyl-Orda region had soared by 174% between 1995 and 2001, while average growth of the region for the whole decade of transition increased by 68%, which was higher than the average level of growth in Kazakhstan. The rapid growth of industrial production in the Kzyl-Orda region was based on the new oil and gas fields of *Kumkol* and *Akshabulak* and the later discoveries of the *Bektas* and *Konys* oil fields at the end of the 1980s and the 1990s, when extraction work developed significantly. In 1990, the Kzyl-Orda region produced 1.9% of total Kazakhstani oil; by 1995, oil production in the region had quadrupled and accounted for 9.5% of the total oil extraction in Kazakhstan. In 2000, the level of oil extraction in the Kzyl-Orda region accounted for 15% of the national level, having grown by 174% since 1995. Thus in 2000 the level of oil extraction in the Kzyl-Orda region was 10.9 times the output of 1990.

In the second half of the decade, Kzyl-Orda also made progress with its light industry after a significant fall in the first half of the decade, despite a substantial decline in the whole of the light industry of Kazakhstan (Figure 2.3.). By 2001, the Kzyl-Orda region had increased its share of the national shoe production from 8.2% in 1990 to 75.9%. The light industry of the region had declined by 99.1% during the first five years of transition, resulting in the threat of the complete termination of production. However, by 2001, the successful improvement of factory privatisation in the middle of the transition decade increased regional production to a level of 16.8 times the output in 1995. Even though the production level of 2001 did not reach the 1990 level, the dramatic decline of light industry in Kazakhstan overall meant that light industry in the Kzyl-Orda region continued to grow as a proportion of total for the country.

The production of other industries in the region fell dramatically during the first decade of transition. The construction materials industry had declined in the production of all of its main output. The timber industry of the Kzyl-Orda region produced 100% of the cellulose produced in Kazakhstan since 1991 and declined dramatically during the first decade of transition due to the fall in demand from former Soviet republics, and in 2000 had to terminate production.

By 2001, industrial production in the Kzyl-Orda region had increased its share of the national industrial output from 1.4% in 1990 to 3.9%. However, despite the high growth in production of the fuel and light industries, the Kzyl-Orda region did not increase its share of regional GDP in 2001 compared to 1990 (Table 2.2.), which stayed at 2.4%. At the same time, in 2001, the level of GDP per head increased compared to 1990 from 59.6% to 79.8% of the average per capita GDP in Kazakhstan. Despite the high growth of the production of some industrial goods and the highest growth rates of industrial production since 1996 (Table 2.4.), the reason for the insignificant growth of the share of the Kzyl-Orda region in GDP can be explained by the very poor initial conditions of the region. Such conditions demanded more time and finances to approach the average Kazakhstani economic development level. The region had a high growth of investment for the development of oil fields, but other industries of the region, except light industry, faced a continuous fall in production. The industrial production of the region began to concentrate on profits in the fuel industry and became highly dependent on world prices of oil and external demand. At the same time, the diversification of industrial production in the Kzyl-Orda region that could maintain the economy of the region during the period of the oil crisis was lost, although the share of other industries would be comparatively small. Thus, transition brought intensive development of the fuel industry to the Kzyl-Orda region which decreased interest in the development of other established industries, and created a growing imbalance in regional development.

The economy of *Southern Kazakhstan* is based on agriculture and heavy industry. However, due to the economic crisis during the first years of transition, the region was considered to be partly agricultural and partly a backward region (Table 2.3.). The share of GDP (Table 2.2.) of the region then declined from 8.9% in 1990 to 4.4% in 1995, while GDP per head decreased from 80.6% of the average Kazakhstani level in 1990 to 35.7% in 1995. Nevertheless, the economy of the region made slight progress in the second half of the transition decade, when the share of GDP increased to 6.9% in 2001, and GDP per capita increased to 43.5% of the average Kazakhstani level. The slight growth in the GDP of Southern Kazakhstan is explained by the growth of industrial production at the end of the first transition decade. In the post-Soviet period Southern Kazakhstan specialised in the extraction of mineral resources, machine-building and chemical industries. In 1990, Southern Kazakhstan had one of the largest oil refineries in Kazakhstan, manufacturing crude oil from the relatively new fields of the neighbouring Kzyl-Orda region. Despite the rapid growth of the fuel industry in the Kzyl-Orda region, the output of the oil refinery in Southern Kazakhstan, *Chimkent*, which was mainly produced for export, fell dramatically during the years of transition. The reason for the decline was that since transition began, numerous oil fields in Kazakhstan, including the prospective fields of Kzyl-Orda were privatised, and their owners had a high interest in profit, which implied attempts at the reduction of production costs. Taking into account the distant location of the Southern Kazakhstan oil refinery from the market, it became unprofitable for oil fields to supply crude oil to the Chimkent refinery. The latter had high production costs with out-dated technology and relatively high transportation costs for final oil products compared to the transportation costs of crude oil. Therefore, the output of the Southern Kazakhstan oil refinery dropped significantly, and the production of many finished products fell by more than 95% over the first transition decade.

Production in the chemical industry in Southern Kazakhstan fell for the same reason as in the fuel industry, where high production costs, out-dated technology and high costs of transporting goods to the Russian market rendered production in Southern Kazakhstan non-competitive. As a result, production of many chemical goods in the region was terminated over the transition period.

Since 1999, other industries of Southern Kazakhstan whose production was based on local sources and was intended for the local Kazakhstani market, became to recover their production. Construction materials, machine-building and mining declined substantially over the whole transition period until 1999-2000, when production started its rapid upturn. The proximity of Southern Kazakhstan to the Almaty region which was the centre of all the economic activities, made it possible for the region to increase the production of goods (mainly construction materials), with a high demand in the Almaty region and relatively low transportation costs compared to other regions.

The light industry of the Southern Kazakhstan region deteriorated dramatically over the transition period. The low quality and high costs of textile production in Kazakhstan significantly reduced demand as customers preferred imports from outside Kazakhstan. Therefore, the production of textiles fell together with the demand from producers of raw materials such as cotton. As a result, cotton production in the region declined by 75% over the transition decade, while by 1998 the production of textiles fell by 76.3% with less cotton textile production in the region. The manufacture of cotton textiles in Southern Kazakhstan was ceased because of the steep fall in the production of cotton, which affected the profitability of textile production due to the fact that only a small proportion of the capacity of factories was used. However, in 2001 there was significant growth in cotton production, which exceeded the production level of 1991 by 50%. This can be explained by the substantial rise in exports to foreign markets, where Kazakhstani cotton had a comparative advantage due to lower costs, as a result of the low costs of local labour given that cotton cultivation relies entirely on manual labour.

The food industry in the Southern Kazakhstan region had favourable conditions for fruit and vegetables. However, at the beginning of transition their production fell by 98.8% as a result of financial difficulties and higher competition from neighbouring Uzbekistan, which had lower costs of production. Nevertheless, the whole food industry increased its production by 3.4 times over the second half of the transition decade, which mainly consisted of the production of finished goods, but their level was much lower than the production level of 1991.

Thus, although richly with natural minerals and favourable conditions for agriculture the Southern Kazakhstan region faced a decline in many of its specialised industries, where the obsolescence of technology and the distant location from foreign markets played a crucial role. Unless the output of the chemical industry and oil refinery could be sold inside the country, their production in the region would not be viable. The only prospect and hope for industries in Southern Kazakhstan were the construction materials and food industries, whose output was designed for local consumption. During the Soviet period, Southern Kazakhstan exported most of its industrial output to other Soviet republics. Transportation costs did not play a crucial role for the Soviet Union because industries were located according to the specialisation of each republic regardless of the transport requirements. The Kazakh SSR was the supplier of mineral resources. However, during the transition period, transport costs became an important factor for Kazakhstan. The owners of enterprises acquired a personal interest in efficient production, which could increase profit. Therefore, it became important to seek local partners, in order to cut transportation costs.

Zhambyl is rich with mineral resources and, like the southern regions, specialises in agricultural production (Table 2.3., Map 5. Regional division by groups of specialisation, 1991-2003). Industrial production in the region during transition was at the same level as Kazakhstani development (Figure 2.7.). It declined in the first half of the decade by 55.8%, and gradually rose by 29.2% over the next five years. The transition had a detrimental impact on the entire economy of the Zhambyl region (Table 2.2.). Its share of national GDP declined from 6.8% in 1990 to 2% in 2001, and while the GDP per head declined from 107.7% to 33.2% over the same period compared to the average level in Kazakhstan.

The heavy industry in the Zhambyl region consists of chemical and machine-building industries. The Zhambyl region has the largest factory in the world for the production of mineral fertilizers with a capacity of 30 thousand tonnes per year (Ermakov, 2001). However, the production of mineral fertilizers and other chemical output declined over the transition period by 95%, with signs of a slight recovery since 2000. The reason for the decline in production of such a powerful industry in the region lay in the high transportation costs. The accumulation of profit on the part of former Soviet managers mandated the search for sources that were located more closely.

The output of machine-building in the Zhambyl region fell continuously, due to the decline and lack of creditworthiness of the chemical and agricultural sectors, which were the main customers for the machine-building industry in the region. However, in other regions the output of the machine-building industry fell even more sharply. Hence, the share of the national output of machine-building in the region grew rapidly. Thus, the production of chemical equipment in Zhambyl increased its share of national output from 10.1% in 1990 to 76% at the end of the transition decade, while the actual volume of production fell.

Output of the light industry in Zhambyl (a specialisation of the region) fell as dramatically as in the rest of Kazakhstan due to the high inflow of competitive goods from outside. In 2001, the food industry of the region managed to exceed the production level of 1990 by 54.9%, while production of the whole Kazakhstani food industry in 2001 was 54.1% lower than its 1990 level. This growth in the food industry was accounted for mainly by the growth in sugar production, a specialisation of the Zhambyl region. In 2001, the Zhambyl region produced 51% of Kazakhstani sugar.

The steep fall in contribution of the Zhambyl region to national output (GDP) can be explained by the dramatic decline in the output of heavy industries in the region, which was highly industrialised prior to the transition period. The GDP per head of the region fell from an above average level in 1990 to the lowest level in Kazakhstan in 2001. Although the chemical and machine-building industries in the region accounted for a growing proportion of the national output, the actual volume of production fell significantly, which left the majority of skilled industrial workers without a job. Thus, industrial regions were left with a specialisation in agriculture. At the same time, a high percentage of the population got involved in the informal business of trading consumer goods, based on the import of textiles from abroad. The critical position of the region with the lowest economic development could be only be

solved by finding a market for the chemical industry of the region or the creation of a local market for its huge potential.

The *Kostanai* region was in part classified as specialising in heavy industry.
The southern part of the region, however, was considered to be in the fourth
group of backward regions (Table 2.3., Map 5. Regional division by groups of
specialisation, 1991-2003). Industrial production in Kostanai declined substantially in the first half of the first decade of transition and underwent constant fluctuations in the second half. As a result industrial production in the
Kostanai region in 2001 attained 50.1% of its 1991 production level (Figure
2.7.). The main specialisation of the Kostanai region is metallurgy; in 2001 the
region produced 88.9% of Kazakhstani iron ore. Although the output of the
metallurgy industry in the region exceeded the level of 1995, it was still 35%
lower than the 1990 production level. The metallurgy industry of the Kostanai
region mainly supplies its output to Russia or to other countries. As a result of
the Russian crisis and the decline in world commodity prices in 1998, iron ore
extraction in the region declined by 40.1% in one year, but later recovered.

The Kostanai region specialised in light and food industries prior to transition.
However, during the transition period the share of the region in the national
output of light industry fell continuously, from 9% in 1990 to 1% in 2000. The
output of the food industry of the Kostanai region also fell substantially over
the transition period, but began to grow in 2000. The production of many
foodstuffs in the Kostanai region had declined during transition. However,
their proportion of the total food production of Kazakhstan increased, as a result of a deeper fall in the average level of Kazakhstani food production. Food
production in the Kostanai region was based on its agricultural production,
which fell steeply at the beginning of transition and fluctuated wildly in the
second half of transition, being highly dependent on climate changes, lacking
improvements in technology and suffering from poor management. The
backward part of the Kostanai region (the Torgai region[44]), depended entirely
on agriculture and did not make any progress in the development of the

---

44   Torgai region was a separate region from Kostanai until 1997, with further divisions
      between Akmola and Kostanai region as a result of regional policy and the combi-
      nation of the backward region with more progressive neighbouring regions.

economy, but declined even further. The economic administration of Torgai and Kostanai were combined and as a result the general indicators of regional statistics were smoothed to provide a less extreme picture.

During the transition period, the Kostanai region retained the specialised industries, which it had prior to transition. Even though these industries had a higher shares of the national production of these industries in Kazakhstan the level of production became extremely low compared to 1990. The sharp fall in the light industry meant the gradual destruction of the whole industry whose level of production technology and quality of output did not enable it to compete with foreign imports. The decline in the food industry reflects the decline of demand from the former Soviet republics, which prioritised the self-sufficiency of their food industries after becoming independent. The production of many foodstuffs in Kostanai, as well as in the whole of Kazakhstan, has grown significantly since 2000, a fact which reflects the success of government measures for the protection of the local food producers through increasing tax on imported food. However, two main specialisations of the Kostanai region, agricultural production and iron ore extraction, are highly dependent on external conditions. Agricultural production is vulnerable to weather conditions due to the low level of technology and obsolete machines, while the extraction of iron ore is dependent on outside demand and world commodity prices. The high dependence of the region on external conditions could be reduced by the development of the production of intermediate and finished goods in the region.

By 2001, industrial production in *Eastern Kazakhstan* had risen by 35.2% since 1995 (Figure 2.7.), following a sharp decline during the first five years of transition, at the end of which the level of industrial production was 46.2% compared to 1990. However, despite growth during the following five years since 1995, in 2001 the industrial production of Eastern Kazakhstan accounted for only 62.5% of the level of 1990. In a way similar to the Kostanai region, Eastern Kazakhstan was connected to two groups of the regional division (Table 2.3.). The eastern part of the region specialised in heavy industry, while the north western part   (the Semipalatinsk region[45]) was considered backward. As the economy of Eastern Kazakhstan specialised in heavy industry, its performance was dominated by the decline in the production of the majority of heavy industrial goods in the first half of the transition decade. However, the second half of the decade was characterised by growth. Eastern Kazakhstan is the region with the largest deposits of non-ferrous metals in Kazakhstan, and one of the largest producers in the CIS[46] countries. However, since the beginning of transition, production in the metallurgical industry has continuously fallen due to the lack of investment and the severing of links with consumers in the former Soviet republics where, for example, steel production in 2001 reached a mere 9.8% of the 1990 production level. Eastern Kazakhstan is the largest producer of zinc in Kazakhstan and in the CIS countries. Its production fell significantly during the first half of the first decade of transition and recovered its production by 50% in the second half of the decade, by establishing trade links for export with Russia and other foreign countries. The endowment of the Eastern Kazakhstan region with mineral resources does not only bring benefits to the region. For example, Ust-Kamenogorsk (the city where the zinc-lead factory in Eastern Kazakhstan is located) is considered as one of the most polluted cities in the world. The lack of financial resources does not allow the region to acquire the appropriate technology for safer production. The cost of the environment degradation is not borne by the government, but by the population of the region which suffers as a result of serious health problems which will affect it for generations to come.

The production of construction materials in Eastern Kazakhstan remained its specialisation. However, the output of many goods in this industry fell by more than 80% over the first ten years of transition, while the average level of production of construction materials in Kazakhstan fell even further. In general, industries in Eastern Kazakhstan, which constituted the region's spe-

---

45   Until 1997, the Semipalatinsk region was separated from the Eastern Kazakhstan region. The statistics of the Eastern Kazakhstan region are described by the combination of these two regions.

46   CIS is the Commonwealth of Independent States, which is the former Soviet Union, except the Baltic states.

cialisation retained more or less the same share of national production during the first decade of transition. However, the volume of production in real terms fell dramatically, where continued production no longer brought any benefits to the region, but instead the burden of huge losses.

In 1990, Eastern Kazakhstan was one of the important producers of light industry, accounting for 22.2% of textile and 15.2% of shoe production in Kazakhstan. However, by 2001, the production of textiles in Eastern Kazakhstan had fallen by 98.8% since 1990, while shoe production fell by 99.3% during the same period. Such a significant fall in the production of light industry in Eastern Kazakhstan and in the whole of Kazakhstan was accompanied, and accelerated, by the increasing inflow of textile products from other countries that had rendered the output of local factories hopelessly uncompetitive with cheaper goods of higher quality. The supply of textile products from abroad was organised by a new generation of self-employed people called *chelnochniki* – "trade people with big bags". They travelled to China, the Arab Emirates, Turkey and Central European countries such as Poland and others and bought textile products in bulk for resale in Kazakhstan. Every year during the transition period more and more people joined this business, as they could get real money for their work without having to face the wage arrears that characterised jobs in their previous places of employment.

In 1990, Eastern Kazakhstan was one of the largest producers of meat and meat products in Kazakhstan, accounting for 14.6% of the total production in Kazakhstan. However, the performance of the food industry in Eastern Kazakhstan was very poor compared to the average growth of the industry. The total food industry of Kazakhstan increased its production by 41.9% between 1995 and 2001, while the output in Eastern Kazakhstan declined by 45.8% during the same period. Despite the growth in the regional food industry since 1999, during the period under consideration (1995-2001) it declined overall due to the steep falls in production in the earlier years. Thus, the total industrial production of the Eastern Kazakhstan region fell substantially during the first decade of transition, becoming dependent on the production of non-ferrous metals, which was relatively successful, thereby losing its industrial diversity.

Prior to 1997, the present Eastern Kazakhstan region comprised two different regions, Semipalatinsk and Eastern Kazakhstan. Semipalatinsk was considered a backward region due to its low level of industrial development. In 1997, the Semipalatinsk region became a part of the Eastern Kazakhstan region following the implementation of the regional policy. Regional unification was explained by the transfer of control over the backward region to the more successful neighbouring Eastern Kazakhstan region. However, the production of goods that was mainly concentrated in the territory of the Semipalatinsk region decreased over the years without recovery. Consequently, the unification of regions on the basis of the regional policy, did not yield the expected results of growth in the backward regions. Indeed, the performance of backward regions was concealed under statistical cover of the more successful Kostanai and Eastern Kazakhstan regions.

The *Atyrau* region was included in the first and fourth groups (Table 2.3.) of the regional division as a region rich with mineral resources, particularly hydrocarbons. At the same time, the agricultural part of the region was considered a backward region due to poor climatic and geographical conditions. Atyrau is one out of two regions that in 2001 exceeded its 1990 level of industrial production (Figure 2.7.). Although industrial production in the Atyrau region fell by 16.7% between 1990 and 1995, the production recovered in the second half of the decade with an increase of 89.5% that resulted in an aggregate regional growth of industrial production over the decade of 57.8%. The Atyrau region is located on the shore of the Caspian Sea and its industrial production is based on the extraction of hydrocarbons, its oil refinery, chemical, machine-building for the hydrocarbon industry, a ship-repair factory and a fish processing factory, which is the largest in CIS. The Caspian Sea is a rich commercial fishing ground that allows surrounding countries to produce more than 85% of the world's sturgeon and 90% of the world's black caviar. It is very important for Kazakhstan and the other Caspian Sea countries to maintain and to improve the environmental conditions of the sea in order to prevent pollution from hydrocarbon production. The Caspian Sea has many of the world's rare and unique species of fish, and the price of a ton of caviar is 20000 times higher (Ermakov, 2001) than that of a ton of oil. The share of Atyrau fishing as a proportion of the Kazakhstani total increased from 20.2%

in 1991 to 66.7% in 2001 due to significant growth in the industry since 1998 and the decline of the Mangistau share of the national fishing industry from 33.2% in 1990 to 3.6% in 2001. Despite the high growth of the fishing industry and the high profitability of its caviar, there is a problem that arises from the fact that the region does not always follow safe rules for the protection and preservation of the stocks of rare fish and has already received warnings from international organisations who refused to import the caviar from Kazakhstan.

Since the beginning of transition, oil production in the Atyrau region has grown substantially. It increased its share in the total oil extraction in Kazakhstan from 9.7% in 1990 to 43.2% in 2001. The extraction of natural gas in the region grew from 8.7% to 53% as a proportion of national output during the same period due to the intensive rate of the development of the hydrocarbon fields[47]. In the middle of the transition decade, the hydrocarbon fields of Kazakhstan were gradually privatised and a large proportion of their shares sold to foreign investors, where main of them were ChevronTexaco, BG pls, Agip and LUKoil. Their main interest was to increase the level of production growth and therefore invested significant funds to enhance the technology in the expectation that this investment would pay off as a result of higher productivity and efficiency.

One of the specialisations of the Atyrau region during the Soviet period was the production of chemical goods using by-products of the oil and gas industry. Indeed, it was one of the largest producers in the Soviet Union. However, in 2000, due to its continuous decline the chemical industry of the Atyrau region produced a mere 1.89% of the 1995 level of output. The reason for such a steep fall, from which it has not recovered, was the obsolescence of technology in the chemical industry of the region. Consequently, it is more profitable to export oil and gas to be refined and for the by-products to be used by indigenous industries in the export countries. Therefore, despite the growth of the extraction of oil and gas, the chemical industry in the region is deteriorating.

---

47   Although the figure of oil and gas extraction growth in the Atyrau region looks impressive in 2001, in Kazakhstan it still did not reach the level of 1989 production.

During the second half of the first decade of transition, Kazakhstani regional policy was designed to enhance the economic conditions of the backward regions by the increasing the production of the specialised sectors of their economy. However, agricultural production in the backward part of the Atyrau region had further declined by 31.2% over these years, while the total agricultural production of Kazakhstan declined by just 6.1% over the same period. The decline in Atyrau was due to the lack of equipment that could slightly improve the agricultural production in conditions of poor soil and lack of irrigation.

The growth of industrial production in the Atyrau region was observed only in the hydrocarbon industry, while the output of other industries that were specialisations of the region, such as chemical industry and livestock farming, fell significantly. The strengthening of the competitiveness of mineral based sectors and the weakening of the competitiveness of non-mineral based sectors is known as the *Dutch decease*. The growing demand for mineral resources leads to the currency appreciation, which in turn leads to the loss of the competitiveness of non-mineral based sectors and of the economy as a whole (Kalyuzhnova, 2002). The share of national GDP of the Atyrau region increased from 5.1% in 1990 to 9.7% in 2001 (Table 2.2.), while per capita GDP increased from 195.5% of the average Kazakhstani level to 395% in 2001 and with a growth of industrial production of 57.7% over the first decade of transition (Figure 2.7.). Nevertheless, these figures disguise the lack of improvement in the backward agricultural part, whose economic conditions had worsened over the decade.

The average salary of workers in the Atyrau region was double that of the average Kazakhstani salary in 2001. This however does not reflect the real situation with regard to the standard of living of the region's population, as the higher salaries of the region are an indicator for the salaries in the hydrocarbon industry which has a substantial proportion of foreign specialists. At the same time, the local population, which is largely not employed in the hydrocarbon industry, is trying to survive at the lowest standard of living.

The *Mangistau* region, which is similar to the Atyrau region was assigned to the first group of regional development as a region endowed with mineral resources, particularly oil and gas, and to the fourth group, due to the backwardness of its agricultural sector. In 1990, the Mangistau region had the lowest share of the national GDP (Table 2.2.), which was 1.8%. However, in 2001 this figure increased to 4.8%, while the level of industrial production declined by 57.9% during the first decade of transition. The industry in the Mangistau region consists of the chemical industry, machine-building for the chemical and hydrocarbon industries and mainly the production of oil and gas. The extraction of oil in the Mangistau region grew extremely fast in the middle of the 1970s due to the discovery of new fields and their high density. This made the extraction easier compared to other fields and reduced its extraction costs. Production continued to grow until the middle of the 1985. After the start of *perestroika* oil production in the region began to decline. In 1990, Mangistau produced 62.6% of Kazakhstani oil, being the largest oil producer in Kazakhstan and one of the largest producers in the former Soviet Union. Between 1990 and 1995, oil production in the region declined by 49.2%. However, by 2000, the level of oil production had increased by 12.3% compared to 1995 with continuous fluctuations over the years. Nevertheless, the share of oil production in the Mangistau region of the total output in Kazakhstan fell to 26.1% due to the significant increase of oil extraction in other oil producing regions. Since transition started, extraction of natural gas has declined in the Mangistau region. The share of the region in the national production of natural gas declined from 39.1% in 1990 to 9.8% in 2001.

Production in the chemical industry of the region rapidly decreased over the transition years and in 2001 reached 0.5% of the 1990 production level. The production was mainly based on mineral fertilizers for agriculture. However, due to the decline in demand from the former Soviet republics and also the decline of local agricultural production, which was due to a reduced level of technology, the chemical industry in Mangistau was in crisis.

Thus, production of all industries in the Mangistau region declined including those that grew in Kazakhstan as a whole (such as natural gas extraction). The part of the Mangistau region that specialised in heavy industry declined much faster than the backward agricultural part of the region due to the initial low level of production of the latter. The share of the region in the national GDP increased over the first decade of transition (Table 2.2.), partly because the national GDP declined overall in Kazakhstan.

The *Western Kazakhstan* region was included in the first and third groups of the regional division (Table 2.3.) as the region endowed with mineral resources, mainly oil and gas. Due to its agricultural specialisation, the region was assigned to the third group. The economy of Western Kazakhstan made relative progress by 2001 because of the deterioration of other regions. Thus, the share of the region in the national GDP increased from 4.3% in 1990 to 4.9% in 2001 (Table 2.2.). The GDP per head increased from 113.1% compared to the average Kazakhstani level in 1990 to 125.4% in 2001, even though it experienced a steep fall in the middle of the decade to 66%. From 1995 onward, industrial production in the region did extremely well, increasing its output by 81.9% by 2001. However, the production level of the region in 2001 was still 23.8% lower than that of 1990 level because output fell by 58.1% during the first five years of transition. Industrial production in Western Kazakhstan consists of the extraction of oil and gas, machine-building (mainly for agricultural production), and light and food industries. Western Kazakhstan has one of the largest gas deposits in the world, *Karachaganak,* which was discovered at the end of the first decade of transition and has a high potential for future development. In 1990, Western Kazakhstan produced 15.7% of Kazakhstani oil (including gas concentrate). However, in 1995, oil extraction in the region declined by 39.1%, and its share of national production fell to a level of 12%. This accounts for the fall of the regional GDP and the average salary in Western Kazakhstan in 1995 (Table 2.2.). Between 1995 and 2000, oil extraction in Western Kazakhstan increased by 87.9%, exceeding the 1990 production level by 14.4% as a result of the discovery of new fields at the end of the decade.

In 1990, Western Kazakhstan was the largest region in terms of the extraction of natural gas, whose share accounted for 57.1% of the national output. Its share of the national output declined to 32.8% in 2001 due to the rapid growth of gas extraction in the Atyrau region. One of the specialisations of the West-

ern Kazakhstan region was machine-building, mainly for the agricultural sector. Thus, in 1990, Western Kazakhstan produced 7.1% of Kazakhstani machinery for the livestock-farming sector, and this proportion grew to 10% in
1993. However, between 1990 and 1995, the production of machine-building
in the region declined by 55.2% and by 91.4% over the following five years.
As a result, in 2000 the level of production of machine-building in Western
Kazakhstan accounted for only 3.9% of the level of output in 1990.

Light and food industries of Western Kazakhstan were based on the production of goods made from leather and wool and meat products. These items
did not account for a significant share of their total production in Kazakhstan
and moreover the level of production of such goods in Western Kazakhstan
fell substantially during transition due to the decline in agricultural activity and
high levels of import from neighbouring Russia. Therefore the production of
light and food industries declined by 82% and 86% respectively during the
first decade of transition. The production of all specialised industries in Western Kazakhstan declined between 1991 and 2001 except for the extraction of
oil and gas, thereby creating a dependence on the hydrocarbon sector. However, on the positive side, in 2001, Western Kazakhstan attracted a 17.7%
share of Kazakhstani investment into fixed capital, which was mainly allocated to the fuel industry *(Kazakhstan: 1991-2002*, 2002).

The *Aktubinsk* region was included in the first group of the regional division
(Table 2.3.) as a region rich with mineral resources including oil and gas. Industrial production in the Aktubinsk region experienced a decline during the
first five years of the first decade of transition, as did many other regions and
indeed the whole country. However, the decline was less severe than that of
other regions (Figure 2.7.) except Atyrau. Industrial production fell by 28.6%
during this period compared to a 51.8% decline in the whole of Kazakhstani
industrial production. Although it grew by 21.6% over the next five years, industrial production of the Aktubinsk region could not reach the 1991 level by
2001. Industrial production in the Aktubinsk region consisted of the production
of hydrocarbon, mining, chemical industry, machine-building, food and light
industries based on local raw materials. The Aktubinsk region is the only region that had maintained its oil extraction volume at the same level during all

the years of transition, while the output of other regions fluctuated significantly. However, natural gas extraction in the region increased by 54.6% over
the same period, although its share of national production remained largely
unchanged.

The mining industry of the region declined over the first five years of transition, but later, the production of many ferrous metals significantly increased
due to their value on foreign markets. The production of construction materials, which is based on minerals, declined by 74.7% over ten years as a result
of a decline in construction all over the country. In 2001, the chemical industry
of the region exceeded the level of production in 1991 by 35% as it was
based on the mining industry, producing rare output not only for Kazakhstan
but for other countries as well, which were ready to invest in local production.

Light and food industries of the region declined in the Aktubinsk region as in
other regions of Kazakhstan. During the first ten years of transition their output fell by 93.2% and by 82.3% respectively. The light industry mainly produced textiles, which could not compete with the high inflow of imports. The
food industry specialised mainly in meat products. The level of production declined due to the attitude of neglect by private owners with respect to their
livestock at the beginning of transition and their personal interest in high and
quick profit. The industrial production of the Aktubinsk region had maintained
and increased the output of oil and gas and some chemical products, while
other industries experienced severe falls in production, making their region
dependent only on a small range of commodities which the region produced.

Prior to 1997, the *Karaganda* region was divided into two separate regions[48],
Karaganda and Zhezkazgan. The Zhezkazgan region is located in the central
and western parts of the new Karaganda region and specialised in agricultural production and the extraction of mineral resources. However, all coal extraction in the newly united region took place in the Karaganda region. As a
result of the regional policy (1996-1998), which sought the equalisation of regional development, the Zhezkazgan region was united with the Karaganda

---

48   In the book these two regions are analysed as one region – Karaganda.

region in order to balance the statistics of regional development, where Zhez-kazgan was designated a backward region, mainly specialising in agriculture. The analysis of the Karaganda region is based on the new division of regions after unification.

The Karaganda region is the largest region of Kazakhstan that is located in its central part; it covers 16% of the country's territory and produced 9.8% of its GDP in 2001. The Karaganda region is the region in Kazakhstan with the largest deposits of mineral resources and as a result it was assigned to the second group of the regional division (Table 2.3.). The agricultural part was assigned to the fourth group of backward regions, due to the crisis of its pro-duction. The industrial production of the region declined during the first dec-ade of transition by 25.3% (Figure 2.7.). However, during the second half of the decade output grew by 47.2%. In 1990, the Karaganda region was the second largest region of coal extraction in Kazakhstan after the Pavlodar re-gion and produced 37.1% of the national coal output. However, the extraction of many mineral resources including coal declined over the transition period, due to reduced demand from the former Soviet republics. Many cities of the Karaganda region were built around mines during their development, but many of those mines are now abandoned due to a cut in production. Whole cities of miners lost their livelihoods.

The extraction of a high variety of other minerals in the region including those required for construction materials experienced a dramatic fall at the begin-ning of transition due to severed links with former customers outside the country and the muddled privatisation programme. However, since the adop-tion of new management under private ownership and the establishment of new trade routes, production began to grow at a rapid pace even though in 2001 the production of many minerals was still below the 1990 level. In par-ticular, the production of construction materials in the Karaganda region had a high potential given its strategic location close to the newly constructed capi-tal of Kazakhstan. The construction work in Astana generated a high demand for the construction materials.

Even though machine-building in the region had the most favourable conditions for development as it was based on all the local inputs, production fell continuously until 1999. The reason for this was the decline in metal extraction in the first half of the first decade of transition. Other factors were the failure of privatisation and the more sophisticated structure of the production process in machine-building that demanded a longer time for recovery compared to the extraction or processing of other mineral resources. However, after 1999, production soared by a factor 20.4. Output in 2001, however, was still lower than the 1990 level, but a high percentage of the population was gainfully employed in the industry.

Regardless of the high attention to the agricultural part of the Karaganda region, which was designated a backward part and was given a priority for investment in development, its production continued to decline at a 32.1% rate during the second half of transition. After the affiliation of the Zhezkazgan region with the Karaganda region, local authorities had to govern a region twice the size of the region they governed before, and as a result, nothing was done for the improvement of agricultural production in the short term, as it took some time for the new authorities to understand and deal with the needs of the territory that had been added to the region. The production of light and food industries declined by 90% during the whole first decade of transition. Food industry was affected by the decline of agricultural production.

Karaganda, as a highly diversified industrial region, was severely affected in the first five years of transition. A high percentage of specialists lost their jobs. Despite the decline of industry as a result of privatisation, there was still significant level of industrial capacity in Karaganda. For example, at the end of privatisation, when fifteen mines and a steel factory were sold to the Indian Ispat company, the steel factory was the 25th largest steel factory (by capacity) in the world (Olcott, 2002). Compared to the pre-transition period, Karaganda had lost some of the diversification of its industrial production. Chemical, light and food industries lost much of their diverse production capacity. On the other hand, heavy industries became even more diverse with the opening of new gold and silver mines in 1997. Being highly dependent on heavy industries, the region entered a critical stage, where the female popula-

tion was left unemployed and the potential of agriculture was not being properly exploited.

The economy of the *Pavlodar* region is based on mineral resources and
heavy industry, which is dependent on local sources, and as a result, the
Pavlodar region was assigned to the second group of the regional division. Its
specialisation was heavy industry (Table 2.3.). Industrial production in the
Pavlodar region declined over the first ten years of transition, albeit with slight
growth (0.3%) in the second half of the decade. The total fall in output over
the first decade of transition amounted to 46.7% (Figure 2.7.).

The Pavlodar region is well known for its large coal reserves and comparatively cheap extraction costs. Prior to 1991, 110 Russian power stations and
the majority of Kazakhstani power stations were run on coal from Pavlodar
(Ermakov, 2001). Being the third largest in the former Soviet Union and the
largest coal producer in Kazakhstan, in 1990, the Pavlodar region produced
62.3% of Kazakhstani coal. Over the ten years of transition, coal production in
the Pavlodar region gradually declined and by 2001 output had fallen by 34%
compared to 1990. However, the region increased its share of Kazakhstani
coal extraction to 72.2% as total Kazakhstani coal extraction fell substantially,
mainly in the Karaganda region, where production costs were higher than in
Pavlodar.

The output of the metallurgical industry of the region declined during the first
five years of transition. However, after the mid-transition crisis the production
of many minerals grew steadily due to the renewal of trade links with
neighbouring Russian regions. At the same time, the extraction of minerals
for the construction materials industry dramatically fell over the years of transition and in 2001 reached 0.01% of the 1990 production level. The extraction
of minerals for the construction materials industry in the Pavlodar region was
very difficult due to the geology of raw material deposits and therefore involved higher production costs. For this reason it was not profitable to use the
output from Pavlodar in the transition period, while neighbouring Eastern Kazakhstan and the Karaganda regions were the main suppliers of these kinds
of mineral resources with lower costs of production.

One of the largest oil refineries in Kazakhstan is located in the Pavlodar region, however it processes oil from neighbouring Russian regions. In 1990,
the Pavlodar region produced 55.4% of the country's petrol, 54% of kerosene
and 26.5% of fuel oil. However, after the collapse of the Soviet Union industrial relations between the newly independent states became more complicated and caused a decline in the output of oil products, which was intensified
by the significant fall in the production of crude oil. The decline in production
was induced by a fall in world oil prices, which nearly resulted in the closure
of the factory. However, in 2000, the Pavlodar oil refinery significantly increased its output (by a factor of 26.3), as a result of the accelerating growth
of oil extraction in Russia.

The production of the chemical industry of the region, which was based on oil
refinery by-products, fell drastically, due to the decline in the output of the refinery, and as a result, in 2001 the production level of the chemical industry in
the Pavlodar region amounted to 0.3% of the 1990 production level. The
chemical industry, in turn, affected machine-building in the Pavlodar region,
which specialised in the production of equipment and machines for the
chemical industry. Thus, by 2001, the production of machine-building had
fallen to 3% of its 1990 production level. However, at the end of transition,
machine-building began to show signs of recovery; it grew by 30%, indicating
that growth in the chemical industry is to be expected.

The Pavlodar region became the largest producer of meat in the food industry
during transition, increasing its share of national production from 5.9% in
1990 to 44.7% in 2001. This was not due to high growth in the volume of production in Pavlodar, but rather due to the fall in the output of other regions. In
fact, production of the food industry in Pavlodar fell by 66.1% over the first
decade of transition, with fluctuations of growth from year to year.

During the Soviet period, the Pavlodar region was one of the industrially developed regions in Kazakhstan. However, in the course of the first decade of
transition, the production of many goods significantly declined, even though in
some cases it managed to increase its share of national production due to the

deeper decline of other regions. Nevertheless, at the end of the first decade of transition a trend towards growth could be observed in Pavlodar, as the production of many industries started to recover. The significant recovery of many industries in the region can be explained by the comparative advantage of the region due to the location on the border with Russia, which is the perfect market for the industrial output of Pavlodar. The first decade of transition was characterised by the establishment of industrial connections between the Pavlodar region and neighbouring regions of Russia, where the proximate location of Pavlodar to raw material sources, played an important role in cooperation to develop efficient production with minimum costs.

Northern Kazakhstan was assigned to the second and third groups of the regional division (Table 2.3.) due to its specialisation in heavy industry and agriculture. Northern Kazakhstan is one of several regions that could not recover its industrial production over the second half of the first decade of transition. In fact, Northern Kazakhstan had the lowest rates of decline in industrial production in the five and ten years of comparison (Figure 2.7.). Despite the attempts to achieve growth in industrial production in the region in 1998 and 2000 (Table 2.4.), the level of industrial production in Northern Kazakhstan in 2001 was 23.1% lower than in 1995 (Figure 2.7.), while the gross decline of industrial production in Northern Kazakhstan over the whole decade amounted to 73.3%. The whole economy of the region was disrupted. This can be seen from the significant fall in per capita GDP of the region, which fell from 97.4% of the average figure for Kazakhstan in 1990 (Table 2.2.) to 70.7% in 2001.

Northern Kazakhstan classification as specialising in heavy industry rested mainly on its machine-building and construction materials industries. Output in both industries fell by more than 90% during the first decade of transition. However, as many regions and industries actually managed to achieve an increase in their production in 2000, the construction materials and machine-building of Northern Kazakhstan also achieved significant growth in that year. Thus, the output of the machine-building industry increased by 65.4%, while the production of construction materials rose by 220% in one year. At the same time, the timber industry of the region also increased its production by

220% over the 1998-2001 period following a precipitous fall in production (i.e. by 99%) at the beginning of transition.

The level of output of the food industry, which was one of the main specialisations of the Northern Kazakhstan region before transition, fell gradually. However, unlike other regions the food production in Northern Kazakhstan did not show any signs of recovery even at the end of the decade. The comparative advantage of Northern Kazakhstan given in the location close to the Russian border. However, it did not play a positive role in the food production of Northern Kazakhstan, because its output was more expensive and of lower quality compared to the food products of neighbouring Russia.

Production in every sector of industry and agriculture of Northern Kazakhstan fell at a higher rate compared to other regions and to the average figures for the whole of Kazakhstan. This moved the region towards the group of backward regions, as it mostly lived on the illegal smuggling of Russian goods to Kazakhstan. However, since 2000, industrial production of Northern Kazakhstan has showed positive signs of slight growth (Table 2.4.) due to the increase of production in the construction materials and machine-building industries to satisfy local demand. However, the volume of growth was insignificant, taking into account the dramatic fall over the whole decade. Therefore, being located next to the Russian border is not always a comparative advantage. In the case of Northern Kazakhstan, it turned out be a disadvantage for the food industry.

In 1996, the *Akmola* region was defined as a region whose specialisation was agriculture. Agricultural production underwent intensive development at the beginning of the 1960s as a result of being in the centre of the *virgin lands* programme. The economy of the Akmola region is similar to that of the neighbouring Northern Kazakhstan region, where the economy declined over the first decade of the transition period. The per capita GDP of the Akmola region declined from 84.1% of the average level in Kazakhstan in 1990 to

61.6% in 2001. However, GDP per head in Astana[49] city (Table 2.2.) was 41.1% higher than the average for Kazakhstan in 2001 due to the transfer of the Kazakhstani capital in 1997 from Almaty to Astana, which boosted the economy of the city artificially. As a result, Astana city accounted for a larger share of national GDP in 2001, than the remainder of the region (6.6% and 3.3% respectively – see Table 2.2.).

Even though the Akmola region was not assigned to the group of regions whose specialisation was heavy industry, the region was one of the largest producers of some product lines of the machine-building, chemical and construction materials industries during the Soviet period. The industrial production of the Akmola region, which was based on the above-mentioned industries, fell by 50% during the first five years of transition (Figure 2.7.) and grew slightly (by 4.6%) over the next five years. At the same time industrial production in Astana city gradually grew since its designation as the capital, such that total growth between 1997 and 2001 amounted to 30.5%.

In 1990, the Akmola region was the largest producer of agricultural machinery in Kazakhstan prior to the collapse of the Soviet Union. It accounted for 55% of Kazakhstani production. By 1999, this production had declined by 85.7% as a result of low investment and insolvency of customers. However, since 2000, production has started to grow again, while the production of machine-building in Astana city has continuously fallen, due to the fact that other industries were given priority in order to promote the development of the new capital.

The chemical industry of the Akmola region serves mainly the agricultural sector. Because of a decline in agricultural production, which prior to transition exported a large proportion of its output to the former Soviet republics, the production of the chemical industry in Akmola also declined. The privatisation of many farms made owners financially responsible for the production, which resulted in low profits due to the lack of expertise of the new owners.

---

49   Astana city is located in the Akmola region and had different names in the past beginning with Akmolinsk, Tselinograd and the latest name of Akmola before it was changed to Astana in 1997, which in Kazak language means - the capital.

Consequently, they could not afford to use the necessary volume of chemicals, and as a result, the production of the chemical industry in the region fell by 98.3% during the first decade of transition.

The output of the construction materials industry in the region constantly declined during the first decade of transition. As a result of the crisis in the whole industry which operated below capacity production in Akmola fell by 82.9% between 1991 and 2001. However, the production of construction materials in Astana city soared since the city was designated as the capital, quadrupling between 1998 and 2001 as a result of the expansive construction work in the city. The geographical location of Astana city places it closer to the construction materials factories of the Karaganda region, than to the factories of its own region. This was the reason for the significant growth in the production of construction materials in Karaganda. However, the fall in the production of construction materials in the Akmola region is not only explained by its location, but also by the inefficient use of resources by local authorities, which employed foreign contractors for the construction of the capital city. Thus, the construction of the new capital supported the industrial development of other countries rather than its own.

Production in light industry fell in the Akmola region during transition as well as across the whole country. However, the output of light industry in Astana city increased by 49.6% between 1996 and 2000, mainly due to the production of furniture, which was in high demand given the high influx of population into the new capital and the availability of local raw materials for this industry.

The main specialisation of the Akmola region is agricultural production which, during the Soviet period, mainly exported its output to former Soviet republics. However, during the first years of transition, production declined by 56.9%, which was the result of lost trade connections and the insolvency of former Soviet republics. Despite this fact, Kazakhstan did not completely cut the wheat supply, but the volume of exports declined significantly. Nevertheless, production recovered after 1996 and had grown by 49.9% in 2001 due to newly established trade links not only with CIS countries but also with others. However, apart from bread products, the food industry of the Akmola region steadily declined over the transition years. Its output fell despite high local demand by the increased population in Astana city. Investment was mainly provided for the expansion of the city infrastructure, and not for the development of local industry.

Industrial production of the Akmola region was in a state of decline, despite the move of the capital city to the region. Even the industries of Astana city did not benefit from the new title, except for construction materials, while other industries continued to decline over the transition period. All investment was directed at developing the city, but very often the resources required for this development were brought from outside Kazakhstan due to their higher quality. The hypothesis that industrial enterprises perform better around the capital city can be rejected for Astana at the present moment, where industry is still in decline.

The *Almaty* region was assigned to the third group of the regional division in the middle of transition as the region specialised in agriculture. However, during the Soviet era, the region was important for the Kazakhstani economy due to its machine-building, ferrous metallurgy, light and food industries. The economy of the Almaty region and Almaty city (the country's capital[50] until 1997) developed unevenly and in different ways. Over the first ten years of transition, the region's share of national GDP declined from 7.8% to 4.9%, while the share of Almaty city increased from 6.6% to 17.2% over the same period (Table 2.2.). In 1990, the GDP per head of the Almaty region was 23.4% lower than the average Kazakhstani level. By 2001, per capita GDP had declined even further to 52.5% below the national average level. However, Almaty city was blooming at that time. Its per capita GDP rose from 112.7% of the average national level in 1990 to 200.9% in 2001. Thus, the share of national GDP of Almaty city was greater than that of any other city or region in Kazakhstan. The industrial production of Almaty city was also in a better situation over the second half of the first decade compared to the

---

50   Even though Astana city was officially announced as the capital city of Kazakhstan in 1997 with all government units' transfer, Almaty city stayed as the cultural and business centre of the country, which later had the unofficial title of Southern capital.

whole region (Figure 2.7.), when the Almaty region grew by 11%, and Almaty city by 86.6%.

In 1990, industrial production in the Almaty region was based mainly on the power industry. This accounted for about 50% of total industrial production in the region. The remainder was made up of light industry with its share of more than 20%, and food, machine-building, construction materials and ferrous metallurgy. At the same time, Almaty city had dominant food and machine-building industries. The machine-building industry was mainly located in Almaty city and specialised in the production of metallurgical and automation equipment. Its production declined by 38% over the first decade of transition due to the fall in production of other sectors of industry that used its output. Production in the metallurgical industry of the region, which was the main customer of the machine-building production, had declined by more than 85% with a slight increase at the end of the first transition decade. The decline in production was caused by the fall in demand of the former Soviet republics. This was in part due to high transportation costs, which had to be paid by private owners, who preferred to find sources closer to home.

In 1990, the Almaty region was the largest producer of reinforced concrete in Kazakhstan for the construction materials industry. It accounted for 21.9% of the national output, where 78.3% of production was coming from Almaty city. During the first five years of transition, production in the industry rapidly fell by 88.6% due to the turmoil of privatisation. However, between 1999 and 2001, production increased by 2.5 times in the region as well as in Almaty city due to the high concentration of financial activities in Almaty city, which increased the wealth of the population, and the substantial growth of private construction during the second half of the first transition decade.

In 1990, the Almaty region was one of the largest producers of the light industry in Kazakhstan. It accounted for 14.2% of the national output of light industry, with 86.8% coming from Almaty city. During the first ten years of transition, production of light industry in the Almaty region as well as in Almaty city fell by more than 90%. Almaty city was a trade centre of Kazakhstan (due to the higher level of wealth of the population), particularly for textile products from other countries, which were bought by the local self-employed population, and had a competitive advantage to local production. Thus, the light industry of the region as well as in the whole of Kazakhstan almost disappeared during the transition period due to the obsolescent technology, which was producing goods at lower quality and higher costs compared to those which were imported.

The situation with production in the food industry was slightly different to the light industry, as the Almaty region made better progress compared to the whole food industry of Kazakhstan. In 1990, the Almaty region was one of the largest producers in the food industry accounting for 15% of the national food production where 79% was coming from Almaty city. The production of the food industry in the region declined by 67% over the first half of the decade. However, during the next five years the Almaty region managed to increase its food production by only 3%, while Almaty city increased its production by a factor of 2.3. Almaty city is the perfect market for the food industry, because the population can afford to consume not only basic products but also a high assortment of other luxury food products. Being located in the middle of the financial centre, it is easier for food enterprises to find investment. However, there is also a higher risk of failure due to strong competition, while enterprises from outside the city have difficulties in entering the market.

Thus, industrial production in the Almaty region declined in the initial transition period with a rise at the end of the decade as many other regions. However, due to the steeper fall in the production of other regions, the region's share of national output of many products significantly increased at the end of the decade. Heavy industry declined during transition, due to the distant location from the market in the former Soviet Union, while construction materials and food industries substantially grew over the second half of the first transition decade. Given that Almaty city is the financial centre of Kazakhstan, one would assume that regional development has to benefit from its proximity. However, the opposite is the case. The high level of competitiveness of trade in the city reduced the opportunity for local industrial enterprises to sell their products. Therefore, the hypothesis that the location of industrial enterprises in the proximity of Almaty city is beneficial must be rejected.

Regional development policy

After the collapse of the Soviet Union, disparities in development between the Kazakhstani regions started to widen significantly (see *Regional development under transition* in this chapter), due to the failure of many industrial enterprises. During the Soviet era, industries of Kazakhstan were developed according to the central plan of the Soviet economy, while the issue of even regional development in Kazakhstan did not exist, due to the priority given by Soviet economic planners to efficient use of Kazakhstani comparative advantage for the growing requirements of the Soviet Union as a whole. During the first decade of transition, some of the industries of Kazakhstan, which are based on mineral resources, very quickly recovered after their initial failure and significantly benefited from transitional changes, increasing the regional share in total GDP (Figure 2.6.). However, the regional development in Kazakhstan was uneven, with growing disparities. For the first time the Kazakhstani government issued a set of reforms for balanced regional development for the years 1996-1998. The aim of the *regional policy* was the development of the Kazakhstani economy on the basis of the effective development and usage of regional resources (Academy of Science, Institute of Economics, 1998). The aims of regional policy were focused on:

- Equalizing the differences in regional development, by increasing standards of living and industrial production in poorer regions;
- Development of economic specialisations of the regions in accordance with the needs of the economy of the country;
- Reducing the disproportions in the regional economic structure;
- Development of rural areas;
- Creation of independent legal, political and economic regional authorities;
- Development of Kazakhstani markets of labour, goods and capital on the basis of regional markets.

Implementation of regional policy was based on the wide development of industrial clusters according to the initial conditions of individual regions and to the needs of the market economy. The implication was that financial support from the government should be balanced between priority-regions[51] and regions with a lower level of development than the average Kazakhstani level. Regional finance authorities were established in order to accumulate financial resources from different sources for the self-financing of economic development.

For the implementation of regional policy, regions were divided into four groups according to their level of development. Some regions were included in two different groups according to their industrial specialisations (section 2.2 The collapse of the Soviet economic system and its impact on the regional development of the Kazakhstani economy, Table 2.3. Division of regions by four groups, 1996).

1.   For the *first group* regions the policy set was focused on:
   • Intensive development of strategic mineral resource fields, mainly oil and gas, using new technologies;
   • Development of an infrastructure for the market economy that would create viable conditions for external market relations and the attraction of foreign investors;
   • Support of the industries – responsible for the creation of a new generation of equipment for oil and gas extraction under extremely difficult conditions.

2.   The main directions of further development for the *second group* of regions were:
   • Development of new generation machine-building on the basis of electronic and laser technology;
   • Development of a production and market infrastructure on the basis of regional allocation benefits.

3.   The regional policy for the *third group* of regions was focused on:
   • Division of regional specialisations in the agricultural sector according to the technological basis of the regions;

---

51   Priority- regions include regions with strategic production for the country for self-sufficiency including goods for world market export.

- Implementation of new generation technology based on biotechnology and on genetics engineering;
- Creation of small and medium enterprises for the manufacture of agricultural goods, in order to reduce the level of unemployment in rural areas and to increase the efficiency of production in distant rural areas.

4. The regional policy envisaged special reforms for the *fourth group* of regions:
   - Prevention of an ecological crisis;
   - Fundamental reconstruction of the economy infrastructure on the basis of local resources;
   - Elevation of living standards in backward regions on the basis of financial support from the government.

Regional policy for the *first group* of regions demanded government support for the creation of a regional infrastructure, in terms of transport links, a market and financial system and in terms of a tax and credit system in order to attract investment. The policy for the *second group* envisaged the creation of a new financial network in terms of the tax system in order to create favourable conditions for the speeding up of scientific technological progress. Reforms for the *third group* had to be implemented under government management and involved the attraction of investment for the modernisation of technology and the creation of the legal and financial infrastructure to support the creation of small and medium enterprises. Regional policy in the *fourth group* of backward regions was completely under the control of the government because of the absence of any legal, financial or technological basis in those regions, which would be required for the recovery of the whole economy.

Despite the elaborated government policy for regional development and the reduction of disparities in regional economies, the situation had not changed during the period proposed for the implementation of regional reform, 1996-1998. Mineral rich regions continued to grow against the background of general decline (Table 2.4.). The failure of the implementation of regional policy was due to the lack of funds for inter-regional development. A number of projects were proposed during that period by the World Bank, the European Bank for Reconstruction and Development (EBRD) and the Asian Development Bank[52]. However, many of them were focused on financial sector adjustments, while a few projects on regional development were mainly based in the Almaty and Akmola regions, designed to take at least ten years to be completed. Both the Asian Development Bank and the EBRD have projects designed to support the rehabilitation of the Almaty - Bishkek road, which is expected to promote regional cooperation in Central Asia. Current projects of international banks are based on the rehabilitation of existing transport links which connect Kazakhstan with other countries, while the development and reconstruction of internal links is supported only in regions rich with mineral resources or the regions containing the two capitals.

Since transition started, the Kazakhstani government has become aware of the necessity of balanced regional development, which requires the development of inter-regional links. However, the implementation of regional policy did not bring results due to the lack of sufficient financial funds. Consequently, geographically isolated regions from economic centres (such as Almaty and hydrocarbon rich regions) and regions which did not have strategic mineral resources, faced an economic decline following the growing gap with the economies of other regions, due to the absence of inter-regional connections and the severed connections with former Soviet republics. Regional policy stayed at the level of rhetoric, while the main aim of balanced regional development was to connect regions from the start. The investment policy is closely linked with the regional policy (being one of its main elements), but it can not be universal for all Kazakhstani regions. According to the perception of the government, backward regions are supposed to have priority for governmental financial support, while regions with developed industries are supposed to develop and extract financial resources from their production (Kenzheguzin and Isaeva, 1998). In reality, we could identify three major dimensions of the policy.

---

52   Project summary documents for the World Bank, the European Bank for Reconstruction and Development, and the Asian Development Bank.

The first dimension is connected with the period of the initial implementation of regional policy (1996-1998). It was characterised by the third phase of privatisation through individual projects where mainly firms with the specialisation of mineral resources were privatised (Kalyuzhnova, 1998). However, the income from privatisation did not reach the regions, but stayed at the level of personal interests of managers.

The second dimension is connected with the move of the capital in 1997, which was transferred to a city in the northern part of Kazakhstan. This fact became a part of the implementation of regional policy by proxy. Because the government did not have financial resources for the capital transfer, the Stolitsa (capital) Fund was created for purposes of the capital city development. Foreign companies with a business interest in Kazakhstan had to invest into the Stolitsa Fund on the "voluntary" basis, otherwise they did not have too much chance to conduct business in Kazakhstan.

The third dimension is related to the obligation of foreign companies to invest in the local regional development. One of the peculiarities of that period was a desire of the government to finance the regional policy via foreign investors. The latest "innovation" which was finally articulated in 2001 is the concept of "Local Content", where foreign investors, as a part of a contract, have to invest into the development of the local region, including the employment of local labour, the usage of local goods and investment in the improvement of social spheres.

During that period the mismanagement of the second phase of privatisation led to the decline in the industrial production of Kazakhstan. Therefore, the government lacked financial resources to invest in regional development. However, oil and gas industries attracted most of the interest of foreign investors. Therefore, the development of oil and gas industries became a priority for Kazakhstan. The high interest in oil and gas industries of Kazakhstan enabled the government to achieve one of the goals of the regional policy, by forcing foreign companies to invest in the social development of the backward part of the region of their operation. This fact became the specific feature of Kazakhstani regional policy.

In 1997 a 40-year production sharing agreement (PSA) covering development development and exploitation of the Karachaganak gas field was signed between the Republic of Kazakhstan and BG International (32.5%), Agip (32.5%), Texaco (20%) and LUK oil (15%). This alliance formed the Karachaganak Integrated Organisation (KIO). The positive impact being made by KIO in the Western Kazakhstan. According to PSA, KIO has a contractual obligation to invest into social projects of the Western Kazakhstan. Prime objectives of social projects included the development of health system, education and improvement of the quality of life of local population. The budge of investments into social projects of the KIO amounted 9 million dollars per annum, which were spent on the construction of numerous hospitals, schools, theatres, roads and others. Some of examples in the Western Kazakhstan could be hospital in Kazytalovka with the budget of 6.5 million dollars, indoor skating rink with the budget of 6.2 million dollars, Kazakh Drama Theatre with the budget of 10.55 million dollars. Therefore, regions with backward territories and rich with mineral resources, mainly oil and gas, benefited from the regional policy. However, regions which were not industrially developed or rich with mineral resources, remained on low economic development. As a result the regional policy, which was directed to the growth of regions and the reduction in the level of disparities of regional development, increased the disparities even more. Oil and gas rich regions significantly advanced in their development while economies of backward regions with no mineral resources deteriorated even more as a result of the absence of the financial support of the government.

Although, the main purpose of regional policy was to raise the development level of backward regions, investment for this purpose significantly fell during transition. Backward regions and regions specialising in industries that were different from mineral resources, could not attract investment due to the underdeveloped infrastructure, while available resources inside those regions were not directed at industrial development but went to profitable financial markets inside or outside the country (Academy of Science, Institute of Economics, 1998). Regions rich with mineral resources attract the main portion of Kazakhstani investments, in 2001 74.4% of all investment in Kazakhstan went to the extraction of oil and gas, whereas in 1990 this figure amounted to only 9.3%. Therefore, the priority accorded by the government of Kazakhstan to the mineral resource industries, which yielded the highest profit, negatively affected the development of other industries by the reduction of investments and consequently the policy to bring about even regional development failed.

The effect of the transfer of the capital

In 1997, the capital of Kazakhstan was moved from Almaty (southeast of Kazakhstan) to the northern part of Kazakhstan – Astana (Akmola region). The political reason given was the fear of Russia, which could make claims on territories of northern and eastern parts of Kazakhstan, which were granted[53] to Kazakhstan by the Russian Federation in 1921 *(Sovetskii Soiuz – Kazakhstan,* 1970). However, the location of the capital in these territories would increase the population of ethnic Kazakhs in the northern regions and decrease the possibility of a conflict about their return. The economic reason was the President's strategy, which diverts the attention of the population and foreign observers from internal economic problems[54]. In addition, there was a geological excuse for the transfer of the capital, as ex-capital Almaty is located in a zone of high seismic activity. From previous experience, it was known that there existed the potential for a major earthquake which could destroy the entire city. In 1887, an earthquake destroyed the whole city of Almaty, and in 1911, another less strong earthquake again destroyed the main part of the city. As a result, movement of the capital became a part of a regional development by proxy, whereby extra funds were allocated to the development of the new capital, which in the long run would involve the development of other northern regions. The construction of the new capital consumed a significant amount of investment that was diverted from other regions of Kazakhstan. Thus, investments into the fixed capital of the Akmola region increased by a

---

53   The transfer of southern regions of Russia to the Kazakh SSR in 1921 was directed by V.I. Lenin in order to make the industrial development of Soviet republics relatively equal. Regions which were attached to the Kazakh SSR, were intensively industrially developed in the mining sector. Consequently, the general level of industrial development of the Kazakh SSR significantly increased.

54   Interview with Dr. Y. Kalyuzhnova.

factor of 4.6 times in 1997, while its share of national investment soared from 3.5% to 15.9%. Investment in Astana city accounted for only 15% of total Kazakhstani investment in 1998 and 1999. Later this share declined to 10%, but investment continued to grow in real terms.

Despite the growth in investment in the development of the new capital, the industrial production of the region did not benefit from this. Growth of industrial production of the Akmola region was only 4.6% higher in 2001 compared to 1995, while in Astana city industrial production increased by 30.5% between 1997 and 2001 (Figure 2.7.). The growth of industrial production in Astana city was entirely due to the growth in demand of the construction materials industry, while other industries declined significantly. (Section 2.3 *Changes in regional concentration of industrial activities*). Nevertheless, production in the construction materials industry in the whole of the Akmola region, and in neighbouring regions, which are rich with mineral resources, declined, because of lower demand for their production in the construction of the new capital. The government invested large amounts for fast and quality construction, employing mainly foreign contractors, who preferred to use input from their own countries. These were of better quality and through this they maintained the industrial production of their own countries, while local production significantly fell in this environment of low demand for local output. However, in the long run, the transfer of the capital to the more central part of Kazakhstan will increase the level of access of other regions to the capital, and therefore will be the centre of finance and information. Information and new technologies are expected to travel with higher speed in the country, than they did with the capital located at the edge of the country. However, these changes could be expected to materialise only in the long run after the development of infrastructure has connected the new capital to other regions.

The development of the market on the basis of existing connections
During the first decade of transition, the development of the Kazakhstani market was based on the location factor such that Almaty city became the centre. The mechanism of the planned economy was inherited by Kazakhstan from the Soviet economic system and was based on plans for the quantity of production and fixed prices created by the central authority of the Soviet Un-

ion. Sensitive tools of the market, such as relations between supply and demand, were not taken into account in central planning. Consequently, economic adjustments took place on the basis of soft budget constraints. After the breakdown of the Soviet system in 1991, the economy of Kazakhstan entered the transition process towards a market economy, where the core drivers of the economy became supply and demand. In order to operate under the new economic conditions, new markets were created, such as financial and legal services, which did not exist during the Soviet era. Prior to transition, the state owned virtually all property. However, since transition started, the privatisation process has created new forms of property ownership of all kinds of economic objects, which immensely increased the demand for property rights and legal services. As a result, proportion of GDP by the service sector increased from 34.8% in 1991 to 50.9% in 2002.

Industrial production became dependent on agreements made between heads or owners of enterprises. Face-to-face negotiations started to play an important role in bringing about the most efficient deals, which illustrated the emergence of market coordination in transition in terms of horizontal linkages (Kornai, 1992 and 1998) between enterprises. Almaty city became the most advantageous location for businesses, due to the high level of qualified labour and negotiation skills. A high percentage of former government employees and academic staff applied their skills to business activities during the transition period, where not only negotiation skills became important in face-to-face dealing, but also the availability of connections with top authorities. Their move to private business was due to the low level of earnings in state organisations; the salary level of academics is 2.5 times lower than the average earning level of Kazakhstan (Koshanov, 2000). In Almaty city, as it was the capital, there was a concentration of government employees and academics with important key skills for conducting business in the newly emerging market. In addition, all main foreign financial companies are located in Almaty. In order to employ local labour, foreign companies organise training courses outside Kazakhstan (Arthur Andersen, 2000), which increases even more the skills level of local labour.

The availability of the right connections became the key priority for success of industrial activity, where connections resulted from the experience of being close to power. If business has the right connections, it may get bank credits in 1-2 months, while for businesses without the right connections, it could take a minimum of 4-6 months (Dauranov, Shishkina, Rudeckix, Shiyanova, Ivanova, 2000). Using entrepreneurial skills, nowadays, the young generation is actively involved in business. However, in the majority of cases the success of their businesses is based on inherited connections from their parents who are top leaders, ties to President Nazarbayev's family or because young businessmen "sufficiently ingratiated themselves" (Olcott, 2002) in the President's family circle. One such example is Bulat Abilov, who became the president of Butya, a large trading company, in his twenties. Therefore, the concentration of business activities in Almaty city is not only explained by the location of the capital, but by the access to important connections. The high concentration of government officials in the central location of Kazakhstan increases the speed of business progress due to the relatively high base in negotiation skills.

Since the transfer of the capital, a concentration of business gradually emerged in Astana following the cautious arrival of businesses and staff with high entrepreneurial skills and connections at government level. However, the level of skilled labour in former capital Almaty does not fall with an increase in migration to Astana. The best quality universities of Kazakhstan are located in the former capital, where main percent of graduates stay in Almaty, where growing business is based on the long way experience of the capital. Therefore, the accelerating success of the business in the former capital increases the level of the skilled labour even more and continues to attract labour from other regions, despite the transfer of the capital. Thus, successful production activity or business is based not only on a location close to sources of raw materials source, such as for example the regions in western Kazakhstan regions, which are based on the production of oil and gas and attract 50% of all Kazakhstani investments (*Kazakhstan: 1991-2002*, 2002). It could also be based on the source of highly qualified labour with entrepreneurial skills, which may not necessarily have been originally acquired in order to conduct business, as in the example of government members.

2.4 Conclusion

This chapter has analysed the changes in industrial activities of Kazakhstan during the first decade of transition. The concentration of industrial activities in Kazakhstan has shown a trend towards centralisation in fewer regions. In general, the production level of all industries except for non-ferrous metallurgy and fuel significantly declined during the first decade of transition due to the loss of trade links with former Soviet Union republics, the unsuccessful privatisation process[55] and the lack of knowledge on which to base action in the system moving towards the market economy. The trial and error behaviour of industrial enterprises was explained by the uncertainty and unpredictability of the market, where many industrial enterprises were forced to cease production after a period of serious decline. Over time, as knowledge and information on the market economy became more accessible, industries started to grow. Regions rich with mineral resources started to concentrate on mineral extraction, abandoning other industries in the region, such as light, chemical, food and machine-building industries. Mineral extraction produced higher profits for the regions, as raw materials could be exported to outside markets, while other industries, such as food and light industry, faced high levels of competition in local markets with imported goods. Many enterprises, particularly of the chemical and machine-building industries, cut production due to being located in the wrong place for internal cooperation. The distant location from the output and input markets became highly disadvantageous, as transportation costs played an important role in the policy to minimise the cost of production, as enterprises became financially responsible for their output. Thus, many regions lost their industrial specialisation, while others lost the diversification of industries as they concentrated on mineral extraction. As a result, the economy of Kazakhstan started to rely more and more

---

55 Unsuccessful privatisation process here means the negative effect of the privatisation on the efficiency of privatised enterprises and as a result the negative effect on the whole economy of Kazakhstan. The rent-seeking behaviour of managers thwarted the main objective of the privatisation, which is to increase the economic efficiency of enterprises. The performance of the private sector and the improvement of bureaucratic procedures in the country are indicators of the successful completion of privatisation (Kalyuzhnova, 2003).

on mineral extraction, becoming increasingly dependent on world commodity prices and external demand.

The regional policy for even regional development did not yield the expected results, due to the lack of funds for the development of backward regions, which faced a significant fall of their industrial production and became geographically isolated from the Kazakhstani market. However, the move of the capital to a more central location turned out to be a policy for regional development by proxy for the long term. Easier access to the capital will allow information and new technology to circulate faster and as a result the growth of regional development has a better chance. At the present time, the concentration of production and business activities is observed mainly in the western Kazakhstan regions due to the oil and gas deposits and in the ex-capital Almaty, which is well endowed with highly qualified human capital with negotiation skills (mainly people with experience in government). Thus, the skills acquired in government posts are turned into entrepreneurial skills for business and industry, where good government connections are a fundamental condition for their success. Therefore, the endowment of regions with qualified human capital whose origins are in government increases the likelihood of regions being able to create thriving businesses and industrial enterprises. The prime example of this phenomenon is the new capital, where a high inflow of government workers has brought negotiation skills and easy access to the necessary connections for business success to create a concentration of new and successful business networks. Due to the high concentration of highly qualified human capital with entrepreneurial skills, Almaty is called the financial and business capital, while Astana is called the official capital. Such a division can be expected to remain in place in the long run due to the *hysteresis* phenomenon, whereby regional activities depend on the previous behaviour of labour markets and capital investment. Therefore, a long term is required for regions to adjust to drastic economic changes, such as the move of the capital city to another location.

The main result of the above analysis is the negative effect of the collapse of the Soviet Union on the industrial development of Kazakhstan, whose infrastructure was designed for cooperation with former Soviet republics, while internal connections were not developed. The sovereignty gained made Kazakhstan realise that its economy was not set up to function efficiently and independently of the remainder of the Soviet Union. However, all attempts to reorganise the regional economy, including the unification of some backward regions with more successful ones, did not yield positive results. The creation of incentives for the increase in industrial production through privatisation disrupted the whole economy of Kazakhstan, while the lack of knowledge of how a market economy behaves depressed production further. At the beginning of transition the disparity between mineral rich and other regions increased. This trend may continue until inter-regional collaboration is developed much further.

The next chapter presents models of the regional economies and explains how appropriate these models are for understanding the economic geography of the transition process.

3　Regional Economy in Transition

3.1　Introduction

Previous chapters discussed the impact of location on the industrial development of Kazakhstan during the Soviet era and its consequences during the transition period. The first chapter analysed the evolution location behaviour of industry in the Kazakh SSR after it was joined with the Soviet Union. The second chapter discussed the effects and consequences of the collapse of the Soviet system on the industrial development of Kazakhstani regions during transition.

By choosing transition towards the market economy, rather than maintaining the socialist system, the ex-soviet countries entered into a process of economic transformation under conditions of uncertainty and the lack of information. The transition process of the ex-Soviet countries is unique and there is no matching experience in the world due to the different initial conditions of different economies.

One of the aspects of the transition process which has been largely ignored in the literature is the extent to which the process of economic adjustment has varied across regions within the individual transition countries. Under the previous regime of state economic planning, the location of many of the activities in these countries was determined explicitly by a process of decision-making. The differing industrial structures of each of the regions of these economies was therefore partly a result of a state planning apparatus, as well as a result of different natural resource endowments. Since the transition process began, the outcomes of these planned schemes have often been found to be inefficient in terms of the requirements of a market-based economy. The result of this is that an individual region's transitional restructuring, depends in part on the initial set of natural and industrial endowments inherited by the region at the beginning of the 1990s, and also on the extent to which the region's industries were optimally located. Given that many of the transition countries are very large, whether we define their size in terms of their population, their land area, or their natural resource base, we ought to observe major differences in the transition process between the individual regions of many of these transition countries.

This chapter presents models of inter-regional factor allocation and growth and attempts to understand how they can be appropriately used for the explanation of location behaviour in transition economies, particularly in ex-Soviet countries.

The chapter begins with the analysis of location planning in the Soviet system in order to understand the inherited system of regional development in Kazakhstan. The economic planning of the regional development in the Soviet Union was based on two key approaches: location production analysis of central planning and input-output analysis of inter-industrial linkages. The allocation of industries in the Soviet Union can be explained by the Weber Location-Production Model, which assumes that input factors are constant for the production of the output and that a firm is the price taker on the output market. The location behaviour of industries in the Soviet Union was governed by central authorities, which used the linear programming in order to find the optimum location. The process of industrial production in the Soviet Union was ruled by input-output analysis. The input-output analysis was based on estimated projections of technological coefficients in order to maintain the production process by delivery of inputs between enterprises.

The regional development combined all republics of the Soviet Union under central planning. Key approaches to regional development were based on central management, while sensitive tools of the market, such as price responsiveness, did not play a role in the production process. Another disadvantage of central planning in the regional development was the ignorance of central authorities in the local inter-regional development of the Kazakh SSR, where industries functioned only as part of the integrated system of the Soviet Union and not for the local population. The main objective for central authorities was to develop the economic activities in order to make the Soviet economy to work as a consistent mechanism integrated across all the republics. Therefore, republics had their regions developed only to promote industries with a comparative advantage in the Soviet economy, in other cases central authorities did not allocate the necessary funds for the inter-regional development.

The chapter continues with an introduction and analysis of neoclassical models of regional growth where the one-sector and two-sector models of regional factor allocation and migration are discussed. The analysis of these models gives an understanding of the possible endpoint of transition economies, where high speed of travel of information and high free mobility of factors, such as capital and labour, play a significant role in determining the outcome. The examination of conditions of neoclassical models of regional growth and evaluation of conditions of the Kazakhstani economy gives an analysis of possible ways of adjustments to the neoclassical approach.

Then the chapter continues with models, which could explain the Kazakhstani economy in the process of transition. The disequilibrium model of inter-regional labour migration, the model of human capital migration and endogenous growth theory are based on the inter-regional migration of labour and on the high level of the human capital, which induces labour to migrate. These models where chosen in order to understand the Kazakhstani economy for the reason of the limited mobility of factors in the transition economy, where labour is the only factor which have higher degree of the mobility. Models explain the mechanism of inter-regional migration of labour and the migration intensification with the growth of the level of the human capital. The high level of response of labour to signals of economic instruments, such as changes in wage, in a transition economy can lead to the development of an unbalanced economy, where more successful regions attract labour with high level of human capital, which leads to the further acceleration of development and growth of disparities between regions.

Following the analysis of labour and human capital migration models and the endogenous growth theory the chapter continues with the investigation of reasons which account for the development of the unbalanced economy in transition. Two main concepts of economic development are underlined in this chapter and they are conditions of uncertainty and lack of information. These concepts are believed to hold transition economies at the level where enterprises develop in the chaotic way without the knowledge of macro changes and without the knowledge of the right way of development for achieving the endpoint of the transition, which is the new unknown type of the economy. However, there are certain incentives, which induce labour and enterprises to migrate to particular locations and to organise industrial or business centres. These incentives are an information centre, local non-traded inputs and a local skilled labour pool. The chapter gives an analysis of agglomeration incentives on the basis of Kazakhstan, where these incentives lead to three definite centres of the migration of labour and enterprises. Further sections investigate different types of such agglomeration centres and analyse the Kazakhstani economy and its three agglomeration centres on the basis of their classification, where agglomeration economies are divided into three types: internal returns to scale, localisation economies and urbanisation economies. The analysis is undertaken in order to understand the nature of the creation of agglomeration centres in Kazakhstan and to investigate possible ways of further regional development towards neoclassical models of the regional growth.

Subsequent sections provide evidence of a process of changes in Kazakhstan, which lead the economy towards urbanisation. The evidence is provided on the basis of *Hirschmann-Herfindahl* and *Location Quotient* indices, which measure the level of industrial concentration and regional specialisation. Other evidence is provided by the difference in wages in regional economies of Kazakhstan, which could be described by the disequilibrium model of interregional labour migration. Differences in wages of Kazakhstani regions lead to the creation of definite centres referring to the centre-peripheral development of the economy where inequalities between centres and peripheries are growing very fast.

In order to understand the state of the transition in Kazakhstan and possible transformation of the economy, this chapter analyses the initial conditions of the Kazakhstani economy, which were inherited from the Soviet system. The analysis of neoclassical models of regional growth indicates the possible endpoint of the transition process in Kazakhstan. The investigation of sources and types of agglomeration process establish links between western econo-mies and Kazakhstani economy, underlining limitations of the intensive de-velopment in Kazakhstan in terms of conditions of uncertainty and lack of in-formation. Analysis of classical models of the regional development and con-ditions of the transition economy prepared the background for the empirical test of Kazakhstani economy on the basis of the micro-econometric ap-proach.

In summary, this chapter begins with the analysis of the initial conditions of the regional development in Kazakhstan on the basis of the Soviet system. It then presents models of regional development, which could describe the endpoint of transition economy and explain its current state. Furthermore, the chapter highlights limitations of development of the regional economies in Kazakhstan as a result of conditions of uncertainty and lack of information and analyses sources and types of agglomeration, which result in an unbal-anced economy in Kazakhstan. Finally, the chapter provides evidence of the unbalanced development of Kazakhstan in terms of industrial concentration and regional specialisation and attempts to explain the Kazakhstani economy by the disequilibrium model of inter-regional labour migration. The conclusion analyses findings of the chapter in terms of understanding the regional econ-omy of Kazakhstan and its future outcome.

3.2 Location planning during the Soviet Union period

During the Soviet era the economy of the Kazakh SSR was under the same conditions of the centrally planned mechanism as the remainder of the Soviet Union. The establishment of Soviet economic sectors in geographical terms began in 1920 (Saushkin, 1962). The government of the newly established Soviet Union determined that small industrial clusters that were distributed among many regions and vertically integrated would not work effectively for a country the size of the Soviet Union. Since various modes of horizontal inte-gration were developed in the economy of the country. The Soviet Union was administratively divided into 15 economic regions where each had its own specialisation. These economic regions were designated as republics, which after the collapse of the Soviet Union in 1991 became independent countries.

The creation of Soviet economic regions[56] was based on the endowment of the republics with input resources. According to the geographic division of labour, the Kazakh SSR was designated as an economic region that specialised in energy and metallurgy. However, as the vertical integration between industrial enterprises of economic regions was established after the creation of the Soviet Union, many industrial enterprises of a particular economic region extracted raw materials or produced intermediate goods for further manufacture in other economic regions. For example, the metallurgical enterprises in the Kazakh SSR extracted raw materials for the production of the machine-building industry in the Russian Federation or the Ukrainian SSR, and then transported some of these finished goods back to the Kazakh SSR for local consumption. Such divisions of labour and resources were present in all other industries of the Soviet Union and constituted an efficient use of the republics' comparative advantages for needs of the Soviet economy. The location of industries in the Soviet Union was not based on competitive prices of finished goods, as there was no competition for lower prices, which were always set by central government.

The formation of economic sectors in the Soviet Union was designed in a rational way for the optimal operation of the Soviet economy. Industries were established in economic regions, which were endowed with input factors for the particular production or in locations that were relatively close to producers of intermediate goods. The regional economic planning system of the Soviet Union was based on two key approaches: location production analysis of central planning and input-output analysis of inter-industrial linkages.

The *first principle* of the regional economic planning system is the Weber Location-Production Model (Friedrich, 1929), which was introduced by Alfred Weber in 1909 and explains the rational and optimum behaviour of the indus-

---

56   The term "Soviet economic regions" means here republics of the Soviet Union

trial location in the centrally planned economy. The main core of this model is the *Weber optimum location* concept, which implies that the location of a firm's costs minimisation is the location where the firm can minimise its input factors and transportation costs. The Weber optimum location concept can be represented by the following equation:

$$TC = m \, i \, n \sum_{i=1}^{n} m_i t_i d_i$$

where,

$i = 1,...., k$ -   inputs used,

$i = k+1,....., n$ - outputs produced;

m_i –   is the weight (tonnes) of inputs and outputs

t_i – transportation costs of the item i per ton-kilometre from the input (output) source location to the firm – producer location;

d_i – is the distance measure from input (output) sources to the firm – producer location.

The Weber Location-Production model assumes that coefficients of input factors are constant for the production of the output, and that the firm is the price taker on the output market. The space is assumed to be homogenous, implying that the price and quality of labour, capital and land are equal everywhere. The model provides a convincing analysis of the behaviour of the Soviet economy. The conditions assumed by Weber coincide with those of the Soviet economy. State owned firms were always price takers, as all prices were controlled and coordinated by the government authorities. The effects of the varying economic conditions across this large and diverse country were suppressed by the use of government subsidies in order to keep the level of output prices equal overall.

The location behaviour of industries under central planning was indifferent to profit maximisation, but was based on the minimisation of the costs of production, as it states in the Weber Location-Production model, so that industries were located as close to input sources as possible. The Weber Location – Production model approach was widely applied in the Soviet economy, where multiple inputs and outputs were evaluated in the cost minimisation equation to determine the optimal location of new industrial enterprises using linear programming. All the decisions of the optimal location of industries were made mainly on the basis of their distance to Russia, which was the centre for further distribution. Such links were further consolidated during the Second World War, when eastern parts of the Soviet Union were occupied and required more support than any other republics. Thus, hydrocarbon rich western regions of the Kazakh SSR were the base for the Soviet oil and gas extraction during the war. However, in the eastern part of the Kazakh SSR, in Pavlodar, another large oil refinery was built which was not designed for crude oil from fields in the Kazakh SSR, but for the processing of oil from neighbouring Russian fields. The output of the Pavlodar refinery was further transported to other economic regions of the Soviet Union[57]. The rational and optimal location of industries was designed to enable the efficient functioning of the economy of the whole country, but not the functioning of republics as separated economic entities. Soviet ministries ignored the needs of the Kazakh SSR. Investing in the industrial enterprises of the Kazakh SSR, which were priorities for the Soviet economy, central authorities did not take into account the needs of the local population (Kunaev, 1992). However, the rational location of industries would not be enough for the efficient functioning of the whole system.

The Soviet economy was governed by central planning, which is different from the market economy. In the latter supply and demand are key tools of the system with a strong responsiveness of enterprises to market prices. However, in the central planning system (Lavigne, 1999) political authorities are decision-makers, and the planning system was designed to develop a strategy to achieve the most efficient output of the national economy for the future. Generally, plans were worked out for a period of 5 years and were called *pyatiletka*. The plans set economic targets for the planned period. These targets included aggregate indicators of the volume of total industrial production, the balance between production and consumption, wages, investment quotas, technical development, international relations and the balance of state budget of its receipts and expenditures (Kornai, 1992). So-

---

57   Chapter 2 *The effect of transition on regional development.*

viet plans were designed for all economic sectors; however, the system was not perfect due to the lack of necessary information, inadequate techniques for data processing and the complexity of the plans (Ellman, 1978). All the information was in the hands of the producers, which was very difficult to collect due to the size of the territory and lack of incentives of producers at the periphery to submit the complete information.

At the same time, central planners did not have any information regarding the preferences of consumers due to the inability to measure the responsiveness of consumers. As a result, the shops in the Soviet Union were full of products, which were not desirable to consumers, while there was a shortage of products, which were highly demanded by consumers. Because of this, the central planning of the vast regionally distributed economy made it difficult to integrate the preferences of consumers and the capacity of producers. Difficulties in obtaining such information did not make it possible to distribute some goods in regions where these goods would be most needed. The Marxist-Leninist theory of central planning (M. Ellman, 1978) was assumed to operate in the deterministic world of the information and economic processes. However, the socialist system was full of stochastic processes, which are difficult to predict. Such plans were not fulfilled in many cases due to the lack of input. Furthermore, in some cases there was a tendency to aim to overfulfil the projected plan, as producers had high incentives to earn bonuses for the excess volume produced. However, in the economic conditions where some producers underfulfilled and others overfulfilled the plan, the efficiency of production could not increase, but on the contrary, there was waste of resources. Producers on the lower line of the vertical cooperation were not always able to use the excessive input produced by other industrial enterprises due to the lack of other inputs. Unfortunately, such information in many cases did not reach the bureaucrats, who were in charge of developing new plans and as a result, there were increasing mismatches in the projections on which the plans were based, resulting in even greater inefficiency in the economy.

The *second principle* of the regional economic planning system is input-output analysis, which represents planning in terms of mathematical and electronic methods, and was founded by Wassily Leontief (1953), but was introduced in the Soviet economy in 1959 by Nemchinov (Ellman, 1968). The classical regional input-output analysis reveals the underlying trading structure of the regional economy in order to construct detailed regional multipliers. The regional input-output analysis in the Soviet Union showed the linear programming of input-output linkages in the industrial economy, where the main task was to project technological coefficients, which were mainly estimated by the projections of experts of future technological changes in the particular industry. However, results of the input-output analysis were not always satisfactory due to the "rough guesswork" (Kornai, 1992) of the planning bureaucracy. The input–output analysis in the Soviet Union was created on the basis of commodity-commodity and not industry-industry, which created a problem (M. Ellman, 1968) for the accuracy of analysis. It was time-consuming to collect information on all commodities for the input-output analysis in order to make projections for a certain period. When the detailed information was collected, analysed and projected, it was becoming out of date, as some commodities, by that time, were no longer in production, while the production of new commodities had begun. Thus, computer-based techniques of the planning analysis were used to balance the economy, even though essential information had been lost during the process of collection. As a result, incorrect projections were being applied on the basis of a guess, while "...the only *computer* capable of that is the market." (Kornai, 1992). "The Statistical Office, can take over from where the mechanism of the market system has left off" (Leontief, 1971), but it does not necessarily accomplish its functions due to the negligent approach.

As we can see in the Soviet economy the geographical allocation of resources was based on principles of classical regional economics, however, the problem was connected with the absence of price responsiveness, so that the evaluation of the whole economy was based on costs and not on market drivers, which would assign values to things. The planning system lacked the sensitive tools of the market, such as price, which would give a signal to enterprises to change their production in terms of quality and quantity.

When the Soviet system was dismantled and its republics entered the transition process, market prices became more important for production. In order to analyse market conditions in transition, we have to incorporate models, in particular, where prices play key roles. In order to understand the allocation of production activities, we have to consider models in which the market assigns values to the marginal productivity of inputs and also allows the allocation of factors to be adjusted. Therefore, some models of regional factor allocation and migration will be discussed in the next section in order to understand the hypothetical implications of these models for the Kazakhstani regional economy and to attempt to link constraints of the transition economy with conditions of the targeted market economy.

3.3 Economic models of regional development

3.3.1 Neoclassical regional growth

3.3.1.1 The one-sector model of regional factor allocation and migration

Moving on from the centrally planned economy, the ex-Soviet republics entered the transition process towards the market economy. For newly independent states, inter-regional development would be an important condition to achieve balanced economic growth so that for the first time input factors would be inter-regionally mobile. However, the free inter-regional mobility of such input factors as labour and capital in the transition economy would not always follow the rules of classical regional theories. Therefore, this section presents four models of inter-regional development in order to help understand the possible outcomes of Kazakhstani regional development during the transition process towards a market economy.

The neoclassical approach (Solow, 1956) of inter-regional development explicitly explains the economy type, which could represent the endpoint of transition. The Solow (1956) model represents the one-sector neoclassical model of factor allocation and migration with assumptions that the economy is competitive, where factors are paid according to their marginal productivity and input factors can be efficiently reallocated within a short period of time. The high free mobility of factors plays a significant role, which affects the speed of their allocation and economic adjustments to new changes.

The one-sector model is based on the principle of variable factor proportions, where the marginal productivity of factors is defined by their relative quantities employed in the production activity using the law of diminishing returns for all input factors as long as other factors are being held constant. It means that the marginal product of the variable will fall with the extra quantity employed of this variable. Assuming that production function[58] of regional economies consists of two complementary input factors of labour and capital in the presence of two regions in the country, the capital labour ratios for both regions will be presented in the following form:

K_A/L_A and K_B/L_B

where, K and L are capital and labour factors, A and B are two regions of the economy. In the case of the capital/labour ratio of region A being higher than the ratio of region B, the marginal productivity of capital in region A will be lower compared to the marginal productivity of capital of region B, while the marginal productivity of labour will be higher in region A due to the diminishing marginal productivity assumption. The neoclassical model of regional factor allocation and migrations implies that in the given example the capital factor will move to region B, while labour will migrate to region A from region B, in order to increase its marginal profits. In the market economy, where input factors are freely mobile, they are going to be reallocated until the moment when capital/labour ratios of regions A and B are equalised. In the case of an economy with three or more regions the mechanism of the reallocation of factors according to their marginal productivity will be slightly more complicated, but is based on the same mechanism as in the case of two regions. Thus, if capital/labour ratios of regions A, B, C are assumed to be related as follows:

---

58   The regional production function presents the Cobb-Douglas production function: Qt=AKαLβ , where Q denotes the regional output at time *t*, A is the constant, K and L are two complementary input factors, where K is the regional capital stock and L is the regional labour stock. α and β are shares of capital and labour stocks respectively in regional economy.

$$\frac{K_A}{L_A} > \frac{K_B}{L_B} > \frac{K_C}{L_C} \qquad (1)$$

the marginal product of capital in region A will be the lowest compared to regions B and C, while the highest marginal product of capital will be observed in region C. However, the marginal product of labour will be at its lowest point in region C, and at its highest level in region A, while region B will be in the middle between A and C regions for marginal products of both capital and labour. In such a situation the perfect reallocation of factors will occur when capital moves from regions A and B to region C, and labour migrates from regions C and B to region A until the capital/labour ratios of all three regions are equalised. The whole national economy gains from reallocations of factors according to their marginal productivity, as in the case of equation (1) the marginal product of capital is low in region A compared to region B and C, while region C has the highest marginal product of the capital and still has a potential for its growth. At the same time the marginal product of labour has potential for growth in region A, while it is very low in region C. By reallocating capital factors from regions A and B to region C, the marginal product of the capital will continue to grow in region C until the moment when capital/labour ratios of all three regions become equal. The same mechanism causes the migration of the labour factor from regions B and C to region A, increasing the marginal product of labour until the point of the equalisation of the capital/labour ratios has been reached, after which the marginal product of labour (or capital) will decline with every additional increase in its quantity.

The gains of the national economy from regional allocation of factors and labour migration in the case of unequal capital/labour rations can be illustrated by Figure 3.1.:

Figure 3.1. Inter-regional possibility frontier[59].

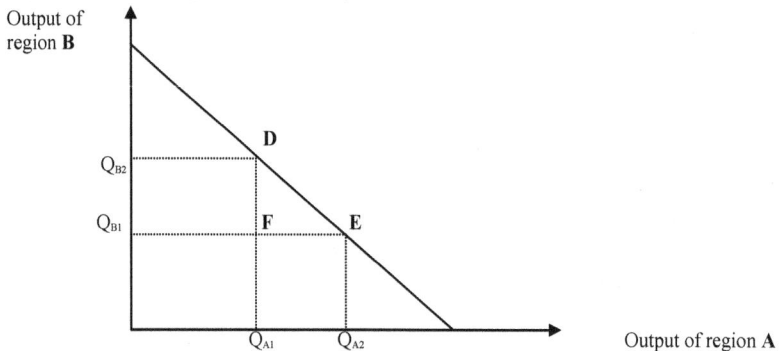

The horizontal axis of Figure 3.1. represents the output of region A, while the vertical axis represents the output of region B. The line DE represents the inter-regional possibility frontier (Borts and Stein, 1964), which shows all possible efficient outcomes of the output combinations for two regions, where all points on this line, including points D and E are Pareto efficient points, while F is the point at which the national economy is operating inefficiently. Rewriting equation (1) for only two regions A and B we obtain equation (2):

$$\frac{K_A}{L_A} > \frac{K_B}{L_B} \tag{2}$$

Equation (2) represents the national economy being located in point F of Figure 3.1., where marginal products of capital and labour factors are different for regions A and B. However, the market economy shifts the factor reallocation towards points D, E or any other point on the DE line. Being located at point F, the capital factor of region A will move to region B for higher marginal profits. Holding the labour constant, the economy will move from point F of Figure 3.1. to point D, where the output Q_{A1} of region A stays the same, while the output Q_{B1} of region B increases to the output Q_{B2}, where the whole economy is better off. In the case of equation (1), if the labour factor migrates from

---

59   Inter-regional possibility frontier is shown on the graph as the stright line, however in reality the the shape may change depending on the economy situation.

region B to region A in order to increase its marginal product, the output of the national economy will move from point F to point E, holding the capital factor constant, where the output Q_{B1} of region B is not changing, while the output of region A is growing from Q_{A1} to Q_{A2}, and increasing the output of the whole economy.

3.3.1.2 The two-sector model of regional factor allocation and migration

The one-sector model was based on the assumption of factors freely moving in opposite directions until they reach the point when their ratios are equalised in the regions under consideration. The one-sector model assumes that all regions have the same production function. Therefore, it cannot be applied to Kazakhstan, because it does not include the factor of mineral resource variations across regions. The two-sector model considers factors, which are also assumed to move freely, but in the same direction. In addition, it is also important to consider the two-sector model, in order to try to understand the inter-regional development in Kazakhstan. Due to the unbalanced regional development, capital and labour could move in the same direction. According to the two-sector model, regions A and B produce a different set of outputs with different production functions. Lets assume that the production of region A is relatively capital-intensive, while the production of region B is more labour intensive. The marginal revenue product (MP) of the capital and labour in both regions will be equal to the product of marginal physical product (MPP) of capital (K) or labour (L) and output price (P)[60]:

$$MP_K = MPP_K \times P$$
$$MP_L = MPP_L \times P$$

---

60   Abbreviation is used on the basis of McCann (2001).

Figure 3.2. Two- sector model of regional factor allocation and migration

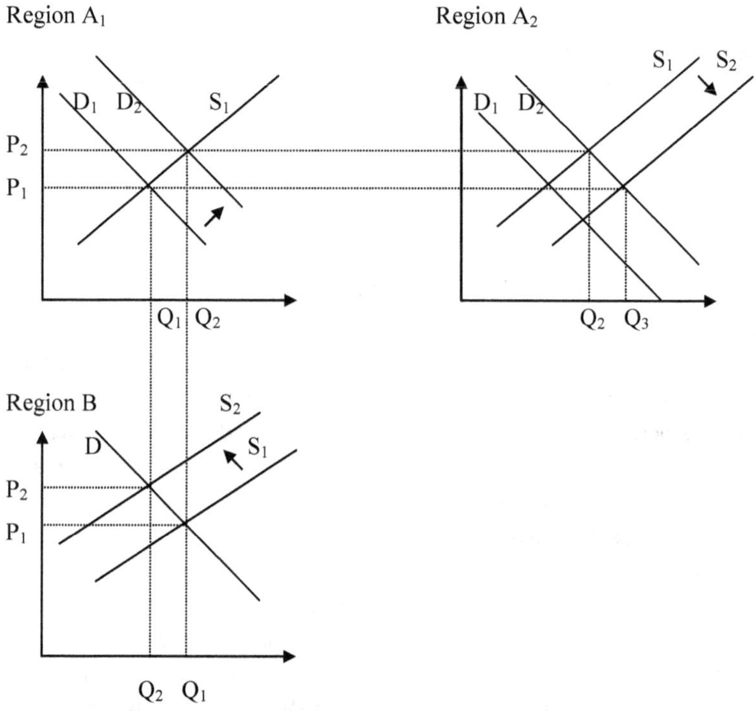

Assuming that the demand on the output of region A increased for the reason of changes in consumers taste, the output price in the region will increase in the short run from P_1 to P_2 (Figure 3.2., Region A_1), while the output price in region B will stay at the same level. Therefore, the marginal revenue product of both capital and labour will be higher in region A relative to region B:

$$MP_K^A = MPP_K^A \times P^A\uparrow \; > MP_K^B = MPP_K^B \times P^B$$
$$MP_L^A = MPP_L^A \times P^A\uparrow \; > MP_L^B = MPP_L^B \times P^B$$

As a result of a higher marginal revenue product in region A, capital and labour of region B will migrate to region A, where the supply curve will move to the right (Figure 3.2., Region A_2) increasing quantity and declining the price in region A, while the supply curve of region B will move to the left (Figure 3.2., Region B) increasing price, due to the decline of production in the region. Consequently the marginal revenue product of capital and labour in region A will decline, and increase in region B.

The two-sector model implies that input factors will migrate across regions until the marginal revenue product is equalised. The one-sector and two-sector models assume the competitive nature of the economy, where factors are paid according to their marginal product and can be freely reallocated across regions until the Pareto efficiency point is reached and can be considered as self-regulating mechanisms of the market economy.

Empirical results of Barro and Sala-i-Martin (1991, 1992) on the example of the European Union, support the argument of the one-sector model of regional convergence over time, however, the process of the one-sector model is very slow especially under certain constraints, such as lack of information and mismanagement. The one-sector and two-sector models are long run models. It is possible that in terms of the Kazakhstani economy, adjustments to the neoclassical approach would be fast if factors quickly respond to changes in the economy. However, it is more likely that the process will be very limited.

The one-sector and two-sector models assume that the market has to be effective and perfect, however, in transition the market is developing very slowly, where due to limitations of knowledge and geography factors respond to economic changes after a long time gap. If a factor responds in the short term, there is a great likelihood that it is human capital. However, there are some exceptions in the Kazakhstani economy, for example, investment flows responded very quickly. These exceptions are the new capital and western part of Kazakhstan, which includes hydrocarbon rich regions, while other regions experience little or no movements at all in factors respond. However, in the case of the new capital the fast responsiveness of investments was artificially defined by the Kazakhstani government and not by market signals. Therefore, it could be more appropriate to adopt the disequilibrium model of inter-regional labour migration.

3.3.2 The disequilibrium model of inter-regional labour migration

The one-sector model of regional factor allocation and migration, which is based on marginal product differences of input factors, shows that the economy will move towards regional equalisation. However, input factors in the Kazakhstani economy have limited mobility, where the factor, which is likely to be most mobile is labour. Therefore, the next model discusses the approach to inter-regional migration of input factors such as labour, based on their free mobility, which is induced by a disequilibrium of real wages between regions. As a result, free labour mobility leads the regional economies to the stabilisation and equalisation of real wages, which is suggested to be one of the significant determinants of the free market economy. This approach is denoted as the "disequilibrium" economy, where real wages of regional economies differ from each other and thereby create the mechanism, which causes the labour factor to migrate until the equilibrium point of real wages is reached at the inter-regional level.

In the case of a duo-regional economy, where A and B are its regions, let us assume that regional wages of the particular industrial sectors are equal:

$$W_{Ao} = W_{Bo} \qquad (3)$$

Let us consider one of the possible examples of change in the production of a particular industrial sector in one or both regions. Assuming that demand for the output of the industrial sector under consideration fell in region A and did not change in region B because of the increase of import substitutes, the labour supply and demand in both regions will take the form of Figure 3.3.

Figure 3.3. The disequilibrium model of inter-regional labour migration.

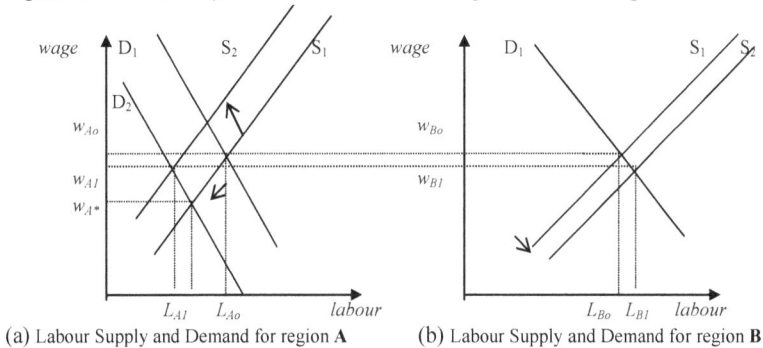

(a) Labour Supply and Demand for region **A**   (b) Labour Supply and Demand for region **B**

As the demand for the output of the industrial sector fell in region A without any changes in region B, the production of this output will eventually decline in region A, with a decline in the demand for labour and its wages. Figure 3.3. shows the original point of the inter-regional economy where wages w_{Ao} and w_{Bo} of regions A and B respectively are equal and original supply and demand curves are represented by S_1 and D_1 in both regions. Because of the fall of demand in region A, the demand curve D_1 moves left towards the D_2 curve, while the wage of region A declines from level w_{Ao} to level w_{A*} (Figure 3.3.). Under the conditions of the market economy, where input factors are freely mobile, labour will migrate to region B, where the level of wages has not changed and still stays at w_{Bo}, which is higher than the new level w_{A*} in region A. When labour migrates from region A to region B, the labour supply declines in region A moving the supply curve S_1 to the left to S_2 curve, while the labour supply in region B increases, moving the supply curve from S_1 to the right towards the S_2 curve. Thus, the decline of the labour supply in region A will slightly increase the wages from the reduced level of w_{A*} to w_{A1}, while the growth in the labour supply of region B, under conditions of unchanged production and demand for input factors, will reduce the wages to w_{B1} level from the w_{Bo} original equilibrium level.

When regional economies are in equilibrium, however, it does not imply that all factor stocks are identical and equal in regions, nor, is it always the case that equilibrium wages are identical. The disequilibrium model assumes real wages to be equal as measured by the comparison of the basic consumer's basket, while the equilibrium model (Graves, 1980) implies that real wages cannot be equal on the regional level as different regions have different amenities and environmental working conditions; regions with more difficult conditions are rewarded by higher wage levels in a market economy. The implication here is that the underdeveloped infrastructure of a region has to be rewarded by higher wage levels relative to other regions in the market economy. However, in Kazakhstan, the economic system is undergoing radical changes towards a market mechanism, where the equilibrium interpretation of regional labour markets would appear to be much less appropriate than the disequilibrium description. Our analysis will now assume that only the disequilibrium model is operative.

3.3.3 Model of human capital migration and endogenous growth theory

The final destination of transition economies is the market economy, which is the only general form of the economy, where every country has its own specialities and therefore its economy develops with its own particular characteristics. Nevertheless, there are main objectives, which have to be attained to properly develop a regional market economy, which are the free allocation of regional factors, free inter-regional labour migration and economic stabilisation. However, economic stabilisation does not imply an unchangeable economy, but the opposite. It assumes continuous changes in the economy, which are self-regulated by market economy mechanisms, which keep the regional economies in equilibrium and the whole economy at a stable level.

Particularly in transition economies labour mobility is associated with human capital at a higher level of education, in which case the disequilibrium model of inter-regional labour migration may not bring regional economies into equilibrium in terms of wages in the short or medium term, therefore, the model could not be appropriate for understanding the behaviour of the Kazakhstani economy. Therefore, we have to consider models where more highly educated labour is taken into account. Therefore, the human capital migration model is focused on the migration of individuals with a higher level of education and can be appropriate for the understanding of the changes in the Kazakhstani economy.

The model of human capital migration is the expansion of the human capital theory discussed by Becker (1964). The argument of the human capital migration model is based on the rational behaviour of individuals, who invest in their education in order to satisfy their lifetime expectations. The model implies that labour with a higher level of education is more likely to migrate in order to find employment with an expected level of wage in order to maximise their returns from their education costs. Labour with a higher level of education has easier access to the information network for job search, through which opportunities for jobs over wider geographical distances increase compared to labour with lower levels of education. As a result, there is a greater likelihood of migration over a wider geographical space for labour with higher level of education. At the same time, easier access to the information network for more highly educated labour allows it not only to cover a larger geographical space but also to respond more quickly to signals of wage changes. Incentives for human capital migration can be explained on the basis of the disequilibrium model of inter-regional labour migration, where Figure 3.4. is constructed on the basis of Figure 3.3.

Figure 3.4. Model of human capital migration.

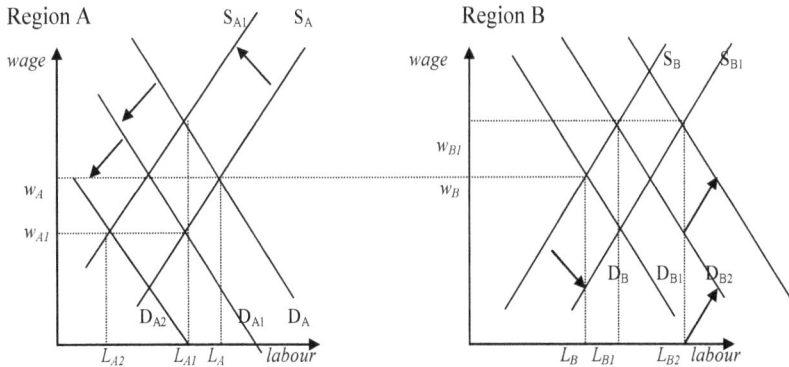

Let us assume that w_A and w_B are equilibrium wages in regions A and B respectively, where L_A and L_B are equilibrium levels of labour. If demand for labour in region A decreases and increases in region B, the wage level of region A will fall from w_A to w_{A1}, while the wage level in region B will grow from w_B to w_{B1}. As a result, according to the disequilibrium model of inter-regional migration, the difference between regional wages will create incentives for labour to migrate from region A to region B. Therefore, the demand of region A will move to the left from D_A to D_{A1}, while supply will also shift to the left from S_A to S_{A1}, when region B will experience growth in demand from D_B to D_{B1}, following the increase in supply from S_B to S_{B1}. The human capital model argues that labour with higher stocks of human capital will respond more quickly to signals of economic tools such as wage changes and will have a higher likelihood of migrating across regions. In the case, if the growth in labour demand of region B is supported by the growth of the physical capital as well, then the labour demand of region B will continue to grow from D_{B1} to D_{B2}. Therefore, the labour demand in region A will fall from D_{A1} to D_{A2} as due to the decline of marginal product of regional capital stock, under the assumption that regional capital stock consists of both human and physical capital.

The illustrated example shows that the model of human capital migration has its limitations where no unique inter-regional equilibrium exists. Therefore, in the case of wage changes due to the expansion of a particular region, including physical capital growth, there is a high likelihood of a high inflow of labour with higher levels of human capital in the short run. This will increase the efficiency level of the economic development in the region, which in time can bring the region to the agglomeration diseconomies of scale due to the unbalanced labour migration and as a result uneven regional development will grow. The effect of changes in internal factors on the regional growth is discussed in the endogenous growth theory, whose approach appears to provide an explanation of the changes in the Kazakhstani economy.

A further development of the human capital framework comes from the endogenous growth theory, which is focused on the economic growth relative to internal regional factors and based on the reconciliation of neoclassical competitive market conditions with localised growth in terms of the analysis of the production function. The neoclassical one-sector model implies that the level of technology diffusion is even and instantaneous across all regions, while in reality the level of technology or innovation are eventually distributed across all regions and industries but with a time gap, where technology can be defined as the combination of production, information and communication frameworks.

One of the main elaborators of the endogenous growth model was Romer (1986, 1987). One of his arguments assumes that the increasing level of regional specialisation leads to increasing returns to scale of the regional production, where the output grows with the increase in specialised input factors of the region (Romer, 1987). Another of Romer's arguments implies that the endogenous growth is induced by the stock of knowledge, where the technology residual in terms of the production growth increases with the growth of the knowledge of firms (Romer, 1986).

The Lucas (1988) approach is also based on the notion of knowledge as a source for endogenous growth, however, Romer's concept of *knowledge* as a source defined it as the product of technological research. Lucas' concept of *knowledge* is based on human capital acquisition, which implies that growth of human capital leads to the increase of output. Lucas argument is based on the Cobb-Douglas production function (footnote 58). After the introduction of the human capital acquisition effect the regional production function is: $Q_t=(uHL)^{1-\alpha}K^{\alpha}J^{\varphi}$, where u is the fraction of time t, which workers spend on the acquisition of human capital H, and J is the external effect of individuals' acquisition of human capital. Following the approach of Lucas the rate of human capital acquisition is: $\Delta H_t = H^{\xi}\delta(1-u)$, where δ is constant, however if ξ is less than unity, the growth of human capital will decline to zero. McCombie and Thirlwall (1994), modified this model assuming that ξ has to be equal or greater than unity, which implies that there are only constant or increasing returns on the acquisition of human capital. After transformations made and derivatives taken for t period of time (McCombie and Thirlwall, 1994) the production function can be written as: $\Delta Q_t = (1-\alpha)\Delta L_{qt} + \alpha\Delta K_t$, where $L^q = H^{\theta}\Lambda$ represents the human capital H of the given level of efficiency and quality Λ. Therefore, from the latter equation it can be seen that the share of output growth which falls on labour, completely depends on the acquisition of human capital.

The development of an unbalanced economy is explained by Myrdal's (1963) approach to the study of the endogenous growth, which differs from neoclassical theory with respect to the reaching of the equilibrium point by regional economies. Myrdal based his explanation on the cumulative causation process, which creates economic and social forces leading economies to disequilibrium. The interregional migration of labour, capital and trade create a gap between regions leading to the backwardness of the weakest ones and slow the development of the whole national economy. Myrdal doubted that migration of input factors in time decreases demand in favoured regions and increasing it in the weakest, which would lead to equilibrium. The approach is based on the mechanism, which produces increasing returns to scale in regions of the in-migration of input factors. Myrdal's hypothesis could be applied to the Kazakhstani situation in the transition stage, where the migration of labour, capital and entrepreneurship to central regions (Almaty, Astana and western Kazakhstan regions) continuously widens gaps in development of central and peripheral regions, increasing the backwardness of the latter. However, the Myrdal approach of the cumulative causation process does not reject the hypothesis that in the long run increasing costs in favoured regions will retard the cumulative causation process when agglomeration will start to emerge in other favoured regions, but still keeping the development lag with weakest regions.

The human capital theory is one justification of the endogenous growth model, which implies that labour with a higher level of human capital is more likely to migrate over a wider geographical space in order to maximise the returns to its education costs. This assumes the higher likelihood of growth in its level of productivity, which affects the total level of production growth of a particular firm and consequently regional growth.

All introduced models of endogenous growth theory imply that output growth is attributed to the growth of local factors, such as inputs of regional specialisation, knowledge and human capital, so that endogenous growth is persistent, based on local factors in the environment of market competition. The one-sector model of regional factor allocation and migration and the disequilibrium model of inter-regional labour migration imply that mobility of factors

leads to regional equalisation. The two-sector model of regional factor allocation and migration is based on the migration of factors in the same direction.
However, unlike human capital and endogenous growth theories, the factor
migration in the two-sector model moves towards the equalisation point of
marginal products. Nevertheless, in reality, the process is very slow and the
equalisation point can only be reached in the long run, while the short or medium terms are characterised by unbalanced regional development. The human capital migration model and the endogenous growth theory imply that
capital and labour are moving in the same direction, which leads to unbalanced economy and could lead to the agglomeration of diseconomies of
scale. Therefore, we have to explain how these things happen and what defines the nature of the migration, which leads to the unbalanced economy.

3.4   Regional development in transition

3.4.1 Drivers of the transition economies behaviour.

The previous theoretical section revises several fundamental questions concerning the nature of the inter-regional transition process, which need to be
addressed. Firstly, to what extent do firms and individuals respond rationally
to market signals? Secondly, if industrial clustering develops, to what extent
will this phenomenon be maintained? Thirdly, although transition economies
undergo continuous changes, is there is any self-regulating mechanism which
would stabilise the economy? Fourthly, what is an appropriate definition of
stabilisation for a transition economy, taking into account the different individual characteristics of transition countries compared to western market
economies? Given the uncertainty about the way of reaching the state at
which an economy can be described as a market economy, transition countries behave chaotically in searching for the right way of development with no
certain knowledge of the length of the road to the market economy. In order
to answer these questions, there are two main concepts of economic and location theory, which we can use to study the rather chaotic behaviour of enterprises in transition economies. The *first* concept is based on conditions of
uncertainty, where enterprises behave irrationally without being certain of the
outcome. The rational way may not be known, but would be the only one

whereby an enterprise could start to generate positive profits. The *second* approach underlines the importance of the information, which plays a crucial role for growth of an enterprise. Success can depend on being close to the centre of information. This is due to the fact that the new information on the reason for the success and failure of other enterprises will take time to diffuse across geographical distances and is more quickly available to enterprises located nearby[61].

The first concept is based on the Alchian (1950) approach, which suggested that individual behaviour is based on "environmental adoption", where the objective is "positive profits" and not "profit maximisation". In the pursuit of "positive profits" under conditions of uncertainty and incomplete information, individuals[62] do not follow the rational or optimal way of target utilisation. Alchian suggested that "positive profits" are targets under uncertainty conditions, as only individuals with positive profits can survive against individuals with losses. Under conditions of uncertainty it is impossible to predict conditions for success, while the basis of past experience and observation of the current position cannot bring logical foresight of future behaviour due to external changes of the characteristics of enterprises, rather than their behaviour. Thus, enterprises that happen to be located in certain places and have the set of characteristics which happen to lead to success, are mostly lucky and appear to survive by chance.

Enterprises that happen to be close to the optimal set of characteristics for success have a high likelihood of achieving positive profits, while other enterprises take the successful enterprises as an example for the achievement of positive profits. However, copying the behaviour of successful enterprises is not always going to bring good results to imitators, due to the set of different external characteristics including their location and the time lag (given that the circumstances which resulted in the success of the original enterprise may no longer pertain). The right time and location can be crucial for the successful

---

61   The second approach will be discussed in the next section as the source of agglomeration economies.
62   It could be understood that by individuals A. Alchian means objects of the economy system.

performance of one enterprise, while the change in one of these two determinants even on a small scale, assuming that all other individual characteristics are constant, can cause the complete failure of an enterprise's performance. When a newly established enterprise follows the example of the behaviour of an enterprise of the same scale located in the same region, but with a different length of experience and period of successful performance, the former enterprise has little chance of success, as the other external characteristics have changed over time. The length of the time lag depends on the scale of the enterprises and is equal to the period between the success of the experienced enterprise and the results of its performance. Even an enterprise, which maintains the same style of management and production without any changes, having had successful performance in the past, has a high chance of failure (as profits turn to losses) under the changeable conditions of uncertainty in the economy.

The Alchian concept of uncertainty conditions can be fully applicable to the case of the transition economies, where the transformation of the centrally planned economy to the market economy created conditions of uncertainty. During the first decade of transition, state-owned enterprises in Kazakhstan were privatised or expected to be privatised with little knowledge of the right way of management for survival. In such an environment, there is no rational or irrational way of managing enterprises. While the economy is moving towards a new system, the market economy, the duration of this process and the nature of the intermediate stage is unknown. Even though there are types of market economy in the world, which transition countries could imitate, the conditions of uncertainty impose many limitations that can cause failure, due to the different set of initial conditions and external characteristics.

Industrial enterprises in transition economies, which appeared to be in the right place at the right time, had a greater chance to achieve positive profits (for example the Caspian Sea regions with rich deposits of oil and gas), therefore, their success depended on the lucky chance of having the optimal set of external characteristics, which would correspond to the optimal set of internal characteristics. However, the right set of characteristics cannot be constant continuously during the whole transition period, as the whole process of transition consists of the "trial and error" of different possible ways, which could make the economy successful through the imitation of western economies. Thus, transition economies have a high probability of failure for a long period because nobody in the transition economies knows the optimal path of transition to the market economy. Nevertheless, there could be many possible predictions of the right approach. However, the high level of uncertainty leads to a high quantity of proposed ways of economic management. Consequently, it is very unlikely that given all these alternatives whose chances of success are not well understood that the adopted path will be the optimal route to success rather than failure.

Not only do enterprises imitate the behaviour of successful enterprises, but also labour likewise follows the behaviour of leaders in businesses. During the transition period many industrial enterprises were closed down or significantly cut their production, which contributed to the increasing level of unemployment in Kazakhstan. Under conditions of uncertainty and the rise in first time of unemployment, which under the Soviet system was always kept at a minimum level, people started to follow the behaviour of other individuals, who were adopting a "trial and error" approach and achieved success. This boosted the service sector where the commercial trade by individuals accounted for most of the activity. At the same time, not only unemployed but also employed people moved into the service sector. Applying the disequilibrium model it could be said that low wage levels constituted a set of incentives that caused labour to move to the service sector, where very often new jobs were not related to the areas of the qualifications of specialists. There was also a high level of labour migration across regions for better job opportunities. The human capital theory and disequilibrium model arguments explain the motivation of human capital to migrate across regions. Thus, the ex-capital Almaty became the centre of a high influx of labour, due to greater opportunities for development.

In many market economies we can observe the behaviour of following the leader, however, in transition economies this type of behaviour on the part of individuals as well as enterprises became the key determinant of attempts to survive under conditions of uncertainty. Nevertheless, the leader-follower behaviour is not a sufficient explanation of the behaviour of transition econo-mies. There is another justification that is keeping people and enterprises in locations to which they migrated. This is the existence of agglomeration economies. This hypothetical concept will be discussed and tested in the next part by applying it to the Kazakhstani economy.

3.4.2 Agglomeration incentives

Marshall's (1920) concept of agglomeration includes several key incentives that encourage enterprises to choose a location in the proximity to clusters or to organise an industrial cluster, where local characteristics are most impor-tant and include access to a variety of local inputs and the existence of local demand. Organised industrial clusters on the basis of those motives listed above, attract other producers to join three possible sources of agglomera-tion, which were emphasized by Marshall, and these are: an information cen-tre, local non-traded inputs and a local skilled labour pool.

Information centre

The allocation of industrial enterprises to locations in close proximity to indus-trial clusters has many advantages. The first of these is the high speed of in-formation travel and its usage. Enterprises that imitate the strategy of their successful competitors with the closest approximation of the mix of individual and external characteristics, have a higher probability of successful perform-ance than enterprises with a different set of characteristics or enterprises that are searching for the successful way of operating through "trial and error". Therefore, we are coming to the point where enterprises that have better ac-cess to the information on the success and failure of others, have a greater likelihood of performing well by applying the filtered information to its own op-erations. The better access to such information sources allows enterprises to compare different cases of the attempts and results of other enterprises and to choose the behaviour, which would most likely produce a positive outcome for the particular set of characteristics. Therefore, the process of agglomera-tion and the endeavour by enterprises to be located in clusters can be ex-plained as the intention to follow the information source that increases the chance of reaching a positive outcome.

Nevertheless, the perceived advantage for enterprises to be close to information centres is so great that it naturally creates high competition around important information centres. Therefore, despite the high share of successful enterprises in the vicinity of the information centres, there is also a high percentage of failing enterprises, which do not survive the competition, despite the access to high-speed information. However, the surviving enterprises are distinguished by advanced ways of management and production, which promote their development even further, in order to beat newcomers and other existing survivors, who also had improved their methods.

Non-traded local inputs

The second source of agglomeration is defined by access to non-traded local inputs, which do not include consumed inputs, but consist of specialist inputs (e.g. legal, software etc.), such as specialist services to enterprises. Non-traded local inputs would be very expensive for an individual firm, however, if there is a group of firms located in the same area, the cost of non-traded local inputs can be divided between them. Nevertheless, non-traded inputs in transition economies differ from those in market economies. Due to their specific character, specialist services are not yet fully developed in transition countries and as a result, prices are not as high as they are in market economies. If one of the reasons for agglomeration in market economies is to decrease the costs for non-traded inputs, the transition economies would have slightly different reasons. For them it is not the price that is most important with regard to the accessibility of non-traded inputs, but the fact that access to non-traded inputs close to their location enables the more advanced development of industrial enterprises.

Local skilled labour pool

The location of industrial enterprises in a certain area allows them to benefit from the local pool of specific skilled labour. In the case of the expansion of production, industrial enterprises in an agglomeration economy would have lower costs for the acquisition of specialised labour. Industrial enterprises located individually, have higher costs for the employment of additional specialised labour because of training costs. Therefore, enterprises in agglomeration economies have a greater opportunity to respond quickly to market changes

by quick adjustments of input factors. The easy access to the local skilled labour pool also plays an important role in transition economies, especially in
those on the edge of survival. The labour pool is the second important reason
for the choice of location in transition economies after the proximity to raw
materials. The perfect example can be given from the Kazakhstani experience in the case of the move of the capital to another location in 1997, which
is distant from the ex-capital. All government departments were moved to the
new capital together with their entire staff. When new positions are filled in
Astana, preference is given to applicants from Almaty city, where the educational level of the labour pool is many times higher than in the new capital. As
a result, employees are offered high incentives in terms of remuneration and
accommodation in order to move to the new capital. However, the local pool
of the skilled labour in Astana may take decades to develop to the level of
Almaty.

Whilst government departments do not have a choice in their location, businesses do have this choice, and even five years after the designation of the
new capital, not many businesses aspired to move to its location. One of the
reasons is the low quality pool of labour in Astana. The former capital Almaty
still is very attractive for new businesses and is still called the business centre
of Kazakhstan, while the new capital is only seen as the seat of government.
In theoretical terms the ex-capital of Kazakhstan can be termed the economy
of urbanisation (McCann, 2001), which agglomerates different industrial sectors, while the new capital of Kazakhstan can be named the economy of localisation, which specialises only on the one particular economic sector, in
our case it is the governmental infrastructure with its departments and institutions. Nevertheless, Astana, the new capital, is not going to be the economy
of localisation for a long time, due to the absence of key incentives for agglomeration. The poor infrastructure and the low level of education of the labour pool are the main problems for the attraction of businesses to the location around the new capital. However, with the transfer of government institutions, many strong universities of the country, which were located in the ex-
capital Almaty, were forced to create branches in the new capital in order to
be able to meet one of the government targets for the educational improvement of the population of the new capital. It takes time to attract reputable

academic staff to new universities and it takes an even longer time for that generation to complete its education so that it would be able to compete with skilled specialists from the labour pool of the ex-capital. Therefore, the wider development of the region in terms of industrial sectors will take time. Eventually the unskilled labour pool will no longer be a problem, and the conditions in the capital will provide desirable incentives for businesses to migrate.

The three possible sources of agglomeration considered above are important for the location of industrial enterprises at the same place. However, their location is classified into three different categories from the point of view of individual enterprises and industries. In order to understand the location behaviour of enterprises, it is important to examine where agglomeration economies appear to occur in terms of individual firms, industries and locations. The classification of agglomeration economies was first defined by Ohlin (1933) and Hoover (1937, 1948), and divided economies into three types: internal returns to scale, localisation economies and urbanisation economies.

Internal returns to scale
An individual firm, which gains efficient economies of scale due to its large size, can be referred to as a firm with internal economies of scale. Besides being the main reason for size of an enterprise, the type of internal economies of scale is location specific. The internal economies of scale can be generated by enterprises at the location, which is maintained by a significant amount of capital investments and skilled human capital, which is the Marshall source of agglomeration. Thus, location specific characteristics, such as investments and labour, allow enterprises to expand their size and to gain the internal economies of scale. In the case of Kazakhstan, hydrocarbon rich regions can be referred to as internal economies of scale, where individual hydrocarbon enterprises gain the internal economies of scale on the basis of the inflow of high investments and the location in the proximity of other hydrocarbon enterprises, which enables them to share the skilled labour pool.

Localisation economies

The second type of agglomeration economies refer to industrial enterprises located at a certain place according to its industrial sector (base sector)[63]. Enterprises located in the same location of the same industry benefit from the agglomeration by easy access to agglomeration sources discussed above, which are information centre, non-traded local inputs and a skilled local labour pool. Industries, which are based on natural resources, are less mobile than those based on other factors, therefore, for the cumulative growth of localisation economies, it is important to have other mobile factors, which would move in the same direction (Böventer, 1975). The Soviet economy was based on planned localisation economies, where industrial enterprises were located on the basis of the proximity to raw material sources in the Kazakh SSR and were connected to enterprises of other industries in other republics of the Soviet Union. The mobility of such input factors as labour and capital was defined by the central planning system, which directed factors to important industries and locations for the Soviet economy. Therefore, the growth of localisation economies in the Soviet system was ensured by the artificial mobility of input factors. Thus, the Karaganda region was referred to as the localisation economy, where enterprises of the mining industry were concentrated, while manufacturers were located in other republics. All other regions of the Kazakh SSR were industrially developed according to their specialisation, which created localisation economies, where enterprises benefited from the diffusion of information on innovations or technologies and from easy access to the pool of skilled labour.

Urbanisation economies

The third type of agglomeration economies defines the location of enterprises in a certain place across different sectors. The localisation economies of industrial enterprises, which achieve internal returns to scale, require other services (non-base sectors[64]) to be maintained for enterprises or labour level in

---

63   The base sector is the industrial sector, which gives the origin for the development of localisation economies. The high concentration of industrial enterprises of a particular industrial sector in a certain location creates the localisation economy.

64   Non-base sectors are economic sectors, which are placed in location of the base sector in order to maintain its work and the living of the population. The growth and

order to keep and continue the clustering. This type of industrial cluster can be considered to be much more self-sufficient because of the production and services provided, and is described as an economy of urbanisation. Urbanisation economies can be defined as city-specific economies. In the case of Kazakhstan, urbanisation economies can be recalled in the ex-capital Almaty, which is based on enterprises of different sectors, achieving internal returns to scale, while other sectors' enterprises are maintaining the level of internal economies of scale for the city.

The presence of natural resources resulted in the creation of localisation economies in many regions of the Kazakh SSR in the middle of the 20th century, which were based on enterprises with specialised productions already located there. Thus, the Central Kazakhstani industrial cluster was based on coal and other mineral resources of the Karaganda region, which enabled the development of such industrial sectors in this cluster as fuel, ferrous and non-ferrous metallurgy, machine-building, construction materials and chemical sector. In addition, on the basis of localisation economies, urbanisation economies were developing, where the food industry was created for the provision of the existing population. The light industry in such locations was developed in order to maintain employment of the mainly female population as the heavy industries were employed mainly the male population. The Eastern Kazakhstan cluster was based on rich resources of non-ferrous ores and hydropower; the Pavlodar cluster was based on coal resources and Western Kazakhstan on the oil and gas[65]. There are many other industrial clusters in Kazakhstan, which were based on deposits of mineral resources, and stimulated the development of other industrial sectors, which were linked to production of the base sector or the provision of the population. Thus, after defining its specialisation with the location of the industrial base sector on the basis of local mineral resources and geological conditions, other industrial sec-

---

development of non-base sectors around base sector organise urbanisation economies. (i.e. non-base sectors could be light, food industries and other industries which are developed on the basis of the base sector, where the latter usually includes extracting industries of natural resources).

65   The detailed explanation of development of Kazakhstani industrial clusters can be found in Chapter 1 *The Development of the Industrial Sector of the Kazakh SSR on the Basis of the Soviet Economic System* of the book.

tors were attracted to the location due to the presence of local demand, which was generated by other producers or by consumers (the population).

Thus, in the Soviet economic system, many planned localisation economies generated sources for the creation of urbanisation economies, which attracted other industries, such as machine-building (for the service of the base industrial sector), construction materials (for the continuous development of construction around the base sector), light and food industries. All additional industries of urbanisation economies maintained production due to the presence of local demand for their output and the proximity to input factors. However, if non-base industries are directly dependent on the work of the base sector, then the success of the whole region depends on the success of localisation economies. One of the reasons for the failure of regional economies after the collapse of the Soviet Union was the dependency of industrial sectors in the cluster on the base sector. For example the sharp fall in demand for coal led to the failure of all other industries in the Karaganda region, such as machine-building, construction materials, chemical and others, which manufactured products for mines or were based on the output of mines. The failure of regional clusters occurred not only in the Karaganda region, but also in many other specialised regions. Therefore, the development of the market economy in Kazakhstan on the basis of the Soviet planned location of localisation and urbanisation economies did not bring positive results of the maintenance of the production growth. This fact may be explained by difference and non-compatibility in operation of two economic systems, socialism and the transition to the market economy, which overlapped in geographical terms. The establishment of localisation and urbanisation economies during the Soviet time to date needs to be restructured for the profitable operation in the market economy.

The Soviet economy was mainly built on planned localisation economies. However, there was an absence of naturally established urbanisation economies, except in locations where decisions of government were made. In a market economy, people can freely move across regions following the change in economies. On the basis of Alchian's argument, the leader-following behaviour of people creates urbanisation economies. In transition, urbanisation economies may become important for development, as existing localisation economies were planned during the Soviet system and after the transition started, they appeared to be located in the wrong places for internal cooperation. Therefore, such localisation economies and planned urbanisation economies appeared to be most vulnerable to the changes in the transition economy. Thus, urbanisation economies, which are developed on the basis of localisation economies and 'follow the leader' behaviour, become very important for the development of a strong economy. Information there travels faster than in other locations, and new service sectors rise up, such as legal, financial and others which did not exist in the Soviet system. In the market economy the development of agglomeration economies can be captured by the changes in the local real estate market rate, where continuous growth of the property rent is a sign of the development of agglomeration economy. However, in the Soviet system agglomeration economies were created artificially through central planning, where all property belonged to the state. The transition economy is a developing market economy where the dominance of private property has significantly increased through the first decade of transition. Therefore, in the case of Kazakhstan, changes in the local real estate market rent became signs of the development of agglomeration economies. In particular, it can clearly illustrate the growth of an agglomeration economy in Almaty city, where property rents are continuously increasing.

The Kazakhstani economy moves towards the development of urbanisation economies. The former capital Almaty and the new capital Astana are referred as sources of agglomeration economies with easy access to information, non-traded inputs and skilled labour pool (Ermakov, 2001). Planned localisation economies in Kazakhstan are mainly facing decline due to their unsuitable location for inter-regional development, chosen originally on the basis of requirements for the functioning of the Soviet system. However, these locations were not efficient for the operation of the Kazakhstani economy. Nevertheless, there were some economies of localisation, such as hydrocarbon rich regions, which were located close to each other and benefited from clustering by the close access to hydrocarbon specific non-traded inputs, the fast travel of information on specific innovations of the oil and gas industry and access to a labour pool with specific skills. As a result, the Kazakhstani economy became highly dependent on such few localised economies.

Changes in the transition process of the Kazakhstani economy can be considered in terms of the agglomeration process where the human capital migration model and endogenous growth theory are most appropriate for understanding the process of changes in the transition economy of Kazakhstan. Since the transition process started, the unbalanced development of Kazakhstani regions has played an important role. The development of internal industrial cooperation would be more efficient for the growth of the economy, than the complete dependence on external links. Following the Lucas argument, regions well endowed with the labour of higher human capital than in other regions, achieve economic growth. In the case of Kazakhstan, the example is the ex-capital Almaty, which is the centre for better opportunities for higher education. As a result, the productivity of labour in the city is higher than in other regions, due to the higher level of human capital stocks. At the same time the human capital migration model assumes that labour with a higher level of human capital is more likely to migrate across regions, which explains the migration of highly educated labour to the new capital Astana. Thus, Kazakhstan has two centres of agglomeration in terms of labour with high human capital, which are Almaty and Astana. Individuals, who acquired a higher than average level of education in a particular region, have an incentive to move to one of the two capitals, in order to maximize the returns of the human capital they acquired. As a result, these two centres benefit from the higher level of education of their labour, which increases the efficiency of production and total regional economic development. However, other regions suffer from an outflow of highly educated specialists and decline of their economic growth.

Romer's argument regarding the increasing level of regional specialisation, which affects the growth of regional production, can be applied to the western part of Kazakhstan which is well-endowed with oil and gas, and which attracts the major percentage of Kazakhstani foreign direct investment. As a result, western regions of Kazakhstan have the highest level of production growth in the country, while other regions face an outflow of specialists and lack investment. The western regions of Kazakhstan have highly specialised industries, requiring skills that cannot easily be acquired in the short term. However due to the wage differential, the migration into the western regions should still occur from low-wage industries of other regions (Sjaastad, 1991). The existing situation of Kazakhstan does not show any signs of the balancing of regional development or tendency towards the equalisation of regional factors, while there are three agglomeration centres of factors, which tend to grow at the cost of other regions.

The sources and types of agglomeration economies analysed above provide a strong argument for the hypothesis that the Kazakhstani transition economy is gradually moving towards urbanisation economies, which is, however, a very slow process. The geography of Kazakhstani industrial production changed across the regions since 1991. It is possible to provide evidence in support of the argument that the Kazakhstani geography of industrial production is changing in response to the agglomeration of the economy towards urbanisation. The evidence can be observed in two types of indices of industrial concentration and regional specialisation.

3.4.3 Industrial concentration and regional specialisation of transition economies and its changes

Regional specialisation is maintained for the relative small changes of the movements of skilled labour supply due to where it was historically based and due to the almost unchangeable nature of the location of industrial clusters. However, the level of regional specialisation and industrial concentration can change in response to the agglomeration process. Thus, *Hirschmann-Herfindahl* and *Location Quotient* indices have been used in the study in order to capture the agglomeration effects on industrial spatial structure and geographical specialisation.

The *Hirschmann-Herfindahl* (*HH*) index measures the extent of the spatial concentration of a certain industry (Ellison and Glaeser, 1997), denoted here as *HH* and can be calculated by using the formula:

$$HH_I = \sum_{j=1}^{J}(s_{Ij} - x_j)^2$$

(11)

where s_{Ij} share of a particular industry I in a region j as a proportion of the national production of the industry I, and x_j is the share of aggregate national GDP in each region j[66]. The HH index, which varies between zero and two, is calculated for each industry separately and captures the extent to which an individual industry is unevenly distributed across an economy, and indicates the extent to which localization economies may be significant for the industry as a whole. The higher value represents a more spatially concentrated industry[67].

The *Location Quotient* (*LQ*) index measures the level of regional specialisation in a certain industry and can be calculated, using the following formula:

$$LQ_{I_j} = \frac{GDP_{I_j}/GDP_j}{GDP_{I_N}/GDP_N}$$

(12)

where LQ_{Ij} is the *Location Quotient* for a particular industry I_j in region j, the subscripts I, j and N represent industry, region and national level, respec-

---

66 SIj can be calculated using the following formula: $\dfrac{V_{Ij}}{V_I}$; where VIj is production of
industry I in region j, and VI is the national production of industry I.

67 The HH index will be equal to 0 in the situation where output is perfectly evenly distributed across all spatial areas. In this case, the difference between SIj and xj will be equal to 0 and consequently the HH index, which is the sum of squares of these differences, will be 0 as well. In the situation where a country consists of 2 regions of identical size and two industrial sectors, and each region is completely specialised in one of the two sectors (such that each region produces all of the national output in a single sector), then the HH index for one of these industrial sectors will be: $(1-0.5)2+(0-0.5)2 = 0.5$, where $SIj = 1$ and $xj = 0.5$ for the first region, where the industry is concentrated and $SIj = 0$ and $xj = 0.5$ for the second region. In the situation where regions remain completely specialised, and one region is 99 times bigger than the other region, then for the industry which is concentrated in the small region $SIj = 1$, but $xj = 0.01$ for the small region and $SIj = 0$, and $xj = 0.99$ for the bigger region. Therefore, $HHI=(1-0.01)2+(0-0.99)2=1.9602$, which is nearly equal to 2 and defines the high level of concentration of a particular industry.

tively. As such, this index reflects the extent to which a particular region benefits from any spatial industrial concentration, as captured by the *HH* index and
whether the region is the importer or exporter of goods and input factors (Ellison and Glaeser, 1997). If *LQ* index value is greater than 1, the region is a
net exporter of a particular industrial production, while a value less than 1
means that the region is a net importer.

Based on the argument that industrial clusters keep their historical location
due to Krugman's key facts[68], the *Hirschmann-Herfindahl* index would stay
similar over years showing that established industrial sectors would not significantly change their location, except for newly developing industrial sectors,
which are in the process of choosing their location. However, in the case of
transition, the regional specialisation in terms of the *Location Quotient* and industrial concentration, *Hirschmann-Herfindahl* index, may undergo more significant changes over the years than in the case of an established western
economy.

---

68   There are two strong forces, which induce the agglomeration process and "... keep
     a manufacturing core in existence...", these two forces are: first is that firms wish to
     locate in places close to larger markets and second that workers wish to be located
     in places with easy access to products produced by other workers. (Krugman,
     1991).

Table 3.1. *Hirschmann - Herfindahl* index for Kazakhstani industrial sectors

Industrial sectors	1990	1996	2001
Chemical	0.089	0.091	0.077
Fuel	0.089	0.089	0.079
Light	0.078	0.097	0.097
Food	0.080	0.084	0.087
Machine-building	0.080	0.092	0.090
Metallurgy	0.089	0.081	0.079
Power	0.087	0.076	0.089
Timber	0.090	0.097	0.098
Construction materials	0.088	0.099	0.099

Source: Indexes are calculated using data from: *Promyshlennost' Kazakhstana: 1990, 1995-1998 goda*, 1999. *Promyshlennost' Kazakhstana: 1990-1997 goda*, 1998. *Promyshlennost' Kazakhstana i ego regionov: 1998-2001 goda*, 2002.

In the case of Kazakhstan, many large industrial factories were shut down, due to the loss of their market and mismanagement after the collapse of the Soviet Union. As a result, *HH* and *LQ* indices may vary over the years of transition. Table 3.1. and Table 3.2. present measures of industrial concentration and location specialisation indices in Kazakhstan over the ten years of the transition period back to the year 1990, which was the last year of the socialist economy in the Soviet Union. A higher value of the *Hirschmann-Herfindahl* index indicates a higher spatial concentration of particular industrial sectors, while a value of zero would correspond to the perfect spatial dispersion of the considered industrial sector.

242   NATALYA SHEVCHIK KETENCI

Table 3.2. Location Quotients[69] for Kazakhstani regions

Regions	1990	1996	2001
Akmola	0.58	0.94	0.42
Aktubinsk	0.80	1.03	1.15
Almaty	1.08	0.50	0.51
Atyrau	0.78	1.48	1.57
Eastern Kazakhstan	1.20	1.21	0.98
Zhambyl	1.17	0.63	0.91
Western Kazakhstan	0.46	0.84	0.64
Karaganda	1.38	1.60	1.27
Kzylorda	0.42	0.96	1.74
Kostanai	0.72	0.94	0.89
Mangistau	0.95	1.55	1.74
Pavlodar	1.18	1.25	1.39
Northern Kazakhstan	0.89	0.41	0.44
Southern Kazakhstan	1.10	0.97	1.04

Source: Indexes are calculated using data from: *Statistical Yearbook of Kazakhstan –
1991*, 1992. *Statistical Yearbook of Kazakhstan – 1997*, 1998. *Statistical
Yearbook of Kazakhstan*, 2001.

Measures of Table 3.1. indicate that the spatial concentration of all Kazakhstani industrial sectors has been changed since 1990. The *HH* index in Table
3.1. gives evidence that the distribution of Kazakhstani industrial sectors is
not even across the regions. Changes in the *HH* index, which appeared
through the transition decade indicate transformation in the spatial concentration of industries and show the rapid tendency of industrial sectors towards
the higher spatial concentration of particular industries[70]. Thus, only the

69   The *Location Quotient* here represents the measure of regional specialisation for
the whole Kazakhstani industry, including all industrial sectors, which are introduced
in Table 3.1, for the measure of *HH* index.
70   As the maximum value of the index can be 2, any small changes in the value of the
index illustrate significant movements of industrial concentration on the basis of a
multi-regional country like Kazakhstan, which consists of 14 regions, while in a
country of 2 regions such changes would be insignificant.

power industry had a value of the HH index in 2001 close to its value for 1990, while the values of the HH index for the chemical, fuel and metallurgy industries declined significantly, which means that the level of concentration of these industries had declined across the regions. Despite the location-specificity of the fuel industry, its level of distribution across regions had increased mainly on account of oil and gas extraction. Regions rich with hydrocarbon resources concentrated intensively on the growth of their production during the transition decade, as it was the only industrial sector which could attract investments to the region. During the transition period, the Kzyl-Orda region joined the hydrocarbon producers group due to the discovery of new oil fields. Oil extraction in the region accounted for 17.1% of the total production in Kazakhstan in 2001.

The coal extraction of the fuel industry also extended its geography, increasing its production in Akmola, Zhambyl and Southern Kazakhstan regions, even though it accounted only for relatively small shares of the total Kazakhstani production. The chemical industry includes the petrochemical sector and extended its geography together with the growth of the hydrocarbon sector, even though the production level had declined by 79% over the first transition decade, and its share of national production fell from 6% in 1990 to 1.3% in 2001 (Chapter 2 The effect of transition on regional development). The non-ferrous sector of the metallurgical industry is one of few sectors which had a higher level of production in 2001 than in 1990. Its growth and the extension of its geography is due to the value of non-ferrous metals for foreign investors. The growth in the level of spatial concentration of other industries – light industry, food, machine-building, timber and construction materials is a consequence of the reduction of output in many regions. The production of many industrial enterprises of these industrial sectors in Kazakhstan declined significantly, and many of them were shut down, due to the collapse of the Soviet system and the severance of industrial links with enterprises of other Soviet republics. As a result, the spatial concentration of these industries had increased not for the reason of the intensification of production, but because of the failure of existing ones.

These activities are also reflected in the changes of the values of the *Location Quotient*. It can be seen in Table 3.2. that the number of regions with high industrial specialisation stayed the same over the first transition decade. However, specialised regions themselves have changed since 1990. Thus, the value of the *LQ* index significantly dropped in the Almaty and Zhambyl regions, which mainly specialised in the *machine-building, construction, light* and *food* sectors. The loss of the industrial specialisation in these regions appeared mainly to be due to the dramatic failure in the whole country of the *machine-building* and *light industry* sectors. The notable growth in the value of the index for the *Atyrau, Mangistau* and *Kzyl-Orda* regions can be explained by the high concentration of regions on hydrocarbon production, which attracts a significant share of Kazakhstani investment. Other industries of these regions experienced continuous decline due to their non-competitiveness with imported goods and the low value of the *LQ* index for the region compared to hydrocarbon industries. The change in the value of the *Location Quotient* as well as that of the *Hirschmann-Herfindahl* index in the transition economy, taking the case of Kazakhstan, was partly due to the reallocation of individual sectors, but primarily a consequence of the decline and even collapse of different sectors in different regions.

Measures of *Location Quotient* and *Hirschmann-Herfindahl* indices from Table 3.1. and Table 3.2. provide additional evidence for the arguments discussed above to the effect that the transition economy is not static, but changeable at every stage. The decline in the level of spatial concentration of the *fuel* industry and the growth of regional specialisation of hydrocarbon-rich regions supports our argument of the agglomeration process in the transition economy, such that the creation of localisation economies can be observed in western Kazakhstan, while urbanisation economies are being generated in capital cities.

Results of changes in the agglomeration process are also reflected in terms of changes in the levels of wages, where additional evidence can be provided in favour of the shift of the Kazakhstani economy towards urbanisation economies.

3.4.4 The disequilibrium model of inter-regional labour migration in transition economies

In the centrally planned economies, real wages in the regions and all republics of the Soviet Union were approximately equal, except in labour intensive
industries such as mines and in distantly located regions with difficult living
conditions (e.g. the cold climate in Siberia or the far northern hydrocarbon-
rich regions of Russia), where higher rates of wages were paid. The production functions were also identical for enterprises from the same industrial sector, as industrial production was allocated across all republics of the Soviet
Union, in a manner which was considered efficient for the Soviet Union as the
whole country. However, the equality of the economies of regions and republics was not maintained by market mechanisms, but by central authorities,
which artificially held input factor and output prices equal. In the case of production losses, the government subsidised such enterprises. Transition
economies lost the central organ of price control and faced with partial market
regulations, where local authorities still determined prices for some important
food products. However, wages were no longer under central control, but
were set by the owners of enterprises, where employees were paid according
to the productivity of enterprises. As a result, locations of higher industrial development had higher levels of wages (Table 3.3.).

Table 3.3. presents an average level of nominal wages across Kazakhstani
regions, where *Rank* columns of the table indicate a higher level of wages
compared to the average in Kazakhstan with the increasing value of a rank.
The 6th and last column of Table 3.3. shows the percentage of relative
change of average wage value. The level of average wage at the beginning of
transition, 1990, was relatively similar in all regions of Kazakhstan (Table
3.3.). However, the level and ranking of regions according to their wage levels
had completely changed over the transition period compared to 1990, such
that regions based on oil and gas extraction joined the group of regions with
high levels of average wages, while regions that had a high level of industrial
development regions under the Soviet system, like Eastern Kazakhstan,
Southern Kazakhstan and Karaganda experienced a reduction in their average wage levels.

Table 3.3. The average regional wages (%, average Kazakhstani wage = 100)

Regions	1990	Rank[71], 1990	1996	Rank, 1996	1996 (1990=100)	2001	Rank, 2001	2001 (1996=100)
Akmola[72]	94	4	87	6	-7	56	1	-36
Aktubinsk	99	8	108	9	9	102	11	-6
Almaty[73]	115	13	63	2	-45	65	4	3
Atyrau	102	10	128	14	25	197	15	54
Eastern Kazakstan	102	9	104	8	2	93	9	-11
Zhambyl	110	12	72	3	-35	62	2	-14
Western Kazakstan	104	11	80	4	-23	109	12	36
Kara-ganda	93	3	118	11	27	89	8	-25
Kzylorda	115	14	112	10	-3	78	7	-30
Kostanai	89	2	102	7	15	69	6	-32
Mangistau	78	1	212	15	172	206	16	-3
Pavlodar	97	5	126	13	30	97	10	-23

71 Rank is given by author on the basis of increasing order of regional wages. The lowest level of rank, with value 1, corresponds to the region with lowest level of wages. Respectively, the highest level of rank with value 15 corresponds to the regions with highest level of wages.
72 Figures exclude capital in 2001.
73 Figures exclude capital for all indicating years.

Regions	1990	Rank[71], 1990	1996	Rank, 1996	1996 (1990=100)	2001	Rank, 2001	2001 (1996=100)
Northern Kazakstan	99	7	82	5	-17	64	3	-22
Southern Kazakstan	119	15	62	1	-48	65	5	5
Astana city	-	-	-	-	-	124	13	-
Almaty city	98	6	120	12	22	126	14	5

Source: Indexes are calculated using data from: *Statistical Yearbook of Kazakhstan – 1991*, 1992. *Statistical Yearbook of Kazakhstan – 1996*, 1997. *Statistical Yearbook of Kazakhstan, 2001*.

Since 1996, average wage levels across regions started to move in different directions, where the highest level was observed in hydrocarbon-rich regions, like Mangistau and Atyrau. By 2001 disparities between regions significantly increased, such that the highest level of the average wage was 3.7 times the lowest level in 2001, 3.4 times in 1996 and only 1.5 times in 1990. Except in the hydrocarbon-rich regions, the growth of average wage levels can be observed in the capitals of Kazakhstan, which had the highest rank of wage levels in 2001 after the Mangistau and Atyrau regions. All regions, whose activity is connected to oil and gas production, have higher than average levels. These regions also include Aktubinsk and Kzylorda, however, the industrial average wage level in these regions is higher than the average Kazakhstani industrial wage level by 20% and 15% respectively, while the average level of the whole economy in these regions is much lower, due to the high concentration on the development of oil and gas industries.

In 1996, Karaganda and Pavlodar had an excessive level of average salary by the standard of the average Kazakhstani level, where coal production had the highest level of wages even in Soviet Union time. However, in 2001 the distortion of average salaries had increased significantly, due to growth in the hydrocarbon-rich regions and the two capitals, and a decline in other regions in terms of the average national salary. A most interesting and paradoxical fact that can be observed by comparing the Akmola[74] and Almaty regions to the capital cities that they contain. It can be seen that the cities of Almaty and Astana have one of the highest levels of average salaries. However, the regions in which the capitals are located have themselves the lowest levels of average salaries in the country. All economic activity is concentrated in the capitals, while their surrounding regions are living by other rules.

Hence transition economies can be described as economies of disequilibrium, where growing differences between wage levels in the regional economies of Kazakhstan can be observed. However, the disequilibrium model analyses the mechanism where differences in inter-regional real wages cause labour to migrate to regions with higher real wages until the point of equalisation with regional real wages is reached. Disparities that have arisen in the transition period encourage labour to move to better regions. However, regions that do not benefit from migration, do not gain from the labour and capital reallocation as the neoclassical and disequilibrium models would describe. Marginal products of labour and capital do not grow because of their lower ratios compare with better performing regions (from neoclassical model), but their industrial production declines even further.

Taking the example of the two Kazakhstani capitals, Almaty and Astana, it can be seen that by offering higher wages in the location of the new capital, authorities attract labour from other regions by creating the disequilibrium in the economy. However, due to conditions of uncertainty, labour does not move very quickly from one region to another, but adjusts to the new information over a time period t, which begins when the individual receives informa-

---

74 Akmola region is the region of the new capital Astana. The region has different name from its central city name for the reason that Astana city had many different names in the past, where one of the most significant for the Kazakhstani history was Akmola. Therefore, after giving a new name to the city as the capital of Kazakhstan, the name of the region stayed as the old name.

KAZAKHSTANI ENTERPRISES IN TRANSITION 249

tion on the better wages offered in other regions, until the moment when he/she decides to move. The Almaty city can be seen as the centre[75] of the Kazakhstani economy at the current moment, as it has a higher average level of wages, and does not require labour with specific skills, as in the case of hydrocarbon-rich regions.

Thus, the example of growing disparities between average wage levels across regions supports the argument, which was discussed in the previous section, that there is an agglomeration process in the Kazakhstani transition economy, which moves towards urbanisation economies. Higher wages in the Kazakhstani capitals attract human and physical capital that maintains the development of urbanisation economies.

The disequilibrium of wages in the transition economy in the example of Kazakhstan (Table 3.3.) refers to the centre-peripheral development of the economy, where intensive development is observed in a few centres, which can be considered as developing localisation economies, i.e. the hydrocarbon regions, and developing urbanisation economies of the Kazakhstani capitals, while other regions are on the edge of survival.

As previously discussed, there are three locations in Kazakhstan which could be considered as centres of the agglomeration economy: they are the ex-capital Almaty, the new capital Astana and the hydrocarbon regions located in western Kazakhstan. Comparing peripheral regions to the three centres of high economic activity in Kazakhstan, it can be seen that the difference between their average wages, which include all sectors of the economy and the wage levels in other regions grew significantly during the first decade of transition (Table 3.3.).

Thus, it appears that the whole economy of Kazakhstan can be described by the concept of the disequilibrium model, where inequalities between centres and peripheries are growing very fast. Despite that, the biggest business cen-

75 The centre here is referred to the centre-periphery model, where the economy of a country has one or few regions, which economics are highly distinguished from other regions by the level of diversification and by higher standards of living.

tre of Kazakhstan - Almaty city - is the most expensive city. It is still the final target for many citizens that are searching for better lives, as the wage level is also higher there. There is a high level of migration to Almaty city from other peripheral regions, which increases every year. The migration especially became one of the characteristics of rural undeveloped areas with young people heading to the central cities for better opportunities. Thus, the disequilibrium exists in transition economies not only on the regional level, but also on the urban and rural levels, as in rural areas the age of the labour pool is significantly increasing. As a result, disparities between urban and rural areas are growing even more rapidly, than between regions. Transition economies, particularly in ex-Soviet countries, have the centre-periphery type of economy, where the best quality labour seeks to move to the centre for its intellectual fulfilment, which in addition to low standards of living, it cannot achieve in peripheral regions.

Western economies have multiple centres, where the periphery and centres are much closer to an equilibrium with the same level of utilities than in transition economies. It will probably take a long time for the equilibrium level to be reached in transition economies, when centres such as Almaty are going to be crowded and expensive enough to inhibit further migration, and other centres will form, such as the artificially created centre represented by Astana city. The new capital is still too young to permit any conclusions about its centrality. It is supposed to be the second centre, however, evidence of wage differentials and enterprises transferring to this location, support the argument of the development of an urbanisation economy. The transformation of transition economies to multi-centre economies, particularly Kazakhstan, will take a long time due to its vast territory, which is considered to be peripheral except for one city – Almaty. Almaty is the centre for easy access to the information on the operation of the market. The concentration of market trading institutions, the highly educated labour and advanced level of the development of businesses allow production activities of surrounding enterprises to grow on the basis of extracted information on the modern development. However, it takes a long time to spread across the regions, so that by the time the information is disseminated it is out of date. In addition, the more distant a location is from the centre, the slower the speed of information and the less risk individuals are ready to take. Having fewer opportunities, peripheries prefer to take less risk in order not to make the situation worse, and to preserve what they already have. Such an attitude in the peripheries makes prolongs the transition period, and creates high regional inequalities, which are very difficult to reduce as the development of the centres progresses further.

Even though peripheral regions do not have opportunities to act themselves in order to reduce the disparities with the centre, the chances of external help are also low. Kazakhstan attracts many international companies, especially, those connected to hydrocarbon production. Branches of all of these international companies and international embassies are located in Almaty, due its position as a capital and as a relatively developed city in Kazakhstan compared to other regions in terms of the infrastructure. Therefore, Almaty attracts foreign investment for the improvement of its infrastructure, providing an adequate telecommunication and transportation network for the faster connections of locally based branches to their headquarters. Most foreign capital is concentrated in Almaty (although part of it is moving to Astana city) and in regions which are sources of valuable mineral resources, while the remaining regions are out of the game. As a result, the disparities between regions that do not receive such attention and investment from abroad and those that do is increasing.

Evidence of the high probability of regional disparities in transition economies was found in research conducted by Petrakos (2001) taking Poland, Hungary, Romania and Bulgaria as a case study. One of the results of the research was that even the best performing transition economies with the centre - periphery model of the economy, would be faced sooner or later with increasing regional inequalities. However, countries with diversified economies have a higher probability of faster adjustments to the market economy with lower costs of the transition than economies with high regional specialisation. Nevertheless, comparing specialised regions and backward regions of a transition economy, highly specialised regions in a particular industrial sector have a greater likelihood of faster development and adjustment to the new economic rules than backward regions. In transition economies, especially taking the case of the former Soviet Union, many industrial sectors faced a dramatic decline of their production and in many cases the termination of the operation of factories. Heavy industrial regions were "drivers" (Bachtler and Downes, 1999) of the economy in the centrally planned system, however, the transition brought unsuccessful experience of the privatisation process and enterprise restructuring in addition to the reorientation of secure subsidised markets to the uncertain market economy system and the loss of subsidies. As a result, highly specialised regions of a particular industrial sector suffered from industrial collapse caused by the transition process. However, these regions have higher chances of developing prosperity than the backward regions of Soviet times, due to the existence of better infrastructure than in backward regions and a higher level of skilled labour, which used to service the prosperous industrial sectors in the Soviet system. The old and almost useless infrastructure will be easier to revive than to build a new infrastructure from scratch.

All the evidence discussed above supports the argument of regional economic theory that the economy is in the state of change. Particular transition economies face changes in all sectors. In the beginning of transition the state property was dominating in the Kazakhstani economy, however by 1999 the share of private property increased to 68.4%, while the share of state property declined to 21.9%, and the remaining 9.7% of property belonged to foreign owners (*Kazakhstan: 1991-2001*, 2001). The extended geography of industrial reorganisation creates growing disparities in regional development. Industries develop intensively and converge in locations in response to market signals. Regional wage disparities (Table 3.3.) provide evidence of the disequilibrium type of model in Kazakhstan, where labour is moving towards locations with higher wage levels, which supports the argument of the development of agglomeration economies in favour of urbanisation economies.

3.5 Conclusions

Regional development is one of the weakest points of transition economies, as neither in the Soviet economy nor in the transition regional development was a priority, even though it plays an important role in the maintenance of economic growth in Kazakhstan. Industrial sectors were mostly developed next to the raw materials base, however, manufacturing and the production of finished goods were allocated in relation to the market demand. Production of finished products was located in territories of different republics of the Soviet Union. However, this was not a problem as this took place under the socialist system, which was based on central planning, governed by the principle of soft budget constraint. Central authorities reduced the power of enterprise management, dampened their initiative and self-sufficiency by sending production orders in the form of compulsory plans and keeping the finances under the control of the government. All excessive profits of enterprises were confiscated by the authorities, while the planned production volume for the next period was increased. At the same time enterprises or projects which were incurred losses, were supported by soft subsidies or credits.

The collapse of the Soviet Union destroyed the centrally planned economy. The newly independent states faced the problem of maintaining the economy and industrial production without the previous links to other ex-Soviet republics and central management. Realising that the industrial allocation of the Soviet Union no longer worked, transition economies entered into a period characterised by the struggle for survival whilst heading for the same goal, the market economy. The regional approach to the market economy is represented in this chapter by the neoclassical one-sector and two-sector models of regional factor allocation and migration, by the disequilibrium model of inter-regional labour migration, where regional factors are freely mobile between regions and by different types and sources of agglomeration economies.

Thus, transition economies seek to become market economies, however, they are still far away from this goal due to the initial disproportional regional development, which created inter-regional economies distortions. A. Alchian's (1950) concept of uncertainty conditions and Marshall's (1920) key incentives of agglomeration process indicate that inequalities between regions of transition economies prolong the transition to the market economy and render it more difficult. The new way of enterprise management was not the standard example to follow, but every enterprise chose its own way of survival or followed enterprise-leaders. Many agglomeration centres, which were created during the Soviet system, were not able to maintain their structure due to the closure of many factories due to the loss of trade connections with ex-Soviet republics. Several industrial centres, which were located around the ex-capital Almaty, Caspian regions producing hydrocarbon and a newly developing centre around the new capital Astana were able to continue.

The case of wage differences across regions provides evidence that the Kazakhstani economy is in the state of disequilibrium, such that human capital and enterprises are converging to higher profit locations. This supports the argument for the shift of the agglomeration process of the Kazakhstani economy towards urbanisation economies. The information on the development and transition to the market economy is circulating very quickly in those active industrial and economic centres. However, the remaining 14 regions of Kazakhstan are operating under uncertain conditions, where there is a time lag for information and capital transfers.

The development of transition has the objective to transform the economy into a market economy, but the conditions of uncertainty make this a long-running process. Ex –Soviet countries are in this special position because they do not only change the system from the socialist to the market economy, but at the same time they learn to live as independent countries and not part of a giant controlling system. Thus, the special position of these countries creates more obstacles to overcome and questions to solve. The most obvious of these is equal development of the regions.

The general types of relationships which can be observed between regional location, density and productivity of Kazakhstan, and the effects of industry and regional location on the transition performance, are broadly similar to those of the economy of Russia as a whole (Hanson and Bradshaw 2000). As such, although Kazakhstan is much smaller than Russia, the spatial economy characteristics of Kazakhstan can be viewed as something of a micro-version of the Russian economy. The regional performance characteristics, which appear to be common to large-area transition economies, seem to be a result of both different interregional industry compositions and different regional geographies. The inter-regional factor allocation and migration in one-sector and two-sector models is highly correlated with the performance of industries of regional specialisation. Therefore, in order to determine which (if any) of macro-economic aspects of regional performance are dominant, requires us to disaggregate both the structural and locational aspects of industry, and to distinguish between the relative contributions of different interregional industry compositions and different regional geographies on the performance of individual firms. This is exactly the purpose of the next chapter. The employed database allows to integrate micro-level firm data with aggregate regional and industry data of both a spatial and a non-spatial nature. Given the data available to us, the most direct econometric technique which can be used to do this is multinomial logit modelling. However, in order to motivate our econometric approach, it is first necessary to specify a theoretical model which is appropriate to both the Kazakh spatial and economic structure and also the particular data set which is at our disposal. The next chapter turns to this issue.

4   The Estimated Model and Results

4.1. Introduction

This chapter aims to investigate regional industrial restructuring within Kazakhstan in order to understand how advantage of location differs across all
fourteen regions of the Kazakhstani economy. The topic has not been previously investigated, except where it concerns discussions of the impact of
Caspian oil and gas endowments on the Kazakhstani economy as a whole
(Kalyuzhnova, 1998).

One of the aspects of the transition process which has tended to be under-
researched in the mainstream literature on transition, is the extent to which
the process of economic adjustment has differed between regions within the
individual transition countries. In the regional economics literature there have
been a number of case studies of the regional aspects of transition (Gorzelak
1996; Artobolevsky 1997; Hanson and Bradshaw 2000), plus some limited
aggregate data analysis of this issue (Myant 1995; Bachtler 1992; Smith
1995, 1998). However, what is largely missing in the transition economics literature is any microeconometric analysis of the regional aspects of the transition process. Yet, from a microeconomic perspective this is a central issue,
because any aggregate changes in regional industrial structures will be the
result of microeconomic changes on the part of individual firms and enterprises. The lack of any widespread microeconometric analysis of the regional
aspects of transition process is largely due to a paucity of reliable data.
Therefore, this chapter aims to make a microeconometric contribution to the
available body of evidence of the nature of the transition process.

In order to test the production behaviour of industrial enterprises in the transition economy using the example of Kazakhstan it is necessary to find a
model, which would test the production behaviour of individual industrial enterprises relative to their characteristics. Several hypotheses are proposed on

the basis of arguments discussed in the previous chapter and will put forward the suggestion that the performance of industrial enterprises and their location in regions with a high industrial production level depends on the set of individual, industrial and location characteristics of industrial enterprises. The *first hypothesis* tested in the study examines the dependence of an enterprise's performance on its individual characteristics, which includes location, industrial and individual specific characteristics. The *second* hypothesis examines the association of characteristics of industrial enterprises in transition economies with their location, testing to what extent characteristics of industrial enterprises in transition economies are statistically different for different locations.

The methodology of the current research is to employ the production function where the profit maximisation changes would reflect changes in the enterprise's characteristics at the individual, industrial and location levels. Empirical results presented in this chapter are obtained by multinomial logit models, which refer to equations 11 and 12 of the current chapter and are deducted from the production function.

Given the data available to the study, the most direct econometric technique which can be used to do this is multinomial logit modelling, which is described in section 4.3 *The background to the model* of the current chapter. Here the response variable is taken as categorical data, while explanatory variables include different types of data, such as categorical, continuous and dummy variables. The logit estimates were generated by the statistical package STATA.

The data for empirical tests combine both national and survey statistics, where the survey statistics consist of a unique micro-level database of 1374 Kazakhstani firms, which consists of 5597 observations, and based on the questionnaire on Kazakhstani industrial enterprises and their qualitative production activity performance conducted in Kazakhstan on a quarterly basis since 1994. Tests of both hypotheses include 20 quarterly cross-sectional estimations based on the same set of industrial enterprises but a different set of enterprises' characteristics between 1997 and 2001. Panel data estimations are impossible in this case due to the inclusion of different sets of enterprises for every observational quarter, even though they belong to the same set of industries and regions. The cross-sectional estimations of the heterogeneous sample of industrial enterprises over time periods are employed in order to distinguish between the sectoral and regional influences on firm performance.

The chapter is organised as follows: section 4.2 provides the description and analysis of the database used in the study, highlighting advantages and disadvantages of the database information. Section 4.3 focuses on the framework of the suggested model and the introduction of variables for the two hypotheses tested in the study. Finally, section 4.4 provides and analyses the results of the tests of two hypotheses based on the framework of the model, introduced in section 4.3.

4.2 The source and processing of the data

4.2.1 Questionnaire

The study is based on a survey, which consists of a set of questionnaires that was given to Kazakhstani industrial enterprises. The purpose of the survey is to provide information on Kazakhstani industrial enterprises, which can then be used to estimate, manage, develop and report on industrial development. The survey was designed and carried out by the Institute of Economic Research under the Ministry of Economy in Kazakhstan and was first conducted in Kazakhstan in 1994. This was then repeated half-yearly in 1994 and has continued on a quarterly basis since 1995. The survey is being used to obtain information, such as data on the growth of individual industrial enterprises, which is not available from other sources. Therefore, the survey is the only comprehensive source of information about the evolution of Kazakhstani industrial firms and the causes of their failures.

Table 4.1. The number of firms who participated in the survey on a quarterly basis.

Year/Quarter	I	II	III	IV
1994	63	0	85	0
1995	86	101	100	93
1996	110	268	282	271
1997	243	320	308	287
1998	279	204	298	234
1999	202	250	205	240
2000	158	150	176	114
2001	112	139	130	117

The survey consists of questionnaires, which have approximately 200 responses from industrial firms for every quarter, even though it varies each time (Table 4.1.).

The questionnaire was presented in Russian, and was translated by the author into English (Table 4.2.). The author also created and designed the electronic form of the database for later research. 1374 different enterprises took part in the questionnaire, creating 5597 observations for the whole period of the survey between 1994 and 2001 except for two quarters in 1994 when the questionnaire did not take place. Every questionnaire has a different set of respondents (i.e. enterprises). Some of these were repeated in several questionnaires as during the time of the survey rapid changes occurred in the industrial life of the country. During this period many enterprises closed down as they were not able to survive after the loss of industrial links with enterprises from other former Soviet republics. At the same time it was during the second and third phases (Kalyuzhnova, 1998) of the privatisation process in Kazakhstan when many state enterprises were privatised, their name changed and sometimes the type of output they produced, and it was therefore difficult to keep track of questionnaires relating to the same enterprise. This is why the research is based on questionnaires from a different set of enterprises over different quarters. The data estimations were based on the assumption that all sets of enterprises were similarly distributed by given categories, which would allow comparisons with each set of enterprises.

The questionnaire itself consisted of a set of questions (the translated version is given in Table 4.2.). Sampled firms were asked to complete the questionnaire on the characteristics of the firm and their production performance. The questionnaire was divided into two main parts. The first one was the introduction and the second part contained questions on the production activity of an enterprise. The introduction was at the top of the page. It always contained the same questions in every quarter on the details of the enterprise and thus read practically like a business card of the enterprise. The questions were as follows:

1. title of the enterprise;
2. regional location;
3. industry;
4. main production output;
5. type of ownership;
6. number of employees;
7. production volume in monetary terms (this question was introduced in the questionnaire from the third quarter of 1997);
8. year and quarter of the survey.

The question *Title of the enterprise* is included in the questionnaire only for reasons of identification for further data estimations, while all enterprises were given a guarantee of confidentiality with regard to the use of the information only for data estimations. *Regional location* of enterprises was represented by 14 regions where the questionnaires were distributed and collected (Table 4.3.), while the *industries* of Kazakhstan are represented by 9 fields that correspond to the division of Kazakhstani industry into different sectors. (Table 4.4.).

Table 4.2.   The translated version of the questionnaire, example of the fourth quarter 1997.

Questionnaire   Quarter IV Year 1997

Title of the enterprise

Location of the enterprise by region

Employment size of the enterprise
<50
51-100
101-200
201-500
501-2000
2001-5000
>5000

Ownership type
State
Joint Venture
Joint Stock
Private
Others

The main output of the enterprise

The industry of the enterprise

The production volume for the previous quarter in the local currency

Current quarter assessment questions	Next quarter assessment questions	Special questions
1. Production of the main output compare to the previous quarter. Growth / Unchanged / Decline	9. Estimation of production activity for the next quarter. Growth / Unchanged / Decline	18. Impediments for the company production activity are: 1. Insufficient domestic demand 2. Insufficient foreign demand 3. Shortage of raw materials 4. Financial difficulties 5. Customers bad debts 6. Unstable tax policy 7. Others
2. Evaluation of the economic situation of the company. Good / Satisfactory / Bad	10. Estimation of the company's economic situation for next quarter. Better / No changes / Worse	19. Changes in investments: a. 1997 compare to 1996 year. Growth / Unchanged / Decline / No investments b. 1998 compare to 1997 year. Growth / Unchanged / Decline / No investments
3. Number of personnel employed compare to the previous quarter. Growth / Unchanged / Decline	11. Expected number of personnel employed in the next quarter. Growth / Unchanged / Decline	Including foreign investments a. 1997 compare to 1996 year. Growth / Unchanged / Decline / No investments b. 1998 compare to 1997 year. Growth / Unchanged / Decline / No investments
4. Main output prices compare to the previous quarter. Strong growth / Slow growth / Unchanged / Decline	12. Main output prices in the next quarter. Strong growth / Slow growth / Unchanged / Decline	
5. Demand for the company's main output in comparison with previous quarter. Growth / Unchanged / Decline	13. Demand estimations for the company's main output for the next quarter compare to the current quarter. Growth / Unchanged / Decline	20. Impediments for the next year investments 1. Low profit 2. Hard budget constrains 3. Difficulties in credit obtaining
6. Company's export compare to the previous quarter. Growth / Unchanged / Decline	14. Estimation of the export in the next quarter. Growth / Unchanged / Decline / No export	21. How do you plan to use investments? 1. Replacement of the new equipment 2. Developing production of existing output 3. Introduction of a new technology
7. Total amount of finished goods in the warehouse. Big quantity / Normal quantity / Small quantity	15. To what extent is your company's capacity used at the present time (% in comparison with full capacity)? 16. For how many weeks you can use your stored raw materials?	4. Energy saving measures 5. Environment protection measures 6. Introduction of new output types 7. Others
8. How did raw material stocks changed compare to the previous quarter? Growth / Unchanged / Decline / No stocks	17. How did prices for raw materials change compare to the previous quarter? Increased / Unchanged / Decreased	22. Competitiveness of the main output at: a. Domestic market. Increased / Unchanged / Decreased b. Foreign market. Increased / Unchanged / Decreased

Table 4.3. Kazakhstani Regions

	Regions
1	Akmola
2	Aktubinsk
3	Almaty
4	Atyrau
5	Eastern Kazakhstan
6	Zhambyl
7	Western Kazakhstan
8	Karaganda
9	Kzyl-Orda
10	Kostanai
11	Mangistau
12	Pavlodar
13	Northern Kazakhstan
14	Southern Kazakhstan

Table 4.4. Industries of Kazakhstan

	Industries
1	Chemical
2	Construction Materials
3	Fuel
4	Light
5	Food
6	Machine Building
7	Metallurgical
8	Power
9	Timber

The main production output denotes the type of an enterprise's main output. For the whole period of the research there are 158 types of main output across the whole range of industry.

Types of ownership of enterprises are represented in the questionnaire by five different categories (Table 4.5.), where the classification of the National Statistics Agency means that *State* type of ownership implies the entire control of the assets and management of an enterprise by the government. *Joint Venture* enterprises have their property and management divided between indigenous (private or public) and foreign owners where the shares of each party are specified in an agreement and vary with each different case. *Joint Stock* (public) type of ownership gives rights to an enterprise to issue and sell its shares publicly, while shareholders do not run the company but have rights to elect the board of directors for its management and control. *Private* enterprises have one or several owners, who control the property of an enterprise and run its management with unlimited liabilities and with no public access to their shares. The category *Others* (Table 4.5.) represents different sub forms of private ownership, particularly the private form of Joint Stock ownership type with limited liabilities, where shares belong only to a limited number of owners. In this category, respondents themselves specified the types of ownership of their enterprises.

However, in order to be able to assess the ownership types in the database, the presentation of different types was rearranged and grouped into four categories according to its increasing order of market orientation in terms of public access to their shares (Table 4.6.). Therefore, *State* enterprises are introduced at the beginning of the ranking because they are closed for market and public access. The *Joint Venture* enterprises are ranked by the second value because the property can still belong to private owners as well as to state and foreign partners. This fact represents the first step of the shift of the state ownership towards the private, but shares are divided between owners and still cannot be sold to the public. *Private* and *Other* types are grouped together indicating the group of enterprises with different types of private ownerships, such as privately owned, family owned or partnership enterprises with limited access by the public to their shares. Private ownership introduces the next stage of the enterprises' openness to the market, where the ownership of the enterprise is completely private and can be divided between several owners. However, access by the public to their shares is closed. *Joint Stock* enterprises represent the final category in the ranking of the market-oriented enterprises in the survey. This is the type of ownership most open to the market compared to other categories, because *Joint Stock* enterprises can have an unlimited number of shareholders, where access to the shares of enterprises shares is unrestricted, both on the stock exchange and to the general public.

Table 4.5. Types of enterprise ownership as entered in the questionnaire

	Ownership type
1	State
2	Joint Venture
3	Joint Stock
4	Private
5	Other (specified by respondents)

Table 4.6. Types of enterprise ownership categorized for database estimations

Rank	Ownership type
1	State
2	Joint Venture
3	Private + Others
4	Joint Stock

The *number of employees* of an enterprise is represented in the questionnaire by a choice of seven different thresholds (Table 4.7.), where an enterprise with 50 or less employees is the smallest and is ranked as 1, while an enterprise with 5000 or more employees is the largest and is ranked as 7. All seven thresholds of the size of the workforce are ordinally ranked according to the increasing order of employment size.

The *production volume in monetary terms* gives information on the output value produced over the previous quarter (relative to the quarter in which the questionnaire was conducted) in local currency terms. However, only 50% of all participants answered this question. There could be several reasons for the reluctance to reveal the true financial situation. Among them could be the fear of information being discovered by their competitors, who could increase the competition against them, and the fear of information being disclosed to tax authorities, in the case of hidden extra profit, which could increase the tax payable. Despite the confidentiality agreement of the questionnaire, enterprises might still be afraid of giving truthful information.

Table 4.7. Size of enterprises by employment

Rank	Employment
1	<50
2	51-100
3	101-200
4	201-500
5	501-2000
6	2001-5000
7	>5000

The second part of the questionnaire, placed in the lower and main section of the questionnaire layout (Table 4.2.), is divided into three sections with different types of questions. The first section is contained 8 questions on the assessment of the current quarter where, with the rare exception of one or two questions, these are not changed over each quarter. The second section also contains 8 questions and asks for information on the forecast of the production activities of an enterprise in the following quarter. Special questions are contained in the third section of the main questionnaire and those questions are changed over different quarters or years. Specific questions in the questionnaire are continuously being added, removed or modified, but the main core of the questionnaire has remained almost unchanged since the beginning. The number of questions has varied every quarter from 22 to 27 questions.

1. *Questions on the firm's current development* are a core part of the questionnaire and evaluate the current conditions of a firm. These are:

- production of the main output compared to the previous quarter;
- evaluation of the economic situation of the company compared to the previous quarter;
- number of personnel employed compared to the previous quarter;
- main output prices compared to the previous quarter;
- demand for the company's main output compared to the previous quarter;
- company's export volume compared to the previous quarter;
- total amount of finished goods in the warehouse compared to the previous quarter;
- how raw material stocks have changed compared to the previous quarter.

Respondents (i.e. enterprises) answer these questions by choosing one optional qualitative answer (*increased, unchanged, decreased*). The same choice is applied to questions relating to the estimations by enterprises of their future performance.

2. The section on the *firms' estimations of their development in the next quarter* is designed to collect unique information on firms' estimations of their future performance. This information shows the companies' plans and abilities to realise these plans. This section includes the following questions:

- estimation of production activity for the next quarter;
- the company's estimation of the economic situation for the next quarter;
- expected number of personnel employed in the next quarter;
- main output prices in the next quarter;
- demand estimations for the company's main output for the next quarter;

- estimation of exports in the next quarter.

3. *Specific questions* are changed on a quarterly basis. These questions provide information which is only needed for intermediate purposes according to
the requirements of economic research and current changes in the economic
environment of the country. Among the specific questions there are three
quantitative questions; the remainder are close-ended with several optional
answers:

- To what extent is your company's capacity used at the present time (%
  in comparison with full capacity)? Quantitative answer specified by re-
  spondents.
- For how many weeks can you use your stored raw materials? Quantita-
  tive answer specified by respondents.
- The rate of using manpower (%) (the rate of working labour to listed la-
  bour)? Quantitative answer specified by respondents.
- How did prices for raw materials change compared to the previous
  quarter?
- Impediments for the company's production activity are: (5-10 options).
- Changes in investment?
- Impediments for next year's investment?
- How do you plan to use your investment?
- Competitiveness of the main output in domestic and foreign markets?
- The number of personnel working in part-time jobs?
- Financial sources of the company's investment?
- Technical level of the company? Possible answers.
- Share in the total volume of production in percentage of main and un-
  profitable output?
- Reasons for continuing the production of unprofitable output?
- Do seasonal factors affect production activity?
- Reasons for the decline in numbers of personnel?
- Do you intend to introduce new technology to the production process in
  your company during the next year?
- Estimation of work places in the next year?

- If you have planned investment for the next year, which fields of production activity will you invest in?
- Do you intend to introduce new types of output?
- How is payment for your output delivery received (with delays or not)?
- Reasons for delayed payments are?
- Do you plan a reorganisation of your company in 1995 (several options for possible reorganisations)?
- Measures for improvement in sales?
- Measures to avoid shortages in raw material stocks?
- Overdue indebtedness in current quarter compared to previous quarter - for debit and credit?
- Which methods of amortisation are used in your company?
- Are you satisfied with the methods of amortisation used?
- Do you use amortisation for non ultimate expenditures;
- Import of input compared to the previous quarter?
- Estimations of import of input for the next quarter in comparison with the previous quarter?
- Reasons for any growth in production?
- Estimations of profit for the current quarter compared to the next quarter?
- Is your company's output competitive with import alternatives in the domestic market?
- Do you plan to introduce projects in 2001-2005 concerning import substitutes and increases in export?
- What are your changes in production costs?
- Do you intend to increase the range of output and to increase production volume in the next year?
- Which competitors are more significant for your production activity, domestic or foreign?

All the questions in the questionnaire are given in the close-single and close-ended form, where the enterprise has to give particular answers to questions on the title of the enterprise, regional location, industry and main production output (close-single questions), while the rest of the questionnaire has close-ended questions with a choice of limited answers. The questionnaire does not have open questions, where respondent (the enterprise) has freedom in the answers, and in this way the data extracted from the questionnaire can be more easily and precisely estimated. Before creating the electronic version of the questionnaire, all responses were coded according to the increasing or decreasing order of the value of responses[76].

4.2.2 Quality Check of Responses

Three questions were used in the estimations of models of the current research and they are:

1. Production of the main output compared to the previous quarter (dependent variable in the first model and independent variable *Production volume* in the second model), (see 1st question in Table 4.2).
2. Main output prices compared to the previous quarter (independent variable *Output price* in the second model), (see 4th question in Table 4.2).
3. Demand for the company's main output in comparison with the previous quarter (independent variable *Output demand* in the second model), (see 5th question in Table 4.2).

Table 4.8. The distribution of answers in the questionnaire to the question *Production volume of the main output compared to the previous quarter, %.*

Years	Growth (1)	No change (2)	Decline (3)	National Statistics*
1997	27	35	37	104
1998	36	35	29	97.6
1999	38	31	31	102.7
2000	46	29	25	115.5
2001	45	28	27	113.8

*National Statistics shows the percentage of growth of industrial production in Kazakhstan on a year-by-year comparison.

---

76   A detailed description of the coding system of the questionnaire, together with the example table, can be seen in Appendix D *Database Design.*

Table 4.9. The distribution of answers in the questionnaire to the question *Main output prices compared to the previous quarter, %.*

Years	Growth (1)	No change (2)	Decline (3)	National Statistics*
1997	15	78	8	111.7
1998	10	76	13	94.5
1999	15	73	12	157.2
2000	17	75	8	119.4
2001	16	75	9	85.9

*National Statistics shows the percentage of growth in industrial prices of producers in Kazakhstan on a year-by-year basis.

Table 4.10. The distribution of answers in the questionnaire to the question *Demand for the company's main output in comparison with previous quarter, %.*

Years	Growth (1)	No change (2)	Decline (3)	National Statistics*
1997	9	64	28	37646
1998	7	66	28	-46904
1999	8	62	30	140068
2000	18	64	18	356077
2001	16	68	16	288244

*National Statistics shows the profit level of industrial enterprises, mln. Tenge.

Table 4.8. shows the distribution of responses of industrial enterprises to the question *Production volume of the main output compared to previous quarter.* Responses are almost evenly distributed in the three categories of answers: *Growth, No Change* and *Decline*, where the balance between answers corresponds to the general trend in the economy of slow growth in 1997-1999 and accelerating growth of production in 2000 and 2001, where the percentage of industrial enterprises choosing the *Growth* answer increased to 46%. At the same time, the growth of total Kazakhstani industrial production increased from fluctuating around 4% in 1997-1999 to a solid 14% in 2001 according to

National Statistics. Figure 4.1. represents[77] the comparison of the growth trends in industrial production on the basis of the National Kazakhstani Statistics. It is apparent that an increasing percentage of industrial enterprises chose *Growth* options in the questionnaire during the later period. It can be seen from the comparison with the maps that there is the same trend towards growth in the answers of industrial enterprises to questions relating to the production of the Kazakhstani industry.

---

77   Maps on the left-hand side with the title *Questionnaire* represent the growth trends in Kazakhstani regions on the basis of responses of industrial enterprises. The colour varies according to the majority of responses. In 1997, in the AKT (Aktubinsk) region the majority of respondents (more than 50% but less than 100%) gave answers of 'no change' with regard to their industrial production. In 1999, in the KAR (Karaganda) region 50% of respondents gave answers of 'growth' and 50% of respondents gave answers of 'no change' with regard to the levels of industrial production. The *National Statistics* section is defined by a slightly different method, where only total changes in regional industrial production can be seen, without the division of the percentage of industrial enterprise performance. Therefore, in 1997, the KOS (Kostanai) region had overall growth in industrial production, while the AKM (Akmola) region had an overall decline in industrial production. National Statistics, in 1998, indicates that ATY (Atyrau) region did not have any change in the total level of industrial production. Maps were created in order to follow the general tendency of change in industrial production on the basis of questionnaire responses in comparison with National Statistics. In this way the gradual move in the *Questionnaire* maps from red towards green and blue, indicates the gradual increase in the percentage of the chosen answers by respondents to the growth in their industrial production. This tendency is compared to National Statistics maps where the same tendency is observed through the years of change in colour from red to green. This indicates that the general trend towards growth in industrial production in Questionnaire responses coincides with the total picture of National Statistics, where through the years an increasing number of regions experienced growth of their industrial production.

Figure 4.1. The growth tendency of regional industrial production in the questionnaire, in comparison with national statistics.

1997

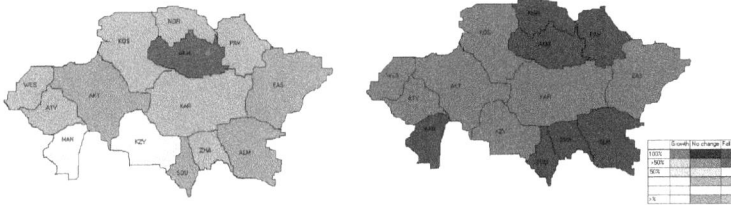

Questionnaire   National Statistics

1998

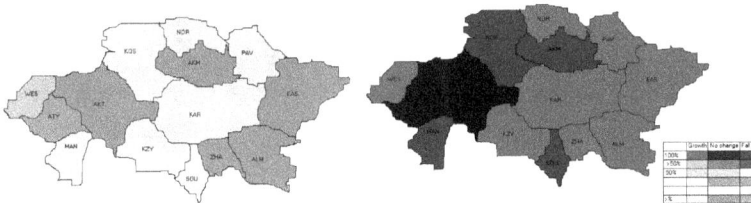

Questionnaire   National Statistics

1999

Questionnaire

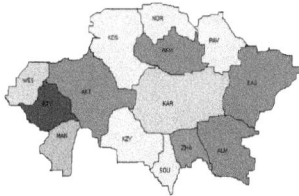

National Statistics

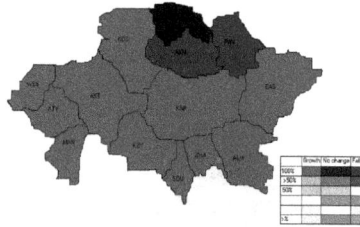

2000

Questionnaire

National Statistics

2001

Questionnaire   National Statistics

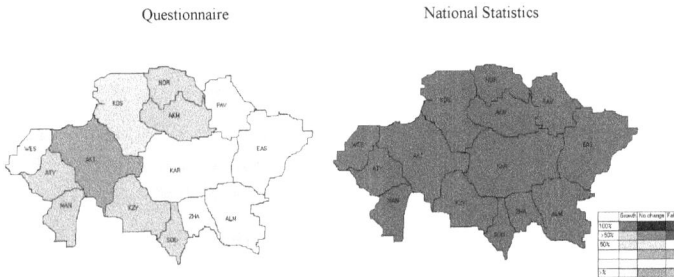

Table 4.9. represents the distribution of responses of industrial enterprises to the question *Main output prices compared to previous quarter*. The main percentage of industrial enterprises, more than 70%, chose the answer *No change* for 1997-2001. However, the National Statistics data shows high fluctuations in prices for industrial producers, where the highest growth was in 1999 (57.2 %) and the steepest decline occurred in 2001 and amounted to a fall of 14.1%. These fluctuations in prices were due to the relative growth and decline of world oil prices at the end of 1999 and 2001, which affected the oil and gas industries. Thus, by the end of 1999 the output prices of oil and gas extraction had increased by more than 150% from the end of 1998, while in 2001 these prices declined by 28.7% compared to the previous year *(Statistical Yearbook of Kazakhstan, 2002)*. Such high fluctuations in industrial production are not reflected in the general tendency of the responses to the questionnaire, because the questionnaire sampled only 5% of hydrocarbon related industrial enterprises. However, despite the small sample, in 1999, 26% of hydrocarbon related industrial enterprises indicated growth of their output prices, while this number declined to 11% in 2001, when the National Statistics also indicated a decline in the prices of industrial producers.

Table 4.10. presents the percentage of answers to the question *Demand for the company's main output in comparison with previous quarter,* where the main percentage of industrial enterprises, more than 60%, chose the answer *No change.* The last column of the table gives figures from National Statistics on the profit level of Kazakhstani industrial enterprises, whose growth could be a proxy for changes in output demand using the assumption that growth in demand increases the profitability of enterprises, *ceteris paribus.* The percentage of industrial enterprises choosing the *Growth* answer, has a tendency to increase between 1997 and 2001. This fact corresponds to the National Statistics figure on the total profit level of Kazakhstani industrial enterprises. In 1998, the profit level of Kazakhstani enterprises was negative, where at the same time the questionnaire has the lowest percentage (7%) of industrial enterprises with *Growth* answers. The low level of profit can be explained by the effect of the Russian crisis rather than a fall in demand. The hardness of the Kazakhstani Tenge until April 1999, made Russian goods relatively cheap compared to local goods as a consequence of the Russian financial crisis in August 1998. However, the float rate of the Tenge since April 1999 and the increase in taxes on imported goods from neighbouring Russia and Kyrgyzstan, increased local demand and the profitability of industrial enterprises by 100-200%. This is reflected in the figures from the questionnaires, where the percentage of industrial enterprises with *Growth* in the demand for their output increased to 16-18% in 2000-2001.

Responses to the analysed questions on Kazakhstani industrial enterprises follow the tendency to economic changes and economic outcomes presented by the National Statistics. Therefore, the analysis of the above questions can be considered as reliable information, based on information of official sources. The model variables combine data from the questionnaire and from National Statistics, which are compatible with the economic analysis.

4.2.3 Sample Representativeness
In order to examine the sample representativeness it is necessary to compare survey data with National Statistics. Appendix represents a comparison of the questionnaire and National Statistics data. Every chart is based on the annual

data and compares the distribution from the sample of the number of industrial enterprises from the questionnaire and from National Statistics, extracting separate data on the level of regions and industries. Figures in Appendix indicate the overall representativeness of the questionnaire sample, where the share of industrial enterprises of the Kazakhstani survey corresponds to the average distribution of industrial enterprises in Kazakhstan on the basis of regions and industries.

4.3 The background to the model

4.3.1 The Theoretical Model of Firm Performance and Location

Modern theories of regional development (Krugman 1991; Porter 1990; Gaspar and Glaeser 1998; McCann 1998) assume that in a market economy, the geographical distance of the firm from specific locations is an essential determinant of its performance. In particular, the relative proximity and accessibility of the firm to specific urban locations, is assumed to be fundamental to the behaviour and performance of the firm. If this assumption is correct, the effects of this should also be observable in the case of a transition economy, which is moving towards a market-based system. In this section, we therefore develop a simple theoretical framework, which is partly based on this assumption, in order to allow the microeconomic effects of geographical location on transition behaviour to be tested, in addition to the effects of non-spatial characteristics of the firm. To my knowledge, in the case of a central Asian transition economy, this is the first piece of microeconometric research, which has explicitly attempted to disentangle the geographical from the non-spatial characteristics of the firm.

The theoretical model which is employed in the study is based on the approach initially set out by Lee (1982, 1990). It studied the location behaviour of the manufacturing firm in developing countries, Colombia and Korea by considering the production function of the firm, which captures the relationship between a firm's performance and its industrial and regional characteristics, with further transformation of the production function into the multinomial logit framework[78]. This type of theoretical model is used in order to provide the justification for the multinomial modelling approach, where performance indicators of the firm are introduced by qualitative response variables[79].

Following Lee's approach, in general terms the production function of a representative firm can be written as:

$$Q = Q[X;A] \qquad (1)$$

where Q represents the firm's output, X is a vector of inputs used, and A is the technology embodied in the firm. A will comprise a vector of the individual firm's characteristics, some of which are firm specific, some of which are industry specific, and some of which will be location specific. Within an explicitly spatial setting, the profit function of the firm located in region j can be written as (Kittiprapas and McCann 1999):

$$\pi_j = \left(P_o - t_o d_{oj}\right)Q(X;A) - \sum_{i=1}^{m}\left(p_i + t_{ij} d_{ij}\right)x_i - \sum_{i=m+1}^{n}(p_{ij} x_i) \qquad (2)$$

where: $(x_1, x_2, \ldots x_m, x_{m+1}, \ldots x_n)$ represents a vector X of inputs, where $(x_1, x_2, \ldots x_m)$ are transported inputs such as intermediate or imported goods, and $(x_{m+1}, \ldots x_n)$ are the location –specific inputs such as labour, land, local services and local raw materials. P_o is the market price of the output goods, p_i is the mill price of each transported unit of input i at region j, and t_{ij} and t_{oj} are the unit transportation cost per km of the transported inputs and outputs, re-

---

78   A similar approach was also used in Kittiprapas and McCann (1999) for viewing the location choice of individual firms in Thailand as a result of the firm having considered the set of characteristics.

79   Although, studies have drawn attention to the Kazakhstani economy, there are only a few highlights of regional industrial perspectives in transition economies and in particular Kazakhstan (see *Introduction* of Chapter 1, *The development of Kazakh SSR industrial sector on the basis of the Soviet economic system*). There is a gap in the area of modelling for industrial enterprises location behaviour in the worldwide literature. Particularly, there is a lack in empirical research for the location behaviour of industrial enterprises in transition economies. The model employed in the current research was applied previously in the literature to such developing countries as Colombia, Korea and Thailand. These types of model are extensively used in economic geography in other economies in order to distinguish between geographical aspects of enterprises performance and non-geographical characteristics.

KAZAKHSTANI ENTERPRISES IN TRANSITION   279

spectively, to and from the regional location j. The unit input cost of each location-specific input at regional location j is given as p_{ij}, and finally the distance from regional location j to each market or input source point is given as
d_{oj}, and d_{ij}, respectively. Rearranging the profit function (2) we have:

$$\pi_j = P_o Q(X;A) - \sum_{i=1}^{m}(p_i x_i) - \sum_{i=m+1}^{n}(p_{ij} x_i) - T \qquad (3)$$

where:

$$T = t_o d_{oj} Q + \sum_{i=1}^{m} t_{ij} d_{ij} x_i \qquad (4)$$

In other words, in equation (3) the total profit of the firm is defined as the total
output value, minus the total input costs and minus the total transactions
costs T, which includes the sum of output and imported input transaction
costs. The profitability of a firm is therefore the result of both spatial and as-
patial cost and revenue considerations.

In order to understand how the profit model (3) can be accommodated within
a real-world spatial economic framework we can begin by using a stylised example employed by Krugman (1991). We can imagine a hypothetical situation
in which all input and output markets are located in the same place, such as a
dominant urban centre denoted as U. In this case both d_{oj} and d_{ij} can be rewritten as d_{Uj}, and t_{oj} and t_{ij} can be rewritten as t_{Uj}. If local factor prices p_{ij} are
invariant across space, the firm will have no incentive to be located elsewhere
other than at U because its profitability will always be lower than at U. The
reason for this is that at U the value of T will be zero, whereas for any other
location, the value of T will be positive. Therefore, in order for a firm to make
equivalent profits at j, where j is any location different to U, the local input factor prices p_{ij} at j must be lower than the local factor prices p_{iU} at U, by an
amount which exactly compensates for the greater transactions costs T associated with being located at j. In this situation where the variation in local factor input prices p_{ij} with respect to p_{iU} is just sufficient to ensure that a firm is
equally profitable at all locations, the spatial economy can be perceived to be
in equilibrium. If the spatial variations in local factor input prices p_{ij} with respect to p_{iU} are less than the required equilibrium values, locations distant

from U will be less profitable than U. On the other hand, if the spatial variations in local factor input prices p_{ij} with respect to p_{iU} are greater than the required equilibrium values, locations distant from U will be more profitable than
U. As such, the profitability per unit of output of the representative firm depends on the interrelationship between the local factor prices and the distance-transactions costs associated with production at any particular location.

For a cross-estimation of firms of different types and different sectors which
produce a range of different outputs, the unit distance-transactions costs t_{Uj}
will be different for each firm type. As such, the equilibrium local factor input
prices p_{ij} at any region j at a distance d_{Uj} from U will be different for different
firms. For any given aggregate spatial variation of local factor prices, the spatial distribution of activities will therefore be different for different types of
firms, reflecting differences in the relative importance of accessibility to U for
different types of firms (Fujita, 1989; McCann, 2001). Firms, whose spatial
transactions costs are significant, will have a higher preference for proximity
to U than firms whose spatial transactions costs are relatively lower.[80] Such
transactions costs will also include the opportunity costs (McCann, 1995;
Gaspar and Glaeser, 1998) associated with distance, time and the need for
face to face contact, as well as the actual transportation financial outlays.
However, many of these opportunity costs are unobservable in reality, because they depend on the technology characteristics A of the firm. Similarly,
for different types of firms, the required optimum input quantities x_i will differ
according to the firm's technology characteristics A, and without additional
specific information, these are unknown to us *a priori*. Consequently, in order
to undertake an empirical analysis of a heterogeneous cross-sectional sample of firms, even in situations where we do have detailed geographical distance measures such as d_{Uj}, it is still usually necessary to employ additional
indirect approaches, in order to capture the relationship between distance-
transactions costs, technology and firm performance. One way of circumvent-
ing these problems of unobservable characteristics is to employ a probabilis-
tic framework, in which the performance of a firm is specified as being a func-

---

80   These transactions costs will also include the opportunity costs associated with dis-
      tance as well as the actual financial outlays (McCann, 1995).

tion of both observable and unobservable characteristics. The simplest and most direct method of doing this is to transform our profit function (3) into a multinomial logit framework.

Suppose there are J regions (j =1,.....J) and the distance between the major urban centre U to each region varies according to the geographical location of the region. If we assume that the market price for inputs and outputs in the dominant urban location U are independent of the distance-transactions costs of transported goods within each individual region, at the optimum output level, then the profit function (3) can be rewritten as:

$$\pi^*_j = g_j \left[X^* \left(A, p_{ij}, d_{Uj} \right) \right]$$ (5)

where X^* represents the optimum input mix, and d_{Uj} represents the distance from each region to the major national urban centre. Assuming that enterprises are operating at or close to their optimum input mix, the general profit maximization condition for the firm can therefore be written as:

$$\pi^{max}_j = g_j \left(A, p_{ij}, d_{Uj} \right)$$ (6)

Introducing a random error of unexplained firm and location variables given as e_j, which are assumed to be Weibull distributed, the profit maximization function now becomes:

$$\pi^{max}_j = g_j \left(A, p_{ij}, d_{Uj} \right) + e_j \quad j \in J$$ (7)

The expected profit function now contains a deterministic portion of observable enterprise and location characteristics and a random portion containing the unobservable attributes of the alternatives. Therefore, the probability that a firm will earn a higher profit in region j rather than any alternative region j' is:

$$P(j / j') = prob \left\{ g_j \left(A, p_{ij}, d_{Uj} \right) + e_j \right\} > \left[g_{j'} \left(A, p_{ij}, d_{Uj} \right) + e_{j'} \right] \right\}$$ (8)

where j' is any alternative region and $j' \neq j$; where $j, j' \in J$. This now allows for a logistic estimation of the probability of the firm achieving higher profits in region j to any alternative region j', according to (Judge 1985) approach:

$$P(j / j') = \frac{\exp \left[g_j \left(A, p_o, p_{ij}, d_{jj'} \right) \right]}{\sum_{j' \in J} \exp \left[g_{j'} \left(A, p_o, p_{ij}, d_{jj'} \right) \right]}$$ (9)

Assuming all parameters are linear, and assuming that we can decompose A into a vector of constituent characteristics defined as $a_1....a_z$, which represent the firm's individual, industry or location-specific characteristics, we can write equation (9) as a mixed logit function of the firm, industrial and regional location attributes as:

$$P(j/j') = \frac{\exp(\alpha_1 + \beta_1 a_1 + ... \beta_z a_z + \beta_{ij} p_{ij} + \beta_{uj} d_{Uj})}{\sum_{j' \in J} \exp(\alpha_1 + \beta_1 a_1 + ... \beta_z a_z + \beta_{ij'} p_{ij'} + \beta_{uj'} d_{Uj'})} \tag{10}$$

where d_{Uj} represents the distance from the location of observable enterprise to the major national urban market centre. With a standard logit transformation (Wrigley 1985) it therefore now becomes possible to estimate the log-likelihood of an individual firm achieving a superior profit at location j relative to location j', in terms of:
(i) the firm-specific or industry-specific characteristics of the firm, defined as $a_1....a_z$,
(ii) the regional location-specific characteristics, defined as p_{ij}, where $j=1,....J$.
(iii) the distance between the regional location of the enterprises and the major urban market, defined as d_{Uj}.

Within the logit transformation of the profit maximisation function, it is now possible to estimate the likelihood of an enterprise located in region j experiencing production growth in connection with the characteristics of an individual enterprise.

Thus, the above theoretical model will be used to test two hypotheses, where the *first* hypothesis examines the dependence of the performance of industrial enterprises in transition economies on their individual characteristics, which include region, industrial and individual specific characteristics. The *second* hypothesis examines the association of characteristics of industrial enterprises in transition economies with their location. Therefore, it tests to what extent characteristics of industrial enterprises in transition economies are statistically different for different locations.

The tests of hypotheses employ the same sets of industrial enterprises over the given period, while characteristics differ. The reason for choosing a different set of characteristics for the test of the second hypothesis is the attempt to employ data purely on the basis of quarterly changes, due to the quarterly origin of the questionnaire data. As such, the second model is trying to test the hypothesis on the basis of quarterly data, which represent more sensitive changes in the economy due to the short-term of their collection. However, it does not mean that the first model yields an inaccurate analysis, even though it is based on quarterly as well as annual data. The annual data employed in the first model are specific industrial, regional and economic characteristics, which do not tend to have significant changes over the quarters. All these variables are described in the following section.

4.3.2 The Model Variables

The data employed in the study are both of a primary and secondary nature, and these are collected and analysed on a quarterly basis. The primary data come from the questionnaire, which is described in section 4.2 *The source and processing of the data*, in this chapter. The secondary data are taken from published Kazakhstani statistics, which are collected on a quarterly and annual basis and provide information for independent variables in the first hypothesis test as well as for the dependent variable in the second hypothesis test. Thus, model estimations combine the firm-level survey information with secondary data from the published Kazakhstani statistics, which provide information on the structure and performance of each of the respective industries at both national and regional scale.

The data we have at our disposal can be characterised in terms of variables of equation (10). For the variables defined above as $a_1....a_z$, there is a range of enterprise-specific, industry-specific and region-specific data. Firm-specific characteristics, *statusid* and *npeid* are included in the list of independent variables for estimations of both hypotheses tests, where the former variable defines ownership status of an enterprise, and the latter variable represents the employment size of an establishment (4.2.1 *Questionnaire*).

4.3.3 Variables for the test of the first hypothesis

In addition to two firm-specific variables, the model which tests the first hypothesis, employs two non-spatial industry-specific variables and two spatial

industry-specific variables. The first of the non-spatial industry-specific variables is the percentage change in national employment in the particular industry on the basis of a year-by-year comparison and is represented by the
variable $empindY_1Y_2$, where Y_1 and Y_2 represent comparison years. The second of the non-spatial industry-specific variables is $gdpsec\ Y_1Y_2$, which is the
percentage change in Kazakhstani GDP by industries on a year-by-year basis.

Apart from the firm specific and the non-spatial industry-specific variables, the
model also employs two spatial industry-specific variables, which are designed to capture the effects of an industry's spatial structure and geographical specialisation on a firm's, or an industry's performance. The first of the industry-specific spatial variables used, is the Hirschmann-Herfindahl index
(Ellison and Glaeser 1997), which indicates the extent to which localization
economies may be significant for the industry as a whole. A higher value
represents a more spatially concentrated industry[81]. In the model, the HH index is represented by the variable $hhindexindY_1$, which shows that the index
is calculated for the year Y_1 on an annual basis. Another measure of HH index is also included in the model - hhY_1Y_2, which represents the percentage
change in the HH index during the period between the beginning of year Y_1
and the beginning of year Y_2.

The second of the industry-specific spatial variables, which is employed in the
first model, is the standard regional industrial Location Quotient Index (Chapter 3), which is used in order to capture any additional region-specific effects
on a firm's performance associated with a particular region's specialisation in
any certain industry. As such, this index reflects the extent to which a particular region benefits from any spatial industrial concentration, as captured by
the HH index and whether the region is the importer or exporter of goods and
input factors (Ellison and Glaeser, 1997). The location quotient is represented
by variable $lq\ Y_1$, and as with HH index, the model also includes an additional

---

81   The detailed explanation of measurement of the HH index can be found in section
      3.4.3. *Industrial concentration and regional specialization of transition economies
      and its changes* in Chapter 3 *Regional economy in transition*.

variable $lq\ Y_1Y_2$ that captures the percentage change in a region's location quotient index on a year-by-year comparison.

The reason for including two regional spatial industrial variables $lq\ Y_1$ and $hhindexindY_1$, defined in levels terms, as well as the two variables $lq\ Y_1Y_2$ and hhY_1Y_2, defined in terms of current rates of change, is very specific. The rationale for this is to distinguish the extent to which current firm performance is determined primarily by the (initial or current) inherited spatial industrial structure, or whether it is actually determined primarily by current changes in these spatial industrial structures. In other words, we are seeking to identify whether it is the historical patterns or the current developments in the spatial industrial structure of Kazakhstan, which are dominant. If the inherited planned system is currently close to a market optimal spatial pattern, we would expect the level variables to dominate, whereas if the inherited system is not close to a market optimum, we would expect the change variables to dominate.

In terms of region-specific variables, the economic performance characteristics of a region which are independent of any particular industry or firm, but which may additionally affect the performance of an individual firm, are captured by a single variable. This variable is defined here as $emplY_1Y_2$, and represents the percentage growth of total employment across all industries in a region between Y_1 and Y_2 years. This variable indicates the extent to which the region as a whole is currently economically buoyant.

Direct regional and industry-specific data on Kazakhstani input costs is not available from published statistical sources, therefore, it is necessary to use an indirect indicator to capture the effects of the location-specific input cost variables defined in equation (10) as $p_{(m+1)j}....p_{nj}$. This variable is the regional GDP per capita for the observable year and is represented in the model by $gdpperheadY_1$. The logic of employing this variable can be understood from the spatial interregional equilibrium, where the local nominal factor input prices must vary in order to compensate for the distance-transactions costs associated with geographic peripherality. For equilibrium profit levels, the GDP per head will therefore tend to vary directly with local nominal input costs. Moreover, if spatial variations in local nominal factor prices also lead to substitution between capital and non-capital inputs, this index adjusts in the correct direction. As such, in the absence of detailed region-specific industry wage and land price data, the regional GDP per head index can be used as an approximation of the nominal level of local labour and land prices, adjusted for regional factor mixes.

The next variable is the mixture of region and industrial specific characteristics of the firm, which comes from the national statistics as a continuous variable - *industrprod* and represents the Kazakhstani industrial production in monetary terms by regions on a quarterly basis. The categorical variable, which is created from the described continuous variable, is introduced in the second hypothesis test as the dependant variable.

Finally, the model employs a purely spatial distance measure of the geographic peripherality of a firm's regional location. The measure is given as the distance in kilometres from the major population centre of each region to the nationally dominant urban centre represented by the Almaty region. Each of the regions is given an ordinal ranking on this basis. In the model, this is represented by *almrank* and has 14 ranks, where the closest region to Almaty has rank 1, which represents the Almaty region itself and the region, which is located at the furthest distance has rank 14. However, in order to allow for the fact that the spatial centre of gravity of the Kazakhstani economy may have moved with the recent relocation of the capital to Astana, we also include an equivalent distance measure to the new capital city of Astana, which is represented in the model by *astrank*.

In the case of cross-sectional data from a transition economy such as Kazakhstan, however, the model specification described by equation (10) must be slightly adapted in terms of the independent response variable employed. The reason for this is that in economic environments undergoing fundamental restructuring and which are not yet close to achieving interregional equilibria (Borts and Stein 1964), the current profits of a firm are not necessarily the best indicator of the medium or long-run profitability or viability of the firm. This is particularly true in the case of transition economies whereby monopoly enterprises are being restructured, and contracts and prices are slowly being established in markets that were previously missing (Hahn 1971). Moreover, such data may often be simply unavailable or at best very unreliable. As such, in these types of changing economic environments, the most appropriate dependent variable to employ for the first hypothesis as an indicator of medium or long-run firm performance may be an alternative indicator such as a firm's current growth. In this case, the current growth performance would be interpreted as the 'best guess' as to the overall future profit performance of the individual firm. Given the absence of any more sophisticated microeconometric data, this is exactly the approach we adopt here.

On the left-hand side of our cross-sectional data response variable is the current output change of the firm, and within the logit modelling technique we estimate the likelihood of a Kazakhstani firm experiencing current output growth as a function of a range of firm, industry and regional variables, as described above by equation (10). We interpret this likelihood of an individual firm's current growth as the best guess of its future performance. Although it is possible that for some firms long-run profit maximisation will be associated with reductions in current output, nevertheless we can assume that this is not the usual case, and that for the vast majority of firms, current output growth will generally be associated with a movement towards long-run profit maximisation. In other words, we assume that the firms which are currently successful (i.e. displaying growing output revenues) precisely because their current production and location characteristics are closer to their particular optimum conditions than those of firms which display current output declines.

The dependent variable of the first hypothesis test comes directly from the survey of Kazakhstani industrial enterprises, representing the categorical variable, which indicates whether a firm's output in real terms had *Growth* (1), stayed *Unchanged* (2), or *Decreased* (3) on a quarterly basis. These response categories are treated as being independent of each other, so there are no problems associated with the independence of irrelevant alternative assumptions.

On the basis of the explanatory and response data, the most appropriate technique is to construct a multinomial logit model with three categories in the response variable. Following the arguments in the previous section, the following logit equation will be estimated:

$$L = \alpha + \beta_1(stausid) + + \beta_2(npeid) + \beta_3(hhindexind) + \beta_4(hhY_1Y_2) + \beta_5(lqY_1)$$
$$+ \beta_6(lqY_1Y_2) + \beta_7(almrank) + \beta_8(astrank) + \beta_9(emplY_1Y_2) \quad (11)$$
$$+ \beta_{10}(empindY_1Y_2) + \beta_{11}(gdp \ s \ e \ cY_1Y_2) + \beta_{12}(gdpheadY_1) + \beta_{13}(industprod)$$

statusid	Ownership status of an enterprise.
npeid	The employment size of an establishment.
hhindexind	Represents the *Hirschmann-Herfindahl* (*HH*) index and measures the extent of the spatial concentration of a certain industry.
hhY_1Y_2	The percentage change in the *HH* index during the period between the beginning of year Y_1 and the beginning of year Y_2.
lqY_1	Represents the Location Quotient (*LQ*) index and measures the level of regional specialisation in a certain industry.
lqY_1Y_2	The percentage change in the *LQ* index during the period between the beginning of year Y_1 and the beginning of year Y_2.
almrank	The distance in kilometres from the major population centre of each region to the nationally dominant urban centre represented by the Almaty region.
astrnak	The distance in kilometres from the major population centre of each region to the nationally dominant urban centre represented by the Akmola region (Astana city).
$emplY_1Y_2$	The percentage growth of total employment across all industries in a region between Y_1 and Y_2 years.
$empindY_1Y_2$	The percentage change in national employment in the particular industry on the basis of a year-by-year comparison,

where Y_1 and Y_2 represent comparison years

$gdpsecY_1Y_2$ The percentage change in Kazakhstani GDP by industries on a year-by-year basis, where Y_1 and Y_2 represent comparison years.

$gdpheadY_1$ The regional GDP per capita for the observable year.

$industprod$ The Kazakhstani industrial production in monetary terms by regions on a quarterly basis.

whereby L is the estimated (logit) likelihood of an enterprise experiencing current output growth as a function of firm, industry and regional variables. The hypothesis being tested here is that the current performance of a firm is a function of the characteristics of the firm, its industry and location.

4.3.4 Variables for the test of the second hypothesis

The second hypothesis test employs different industrial and region specific variables compared to the first considered hypothesis. The next firm-specific categorical variable after the ownership type and employment size of an enterprise, which was also represented in the model of the first hypothesis, is – *productionvolume*. The variable came from the questionnaire and describes changes in the output of an enterprise, representing the response of enterprises to changes in their output compared to the previous quarter, where possible options were *Growth, Unchanged* and *Decline* with ascending ranking 1, 2 and 3 respectively. This variable was presented as the dependant variable in the model of the first hypothesis test, while it is the independent one in the second hypothesis test.

The categorical variable *outputdemand* represents the combination of firm and industrial specific characteristic, which is taken from the questionnaire and describes the change in the demand for an enterprise's output by three response options *Growth, Unchanged* and *Decline* with ordinal ranking 1, 2 and 3 respectively.

The output price p_o of equation (10) is performed in the model by the categorical variable *outputprices*, which is taken from the questionnaire and represents changes in the main output prices of an enterprise in comparison with the previous quarter, where categories of the variable are given by the ordinal rank of *Growth, Unchanged* and *Decline*.

Direct regional and industry-specific data on Kazakhstani input costs on a quarterly basis is not available. Therefore, it is possible to use an indirect indicator to capture the effects of the location-specific input cost variables defined in equation (10) as $p_{(m+1)\,j}\ldots.p_{n\,j}$. The chosen variable is the regional average nominal wage per employee on a quarterly basis and is represented in the model by *wage*. The logic of employing this variable is similar to the employment of the GDP per capita variable in the model of the first hypothesis, where the regional average wage per employee tends to vary directly with local nominal input costs for equilibrium profit levels. Therefore the regional wage is taken as an approximation of the nominal level of local industrial labour and land prices, adjusted for regional factor mixes.

Finally, a purely spatial distance measure of the geographic peripherality of a firm's regional location was employed in the model. In terms of the notation employed in equation (10) this is represented by $d_{jj'}$. On the basis of the arguments set out before, the simplest measure is given as the dummy variable *russianborder*, which divide all regions of Kazakhstan into two groups: regions that are located on the border with Russia and the remaining regions ranking 1 and 0 respectively in both groups. Another dummy variable *hydrocarbon* represents the mixed measure of distance, which is the regional and industrial specific characteristics and denote whether the region is endowed with hydrocarbon.

The employed dependent variable in the logit analysis comes from the national statistics as a categorical variable and divides the set of Kazakhstani regions J into three groups according to the level of regional industrial production in monetary terms. Thus, regions are distributed in groups with *High*, *Medium* and *Low* industrial production, which are ordinally ranked as 1, 2 and 3 respectively. The distribution of regions into these groups is changing through all quarters on the basis of changes in industrial production, where some regions can move from one group to another or stay in the same category if their industrial production did not change significantly compared to other regions.

The variables of the logit model represent data that consider regions in groups and not individually because otherwise the sample for estimations would be too small.

On the basis of the dependent and independent variables introduced above, the most appropriate technique is to construct a multinomial logit model with three categories in the dependent variable as listed above. Following the arguments in the previous section, the following logit equation will be estimated:

$L=\alpha+\beta_1(statusid)+\beta_2(npeid)+\beta_3(productionvolume)+\beta_4(outputprices)+$
$+\beta_5(outputdemand)+\beta_6(wage)+\beta_7(russianborder)+\beta_8(hydrocarbon)+$
$+\beta_9(astana)+\beta_{10}(almaty)$ (12)

statusid	Ownership status of an enterprise.
npeid	The employment size of an establishment.
productionvolume	Changes in the output of an enterprise in comparison with the previous quarter.
outputprices	Changes in the main output prices of an enterprise in comparison with the previous quarter.
outputdemand	Change in the demand for an enterprise's output in comparison with the previous quarter.
wage	The regional average nominal wage per employee on a quarterly basis.
russianborder	Dummy variable represents regions located on the border with Russia.
hydrocarbon	Dummy variable denotes whether the region is endowed with hydrocarbon resources.
astana	Dummy variable defines regions which belong to Akmola region (Astana city is the centre of the region).
almaty	Dummy variable defines regions which belong to Al-

maty region.

whereby L is the estimated (logit) likelihood of an enterprise located in the group of regions with higher industrial production rather than in the group with lower industrial production in monetary terms in connection with its characteristics. The hypothesis being tested here is that the regional location of an industrial enterprise in the well-performed regional group is a function of the characteristics of the enterprise, its industry and the location.

4.4 Result of the Estimations

4.4.1 The test of the first hypothesis
The hypothesis of the first model is that the performance of industrial enterprises in transition economies, in the example of Kazakhstan, depends on the set of spatial, industrial and individual specific characteristics.

Table 4.11. Expected signs of variables marginal effects on probabilities of changes in enterprises' production.

Probability (1)	Expected sign	Marginal effect signs of estimated significant variables
Statusid	+	-, +
Npeid	+, -	+
Hhindexind Y_1	+	-
Lq Y_1	+	-
Almrank	-	+
Astrank	-	Not significant
Empl Y_1 Y_2	+	-
Emplind Y_1 Y_2	+	-, +
Gdpperhead Y_1	+	Not significant
IndustProd	+	+, -
Probability (2)	Expected sign	Marginal effect signs of estimated significant variables
Statusid	-	-
Npeid	+, -	-
Hhindexind Y_1	-, +	+
Lq Y_1	-, +	+, -
Almrank	+	-, +
Astrank	+	Not significant
Empl Y_1 Y_2	-	Not significant
Emplind Y_1 Y_2	-	-
Gdpperhead Y_1	+, -	Not significant
IndustProd	+, -	+, -

Probability (3)	Expected sign	Marginal effect signs of estimated significant variables
Statusid	+	+, -
Npeid	-, +	-
Hhindexind Y_1	+	+
Lq Y_1	+	+, -
Almrank	+	+, -
Astrank	+	-
Empl $Y_1 Y_2$	-	+, -
Emplind $Y_1 Y_2$	-	+
Gdpperhead Y_1	-	+, -
IndustProd	-	-

Notes:

- Probability (1) – the probability of an enterprise having an increase in the production volume of output on a quarterly basis.
- Probability (2) – the probability of an enterprise not having any changes in the production volume of output on a quarterly basis.
- Probability (3) – the probability of an enterprise having a decline in the production volume of output on a quarterly basis.

Table 4.11. represents the signs of the marginal effect of variables employed in the model, and signs which could be expected on the basis of the analysis, given below. The table is horizontally divided into three main parts (*Probability (1), Probability (2), Probability (3)*) where predicted signs of marginal effect for every outcome of the dependent variable are given in the second column *Expected sign*. The third column *Marginal effect signs of estimated significant variables* present actual signs of variables estimations[82].

---

82 The multinomial logit model is presented by the log-linear equation: $\log_e \frac{P_j}{P_{j'}} = \alpha + \beta X_i$ with further transformation to equation (10). The marginal effects of variables estimates in the logit model cannot be interpreted from run of the logit

Probability (1) predicts and introduces signs of marginal effects of model variables when dependent variable takes value *1*, growth of enterprises' production volume. On this basis, the analysis will be made on the effect of enterprises' characteristics on the probability of growth in the production volume of industrial enterprises. *Probability (2)* defines the probability of enterprises' production staying with no changes, while *Probability (3)* examines the dependence of the probability of decline in the production of enterprises on their characteristics.

The marginal effect of the *Statusid* variable is expected to have a positive sign for the probability of production growth and decline and a negative sign for the probability of no changes in production volume. The higher the level of market orientation and liberalisation of an enterprise, the higher the probability that this enterprise will have a higher economic level of activity, which can lead to growth in the production activity as well as to its decline (in the case of failure). Consequently, a negative sign is expected for the probability of no change in the production due the negative effect of higher economic activity on the production stability of active enterprises.

The marginal effect of the *Npeid* variable could be expected to be positive as well as negative for the probability of the enterprises' production growth. Taking Alchian's argument, larger enterprises tend to dominate the market, having easier access to information sources, which could be used for their own advantage. Therefore, it could be expected that in larger enterprises there is a greater probability of growth of production, while under the conditions of heterogeneous firms and imperfect information, smaller enterprises would imitate the behaviour of market leaders (i.e. larger enterprises), due to their significant contribution to the market. However, there could be an alternative viewpoint in the conditions of the transition economy where there would be a low probability of production growth in larger enterprises, which were established in the pre-transition period, due to their lower flexibility to respond to

model. Therefore special computations were made for the derivation of the marginal effect on probabilities of event.

frequent and substantial changes due to the process of transition. The low flexibility of large enterprises would be expected because of hardening budget constraints in the course of transition, where the enterprises of a smaller size would be expected to engage in faster restructuring to achieve higher level of production. Therefore, the probability of the decline in production in large enterprises could be high during the transition period as a result of the time gap in the response to the transition innovations due to their larger size, which makes it difficult to react more quickly than enterprises in the market with a smaller workforce. However, the sign of the marginal effect on the probability of no change in the output of enterprises is doubtful and can be positive as well as negative.

The *Hhindexind* Y_1 variable indicates the spatial concentration of industries, where the higher value of the index denotes the higher level of the spatial concentration of the industry to which the particular enterprise belongs. Expected signs of the variable for the case of the transition economy may well differ from those of the case of a stable economy. Being part of a highly concentrated industry can be beneficial for enterprises as information on innovation can be communicated more rapidly between its enterprises. At the same time enterprises are more likely to be integrated horizontally as well as vertically. Enterprises of a highly concentrated industry may share the same sources of input as well as information. Therefore, the expected sign of the marginal effect of the variable on the probability of the growth of production is positive. However, under the conditions of the transition period, which is indicated by the high rate of change in the economy, enterprises of a highly concentrated industry are more affected by those changes than enterprises of industries that are more evenly spatially distributed. In the pool of enterprises of a particular industrial concentration, negative external elements affect the activities of enterprises as well as their input sources, which pull down the rest of the companies. Therefore, under the conditions of transition economy, the expected sign of the marginal effect of the variable on the probability of the production decline can be expected to be positive. The effect of the *Hhindexind* Y_1 variable on the probability of no change in the production volume can take both signs in dependence on the stage of transition under consideration. Thus, at the beginning of the transition decade, the effect of the variable on the probability of no change in the production can be negative due to the higher probability of the decline in the production of enterprises. However, in the middle of transition the sign of the marginal effect is likely to be positive with a following change to the negative sign at the end of the transition decade due to the recovery process, where the output of enterprises of a more highly concentrated industry is likely to grow.

The $Lq\ Y_1$ variable indicates the level of specialisation of a region in the particular industry, where a higher value of the index indicates a higher specialisation of the region. The marginal effect of the variable on the probability of production growth can be positive, assuming that enterprises located in the higher specialised regions and which do not belong to the industry of the region's specialisation, benefit from the proximity to industrial clusters through the regional infrastructure or by attracting other profits to the region. Nevertheless, the sign of the marginal effect is also expected to be positive for the probability of the production decline. Taking into account the instability of the transitional process of the country, all benefits resulting from the concentration of industry in the particular region, may be lost as a result of the negative effect of transition changes that were described above in the case of the $Hhindexind\ Y_1$ variable. The marginal effect of the $Lq\ Y_1$ variable on the probability of no change in the production can have negative as well as positive signs in accordance with the transition period phases. However, it is more likely to have a negative sign due to the high economic activity during transition, which would increase or decrease the production of enterprises rather than leave it unchanged.

The next spatially specific variables $Almrank$ and $Astrank$ are expected to have negative effects on the probabilities of the rise in the production and positive effects on the probabilities of the decline in production. The reason for this is that Almaty, the former capital and Astana, the new capital, are the two main transaction centres of the country where enterprises located nearby, have better access to finances and information for further development. As a result, industrial enterprises located at a distance from these two centres would have less access to finances and information for new research and development. For this reason industrial enterprises located a significant distance away from the former and new capital cities would be expected to have a low probability of growth of industrial production, and be more likely to experience decline or no change. The study covers the period between 1997 and 2001, which is at the end of the privatisation period and the beginning of the post-privatisation era. Consequently, during the period under consideration many industrial enterprises were in a very poor state with negative performance. Therefore, the unchanged level of their production through the quarters does not necessarily mean that enterprises are viable. It could mean that enterprises are kept going despite their poor performance in order to prevent their closure. Therefore, the probabilities of no change or a decline in the production of industrial enterprises located a long way from Almaty and Astana are expected to be high with a positive significance of variables.

The $Empl\ Y_1\ Y_2$ variable defines the overall employment growth of regions across industrial sectors. Therefore, $EmplY_1Y_2$ indicates the total growth rate of employment on a regional level. The higher level of regional employment growth would reflect the improvement of the regional economic situation, which would lead to a rise in production volume of enterprises located in a particular region, where the marginal effect of the $EmplY_1Y_2$ variable on the probability of an increase in the production of an enterprise would be expected to be positive. The probabilities of no change and decline in the production of industrial enterprises are expected to decrease as a result of regional employment growth, assuming that increases in regional production leads to positive changes of the activities of an enterprise.

The national growth in employment of a certain industry, which is defined by the $Emplind\ Y_1\ Y_2$ variable, is expected to have a positive effect on the production level of an enterprise. It is assumed that the expansion of the workforce of enterprises is based on increasing returns to scale in the transition economy, where more responsibility is assumed by enterprises for their productivity. Therefore, the marginal effect of the $Emplind\ Y_1\ Y_2$ variable is expected to be positive on the production growth and negative on the decline of the level of output of enterprises.

The last two variables Gdpperhead Y_1 and IndustProd are both specific regional characteristics of industrial enterprises and are expected to affect probabilities of production change in the same way. The Gdpperhead Y_1 variable indicates the level of GDP per capita in a region for the period Y_1. The higher level of GDP per head in a region would suggest a better economic environment for industrial enterprises located in this region compared to other regions. Therefore the marginal effect of the Gdpperhead Y_1 variable on the probability of the growth or stability of production of enterprises would be expected to be positive, while the effect of the variable on the probability of the decline of the production of enterprises would be expected to be negative.

The IndustProd variable indicates the level of industrial production in a region. The higher level of industrial production in a region consists of the higher level of production of its enterprises compared to other regions. Following the Alchian argument, enterprises of a larger size (in our case, size is defined by the level of production) have easier access to sources of information due to their market domination. Such enterprises have a higher probability of growth, than of decline. Thus, the higher level of industrial production of a region would positively affect the probability of industrial enterprises, located in the region, to achieve growth and negatively affect the probability of the production of these enterprises to decline.

Therefore, industrial enterprises located in regions with higher GDP per head and belonging to an industry with higher industrial production, would be expected to perform better.

Results of the test of the first hypothesis were obtained with the full set of variables introduced in section 4.3.3 Variables for the test of the first hypothesis. However, these results cannot be explained due to the statistical complications that were found in the data set, which caused the multicolinearity problem in the model. Three variables were found to be highly correlated with other variables that could affect the overall estimations results. These variables are:

- $gdpsecY_1Y_2$ – percentage changes in the volume of industrial production in monetary terms by industries over the year, where Y_2 is the year of observation and Y_1 is the comparison year.
- hhY_1Y_2 – percentage changes in the Hirschmann-Herfindahl index by industries over the year.
- lqY_1Y_2 – percentage changes in the Location Quotient Index by regions over the year.

Due to the multicolinearity problem, it was necessary to omit these variables from the model in order to obtain reliable results from the logit estimation. The omission of these variables does not invalidate the model. After omitting the $gdpsecY_1Y_2$ variable from the model, another alternative variable of this kind remains in the model and is represented by the $empindY_1Y_2$ variable. This variable is the industry specific characteristic and defines the percentage change in national employment by industries on the basis of a year-by-year comparison and is represented by the variable, where Y_1 and Y_2 are comparison years. This variable represents the relationships between the performance of an enterprise and its industrial specific characteristic.

Indices hhY_1Y_2 and lqY_1Y_2 represent alternatives to indices hh and lq, which are presented in the model and capture the spatial industry-specific effect of the behaviour of enterprises on a comparison basis with the previous year. The second category of the dependant variable is taken as the base category, which represents *No Change* in the production of the observable enterprise, while the first and third categories represent respectively *Growth* and *Decline* in the production of an enterprise.

Results of the multinomial model estimations for the first hypothesis.
In order to explain the effect of chosen variables on the probability of an enterprise's production performance, it is necessary to analyse estimations of variables marginal effects, which are presented in Table 4.12. The table is horizontally divided into three parts, which present measures of variables marginal effects on the probability of each category of dependent variable, which are: *Growth* (1), *No change* (2) and *Decline* (3) in the production of in-

dustrial enterprises on a quarterly basis. Each cell of the table contains a coefficient of the estimated variable marginal effect, standard error and z-statistics with significance levels (* for 1%, ** for 5% and *** for 10%).

Table 4.12. Marginal effect estimations of the first model

Year/Quarter	1997:I	1997:II	1997:III	1997:IV	1998:I	1998:II	1998:III	1998:IV	1999:I	1999:II	1999:III	1999:IV	2000:I	2000:II	2000:III	2000:IV	2001:I	2001:II	2001:III	2001:IV
Probability (1)	0.198	0.293	0.282	0.267	0.333	0.392	0.387	0.307	0.309	0.363	0.485	0.370	0.462	0.508	0.483	0.489	0.348	0.589	0.474	0.524
Pseudo R2	0.065	0.062	0.065	0.076	0.104	0.053	0.039	0.089	0.041	0.082	0.048	0.058	0.112	0.054	0.099	0.105	0.140	0.081	0.050	0.089
statsind	-.011	.061	.023	-.042	.014	.019	.032	.049	-.001	.066	-.002	-.033	-.152	.117	.127	.092	.049	.005	.002	-.048
rapind	.024	.033	.009	.031	.032	.038	.036	.04	.047	.054	.051	.045	.065	.079	.058	.073	.072	.078	.055	.067
	-0.46	1.82***	0.79	-1.34	0.44	-0.51	1.45	-1.24	-0.01	1.22	-0.04	-1.17	-2.34**	1.48	2.17**	-1.26	-0.69	0.06	0.03	-0.72
	.038	.01	.079	.086	.043	.031	.001	.086	.027	.049	.024	.052	.028	-.029	.024	.105	.024	-.024	.023	.047
	.019	.02	.019	.021	.029	.03	.022	.04	.025	.024	.031	.025	.035	.035	.033	.045	.039	.035	.034	.039
	1.95***	0.50	3.98*	4.24*	1.48	1.02	0.06	3.56*	1.07	2.03**	0.79	2.02**	0.79	-0.83	0.72	2.37**	0.63	-0.70	0.74	1.22
bhindexind Y1	-2.894	-6.933	2.91	-5.282	-16.93	7.867	-3.48	9.846	2.631	-.537	-1.822	-13.43	-7.402	.633	-3.657	4.287	3.958	4.585	-3.703	2.757
	4.227	4.134	4.138	3.973	4.912	5.77	4.871	4.931	5.568	5.167	5.839	5.461	4.215	3.704	3.851	4.168	8.108	7.053	8.865	8.181
	-0.68	-1.68***	0.70	-1.33	-3.45*	1.36	-1.12	-2.00***	0.48	-0.10	-0.31	-2.46***	-1.76***	0.17	-0.95	1.03	0.49	0.65	-0.98	0.34
lq Y1	-.138	-.562	.086	-.077	-.404	.083	.0255	-.137	-.144	-.015	.149	-.111	-.11	-.037	.124	.051	-.097	.092	-.031	.32
	.206	.221	.168	.126	.168	.183	.131	1.246	.139	.122	.167	.131	.198	.171	.177	.21	.176	.153	.172	.19
	-0.67	-2.55**	0.51	-0.61	-2.39**	0.45	0.19	1.10	-1.03	0.12	0.39	-0.83	-0.56	-0.22	0.70	0.24	-0.55	0.60	-0.18	1.68***
almrank	.012	.034	-.012	.012	.039	.025	.023	-.008	.024	.021	-.015	-.008	.067	.028	-.028	.018	.022	.001	.001	-.06
	.016	.014	.014	.015	.014	.022	.011	.015	.021	.013	.015	.012	.027	.023	.019	.024	.024	.026	.026	.033
	0.72	1.83***	-0.85	0.77	2.98*	1.18	2.04***	-0.57	1.14	1.60	-0.98	-0.68	2.51**	1.24	-1.43	0.72	0.92	-1.30	0.03	-1.82***
asrtrank	.005	-.014	.001	-.003	.005	.011	.023	-.012	-.012	.018	-.009	.003	.021	.005	.001	.023	.019	-.002	-.003	-.003
	.017	.015	.017	.014	.01721	.016	.012	.015	.013	.014	.015	.013	.024	.022	.019	.033	.013	.014	.014	.018
	0.30	-0.94	0.06	-0.21	0.27	1.36	1.92***	-0.80	-0.93	1.35	-0.57	0.24	0.88	0.25	1.07	0.11	1.07	-0.13	-0.45	-0.15
empl Y1Y2	-.019	-.033	-.004	.002	.013	.01	-.008	-.005	.049	-.017	.018	.025	-.007	-.017	.013	-.036	-.016	-.001	-.003	.025
	.009	.016	.009	.013	.012	.008	.0026	.003	.036	.024	.031	.023	.059	.042	.042	.052	.013	.012	.013	.014
	1.07	2.34**	-0.40	0.29	1.05	1.16	0.27	-1.48	1.34	-0.74	0.58	1.08	-0.11	0.06	0.32	-0.71	-1.17	1.00	-0.27	0.54
gdpperhrind Y1	.003	-.002	.002	-.001	.013	-.003	-.008	.005	-.001	.003	-.001	-.005	-.007	-.017	.013	-.023	-.007	-.011	-.001	.025
	.00001	.00001	.00001	.0002	.00001	.008	.001	.008	.0002	.002	.004	.004	.018	.013	.001	.002	.012	.011	.001	.001
	-1.43	-1.16	1.41	-0.88	1.77***	1.16	-1.11	0.56	-0.12	0.88	-0.18	-1.44	-2.04**	-1.38	0.00	0.89	-0.61	1.00	0.68	2.33**
Indusfprod	5.22e-06	.00003	-.00001	-1.52e-06	.00002	3.01e-07	6.53e-06	9.15e-06	.00002	-2.66e-07	-2.82e-06	7.05e-08	.00000104	1.83e-06	-7.31e-06	1.41e-06	-4.16e-06	-8.62e-06	-3.30e-06	-8.57e-06
	.00001	.00001	.00001	.00001	.00001	3.71e-07	.00001	.00001	.00001	.00001	.00001	.00000	.0001	.00000	.00001	.00001	.00001	.00001	.00001	.00001
	0.47	2.17**	-1.34	-0.18	1.77***	0.03	1.05	-1.17	1.19	-0.04	-0.51	0.02	2.18**	0.37	-1.52	0.23	-0.76	-2.02**	-0.67	-1.44

Year-Quarter	1997-I	1997-II	1997-III	1997-IV	1998-I	1998-II	1998-III	1998-IV	1999-I	1999-II	1999-III	1999-IV	2000-I	2000-II	2000-III	2000-IV	2001-I	2001-II	2001-III	2001-IV
Probability (2)	0.353	0.354	0.386	0.326	0.332	0.373	0.385	0.387	0.373	0.305	0.284	0.271	0.285	0.288	0.296	0.322	0.347	0.190	0.308	0.294
Pseudo R2	0.065	0.062	0.065	0.076	0.104	0.053	0.039	0.089	0.041	0.082	0.048	0.058	0.112	0.054	0.099	0.105	0.140	0.081	0.050	0.089
statusnd	.009 / .024 / .28	-.029 / .033 / -0.88	-.034 / .034 / -1.02	.002 / .038 / .04	.032 / .034 / -0.92	.007 / .039 / .18	.034 / .037 / .91	-.048 / .046 / -1.04	-.007 / .054 / -0.13	.031 / .051 / .60	.036 / .045 / -0.80	-.003 / .039 / -0.07	.08 / .061 / 1.32	.063 / .065 / -0.97	-.153 / .045 / -3.40*	-.036 / .066 / -0.54	.151 / .077 / 1.96**	-.089 / .047 / -1.91***	.008 / .049 / .16	.039 / .063 / .63
npeed	-.0001 / .024 / -0.01	.028 / .021 / 1.35	-.089 / .022 / -4.04*	-.061 / .022 / -2.78**	-.038 / .026 / -1.47	-.035 / .028 / -1.25	-.014 / .022 / -0.61	-.003 / .028 / -0.11	.014 / .029 / .48	-.028 / .023 / -1.26	-.056 / .028 / -2.03**	-.026 / .025 / -1.03	-.005 / .03 / -0.15	-.024 / .031 / -0.79	-.068 / .03 / -2.25**	-.063 / .044 / -1.45	-.023 / .049 / -0.45	.015 / .029 / .52	-.028 / .032 / -0.88	-.068 / .032 / -2.12**
hhanddemand Y1	2.604 / 5.166 / 0.50	9.416 / 4.349 / 2.17**	1.937 / 4.409 / 0.44	-2.240 / 4.431 / -0.51	1.113 / 4.951 / 0.22	1.344 / 5.388 / 0.25	6.038 / 4.784 / 1.26	-2.072 / 5.328 / -0.39	.189 / 6.334 / 0.03	-.547 / 5.022 / -0.11	3.15 / 5.68 / 0.55	6.542 / 4.916 / 1.33	-2.409 / 3.707 / -0.65	-3.919 / 3.966 / -0.99	-1.804 / 3.477 / -0.52	-5.441 / 3.563 / -1.53	-18.526 / 9.868 / -1.83***	-.983 / 5.952 / -0.17	-.393 / 7.398 / -0.05	-3.646 / 7.129 / -0.51
lq Y1	-.425 / .285 / -1.49	.025 / .227 / .11	.356 / .191 / 1.87***	.349 / .136 / 2.56**	.238 / .138 / 1.73***	-.034 / .207 / -0.17	.075 / .129 / .58	-.121 / .136 / -0.89	-.046 / .115 / -0.40	-.348 / .108 / 3.23*	-.129 / .135 / -0.96	.184 / .121 / 1.52	.332 / .216 / 1.54	-.022 / .163 / -0.13	-.267 / .187 / -1.43	.043 / .173 / .25	-.251 / .197 / -1.27	.032 / .108 / .30	.157 / .16 / .98	.016 / .173 / .09
almrauk	.013 / .022 / .60	.002 / .019 / .08	-.018 / .015 / -1.20	-.036 / .016 / -2.26**	-.015 / .022 / -1.25	-.022 / .022 / -0.99	-.019 / .011 / -1.67***	.003 / .014 / .21	-.018 / .017 / -1.03	.003 / .013 / .24	.018 / .013 / 1.34	-.008 / .012 / -0.71	-.057 / .031 / -1.86***	-.008 / .022 / -0.35	.005 / .017 / .29	.003 / .023 / .13	.06 / .028 / 2.12**	-.011 / .017 / -0.64	.009 / .024 / .38	.005 / .028 / .17
arirauk	.028 / .022 / 1.27	.027 / .017 / 1.59	.036 / .019 / 1.83***	.032 / .016 / 1.94***	.032 / .017 / -0.78	-.009 / .018 / -0.50	-.005 / .013 / -0.35	.032 / .015 / .76	.009 / .013 / .71	-.005 / .014 / -0.38	.014 / .013 / 1.09	-.007 / .011 / -0.38	-.024 / .027 / -0.88	.006 / .022 / .29	.036 / .02 / 1.79***	-.019 / .02 / -0.92	-.023 / .019 / 1.55	.017 / .011 / 1.54	.013 / .13 / 1.57	-.001 / .016 / -0.04
empl Y1Y2	-.028 / .019 / -1.10	-.004 / .012 / -0.19	-.005 / .012 / -0.42	-.001 / .014 / -0.08	-.005 / .009 / -0.51	.004 / .016 / .28	.0001 / .002 / .06	.005 / .003 / 1.57	-.037 / .03 / -1.23	.016 / .023 / .68	-.004 / .028 / -0.13	.025 / .02 / 1.25	.028 / .051 / .54	-.028 / .046 / -0.62	.051 / .044 / 1.17	-.031 / .044 / -0.71	-.017 / .015 / -1.19	.002 / .009 / .20	.006 / .013 / .51	-.005 / .013 / -0.37
emplind Y1Y2	.015 / .013 / 1.11	-.005 / .012 / -0.46	-.015 / .009 / -1.55	-.024 / .009 / -2.71*	.011 / .008 / 1.35	-.011 / .009 / -1.06	.005 / .007 / .70	-.008 / .009 / -0.90	.004 / .003 / 1.16	.001 / .003 / .30	-.002 / .003 / -0.49	-.002 / .003 / -0.61	.022 / .015 / 1.47	.011 / .011 / 1.00	-.001 / .012 / -0.10	.013 / .015 / .89	-.009 / .013 / -0.76	-.011 / .008 / -1.37	.011 / .11 / -0.99	-.005 / .13 / -0.42
gdppotbrend Y1	-.004 / .003 / -1.49	-.001 / .002 / -0.36	.001 / .002 / .62	.002 / .002 / 1.03	.0003 / .001 / .25	.001 / .002 / .86	.001 / .001 / .69	.001 / .001 / .49	-.0003 / .002 / -0.20	-.001 / .001 / -0.83	.0002 / .001 / .11	-.0001 / .001 / -0.07	.002 / .001 / 1.41	-.0001 / .001 / -0.13	-.002 / .001 / 1.30	.001 / .001 / .001	-.002 / .0001 / -1.83***	-.0002 / .0000 / -0.30	-.001 / .0001 / -0.99	.0003 / .001 / .41
IndustProd	.00003 / .00002 / 2.14**	1.89e+06 / .00001 / .16	-1.95e+06 / .00001 / -0.22	7.93e+06 / .00001 / -0.87	-.00001 / .00001 / -1.75***	6.10e+06 / .00001 / .38	-2.58e+06 / .00001 / -0.51	4.52e+06 / .00001 / .62	-2.07e+06 / .00001 / -0.20	.00001/39 / .00001 / 2.11**	8.34e+06 / .00000 / 1.84***	-1.55e+06 / .00000 / -0.40	-.00001 / .00000 / -2.04**	1.81e+06 / .00001 / .33	8.54e+06 / .00000 / 1.90***	7.14e+06 / .00001 / -1.28	.00001 / .00001 / 2.04**	3.00e+06 / .00000 / .90	3.55e+06 / .00001 / .69	3.55e+06 / .00001 / .64

304   NATALYA SHEVCHIK KETENCI

Year-Quarter	1997-I	1997-II	1997-III	1997-IV	1998-I	1998-II	1998-III	1998-IV	1999-I	1999-II	1999-III	1999-IV	2000-I	2000-II	2000-III	2000-IV	2001-I	2001-II	2001-III	2001-IV
Probability (5)	0.448874	0.353127	0.332173	0.407	0.335	0.234	0.227	0.306	0.318	0.332	0.231	0.360	0.253	0.204	0.222	0.189	0.305	0.221	0.218	0.182
Pseudo R2	0.0652	0.0619	0.065	0.076	0.104	0.053	0.039	0.089	0.041	0.082	0.048	0.058	0.112	0.054	0.099	0.105	0.140	0.081	0.050	0.089

Industrial enterprises with ownership of a higher order of market orientation and liberalisation were found to have fluctuations in their production performance. The probability that the production of these enterprises would rise was lower at the beginning of 2000 and higher at the end of the same year, while the probability of a stable level of industrial production declined due to the higher likelihood of production growth. At the same time the probability of a decline in output of industrial enterprises increased with the increase in the number of enterprises whose ownership type is strongly associated with a market orientation at the end of 1998 during the Russian crisis. However, in the second quarter of 1999 recovery after the Russian crisis led to the probability of decline in output production of industrial enterprises with the enterprises whose ownership reflect a greater market orientation. As a result, Kazakhstani industrial enterprises are found to have a tendency to benefit from the private ownership type, which led to growth in their production. At the same time, private ownership led industrial enterprises into a more vulnerable situation under the effects of an external crisis, while enterprises with a lower degree of market orientation were less vulnerable.

Results of estimations for all industrial enterprises of the Kazakhstani survey show that industrial enterprises with a larger workforce (*npeid* variable) tend to have a higher probability of an increase in their output and a lower probability of being stable or experiencing a decline in production. This indicates that Kazakhstani industrial enterprises with a larger workforce could be less sensitive to other external and internal factors in their production activity compared to firms with a smaller workforce. The latter could find it more difficult to increase their level of production due to a smaller share of the market, so that the probability of being stable is higher than growth. The tendency for a decline in smaller enterprises was significant only over one quarter compared to the growth of output. Thus, industrial enterprises with a larger workforce appear to be more stable in the market, and less vulnerable to economic changes, which affect production.

The *HH* index (*Hhindexind* Y_1 *variable*), which represents the non-spatial industrial specific characteristic, was found to be strongly significant in relation to the production level of enterprises. The results of estimations show that industrial enterprises, which belong to higher spatially concentrated industries, have a higher likelihood that their production volume will stay at the same level or will decline in the subsequent quarter, rather than grow. Industries based on mineral resources would be expected to have a higher level of industrial concentration, such as fuel or metallurgy. However, Kazakhstan, as a country endowed with mineral-resources reveals a different picture. HH index (Figure 4.2.) of the Kazakhstani industrial concentration shows that the lowest level of industrial concentration is observed exactly in fuel and metallurgical industries, which are more evenly distributed across regions than other industries, which is explained by the high dispersion of mineral resources in Kazakhstan. Such industries as light industry, timber and construction materials were found to be highly concentrated in Kazakhstan over the years of the survey, when there was a collapse in production in many regions during the first transition decade as a result of the fall in demand in internal and external markets, and a high level of competition from imported goods. Therefore, the conclusion of HH index estimations indicates that industrial enterprises that belong to industries of the lowest level of industrial concentration, such as fuel or metallurgy (Figure 4.2.) tend to have a higher probability of production growth, rather than being stable or facing decline. Results of the estimations of the HH index reflect the real situation in Kazakhstan, where high interest from foreign investors is observed towards industries based on mineral resources, which increases the level of investment and as a result raises the level of production leading the economy to the *Dutch decease* effect (Kalyuzhnova, 2002). (Chapter 2, part 2.3 *Changes in regional concentration of industrial activities*). Therefore, such uneven distribution of investments increases disparities between the production levels of different industries. Industries based on mineral resources outperform other industries which are mainly based on local consumption.

Another industrial specific spatial variable – LQ index (*Lq Y₁* variable) was found to be negatively significant for the production growth in two quarters (second quarter of 1997 and the first quarter of 1998). This means that Kazakhstani industrial enterprises located in highly specialised regions, tend to have a lower probability of production growth than industrial enterprises located in other regions and a higher likelihood of decline or stability of production. The high probability of decline in the production activity of industrial enterprises which are located in highly specialised regions was found in the first two quarters of the year 1997 and in the second quarter of the year 1999. However, at the end of the observational period, in the fourth quarter of 2001, the probability of production growth in industrial enterprises located in specialised regions was found to be significant.

Figure 4.2. HH Index of the Kazakhstani industrial concentration

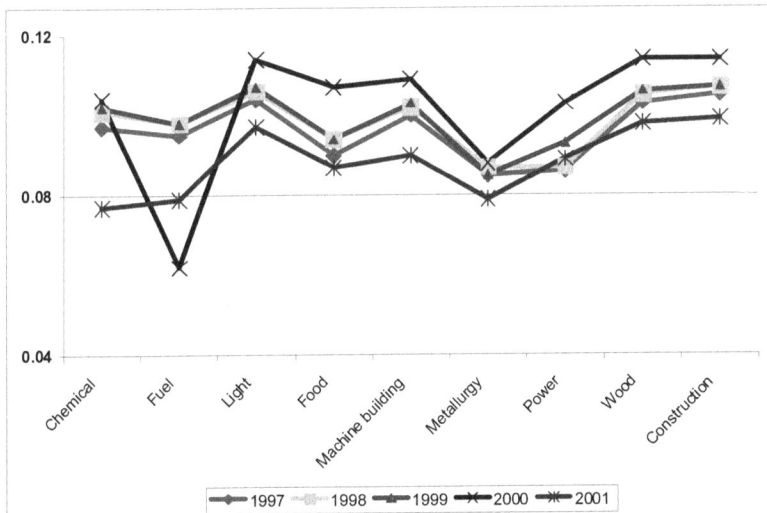

Source: Data are measured from: *Regiony Kazakhstana: 1996-1999*, 2000. *Regiony Kazakhstana: 1997-2000*, 2001. *Regiony Kazakhstana- 1998*, 1999. *Kazakhstan: 1991-2002*, 2002.

Figure 4.3. represents *LQ index* of Kazakhstani regions over the years of the survey, where an index lower than 1 means that the region is a net importer of industrial goods, while the region with an LQ index higher than 1, exports the output of the specialised industry inside the country as well as outside (McCann, 2001). It can be seen from Figure 4.3., that the Atyrau, Mangistau, Kzyl-Orda and Karaganda regions are highly specialised in a particular industry, which is fuel. However, from Figure 2.3. *The growth rates of Kazakhstani industries on a year-by-year comparison* of Chapter 2 *The effect of the transition on the regional development*, it can be seen that the fuel industry grew continuously after 1997. Therefore industrial enterprises located in regions of higher specialisation, and which do not belong to the specialised industry of a region, tended to experience a decline of production compared to enterprises located in regions of lower specialisation in 1997, 1998 and 1999, until estimations illustrated a different picture in the last quarter of 2001. This could mean the gradual production growth of enterprises of non-regional specialisation. However, conclusions can be made after the extension of estimations for the following period.

Figure 4.3. LQ Index of the regional specialisation

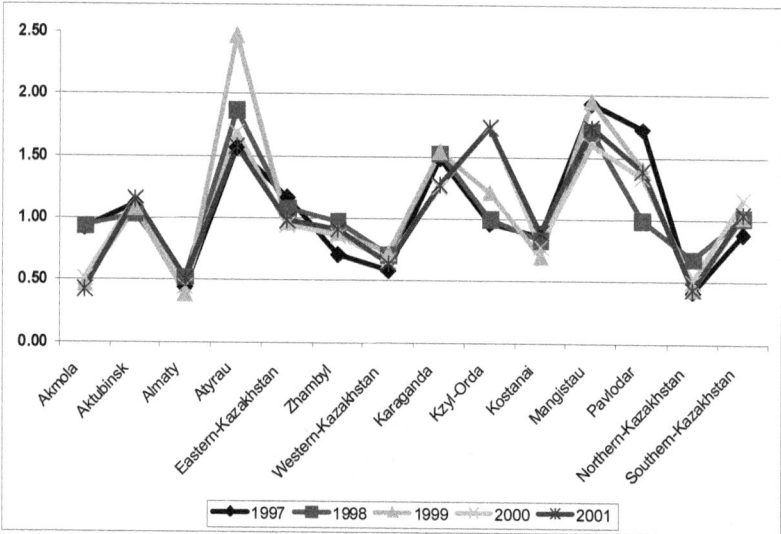

Source: Data are measured from: *Regiony Kazakhstana: 1996-1999*, 2000. *Regiony Kazakhstana: 1997-2000*, 2001. *Regiony Kazakhstana- 1998*, 1999. *Kazakhstan: 1991-2002*, 2002.

As the high level of specialisation is observed only in regions rich with mineral resources, which are a profitable commodity for export, these regions put a lot of effort into increasing the production of these commodities, in order to increase the level of income. At the same time, other industries of these regions, such as food or light industries, lacked investment, so that unskilled labour prefers to migrate to industries of specialisation with a higher level of income and the younger generation prefers to obtain the qualifications of specialised industries to others because of income. Consequently, the production level of industrial enterprises of non-regional specialisation falls, increasing the cost of production. As a result, it is becoming cheaper to import goods from these industries from other regions or countries, while local industries, which do not belong to the regional specialisation, deteriorate at a higher speed. (Chapter 2 *The effect of transition on regional development*, section 2.3 *Changes in regional concentration of national industries*).

Purely spatial distance measures in the model, which are introduced by *almrank* and *astrank* variables and are represented as the distance from regions to the capitals of Almaty and Astana respectively on the basis of ordinal ranking, appear to be significant in different groups of estimations. Thus, industrial enterprises located close to the Almaty region were found to have a low likelihood of growth in their production and at the same time they have a low likelihood of decline in their production, compared to industrial enterprises located in distant regions from the ex-capital Almaty. Therefore, it can be concluded that industrial enterprises located in proximity to the ex-capital city tend to have higher stability of their production, than enterprises of other regions. This fact could be explained by time lags of the privatisation process between the Kazakhstani regions. By the middle of the first transition decade, in 1996, the privatisation of enterprises had a higher level of activity in economically developed regions, such as Almaty, Southern Kazakhstan and Karaganda[83], while in less developed regions such as Northern Kazakhstan and others privatisation proceeded at a slower paces (Kalyuzhnova, 1998). Therefore, the majority of industrial enterprises were privatised in economically developed regions by the beginning of the period of estimation of this study in 1997. The production level relatively stabilised in those regions compared to other less developed regions, which appeared mainly to be distantly located from the ex-capital city and were privatised later due to the lack of

---

83   The higher level of the privatisation activity in economically developed regions, such as Almaty, Southern Kazakhstan and Karaganda did not have effect of the strong correlation between these locations and type of ownership of industrial enterprises (*statusid* variable), the problem of multicolinearity in this case does not exist.

development and the lack of information from the central authorities. As a result their production activity is found to be relatively dynamic during the period of estimation, compared to industrial enterprises located in economically developed regions and close to the Almaty region.

Astana city became the new capital of Kazakhstan in 1997. A high inflow of investment into the development of the whole Akmola region would therefore be expected. However, the results of estimations of the *astrank* variable contradict this hypothesis and show that industrial enterprises, which are closely located to the Akmola region, have a higher likelihood of decline in production, than industrial enterprises which are located in regions distant from the Akmola region. The phenomena could be explained by a high investment into new capital development, which involves the demand in use of high quality goods, which are imported from the neighbouring Russian market or other countries. At the same time, there is no sufficient demand for goods produced by local industries due to higher production costs and lower quality (Chapter 2 *The effect of transition on regional development*, section 2.3 *Changes in regional concentration of national industries*).

Results of estimations from the sample of industrial enterprises show that employment growth on the regional (*emplY$_1$Y$_2$ variable*) and industrial level (*emplindY$_1$Y$_2$ variable*) respectively, negatively affects the production growth of enterprises, which contradicts the expectations expressed above (Table 4.11.). However, considering the data more closely it can be seen that it is necessary to explain the results on the basis of the reduction in the fall of industrial employment rather than its growth. Thus industrial enterprises located in regions with a lower decline in industrial employment were found to have a higher likelihood of decline in their production, which contradicts the expected sign of this variable coefficient (Table 4.11.). Apparently, the reduction in the fall of industrial employment does not necessarily mean its growth. It could indicate the worsening of the situation where industrial employment was falling over quarters and there was a depletion of labour input, so that the high probability of decline in production is the natural way of responding to the depletion of resources.

The growth of total regional employment, $emplY_1Y_2$, was not found to be a positive characteristic for the production growth of industrial enterprises. The likelihood of decline changed over the whole period of estimations. The reason for the decline in production of industrial enterprises in regions with a high growth of total employment could be the reorientation of labour from low-income and declining industries, mainly food and light, to the business of importing goods to Kazakhstan from Russia or other countries.

The GDP per capita index (*Gdpperhead Y_1 variable*) was used to capture the effects of the location-specific input cost variables and was found to have a positive effect on the growth of production of industrial enterprises. However, surprisingly higher levels of regional GDP per head increased the probability of decline in the output of industrial enterprises at the beginning of 1997 and 1999. This could be explained by the negative effect of the Russian crisis at the end of 1998 on Kazakhstani industrial enterprises. Nevertheless, the trend changed at the end of 2000 and 2001 when the higher level of regional GDP reduced the probability of industrial enterprises experiencing a decline in their output, as a result of the recovery of the total economy.

However, a higher level of GDP per head in a region does not give an advantage to all industries located in this region. The location specific characteristic (*LQ Y_1*) of industrial enterprises was found to negatively affect the production growth of industrial enterprises in highly specialised regions. Highly specialised regions tend to be regions rich with energy sources such as coal, oil and gas, which constitute a large percentage of Kazakhstani GDP. Therefore, the value of GDP per head in these regions is high[84] as a result of the concentration of economic activity on energy industries. Results of the estimation of the *Gdpperhead Y_1 variable* yield additional evidence to support the argument discussed in the analysis of the estimations of the *LQ* variable. Location specific characteristics capture the decline of production of industrial enterprises which do not belong to a regional specialisation, such as the food industry in

---

84   During transition, hydrocarbon rich regions, Atyrau, Western Kazakhstan and Mangistau had the highest level of GDP per head including Almaty city. (Table 2.2. *Kazakhstani GDP structure by regions, 1990-2001, %. Chapter 2 The effect of transition on the regional development*).

the region whose specialisation is fuel (*Dutch disease* effect). The higher GDP per head is an advantage for enterprises of the region's specialisation industry, however their dominance negatively affects industries that do not belong to the specialisation of the region in which they are located. The exception of the high level of GDP per head with low level of regional specialisation is Almaty city, where a high concentration of financial resources gives a higher opportunity for all industrial enterprises to increase their production.

The measure of the purely industrial production volume of regions (*IndustProd variable*) indicates the direct positive significant effect to the probability of an increase in industrial enterprises' output through the quarters and the negative effect on the probability of decline in their output. Thus, industrial enterprises located in regions with a high level of industrial production tend to have a higher likelihood of a rise in their output and a lower likelihood of decline. However, in the second quarter of 2001 the high level of industrial production appeared in estimations to have a negative effect on the production growth of industrial enterprises. This could be explained by the slowdown and decline of industrial production in regions with high overall level of production. Thus, the production of the Western Kazakhstan and Pavlodar regions declined by 17% and 7% respectively in the second quarter of 2001 as a result of the decline in 2000 of oil and other mineral commodities prices. Apart from the effect of world commodity price falls, the level of industrial production in Kazakhstani regions was found to be highly dependent on the growth of the production of industrial enterprises.

The hypothesis that the performance of industrial enterprises of Kazakhstan depends on the set of spatial, industrial and individual specific characteristics can be accepted considering the results of the estimations. However, these results also show that the performance of Kazakhstani industrial enterprises is changing over the period under consideration. Strong relationships of performance with spatial, industrial and individual specific characteristics continue to exist, but there are indications of change in some of them. The results indicate the unstable behaviour of industrial enterprises which could be the result of transitional transformations in the country. Such transformations are found to be the most sensitive for production behaviour of industrial enterprises on the regional level, where such variables as LQY_1, $EmplindY_1Y_2$, $EmplY_1Y_2$, $GdpperheadY_1$, which denote the location quotient, growth of regional industrial employment, growth of total regional employment and the regional GDP per head respectively affect the fluctuations of the signs of significant z-statistics. This shows that regional economies are still in the process of development and are economically active. At the same time the ownership type was found to correspond to sign fluctuations, which indicate the weak level of establishment of the new system of ownership types in the economy where enterprises were still getting accustomed to new systems of operation at management level.

Expected signs of the marginal effects of variables mainly coincide with those expected in Table 4.11., at the beginning of section 4.4.1, where the last column shows signs of variables marginal effects that appeared to be significant. However, in some cases the instability of the transition process in Kazakhstan affected the stability of production activities of industrial enterprises. As a result, the sign of marginal effects fluctuates through the quarters, which were associated with most of the significant changes in the economy. Thus, distribution of the means of variables do not change frequently, while the marginal effect of every single variable fluctuates over the whole period of the survey with changes in signs.

Summary
The model used in the study estimates the probability of industrial enterprises being dependent on their individual, industrial and regional specific characteristics in terms of short-term production. Results of econometric estimations represent the high volatility of signs of the coefficients of variables. One explanation of such signs of instability could be that the sample of industrial enterprises is somewhat different for every quarter. However, the general properties of enterprises are the same, and as can be seen from section 4.2.3 *Sample representativeness*, the distribution of enterprises by their individual specific characteristics, such as region and industrial sector, largely has the same structure over all quarters of observation.

Observing the sample of industrial enterprises we have, it can be seen that, enterprises, which repeatedly responded to the questionnaire over the quarters, experienced continuous changes in their industrial production on the qualitative level. The continuous changes in growth and decline of enterprises' output across all quarters of the survey are not distinctive characteristics of a particular enterprise and independent on the regional or industrial specific characteristics of enterprises, but are applied to all surveyed industrial enterprises. Therefore, the much more plausible reason for the high signs of instability of the coefficients of variables may be explained by the enterprises' inherent behavioural instability over the successive quarters of the uncertain transition period. The transition process is defined by the restructuring of the whole economy from the Soviet planning system towards the market economy, as former Soviet republics became independent from the central management. The transition appears to be a highly unstable rather than a smooth process. This is due to the fact that changes are made randomly due to the lack of information that would enable enterprises to restructure appropriately and thereby achieve continuous production growth.

In the transition economy, industrial enterprises adopt the leader following behaviour, imitating the strategy of industrial enterprises who achieve growth of production. However, such an approach does not always bring the expected results. Other determinants play an important role in their performance, such as individual specific, regional specific and industrial specific characteristics, which are estimated in the current study. Therefore, due to uncertain conditions in the transition economy, industrial enterprises face continuous and unpredictable changes.

Thus, the analysis of estimations of marginal effects permits the extraction of information, which could present a general picture of the relationship between production activities of industrial enterprises of the Kazakhstani transition economy and the specific characteristics of the enterprises.

Nearly every firm in the survey exhibited large instability in terms of the short-term production from quarter to quarter, where continuous changes affect the general performance of industrial enterprises on regional and sectoral levels.

Therefore, on the basis of current estimations the conclusion can be drawn that the transition process is characterised by high instability on the micro-economic level. The U-shape of growth theory is not defined by the smooth process in transition economies where the production activity falls sharply, followed by recovery, but by continuous fluctuations. The transition process in Kazakhstan moves the economy from central planning towards the market. This process cannot be completed in the short term due to conditions of uncertainty, while the long-term process is defined by a constant search for the achievement of growth. Lack of information results in many firms resorting to "trial and error" behaviour, while other firms follow the leader of the market. Many enterprises are successful in their production, but many other enterprises fail, which is a consequence of the uncertainty and unpredictability of the transition economy. The results of the estimations show that the transition of the developing market is not strictly divided between enterprises that constantly succeed and those that are failing. It indicates that industrial enterprises, who maintain their production process, continuously experience fluctuations of their production which determine the nature of the transition process.

4.4.2 The test of the second hypothesis

The second hypothesis of the estimated model examines the association of the characteristics of enterprises with their location in transition economies. The hypothesis tests to what extent the characteristics of industrial enterprises are statistically different for different locations. These are divided into three groups: (1) – regions with the highest level of industrial production in monetary terms, (2) – regions with a medium level of industrial production, and (3) – regions with the lowest level of industrial production. The grouping of these regions in terms of their industrial production was defined according to their performance in monetary terms. Regions with a significantly high level of industrial production were included in the first group; regions with a significantly low level of industrial production were included in the last group, while the remaining regions were assigned to the group of the medium industrial production level. The assignment of regions by groups is based on every quarter, where regions change from one group to another every quarter according to their production performance. In the transition period, not only individual characteristics of enterprises are changing, but also industrial and regional characteristics.

Table 4.13. Expected signs of variables marginal effects on the probabilities of industrial enterprises being located in regions with higher industrial production

Probability (1)	Expected sign	Marginal effect signs of estimated significant variables
Statusid	+,-	+,-
Npeid	+	+,-
Production volume	-	+,-
Output price	-	+,-
Output demand	-	+
Russian border	+	+,-
Hydrocarbon regions	+	-,+
Probability (2)	Expected sign	Marginal effect signs of estimated significant variables
Statusid	-	-
Npeid	+,-	+
Production volume	-	+,-
Output price	+,-	+,-
Output demand	+,-	+,-
Russian border	+,-	+,-
Hydrocarbon regions	-	+,-

Probability (3)	Expected sign	Marginal effect signs of estimated significant variables
Statusid	+,-	+,-
Npeid	+	-
Production volume	-	+,-
Output price	+	+,-
Output demand	+	+,-
Russian border	+	+,-
Hydrocarbon regions	+	+,-

Notes:
- Probability (1) – the probability of an enterprise being located in a region with high industrial production in monetary terms.
- Probability (2) – the probability of an enterprise being located in a region with medium industrial production in monetary terms.
- Probability (3) – the probability of an enterprise being located in a region with low industrial production in monetary terms.

Table 4.13. presents the expected signs of marginal effects of chosen variables on the probability of industrial enterprises being located in regional groups with high, medium and low industrial production volume respectively. The Statusid variable defines the ownership type of an industrial enterprise, where the sign of the significant variable could be positive as well as negative for all the categories of probability. However, the increasing order of market orientation in terms of ownership type would be expected to locate industrial enterprises in the group of regions with a higher or lower industrial production volume rather than in the medium one. Industrial enterprises with a higher order of market orientation in terms of ownership type are enterprises who changed their ownership types during the transition period or who have been created during transition. Their industrial production, therefore, is undergoing changes all the time and, due to high activity, these enterprises could be located in regions with a high or low industrial production level rather than with a medium one. In terms of the Statusid variable, there is no one-way causality. However, if we think of alternative arguments, we would expect that

Statusid would highly reflect market changes. On one side it could be expected that higher market orientation in the transition economy would lead to a higher dynamic of enterprise production behaviour, which could lead to production growth. However, on another side it could be expected that areas of high growth and high production level would attract enterprises of a more flexible entrepreneurial nature in terms of the ownership.

The *Npeid* variable is expected to be positively dependent on the probability of industrial enterprises with a larger workforce to be located in the region with higher industrial volume assuming that industrial enterprises with a larger workforce are operating under the optimum input mix. However, privatisation had a negative effect on the production performance of industrial enterprises, so that large-scale enterprises are less flexible to short-term changes and experienced the most significant changes in their structure which affected their production performance. Therefore, it can be expected that the greater size of the workforce of industrial enterprises could increase the probability of enterprises being located in regions with lower industrial production due to the fact that larger enterprises are less flexible to bring about quick transformations and responses to changes in the economy due to transition. During the period of the Soviet planning system many industrial enterprises were created on the basis of the needs of the Soviet Union. Thus, large-scale industrial enterprises were mainly connected to enterprises or markets outside the Kazakh SSR. However, after the collapse of the Soviet Union, most large-scale enterprises were negatively affected by the loss of industrial links.

The *Production volume* variable indicates qualitative changes in actual values being produced by industrial enterprises on the basis of three categories: *Growth*, *No change* and *Decline*, where the higher value of the variable denotes decline in production, and the lower value denotes growth[85]. Therefore, the variable is expected to be inversely related to the probability of an enterprise being located in the regions with high and medium industrial production and positively related to the probability of an enterprise being located in the

---

85   Values for the *Production volume* variable are extracted from the questionnaire, where value 1 denotes the growth of enterprise production, 2 - no change, and 3 - decline.

regional group with a low level of industrial production. Industrial enterprises with declining output would be expected to be in the group of regions with low industrial production volume, while industrial enterprises that experience growth or no change would be expected to have a higher likelihood of belonging to a group of regions with high or medium industrial production.

The variable *Output price* indicates changes in prices for the main output of an individual industrial enterprise, where the higher value of the variable denotes the decline in output prices[86]. Thus, considering the theory of supply and demand, if an increase in prices is associated with growing demand[87] then the volume produced would be expected to grow. It would consequently increase the likelihood of an industrial enterprise being located in the group of regions with higher industrial production, presenting relations between variable and considered probability in a negative way. Lower prices of main output could lead to a decline in production of industrial enterprises, with the probability of such enterprises being located in the group of regions with lower industrial production rises. Relations between the variable and the probability of industrial enterprises being located in a group of regions with a medium level of industrial production can be positive as well as negative, depending on the starting point of an enterprise.

---

86   In *Output price* variable the higher value of the variable denotes the decline in output prices, where *Growth* in prices has value 1, *No change* in prices has value 2 and *Decline* in prices has value 3.

87   In the case of a shortage of supply, the growing price of output would be associated with a decline or no changes in the quantity produced. In the case of Kazakhstani economy such situation could be associated with outdated technology and high level of competition from neighboring countries. This does not allow to local producers to sell their output and on the basis of obtained profit to improve the technology level, which could cut the cost of production and consequently prices of output. Therefore, an increase in output prices of local producers may affect the likelihood of industrial enterprises being located in regions with a low level of industrial production. However, continuous changes in the transition process (during the period of estimations 1997-2001) move the Kazakhstani economy towards the market very fast, where growing prices of output are more often became to be associated with growing demand of consumers, which increases the likelihood of enterprises with growing output price to be located in regions with high level of production.

The variable *Output demand* is defined in terms of qualitative changes in the quantity sold of an individual industrial enterprises output. The variable is presented in the same way as the previous variable where decline in demand corresponds to the higher value (3) of the variable, while growth in demand is associated with the lowest value (1) of the variable under consideration. Variables *Production volume* and *Output demand* are not correlated, as the former defines qualitative changes in the output produced by an enterprise, while the latter defines qualitative changes in the quantity sold of an enterprises output. Thus, industrial enterprises produce a certain volume of output, expecting a particular level of demand, but, as the transition process is defined by conditions of uncertainty and short-term volatility, the expected quantity of demand often does not coincide with the real one. The *Output demand* variable is expected to be negatively related to the dependent variable, as the higher demand for the output of enterprises could lead to price increases and consequently to growth in the industrial production. An enterprise could therefore have a high likelihood of being located in a group of regions with high industrial production. The decline in demand does not necessarily lead to a decline in output prices, but it can lead to a decline in production in the long run. Therefore, with a decline in demand, the value of the variable grows, so that the probability of industrial enterprises being located in the group of regions with lower industrial production increases.

Russian border is a dummy variable, which denotes industrial enterprises located in regions which have a common border with Russia. Industrial enterprises located in regions on the border with Russia are expected to belong to the group of regions with higher industrial production, due to the fact that these enterprises have easy access to both Kazakhstani and Russian output markets. This is especially important for industrial enterprises, whose production is based on mineral resources due to the high demand for such goods in the Russian market. Taking into account the situation that Russian goods of the *light* and *food* industries are of greater quality and have a higher demand on the Kazakhstani market, the probability of these enterprises being in the group of low production also grows.

Hydrocarbon regions is a dummy variable for industrial enterprises that are located in Kazakhstani regions rich with oil and gas resources. Hydrocarbon rich regions are defined by five regions, which are all located in the western part of Kazakhstan: Aktubinsk, Atyrau, Western Kazakhstan, Kzyl-Orda and Mangistau. Production of oil and gas in Kazakhstan accounts for a large proportion of the industrial production in monetary terms. The location of industrial enterprises in regions producing hydrocarbon is therefore expected to be associated with a high level of regional industrial production. Despite these expectations, the output level of hydrocarbon rich regions constantly fluctuates, which means that they do not constitute an exception to the principles governing the remainder of the economy undergoing transitional transformation.

Estimations results

Estimations of the multinomial logit model with a full set of variables described in section 4.3.4 *Variable for the test of the second hypothesis*, cannot be presented due to the multicolinearity problem, which caused the omission of the *Wage, Astana* and *Almaty* variables. The reason for excluding the two latter dummy variables was associated with the relatively small sample of industrial enterprise observations from the Astana region, while estimations made including only the *Almaty region* variable demonstrated the lack of industrial enterprises with sufficient results. After omitting this highly correlated variable, estimations were made on the basis of the given set of variables.

In order to test the hypothesis, it is necessary to make detailed estimations, which would present the marginal effect of a chosen set of variables with certain probabilities. Table 4.14. shows the results of the marginal effect estimations of the second hypothesis test. Each cell gives information on the marginal effect coefficient, standard error and z-statistics with significance levels (* for 1%, ** for 5% and *** for 10%). Three horizontal divisions of the table present separately marginal effects of variables on three different probabilities. The *first* division of the table shows the marginal effect of variables on the probability of industrial enterprises being located in the regional group with a high industrial production volume, the *second* division gives the results of the marginal effect of variables on the probability of industrial enterprises being located in the regional group with a medium industrial production. Finally, the *third* division of the table presents the probability of industrial enterprises being located in the group of regions with a low industrial production level.

Table 4.14. Marginal effect estimations of the second model

Year-Quarter		1997:I	1997:II	1997:III	1997:IV	1998:I	1998:II	1998:III	1998:IV	1999:I	1999:II	1999:III	1999:IV	2000:I	2000:II	2000:III	2000:IV	2001:I	2001:II	2001:III	2001:IV
High level of industrial production (Probability)		0.26768	0.25619	0.542116	1.59E-05	0.253128	0.600691	0.365787	0.550195	0.361782	0.423509	0.431826	0.352658	0.695217	0.547444	0.834879	0.713446	0.775096	0.656254	0.388422	0.294782
Pseudo R²		0.0404	0.0662	0.1489	0.2139	0.2783	0.3755	0.1377	0.2344	0.2111	0.172	0.1748	0.1365	0.1547	0.0961	0.265	0.2123	0.2264	0.1832	0.1828	0.2051
Statused	coef	-.067	-.042	.043	4.72e-06	.024	.085	.125	.015	.095	-.002	.004	.099	.138	-.006	.045	.125	.089	.138	-.021	-.115
	se	.035	.035	.037	.00000	.034	.053	.042	.045	.053	.041	.047	.038	.048	.035	.04	.082	.087	.068	.049	.051
	t	-1.95***	-1.20	1.15	1.87***	.69	1.60	2.95*	.33	1.81***	-0.04	0.08	2.61*	2.83*	-.11	1.12	1.53	1.02	2.03**	-0.42	2.25**
Nperid	coef	.007	-.01	-.043	-1.93e-06	.009	.00004	-.025	-.019	.102	-.039	.068	-.024	-.037	.013	.021	-.041	-.013	-.007	.006	.043
	se	.023	.021	.024	.00000	.026	.00000	.024	.029	.031	.029	.035	.027	.03	.034	.021	.046	.035	.037	.043	.039
	t	0.32	-0.50	-1.99**	-1.26	.37	0.00	-1.06	-0.67	3.19*	-1.35	1.96**	-0.91	-1.25	.40	1.45	-0.90	-0.36	-0.18	0.84	1.10
Production volume	coef	.117	.017	-.051	-4.46e-06	.043	.081	.024	-.032	-.069	.034	.006	-.045	-.069	.066	.039	-.162	.028	.039	.033	-.062
	se	.041	.038	.048	.00000	.039	.068	.041	.035	.036	.032	.039	.044	.046	.038	.046	.093	.067	.066	.075	.071
	t	2.86*	0.46	-1.05	-1.56	1.08	1.19	0.38	-0.38	-1.22	0.65	0.11	-1.02	-1.50	1.12	0.83	-1.74***	0.43	0.60	0.44	-0.87
Output price	coef	-.011	.049	.043	4.90e-06	.123	.074	.018	.038	-.237	-.189	-.149	-.063	.009	-.024	-.006	.155	.059	.129	-.214	-.101
	se	.037	.062	.08	.00000	.063	.089	.067	.089	.093	.074	.084	.068	.074	.091	.084	.129	.123	.108	.102	.107
	t	-0.19	0.81	.53	1.09	1.96**	.83	.27	.42	-2.54**	-2.55**	-1.77***	-0.93	0.13	-0.26	-0.07	1.20	0.48	1.20	-2.09**	-0.94
Output demand	coef	-.043	-.034	.217	4.67e-06	.415	.657	.043	.238	.165	-.134	.241	-.149	-.126	-.056	-.018	-.118	.053	-.318	-.409	-.581
	se	.037	.047	.07	.00000	.063	.069	.063	.082	.076	.071	.083	.068	.083	.075	.067	.113	.099	.098	.083	.083
	t	-0.76	-0.71	3.08*	1.17	6.62*	9.48*	0.68	2.91*	2.17**	-1.89***	2.90**	-2.21**	-1.52	-0.74	-0.27	-1.04	0.58	-3.23**	-6.02**	-6.83*
Russian border	coef	.012	.193	-.467	-3.09e-06	-.412	-.774	-.426	-.638	-.426	-.455	-.477	-.26	-.152	-.258	-.245	-.313	-.215	-.107	-.229	.319
	se	.07	.054	.038	.00000	.046	.115	.049	.054	.059	.039	.067	.069	.127	.098	.099	.12	.118	.122	.059	.187
	t	0.17	3.56*	-12.14*	-0.75	-8.97*	-6.72*	-8.61*	-11.82*	-7.13*	-7.69*	-6.51*	-3.79*	-1.20	-2.64*	-2.47**	-2.61**	-1.82***	-0.88	-2.33**	1.71***
Hydrocarbon regions	coef	-.102	-.117	-.553	.038																.187
	t	-1.45	-2.37**	-10.15*																	

Year-Quarter	1997-I	1997-II	1997-III	1997-IV	1998-I	1998-II	1998-III	1998-IV	1999-I	1999-II	1999-III	1999-IV	2000-I	2000-II	2000-III	2000-IV	2001-I	2001-II	2001-III	2001-IV
Medium level of industrial production (Probability)	**0,42395**	**0,39008**	**0,189957**	**0,441397**	**0,593422**	**0,394493**	**0,239319**	**0,235966**	**0,098662**	**0,230497**	**0,145245**	**0,366628**	**0,108458**	**0,142293**	**0,164975**	**0,285592**	**0,224834**	**0,343574**	**0,373809**	**0,437437**
Formula R²	**0,1404**	**0,0662**	**0,1489**	**0,2139**	**0,2783**	**0,3755**	**0,1377**	**0,2344**	**0,2111**	**0,172**	**0,1748**	**0,1565**	**0,1547**	**0,0961**	**0,265**	**0,2123**	**0,2264**	**0,1832**	**0,1828**	**0,3051**
Statused	.047 / .042 / 1.12	.007 / .043 / .015	-.033 / .028 / -1.17	.001 / .043 / .03	.028 / .035 / .78	-.085 / .053 / -1.60	-.089 / .034 / -2.64*	-.109 / .037 / -2.94*	-.026 / .025 / -1.04	-.063 / .037 / -1.69***	.027 / .032 / -.84	-.111 / .038 / -2.91*	-.086 / .029 / -2.88**	-.026 / .034 / -.75	-.045 / .04 / -1.12	-.126 / .082 / -1.53	-.089 / .087 / -1.02	-.138 / .068 / -2.03**	.017 / .045 / .38	.025 / .058 / .44
Mpaid	-.006 / .025 / -0.25	.037 / .023 / 2.51**	.055 / .019 / 2.93*	.074 / .028 / 2.68*	.049 / .028 / 1.78***	.0004 / .037 / .01	.091 / .019 / 4.65*	.043 / .028 / 1.55	.043 / .019 / 2.21**	.063 / .022 / 2.86*	-.005 / .02 / -.26	.041 / .027 / 1.51	.021 / .018 / 1.17	-.024 / .019 / -1.23	-.031 / .021 / -1.45	.042 / .046 / .91	.013 / .035 / .36	.007 / .037 / .18	.001 / .033 / .04	-.015 / .037 / -.41
Production volume	-.072 / .044 / -1.63	-.102 / .039 / -2.62*	.009 / .032 / .28	.109 / .052 / 2.12**	.053 / .044 / 1.21	-.081 / .068 / -1.19	.018 / .036 / .48	.018 / .049 / .35	-.005 / .029 / -.18	.044 / .039 / 1.12	-.025 / .039 / -.64	.001 / .044 / .02	.03 / .034 / .89	-.065 / .036 / -1.81***	-.039 / .046 / -.83	.162 / .093 / 1.74***	-.029 / .067 / -.43	-.039 / .066 / -.60	-.065 / .073 / -.87	.131 / .089 / 1.48
Output price	.065 / .072 / .91	.009 / .063 / .15	.119 / .049 / 2.43**	-.108 / .075 / -1.44	-.098 / .038 / -1.69***	-.074 / .089 / -.82	-.005 / .054 / -.09	.061 / .071 / .87	-.02 / .066 / -.31	.061 / .037 / 1.06	.012 / .032 / .22	.017 / .062 / .27	.028 / .038 / .73	.025 / .034 / .46	.006 / .084 / .08	-.154 / .129 / -1.19	-.058 / .123 / -.48	-.129 / .108 / -1.20	.176 / .089 / 1.96**	.086 / .12 / .71
Output demand	-.061 / .064 / -0.95	.012 / .056 / .22	.0003 / .048 / .01	.079 / .066 / 1.19	.037 / .064 / .57	-.024 / .094 / -.25	.002 / .05 / .05	-.004 / .064 / -.07	.053 / .04 / 1.31	.059 / .048 / 1.24	-.069 / .039 / -1.76***	-.012 / .062 / -.19	-.029 / .042 / -.69	.077 / .044 / 1.74***	.025 / .075 / .33	-.106 / .102 / -1.04	.093 / .098 / .95	.072 / .103 / .69	.093 / .103 / .90	.039 / .119 / .33
Russian border	.123 / .091 / 1.36	-.271 / .059 / -4.61*	-.049 / .053 / -.93	.305 / .078 / 3.93*	-.106 / .079 / -1.34	.339 / .068 / 4.95*	.016 / .054 / .29	.256 / .077 / 3.32*	.04 / .05 / .80	.069 / .058 / 1.20	.173 / .054 / 3.17*	.368 / .062 / 5.94*	-.015 / .048 / -.32	.039 / .052 / .76	.018 / .067 / .26	.118 / .113 / 1.05	-.058 / .099 / -.58	.318 / .098 / 3.23*	.133 / .085 / 1.56	.678 / .07 / 9.63*
Hydrocarbon regions	-.119 / .096 / -1.25	.006 / .072 / .08	.196 / .065 / 3.03*	.232 / .071 / 3.27*	-.182 / .079 / -2.31**	-.226 / .037 / -6.03*	.265 / .071 / 3.71*	-.103 / .066 / -1.56	-.083 / .039 / -2.08**	.169 / .073 / 2.34**	.182 / .063 / 2.89*	.19 / .074 / 2.71*	.377 / .118 / 3.19*	.396 / .096 / 4.14*	.635 / .089 / 7.13*	.659 / .115 / 5.74*	.576 / .108 / 5.35*	.424 / .12 / 3.53*	.226 / .112 / 2.02**	-.158 / .131 / -1.20

Year-Quarter	1997-I	1997-II	1997-III	1997-IV	1998-I	1998-II	1998-III	1998-IV	1999-I	1999-II	1999-III	1999-IV	2000-I	2000-II	2000-III	2000-IV	2001-I	2001-II	2001-III	2001-IV
Low level of industrial production (Probability)	0.30837	0.35373	0.267927	0.558589	0.153449	0.004379	0.394894	0.213839	0.539556	0.345995	0.422929	0.260714	0.196325	0.310263	0.000146	0.000962	7.02E-05	0.000173	0.237769	0.267781
Pseudo R²	0.0404	0.0662	0.1489	0.2139	0.2783	0.3755	0.1377	0.2344	0.2111	0.172	0.1748	0.1365	0.1547	0.0961	0.265	0.2123	0.2264	0.1832	0.1828	0.3051
Statused	.021	.035	-.01	-.001	-.031	-.0001	-.035	.095	-.069	.065	.023	.012	-.052	.032	.0001	.0002	.00004	.00004	.004	.089
	.038	.033	.027	.042	.026	.001	.036	.037	.057	.052	.045	.038	.039	.052	.00003	.0003	.00002	.00005	.04	.055
	0.55	1.08	-.37	-.03	-1.93***	-.20	-.98	2.56**	-1.23	1.25	.52	0.30	-1.35	0.61	1.45	0.63	1.81***	0.81	0.10	1.64
Hyprid	-.001	-.046	-.006	.074	-.059	-.0003	-.065	-.023	-.144	-.024	-.063	-.016	.017	.03	9.83e-06	-.0003	7.78e-06	.00002	-.037	-.027
	.025	.02	.018	.028	.019	.001	.023	.025	.035	.024	.03	.021	.025	.03	.00002	.0002	.00001	.00003	.033	.029
	-.04	-2.30**	-.35	-2.68*	-3.05*	-.47	-2.82*	-.94	-4.12*	-1.02	-2.08**	-.78	.69	0.36	-0.47	-1.80***	0.58	0.85	-1.13	-.096
Production volume	-.045	.084	.042	-.109	-.096	.0004	-.042	.014	.074	-.078	.019	.044	.039	-.001	-.0001	.0002	.0002	.00003	.033	-.069
	.044	.039	.042	.052	.032	.002	.042	.046	.061	.046	.055	.037	.036	.055	.00004	.0003	.00002	.00015	.059	.069
	-1.02	2.18**	.99	-2.12**	-3.03*	.26	-.99	0.31	1.21	1.70***	0.34	1.18	1.07	-0.01	1.48	0.83	0.99	0.53	0.55	-0.99
Output price	-.054	-.039	-.161	.108	-.026	-.0004	-.013	-.099	.257	.129	.137	.047	-.038	-.001	-.0001	-.001	-9.44e-06	-.00002	.038	.115
	.068	.039	.077	.075	.04	.002	.069	.077	.103	.065	.075	.068	.066	.08	.0001	.001	.00004	.0001	.08	.137
	-0.80	-1.00	-2.09**	1.44	-.64	-.20	-.19	-1.29	2.51**	1.98***	1.84***	0.69	-0.38	-0.02	-1.37	-1.17	-0.26	-0.31	0.47	.11
Output demand	.104	.021	.009	-.078	-.129	-.001	-.044	-.0001	.13	-.193	-.172	.081	.029	-.021	.0001	-.0002	-.0001	-.0001	-.143	-.152
	.065	.036	.055	.066	.043	.002	.06	.065	.075	.065	.082	.069	.06	.074	.0001	.0004	.00003	.0001	.089	.092
	1.61	0.38	0.18	-1.19	-3.01*	-.23	-.72	-.00	-1.74***	-2.97*	-2.12**	-1.16	0.49	-0.29	1.96**	-0.43	-0.36	-0.93	-1.61	-1.65***
Russian border	-.133	.078	-.167	-.305	-.309	-.996	-.039	-.494	-.206	-.067	.139	-.219	.142	.066	.001	.0002	.0004	.001	.367	-.097
	.079	.066	.059	.078	.062	.007	.064	.078	.087	.071	.078	.063	.073	.085	.001	.001	.0004	.0001	.074	.063
	1.19	1.18	2.81*	3.93*	4.96*	-151.51*	-.92	-6.33*	-2.37**	-0.94	1.78***	-3.50*	1.93**	0.78	2.04**	0.43	1.09	1.55	4.97**	-1.04
Hydrocarbon regions	.222	.111	.357	.235	.593	.999	.161	.742	.509	.285	.255	.061	-.225	-.138	-.389	-.346	-.962	-.316	.104	-.16
	.095	.073	.072	.073	.073		.072	.095	.063	.078	.082	.066	.052	.091	.045	.052	.056	.047	.091	.135
	2.33**	1.52	4.93*	3.26*	8.12*		2.23**	7.79*	7.78*	3.65*	3.06*	0.92	-4.33**	-1.52	-8.57*	-6.67*	-6.43*	-6.75*	0.04	-1.18

Marginal effects in many cases do not have many signs fluctuations as could be observed in the first hypothesis estimations. However, some variables have changeable effects over the whole period of estimations and the overall picture after the results are obtained can be presented in the following way.

The increasing order of market orientation and liberalisation in terms of ownership type in most cases was found as the positive individual characteristic of industrial enterprises which leads to the rise in the probability of industrial enterprises being located in the group of regions with high industrial production. At the same time it decreases the probability of these enterprises being located in the group of regions with medium and low levels of industrial production. Even though the mean distribution of the *Statusid* variable increased towards the growth of market orientation and liberalisation of ownership type over the considered period of quarters, the variable stayed positively significant across most quarters, except first quarter of 1997 and the last quarter of 2001. The first quarter of 1997 can be denoted by still low level of privatised enterprises, where personal interest of income was in high priority for managers of many privatised enterprises rather than production growth. The negative effect of the last quarter of 2001 has to undergo further estimations in order to explain this change. However, the general picture shows that privatised industrial enterprises, have a higher likelihood of being located in more successful regions in terms of industrial production and by their growth of production enterprises tend to increase the level of regional industrial production. Results of the test of the first hypothesis, described in section 4.4.1, indicated the vulnerability of private enterprises to external factors, but tended to increase the production volume in the absence of external negative factors, such as a financial crisis or a fall in world commodity prices. Therefore, the regional group with a high level of industrial production appears to be strongly associated with the domination of private industrial enterprises.

The larger size of the workforce, denoted by *Npeid* variable, appeared to have a positive individual characteristic of industrial enterprises across all quarters, (except third quarter of 1997) with an increase in the mean distribution. The general tendency of obtained estimations illustrates that the larger size of industrial enterprises leads to an increase in the probability of indus-

trial enterprises being located in regions with high or medium industrial production levels, while the probability of these enterprises being located in regions with low industrial production level is low. Results of the first hypothesis
test show that industrial enterprises have strong positive relations between
the size of their workforce and production growth. Therefore, the conclusion
can be made that large-scale industrial enterprises tend to increase the probability of a region to sustain high or medium levels of industrial production.

Despite the fact that the marginal effect of the *Production volume* variable on
all three probabilities is shown as highly fluctuating the significance of the
variable was found to have a stable sign, even though only in two quarters.
The higher value of the variable represents the decline in output of industrial
enterprises, which is an individual characteristic of enterprises. At the beginning of 1997 the results indicated that industrial enterprises with a decline in
their output were associated with regions of a high level of production. However, later in 2000 this tendency changed, where industrial enterprises with
the decline in output were mainly associated with regions of a medium level
of production. The mean distribution of the variable in the sample shows the
general tendency of industrial enterprises to have growth rather than decline
of their industrial production.

The results of estimations obtained do not describe the general trend of the
location of industrial enterprises, as the variable was found to be significant
for only two quarters. However, they can be explained on a temporary basis,
namely that industrial enterprises with high industrial production experienced
decline, which was not significant for the effect of regional weight in the total
industrial production of Kazakhstan. At the same time, there could be another
explanation of such results, which would indicate that industrial enterprises
located in regions with enterprises of high production volume at a level significant for the region and Kazakhstan as a whole, experienced a decline in
their production at the beginning of 1997 under the shadow of large enterprises. For example, we can consider the Atyrau region, which is the region of
high industrial production levels due to oil and gas production. Enterprises of
other industries of this region, however, suffer from low and insufficient levels

of development due to its remoteness from the central regions and the lack of resources for their development.

The higher value of the *Output price* variable denotes the decline in the prices of the main output of an individual enterprise. The fluctuation of signs of the variable was found to be divided in two terms. In 1997 and in 1998 industrial enterprises experiencing a growth in main output prices had low likelihood of being located in the group of regions with high industrial production and high likelihood of being located in the group of regions with low industrial production. However, since 1999 and onwards industrial enterprises experiencing a growth in main output prices had a high likelihood of being located in the group of regions with high industrial production, but a lower probability of belonging to the regional group of low industrial production levels. Thus, the increase in output prices could lead industrial enterprises to increase their production level, positively affecting the production level of the whole region, which is found to belong to the group of a high level of industrial production. The opposite tendency, which was found in 1997 and 1998, could be explained by the introduction of new currency Tenge, where an increase in prices did not imply the growth in production of industrial enterprises, where new currency became an obstacle in inter-republican trade.

The *Output demand* variable was found to be significant in most quarters throughout the whole period of observations, particularly in the years 1998 and 1999. The significance of the variable appeared to be positive for industrial enterprises with declining output demand being located in regions with a high level of industrial production and, at the same time, the likelihood of these enterprises being located in regions with a low level of industrial production is very low. The reason could be the temporary decline of output demand of industrial enterprises defining high industrial production. However, for the period, when significance appeared, another explanation is that industrial enterprises located in groups of regions with a high level of industrial production and experiencing decline in their output demand, could be enterprises that do not define a regional specialisation. These could be enterprises of other industries that do not have support for their development because the all efforts of economic development are directed towards industries of specialisation, such as for example the *light* industry in the Atyrau region, which specialises in hydrocarbon production.

A *Russian border* dummy variable was found to be significant in the majority of considered quarters, but there was a volatility of signs. Prior to the first quarter of 1999, industrial enterprises of Russian border regions were more likely to be associated with regions of a high level of industrial production than with regions of medium or low levels of industrial production. However, after the Russian financial crisis in 1998, regions on the border with Russia were negatively affected and estimations show that since the last quarter of 1999 until the end of the period under consideration, these regions were found to be strongly associated with regions of low levels of industrial production. The results of estimations showed that despite the high competition from Russian markets, where goods are cheaper and of better quality, industrial enterprises located in regions on the Russian border were found to benefit from the proximity to both Russian and Kazakhstani markets. However, they were found to be more vulnerable to the Russian crisis than enterprises of other regions. After the Russian crisis occurred, prices of Russian goods became cheaper compared to Kazakhstani prices because the Kazakh currency remained fixed until April 1999. As a result of being unable to compete, the production of Kazakhstani enterprises located on the Russian border significantly fell after the Russian crisis.

The results of the marginal effect of a *Hydrocarbon regions* dummy variable are divided into two periods, where the first period runs from the first quarter of 1997 until the first quarter of 2000. The first period was characterised by the high likelihood of industrial enterprises of hydrocarbon-specialised regions being associated with regions of low industrial production level rather than with the group of a high or medium level of industrial production. The second period starts from the first quarter of 2000 until the end of the period under consideration and indicates the large probability of hydrocarbon regions belonging to the group of regions with a high or medium level of industrial production rather than to the group with a low level of production. The association of hydrocarbon regions with the group of regions of high level of industrial production was found only in the last quarter of 2001. The second period for which results were obtained reflects the position when Kazakhstan recovered from the drastic fall in oil prices in 1999, with a consequent growth of investment in highly promising regions. The first period was characterised by the negative effect of privatisation 1996-1998, when many large energy and hydrocarbon enterprises were privatised, but whose production declined in the short-term due to mismanagement on the part of the new owners (Kalyuzhnova, 1998). Hydrocarbon enterprises were privatised very quickly, while contracts for the collaboration between shareholders and for production strategy were drawn up in the course of a very slow process. As a result, the production of these enterprises was negatively affected.

Summary
The results of estimations provided strong evidence in favour of the hypothesis that the location of industrial enterprises in regions with higher industrial production level in monetary terms depends on its individual, industrial and spatial characteristics. The volatility of signs of significant variables was not as strong as in the test of the first hypothesis, but some characteristics (variables) were affected by external factors. Thus, at the beginning of the survey period, regions on the Russian border were associated with regions of high levels of industrial production. However, their level of industrial production has declined since the Russian financial crisis in 1998 due to the hardness of the Tenge, and a lack of competitiveness of production with neighbouring Russian regions. As a result, these regions became associated with regions of low levels of industrial production. Hydrocarbon regions underwent similar changes, but the result of these changes was due to the turmoil of privatisation and low oil prices in 1999, which kept these regions in the group of a low level of industrial production until 2000, when industrial production completely recovered. Estimations show that the perfect example of industrial enterprises located in the region with high level of industrial production would be private enterprises with a large workforce, growing output prices and located in hydrocarbon regions in the second half of the survey period or in the Russian border regions prior to the Russian financial crisis.

4.5 Conclusion

The chosen multinomial logit framework of the production function allows the examination of relationships between the production behaviour of industrial enterprises and their individual, industrial and location characteristics. The first hypothesis suggested the dependence of the production performance of industrial enterprises on the set of given characteristics, while the second hypothesis suggested the relationship between the location of industrial enterprises, relative to the group of regions with high, medium and low industrial production, and the characteristics of enterprises. Tables 4.11. and 4.13. of this Chapter, in section 4.4, *Result of estimations*, show that results of the estimations of the production and location behaviour of industrial enterprises do not always coincide with the expectations of their behaviour. At the same time the research indicated the tendency of many estimated independent variables to exhibit a volatility of their signs over quarters, which is not related to problems of econometric estimations, as they were corrected over the estimations.

This chapter confirms that the performance of Kazakhstani industrial enterprises varies relative to their location, where industrial and individual characteristics also affect their production performance, while many of them are regionally divided. The first model attempted to capture the relationships between production performance of Kazakhstani industrial enterprises and their specific characteristics. The production performance was denoted in terms of three possible outcomes: *Growth* of production volume, *No change* and *Decline*.

Results of the estimations based on the model demonstrate that *growth* of production is more likely to be observed in industrial enterprises with a larger workforce, if industrial enterprises belong to industries of low industrial concentration; if they are located in regions of low industrial specialisation with a low growth of regional employment and which are at a distance from the ex-capital Almaty city. *No change* in production is most likely to occur in industrial enterprises that are either wholly or partly owned by the state, with a smaller workforce in areas with low growth of regional industrial employment.

However, the concentration of particular industries is most likely to be higher than industries where enterprises face instability in production. Finally, the *decline* in production was mostly detected in industrial enterprises with a smaller workforce, but with high regional industrial employment growth, commonly in regions located closer to the new capital with high industrial concentration, but with low levels of industrial production compared to other regions.

The results provide evidence of the negative effect of the previous industrial concentration and regional specialisation on the production performance of industrial enterprises, which indicates the poor state of industries of Kazakhstan, developed in the past at certain locations because of the comparative advantages of the chosen regions. However, it seems that these previously existing comparative advantages no longer exist or a more powerful force exists, which pulls down many of the spatially concentrated industries. Highly concentrated industries are dependent on unique input factors, such as mineral resources, which are found only in a few regions, but at the same time these industries are highly dependent on demand for their output. The development of industries was not designed for the local consumption in Kazakhstan but for the whole Soviet market, as Kazakhstan possesses rare mineral resources. Therefore, after the collapse of the Soviet Union, Kazakhstan faced a significant fall in industrial production due to the fall in demand from the ex-Soviet republics. Kazakhstan later renewed some of its established links in industrial cooperation, and Russia continued to be the largest market for the output of Kazakhstani heavy industry. Data results indicate the negative effect of the industrial concentration on industrial enterprise performance in the period from the first quarter of 1998 until the first quarter of 2000, which is the period where the Russian crisis of 1998 had its negative effect not only on Kazakhstan but also on other neighbouring countries.

The effect of the regional specialisation on the decline in the production of industrial enterprises did not appear to be the same over the whole survey period. At the end of 1998 and in the second quarters of 1997 and 1999, the effect of regional specialisation on the performance of industrial enterprises was negative. The likelihood of a decline in their production was high, which appeared to be caused by the effect of the Russian crisis and the management of privatisation at the beginning of 1997. However, in the third quarter of 1997 and the fourth quarter of 2001, the effect of regional specialisation was positive, so that industrial enterprises located in regions of high industrial specialisation had a low likelihood of a decline of production. Highly concentrated industries and highly specialised regions do not correlate with growth in production of industrial enterprises. These characteristics affect the decline of industrial production significantly even compared to industrial enterprises of industries of low concentration and located in not highly specialised regions.

The regional location of industrial enterprises appears to be significant from the empirical results, but the effect is slightly different from the one expected. Industrial enterprises located in regions close to the former capital city of Almaty were found to have a low probability of growth in their production, while Almaty was considered to be the business centre of the country and at the centre of quick access to information, where industrial enterprises were supposed to grow. At the same time, results show that industrial enterprises located in regions close to the Almaty region also have a low probability of a decline of their production, except in the first quarter of 2001. Industrial enterprises located at a distance from the Almaty region are very active and have a high likelihood of achieving production growth as well as production decline. The conclusion can be drawn that industrial enterprises located in regions close to the Almaty region have a relatively stable production process compared to distant regions.

The interpretation of the results described above can be seen as the active development of peripheral regions of the country, which contradicts the centre-peripheral theory if we take the capital as the centre of the economy. Kazakhstan has three centres of high economic activity (Chapter 2 *The effect of transition on the regional development*). These are the ex-capital Almaty, new capital Astana and western Kazakhstan (the hydrocarbon rich regions), where the regions of western Kazakhstan are the most distant regions from the Almaty region. When results show high production activity in both directions of industrial enterprises located in distant regions from the Almaty region, these regions can be considered as regions of western Kazakhstan, which are Western Kazakhstan, Atyrau and Mangistau. The location specific character-

istic *almrank* of industrial enterprises demonstrated the activity level of industrial enterprises in hydrocarbon-rich regions compared to the business-centre
of the country Almaty city and its proximate regions.

Another location-specific characteristic of industrial enterprises is the proximity to the new capital city, where results provided evidence of a high probability of production decline in industrial enterprises located in regions close
to the new capital Astana, while more distant regions have a low probability of
production decline in their industrial enterprises. Despite the high-speed development of the new capital city, there is not much attention being paid to industrial development and support of the surrounding region of the new capital. The regions close to the new capital are central Kazakhstan and the
northern regions, which have a common border with Russia and mainly specialise in light and food industries. In addition to the lack of support from the
government, results illustrate that industrial enterprises of the northern regions were extremely vulnerable to the Russian financial crisis, when prices
for Russian goods became lower than those of Kazakhstan. This resulted in a
significant decline in the production level of industrial enterprises in regions
on the Russian borders because of the low competitiveness of Kazakhstani
goods.

The size of the workforce of the industrial enterprises appeared to be strongly
significant over many quarters throughout the whole period of estimation
compared to other variables. Thus, it appeared that an industrial enterprise
with a larger workforce has a higher probability of production growth, rather
than a stable production or a decline. At the same time, the results of the estimations provide evidence of the negative effect of industrial employment
growth on the production performance of industrial enterprises, which appeared in the last two quarters of 1997 and at the end of 1999. In 1997, only
two regions of Kazakhstan had growth of industrial employment. These are
Atyrau and Mangistau which are hydrocarbon-producing regions. However,
despite the growth of regional industrial employment, which was mainly in the
hydrocarbon industries, other industries located in the regions experienced a
decline of production. This is proved by the database data, where 78% of industrial enterprises reported a decline in their industrial production in the sec-

ond half of 1997, which were the non-hydrocarbon industries. Thus, all resources for development are channelled to the hydrocarbon industries of
western Kazakhstan regions, while other industries such as food and light fail
to compete with neighbouring Russian goods and their production is in decline. In 1999, the Kzyl-Orda region had 19.85% growth in industrial employment, and was connected to the latest development of hydrocarbon fields in
the region, while the production of industries such as the food and light industries fell. The growth in regional industrial production can negatively affect industrial enterprises, which are not sources of employment growth, being outside the development concentration of particular industries. However, established industrial enterprises with a large workforce are in a more advantageous position compared to smaller enterprises in terms of the likelihood of
production growth.

The regional *Industrial production* variable was found to be significant for the
growth of the production of industrial enterprises, which indicates that industrial enterprises located in regions with a higher volume of industrial production have a higher likelihood of production growth or stability rather than their
decline. Results from the second quarter of 2001 indicated the negative effect
of the variable on production growth of industrial enterprises. National Statistics show the slight decline of industrial production in some regions, especially hydrocarbon rich regions, which were still regions with the highest industrial production, but experienced a slight decline of output due to the oil
price fluctuations in that period.

The type of ownership of industrial enterprises, which is categorized by its
proximity to market orientation, is evidence of the high production activity in
industrial enterprises and to the higher level to market orientation. Thus, private or partly private industrial enterprises have a lower likelihood than their
state counterparts of not having a change in their level of production and
have a high likelihood of high production activity, which includes growth as
well as decline. It can be concluded from these results that private enterprises
are more flexible with regard to changes in production processes in order to
reach the management target of higher profits or a greater share in the mar-

ket, while experiencing at the same time, continuous changes in the volume of production (both up and down), as a result of the trial and error approach.

The regional GDP per head was not found to have a constant effect on industrial enterprises. In the first quarter of 1997 and the second quarter of 1999, the higher level of regional GDP per head is correlated with a greater probability of a decline in the production of industrial enterprises. However, the third quarter of 1997 and fourth quarters of 2000 and 2001 indicate the opposite result, where industrial enterprises had a low probability of production decline, if they located in regions with a higher GDP level per head. Regions with a higher level of GDP per head are more vulnerable to declines in the economy which were caused by the Russian crisis in 1998.

The second model tests the association of the location of industrial enterprises in regions with higher or lower industrial production with characteristics of industrial enterprises of individual, industrial and spatial nature. Empirical results give evidence of the general trend of industrial enterprises location relative to the regional production level. Thus, industrial enterprises located in regions with a high level of industrial production tend to have a type of ownership of the higher order to market orientation, while industrial enterprises with ownership type of the lower order to market orientation tend to locate in regions with medium and low levels of industrial production. As such, the private type of ownership positively affects the industrial production growth of a region. The last quarter of 2001, however, showed that private industrial enterprises had a low probability of being associated with regions of a high level of industrial production. This could be due to the particular set of industrial enterprises used, or it could presage changes in the economy which would manifest themselves more clearly in data for quarters after the period under consideration in this study.

Results of the effect of changes in production volume and the demand for output of industrial enterprises appeared to be contrary to expectations, where growth of these variables would be expected positively affect the location of industrial enterprises in regions with a higher level of industrial production. Empirical results give evidence of the positive effect of the decline in the

volume of production and in output demand on the location of industrial enterprises in regions with higher levels of industrial production, while having a
low likelihood of being located in regions with a low level of industrial production. The results discovered do not represent the general tendency, as they
were found over only few quarters in groups of estimations. Results were received only at the beginning and at the end of 1997 and at the beginning of
1998 with no signs of significance for the following years. Oil and gas producing regions are mainly in the group of a high industrial production level in
monetary terms, while in 1997 and 1998 they were characterised by the decline in oil and gas prices. This could lead to the decline in production of industrial enterprises of the fuel industry, while decline in output demand was
mainly in the food and light industries, due to the extensive supply of the
products of these industries from outside Kazakhstan. However, in the last
quarter of 2000 results show the positive association of industrial enterprises
experiencing growth with the group of regions of high level of industrial production. This result could be explained by the recovery of enterprises in the
fuel industry.

Growth of prices for the output of industrial enterprises increases the likelihood of this enterprise being located in the region with the highest level of industrial production rather than in the region with a medium level of industrial
production. The results received coincide with the expected ones where the
growth in the price of output would lead to a general increase in industrial
production levels. For the first quarter of 1998, however, the estimation
showed, that industrial enterprises faced a decline in their output prices and
were located in regions with a high level of industrial production. These were
mainly regions specialised in the power industry such as Karaganda and
Eastern Kazakhstan and faced temporary decline in their output prices. Output demand data gave additional evidence of the decline in output demand of
industrial enterprises located in regions with high levels of industrial production during the period of the Russian crisis. The third quarter of 2000 was
characterised by a decline in output demand of industrial enterprises located
in regions with low level of industrial production, which could be a result of the
continuous fall in industrial production, which downgraded regions to low production levels.

The effect of the size of the workforce of industrial enterprises on their location, supports the results obtained from the previous model, where industrial enterprises of larger employment size, tend to achieve production growth or remain stable rather than decline. The results of the current model illustrate the positive effect of a larger workforce of industrial enterprises on their location in regions with a higher level of industrial production, while the probability of such enterprises being located in regions with medium and low levels of industrial production, is very small. Taking into account the results of the previous model, where large-scale industrial enterprises tended to perform better than smaller enterprises, it can be concluded that industrial enterprises with a larger workforce contribute more to the regional level of production than the whole pool of smaller enterprises.

The location specific characteristics of industrial enterprises did not appear to have a constant effect on industrial enterprises location, having changed over some periods. Industrial enterprises located in regions bordering Russia were found to have a high likelihood of belonging to the group of regions with high or medium levels of industrial production, rather than to the group with low levels of industrial production for the period covering 1997, 1998 and the first quarter of 1999. However, results of estimations indicate the opposite effect after the third quarter of 1999, where industrial enterprises located in regions on the border with Russia, were found to have a tendency to belong to regional groups with low levels of industrial production. Despite the Russian crisis in 1998, industrial performance in neighbouring Kazakhstani regions was better than other regions until the first quarter of 1999. However, the negative effect of the Russian crisis came later, when the hardness of the Tenge made Russian goods cheaper, which reduced the level of output of Kazakhstani enterprises due to their low level of competitiveness.

Hydrocarbon regions were in opposite groups to regions on the Russian border over the whole period of estimations. From the second quarter of 1997 until the first quarter of 1999, hydrocarbon regions were in the group of low industrial production. However, from the third quarter of 2000 onward they continuously maintained a level of high industrial production in Kazakhstan.

The fall in oil and gas prices in 1998 and 1999[88] had a negative effect on the state of regions rich with hydrocarbon deposits, whose main source of industrial production is the oil and gas industry. The growth of world hydrocarbon prices in 2000 led the output production of Kazakhstani hydrocarbon enterprises to increase, which kept regional production at a higher level compared to other regions.

The theory of regional economics discussed in Chapter 3 *Regional economics in transition* underlines the proposed reasons for the irrational behaviour of enterprises in transition economies. The main point is the uncertain conditions (Alchian, 1950) of the economy, and the lack of information (Marshall, 1920) required for rational behaviour in the transition period when the economy is transformed into a market economy. Results from the data estimation received demonstrate continuous changes in the behaviour of individual industrial enterprises relative to their individual, industrial and location characteristics, which emphasises the high level of fluctuations in the production activity of enterprises in the search for survival under conditions of uncertainty and lack of information. Despite the volatility of the signs of coefficients of independent variables, both hypotheses presented in this chapter, can be accepted due to the significance of many independent variables over the period of estimations, where the volatility of signs gives additional evidence that transition economies are going through a stage of continuous change. Independent variables were found to be significant in some particular quarters over the period of observation and were interpreted with caution on the basis of national statistics, the facts and economic events of the relevant periods. However, in order to confirm the findings of the study it is necessary to continue this research, which may in future include the extraction of a homogeneous set of industrial enterprises from the database for the panel data estimations.

---

88   BP statistical review of world energy 2002.

Appendix   The representativeness of industrial enterprises in the questionnaire versus National Statistics, %

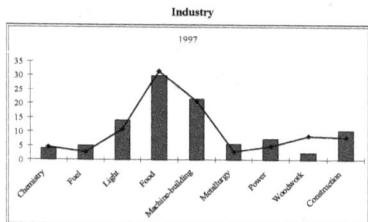

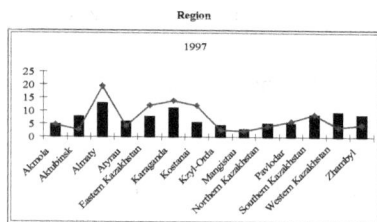

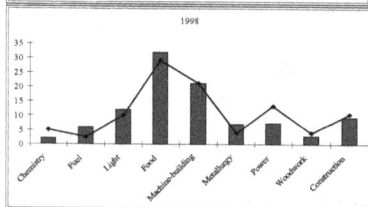

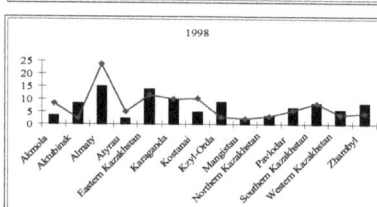

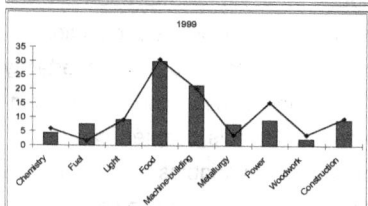

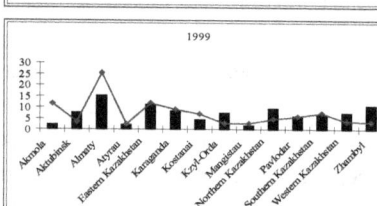

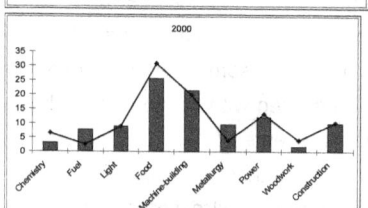

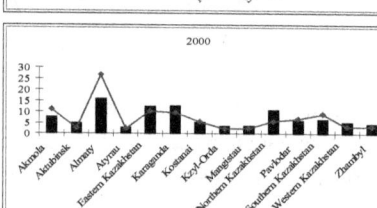

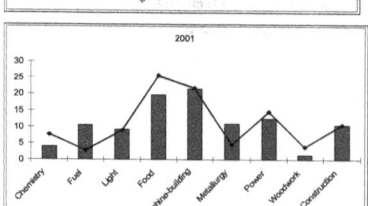

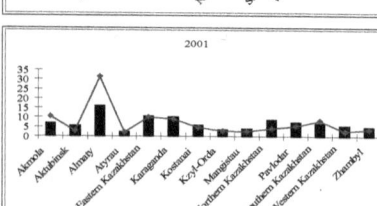

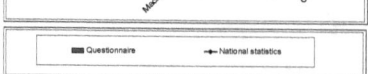

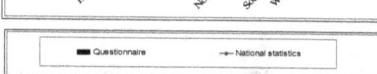

Conclusion

The study first provides an overview of regional economic conditions and spatial concentration problems in terms of industrial development in Kazakhstan during the Soviet period and the first decade of transition. (Chapters 1 *The Development of the Industrial Sector of the Kazakh SSR on the Basis of the Soviet Economic System* and Chapter 2 *The effect of Transition on Regional Development*). It shows that Kazakhstani economic development, to date, has faced structural changes in the economy, which increased the level of centralisation of economic activities, located mainly in the former capital Almaty, Western Kazakhstan (rich with oil and gas) and the gradual growth of economic activities in the new capital Astana. However, industrial growth occurred mainly in Western Kazakhstan and particularly in the hydrocarbon industry, while other industries in these locations gradually deteriorated due to the high competition from imported goods and low levels of investment.

The study investigates the trends of industrial development in the Kazakh SSR as part of the Soviet economy. The investigation of changing patterns of industrial allocation and its performance before and after the collapse of the Soviet Union prepared the background for the analysis of the sectoral and regional influences on firm performance in transition for the case of the Kazakhstani economy. Industries and industrial clusters of the Kazakh SSR were established on the basis of good transport links with other Soviet republics, especially the Russian Federation, while inter-regional connections between industrial enterprises of the Kazakh SSR rarely existed. However, the collapse of the Soviet Union severed the links between its former republics. The whole organising principle of the Soviet economy, which integrated production dispersed across the whole territory of the union into a single economy based on a central plan, suddenly ceased to operate. Consequently, industrial links between former Soviet republics were destroyed, while the market for indigenous products became confined to the local consumers. As such, the demand for the production of Kazakhstani industries significantly fell during transition, while internal links for the local consumption of indigenous production had not been developed during the Soviet period. As a result, the production of all industries of Kazakhstan was substantially reduced, negatively affecting the growth of the Kazakhstani economy.

The study also discusses trends of the changing concentration of industrial sectors in each region of the Kazakh SSR in the Soviet period as well as in the first decade transition. This provided an understanding of the general trend of industrial performance to decline in peripheral regions and to significantly increase in central regions in terms of economic activities. These central regions are the Kazakhstani capitals and regions rich with hydrocarbon deposits, which became the main industrial regions capable of generating of profit for the Kazakhstani economy.

The study represented and analysed models of inter regional factor allocation and growth and attempted to understand how they can be appropriately used for the explanation of location behaviour in transition, particularly with regard to Kazakhstan (Chapter 3 *Regional Economy in Transition*).

Regional development is one of the weakest points of transition economies, which emerged from the centrally planned economy. The collapse of the Soviet Union resulted in the abolition of the centrally planned economy. Newly independent countries faced the problem of maintaining the economy and industrial production without connections to other ex-Soviet republics and central management. Transition economies entered into a period where they were effectively struggling to survive in their effort to move towards a market economy. The regional approach to the market economy is represented in the chapter by the neoclassical one-sector and two-sector models of regional factor allocation and migration, by the disequilibrium model of inter-regional labour migration, where regional factors are freely mobile between regions and by different types and sources of agglomeration economies. All presented models of endogenous growth theory imply that the output growth is attributed to the growth of local factors, such as inputs of the regional specialisation, knowledge and human capital, showing that the endogenous growth can constantly persist based on local factors, even in environment of the market competition. The one-sector model of regional factor allocation and migration and disequilibrium model of inter-regional labour migration show that mobility of factors leads to regional equalisation model. The two-sector model of regional factor allocation and migration is based on the migration of factors in the same direction. However, unlike predictions of the human capital theory and endogenous growth theory, according to the two-sector model the factors migration is directed at the equalisation point of marginal products. Nevertheless, in reality, the process is very slow and the equalisation point can only be reached in the long run, while the short or medium terms are denoted by unbalanced regional development. The human capital migration model and endogenous growth theory imply that capital and labour are moving in the same direction, which results in an unbalanced economy and could lead to the agglomeration diseconomies of scale, particularly in conditions of uncertainty in transition.

Alchian's (1950) concept of uncertainty conditions and Marshall's (1920) key incentives of the agglomeration process indicate that inequalities between regions of transition economies prolong the transition to the market economy and render it more difficult and longer. The new way of the management of enterprises was not the standard example to follow, but every enterprise chose its own way of survival and often followed leading enterprises. Many agglomerations centres, which were created in the Soviet system, were not being able to maintain their structure due to the closure of many factories as a result of the loss of trade links between former Soviet republics. Only several industrial centres were maintained, which happened to be located around the ex-capital Almaty, in the Caspian regions producing oil and gas and the newly developing centre around the new capital Astana.

The chapter concluded that the transition development leads towards the market economy, however, conditions of uncertainty mean that this process will only be completed in the long term. Ex –Soviet countries are in a special position because they are not only changing the system from a socialist to the market economy, but at the same time they learn to live as independent countries and not as part of a giant controlling system. Thus, the special posi-

344 NATALYA SHEVCHIK KETENCI

tion of these countries raises more obstacles to overcome and questions to solve, of which the equal regional development is particularly important.

The analysis of the industrial development of Kazakhstan in the Soviet economy permitted an understanding of the causes of growing disparities on the Kazakhstani inter-regional level in transition. Consequently, the unbalanced development of Kazakhstani regions in the Soviet economy was analysed in the second chapter exploring the effect of industrial decline on the degradation of regional economies. Economic models of regional development in the market economy, which are presented in the third chapter, were analysed on the basis of the background of the Kazakhstani economy that had been provided in previous chapters. This showed that models of inter-regional development in the market economy can not be applicable to the transition economy, where the process of transformation is very slow. Therefore, in order to examine specific characteristics of the inter-regional development of Kazakhstan, it is necessary to make assumptions regarding the uncertain conditions of development in transition. The empirical research was presented in the fourth chapter on the basis of the analysis in previous chapters: on the initial conditions of Kazakhstani economy in the Soviet system; the consequences of Soviet planning for the unbalanced development of Kazakhstani regions in transition and the evaluation of possible applicable models of the inter-regional development under conditions of uncertainty.

The empirical study of the research is based on the mixture of a data of national statistics and questionnaires from a survey on individual Kazakhstani industrial enterprises, in order to analyse the relationship between firm performance and the interregional structure of the economy.

The study develops a simple theoretical framework, in order to allow the microeconomic effects of geographical location on transition behaviour to be tested, in addition to the effects of non-spatial firm characteristics. The theoretical framework is based on the production function of the firm, which captures the relationship between a firm's performance and its industrial and regional characteristics, with further transformation of the production function into the multinomial logit framework. This type of theoretical model is used in order to provide the justification for the multinomial modelling approach, where firm performance indicators are introduced by qualitative response variables.

Econometric estimations are conducted for every quarter where the set of industrial enterprises differs across all quarters, while the distribution of the set of their characteristics is analogous for every quarter. The cross-section estimations for 20 chronological quarters permitted the estimation of the general tendency of production performance of Kazakhstani industrial enterprises in connection with their individual, industrial and location characteristics.

Two hypotheses were introduced in the study. The *first hypothesis* states that the performance of Kazakhstani industrial enterprises in terms of their production growth depends on the set of enterprises characteristics, such as individual, industrial and location. The *second hypothesis* suggests the association of characteristics of Kazakhstani industrial enterprises with their location, testing to what extent characteristics of industrial enterprises in transition economies are statistically different for different locations.

The test of both hypothesises employed the logit framework. The multinomial logit estimations of the *first hypothesis* were conducted in order to examine characteristics of industrial enterprises that are likely to perform production growth. The multinomial logit estimations of the *second hypothesis* were conducted to explore characteristics of industrial enterprises located in regions of high level of the industrial production.

The results of testing the *first hypothesis* demonstrate that the *growth* in production is more likely to be observed in Kazakhstani industrial enterprises, which present the following comparative characteristics: a larger workforce, a low level of industrial concentration of the industry that an enterprise is a part of, and the location of an enterprise in regions of low industrial specialisation, with low growth of regional employment and which is far from the ex-capital Almaty city. The production with *no changes* is most likely to occur in industrial enterprises owned or partially owned by the state and a comparatively small workforce in enterprises, while regional industrial employment is experiencing low growth. However, the concentration of particular industries is most likely to be higher than that of industries where the output of enterprises fluctuates. Finally, the *decline* in production was mostly detected in industrial enterprises with a smaller workforce, but under conditions of high growth of regional industrial employment, commonly in regions located closer to the new capital with high industrial concentration, but with a low level of industrial production compared to other regions.

The results of testing the *second hypothesis* show that regions with a *high level of industrial production* are generally associated with industrial enterprises of higher order of ownership in terms of market orientation, such as private and joint stock enterprises. The high level of industrial production of regions is also associated with industrial enterprises that have a larger workforce and with growing demand for their output. The Almaty region was found to be highly associated with a high level of industrial production across all quarters except the beginning of 1997, where the turmoil of privatisation may have affected industrial production. Until 1999, regions located on the Russian border were found to be associated with a high level of industrial production. However, since 1999, the Russian financial crisis (1998) changed this pattern and regions located on the border with Russia started to be strongly associated with regions with a low level of industrial production. Hydrocarbon regions were found to be highly dependent on external effects such as variations in world oil and gas prices. Thus, these regions were found to be highly associated with a high level of industrial production only since the third quarter of 2000 when world oil and gas prices started to rise.

Regions with a low level of industrial production were found to be strongly associated with enterprises located in the new capital region - Astana, where investment was highly concentrated on the construction of the city using of foreign companies, while local industrial enterprises can not compete with higher quality imported goods.

The results of the data estimation demonstrate continuous changes in the behaviour of individual industrial enterprises relative to its individual, industrial and location characteristics, which proves their irrational behaviour in the search for survival under conditions of uncertainty and lack of information for the rational behaviour. Despite of volatility of signs of coefficients of independent variables, both hypotheses advanced in the study, can be accepted due to the strong significance of many independent variables over the period of estimations, where the volatility of signs constitutes additional evidence that transition economies are in the state of continuous changes.

The database employed in the study gives numerous opportunities for conducting new research on Kazakhstani industrial enterprises. It is also possible to continue and extend the research already started, which is presented in this study. The current research had certain limitations, which would not need to apply to a more extended study. The different set of enterprises employed for every quarter of estimations could negatively affect the fluctuation of obtained signs of estimated coefficients and variations in their significance. Therefore, future research could be focused on the filtering of the set of industrial enterprises for creating the panel data, estimations of which could give results that are more solid.

Bibliography

A. Alchian, "Uncertainty, Evolution and Economic Theory", *Journal of Political Economy* 58 (1950): 211-221.

A. Andersen, "Professional'noe obuchenie ot Arthur Andersen," *Al-Pari* 3-4 (2000).

A. E. Esentugelov, *Institucionalnye i strukturnye izmeneniia v Kazakhstanskoi ekonomike* (Almaty: Ministry of Economy of Kazakhstan, Research Institute of the Economy and Market Relations, 1994).

A. Epbaeva, "Investitsionnye vozmozhnosti Kazakhstanskikh regionov," *Economics and Statistics* 4 (2001): 32-38.

A. Koshanov, "Kadry nauki: vyzhivanie i preemstvennost'," *Al-Pari* 3-4 (2000).

A. Koshanov, M. Isaeva and A. Yesentugelov, eds., *Economika regiona v usloviyakh perekhoda k rynku* (Almaty: Natsionalnaia Akademiia Nauk Respubliki Kazakhstan Ministerstvo Ekonomiki Respubliki Kazakhstan, 1993).

A. Marshall, *Principles of Economics* (London: Macmillan, 1920).

A. Peck, *Economic Development in Kazakhstan: The Role Of Large Enterprises And Foreign Investment* (London: RutledgeCurzon, 2003).

A. Smith, "Regulation Theory, Strategies of Enterprise Integration and the Political Economy of Regional Economic Restructuring in Central and Eastern Europe: The Case of Slovakia," *Regional Studies* 29:8 (1995): 761-772.

A. Smith, *Reconstructing the Regional Economy* (Cheltenham: Edward Elgar, 1998).

A. Tokbergen, G. Sulejmenova and P. Turegeldieva, "O prichinakh sokhraneniia ubytochnosti predpriiatii v Kazakhstane," *Al-Pari* 1 (1998): 46-48.

Academy of Science, Institute of Economics, *Ocherki ekonomicheskoi istorii Kazakhskoi SSR* (Alma-Ata: Galym, 1974).

Academy of Science, Institute of Economics, *Regional'naya politika Respubliki Kazakhstan: Ekonomicheskii mekhanizm realizatsii* (Almaty: Galym, 1998)

Academy of sciences, Institute of economics, *Effektivnost' regionalnoi ekonomiki Kazakhstana* (Almaty: Nauka, 1977).

B. Atamkulov, M. Isenov, "Svet i teni investitsionnoi politiki," *Al-Pari*. (1998).

B. Bajtanaeva, "Gosudarstvennaia podderzhka razvitiia predprinimatelstva v Kazakhstane," *Al-Pari* 6 (2000): 19-22.

B. Ohlin, *Interregional and International Trade* (Cambridge: Harvard University Press, 1933).

British Petroleum Statistical Review of World Energy 2002.

C. Friedrich, *Alfred Weber's Theory of the Location of Industries,* (Chicago: University of Chicago Press, 1929).

Central Statistical Department of USSR, *Ekonomika Sovetskogo Soiuza v 1980 gody,* (Moscow: Financy i Statistika, 1981).

D. Kunaev, *O moem vremeni* (Almaty: Deuir and Yntymak, 1992).

E. Böventer, "Regional Growth Theory", *Urban Studies* 12:1 (1975): 1-29.

E. Maskin and C. Xu, "Soft Budget Constraint Theories: From Centralization to the Market," *Economics of Transition* 9:1 (2001): 1-27.

E.K. Smirnickii, *Ekonomicheskie pokazateli promyshlennosti* (Moscow: Ekonomika, 1980).

E.M. Hoover, *Location Theory and the Shoe and Leather Industries* (Cambridge: Harvard University Press, 1937).

E.M. Hoover, *The Location of Economic Activity* (New York: McGraw-Hill, 1948).

Ekonomicheskaia Enciklopediia, *Promyshlennost' i stroitel'stvo – 3* (Moskva: Sovetskaia Enciklopediia, 1965).

Ekonomicheskaia Entsiklopediia, *Promyshlennost' i stroitel'stvo – 1* (Moskva: Sovetskaia Entsiklopediia, 1962).

Ekonomicheskoe razvitie Kazakhskoi SSR (Alma-Ata: Kazakhskoe Gossudarstvennoe Izdatel'stvo, 1960).

Ekonomika Kazakhstana za 60 let: 1917-1977 (Alma-Ata: Nauka, 1977).

F.H. Hahn, "Equilibrium with Transactions Costs," *Econometrica* 39:3 (1971): 417-439.

G. Ellison and E.L. Glaeser, "Geographic Concentration and in US Manufacturing Industries: A Dartboard Approach," *Journal of Political Economy* 105 (1997): 889-927.

G. Gorzelak, *The Regional Dimension of Transformation in Central Europe* (London: Jessica Kingsley, 1996).

G. Myrdal, *Economic Theory and Underdeveloped Regions* (London, Duckworth, 1957).

G. Petrakos, "Patterns of Regional Inequality in Transition Economies," *European Planning Studies* 9:3 (2001).

G.A. Kaliev, *Agrarnye problemy na rubezhe vekov.* (Almaty, 2003).

G.G. Judge, *The Theory and Practice of Econometrics* (New York: John Wiley and Sons, 1985).

G.H. Borts and J.L. Stein, *Economic Growth in a Free Market* (New York: Columbia University Press, 1964).

G.S. Becker, *Human Capital: A Theoretical and Empirical Analysis with Special Reference to Education* (Chicago: Chicago University Press, 1964).

I. Dauranov, A. Shishkina, A. Rudeckikh, E. Shiyanova and N. Ivanova, "Malyi biznes: problemy oformleniia kredita," *Al-Pari* 5 (2000).

International Monetary Fund, *Economic Review Kazakhstan* (Washington, D.C: International Monetary Fund, 1992).

J. Bachtler and R. Downes, "Regional Policy in the Transition Countries: A Comparative Assesment", *European Planning Studies* 7:6 (1999).

J. Bachtler, "Regional problems and Policies in Central and Eastern Europe", *Regional Studies*, 27:7 (1992): 665-671.

J. Gaspar and E.L. Glaeser, "Information Technology and the Future of Cities," *Journal of Urban Economics* 43 (1998): 136-156.

J. Kornai, "From Socialism to Capitalism: What is meant by the "Change of System," *The Social Market Foundation, Centre for Post-Collectivist Studies* (June 1998).

J. Kornai, *Economics of Shortage* (Amsterdam: North-Holland, 1980).

J. Kornai, *The Socialist System: The Political Economy of Communism* (London: Clarendon Press, 1992).

J.G. Saushkin, "Economic Geography in the U.S.S.R," *Economic Geography* 38:1 (1962): 28-37.

J.S.L. McCombie and A.P. Thirlwall, *Economic Growth and the Balance-of-Payments Constraints* (Basingstoke: Macmillan, 1994).

K.S. Lee, "A model of intraurban employment location: an application to Bogota, Colombia," *Journal of Urban Economics* 12 (1982): 263-279.

K.S. Lee, "A model of intraurban employment location: estimation results from Seoul data," *Journal of Urban Economics* 27 (1990): 60-72.

Kazakhstani Academy of sciences, *Dolgostrochnyi prognoz razvitiia promyshlenykh otraslei* (Almaty: Nauka, 1976).

L.A. Sjaastad, "The costs and returns of human migration," *Urban and Regional Economics* (1991): 263-76.

M. B. Olcott, *The Kazakhs* (Stanford, California: Hoover Institution Press, Stanford University, 1995).

M. E. Porter, *The Competitive Advantage of Nations* (New York: Free Press, 1990).

M. Ellman, "The Fundamental Problem of Socialist Planning," *Oxford Economic Papers* 30:2 (July 1978): 249-262.

M. Ellman, "The Use of Input-Output in Regional Economic Planning: The Soviet Experience," *The Economic Journal* 78:312 (December 1968): 855-867.

M. Fujita, *Urban Economic Theory* (Cambridge University Press: Cambridge,1989).

M. Kaser, *The Economies of Kazakstan and Uzbekistan*, (London: The Royal Institute of International Affairs, 1997).

M. Lavigne, *The Economics of Transition: From Socialist Economy to Market Economy* (London: Macmillan Press Ltd, 1999).

M. Myant, "Transforming the Czech and Slovak Economies: Evidence at the District Level," *Regional Studies* 29:8 (1995): 753-760.

M.B. Kenzheguzin and M.G. Isaeva, eds., *Regionalnaia politika respubliki Kazakhstan: Ekonomicheskii mekhanizm realizatsii* (Almaty: Ministerstvo nauki – Akademiia nauk Respubliki Kazakhstan, Institut Ekonomiki, 1998).

M.B. Olcott, *Kazakhstan: Unfulfilled Promise* (Washington, D.C: Carnegie Endowmnet for International Peace, 2002).

Ministry of Economy of Kazakhstan, Academy of Sciences, Institute of Economics, *Regional'naia ekonomika v perekhodnom periode* (Almaty, 1993).

Ministry of Economy of Kazakhstan, Research Institute of the Economy and Market Relations, *Razvitie ekonomicheskogo kompleksa Kazakhstana v perekhodnom periode* (Almaty, 1994).

Ministry of Economy of Kazakhstan. Research Institute of the economy and market relations, *Ekonomika Kazakhstana na puti ustanovleniia i progressa* (Almaty, 1994).

N. Amrekulov and N. Masanov, *Kazakhstan Mezhdu Proshlym i Budushchim* (Almaty, 1994).

N. Masanov, *Kochevaia Tsivilizatsiia Kazakhov* (Almaty: Socinvest; Moscow: Horizont; 1995).

N. Wrigley, *Categorical Data Analysis for Geographers and Environmental Scientists* (London: Longman, 1985).

National Academy of science of Kazakhstan, Institute of Economics, *Issledovatel'skii otchet: Ekonomicheskii mekhanizm territorial'nogo razvitiia respubliki Kazakhstan i ego differentsiatsiia po regionam* (Almaty, 1995).

National Statistical Agency of Kazakhstan, *Ekonomika Kazakhskoi SSR v 1968* (Almaty, 1970).

National Statistical Agency of Kazakhstan, *Ekonomika Kazakhskoi SSR* (Almaty, 1968).

National Statistical Agency of Kazakhstan, *Kazakhstan i drugie strany* (Almaty: Kazinformtsentr, 1993).

National Statistical Agency of Kazakhstan, *Kazakhstan i strany SNG, 2001* (Almaty, 2002).

National Statistical Agency of Kazakhstan, *Kazakhstan v tsifrakh* (Almaty, 1987).

National Statistical Agency of Kazakhstan, *Kazakhstan: 1991-2001* (Almaty, 2001).

National Statistical Agency of Kazakhstan, *Kazakhstan: 1991-2002* (Almaty, 2002).

National Statistical Agency of Kazakhstan, *Kazakhstanu 40 let, 1960* (Almaty, 1961).

National Statistical Agency of Kazakhstan, *Narodnoe xoziaistvo Kazakhskoi SSR za 25 let* (Alma-Ata, 1945).

National Statistical Agency of Kazakhstan, *Narodnoe xoziaistvo Kazakhstana za 70 let* (Alma-Ata, 1990).

National Statistical Agency of Kazakhstan, *Narodnoe xoziaistvo Kazakhskoi SSR* (Almaty,1987).

National Statistical Agency of Kazakhstan, *Promyshlennost Kazakhstana:*
1920-1999 goda (Almaty, 2000).
National Statistical Agency of Kazakhstan, *Promyshlennost' Kazakhstana i*
ego regionov: 1998-1999 goda (Almaty, 2000).
National Statistical Agency of Kazakhstan, *Promyshlennost' Kazakhstana i*
ego regionov: 1998-2001 goda (Almaty, 2002).
National Statistical Agency of Kazakhstan, *Promyshlennost' Kazakhstana:*
1990, 1995-1998 goda (Almaty, 1999).
National Statistical Agency of Kazakhstan, *Promyshlennost' Kazakhstana:*
1990-1997 goda (Almaty, 1998).
National Statistical Agency of Kazakhstan, *Regiony Kazakhstana - 1995* (Almaty, 1996).
National Statistical Agency of Kazakhstan, *Regiony Kazakhstana - 1996* (Almaty, 1997).
National Statistical Agency of Kazakhstan, *Regiony Kazakhstana - 1997* (Almaty, 1998).
National Statistical Agency of Kazakhstan, *Regiony Kazakhstana - 1998* (Almaty, 1999).
National Statistical Agency of Kazakhstan, *Regiony Kazakhstana – 1991* (Almaty, 1992).
National Statistical Agency of Kazakhstan, *Regiony Kazakhstana – 2001* (Almaty, 2002).
National Statistical Agency of Kazakhstan, *Regiony Kazakhstana: 1991-1997*
(Almaty 1998).
National Statistical Agency of Kazakhstan, *Regiony Kazakhstana: 1995-1998*
(Almaty, 1999).
National Statistical Agency of Kazakhstan, *Regiony Kazakhstana: 1996-1999*
(Almaty, 2000).
National Statistical Agency of Kazakhstan, *Regiony Kazakhstana: 1997-2000*
(Almaty, 2001).
National Statistical Agency of Kazakhstan, *Sotsial'no-ekonomicheskoe poloz-*
henie Kazakhstana - 1998 (Almaty, December 1999).
National Statistical Agency of Kazakhstan, *Sotsial'no-ekonomicheskoe poloz-*
henie Kazakhstana - 1999 (Almaty, December 2000).

National Statistical Agency of Kazakhstan, *Sotsial'no-ekonomicheskoe polozhenie Kazakhstana - 2000* (Almaty, December 2001).

National Statistical Agency of Kazakhstan, *Statistical Yearbook of Kazakhstan – 1991* (Almaty, 1992).

National Statistical Agency of Kazakhstan, *Statistical Yearbook of Kazakhstan – 1992* (Almaty, 1993).

National Statistical Agency of Kazakhstan, *Statistical Yearbook of Kazakhstan – 1995* (Almaty, 1996).

National Statistical Agency of Kazakhstan, *Statistical Yearbook of Kazakhstan – 1996* (Almaty, 1997).

National Statistical Agency of Kazakhstan, *Statistical Yearbook of Kazakhstan – 1997* (Almaty, 1998).

National Statistical Agency of Kazakhstan, *Statistical Yearbook of Kazakhstan – 2000* (Almaty, 2001).

National Statistical Agency of Kazakhstan, *Statistical Yearbook of Kazakhstan - 2001* (Almaty, 2002).

P. Desai, "Soviet Growth Retardation", *The American Economic Review* 76:2 (May 1986): 175-180.

P. Hanson and M. Bradshaw, eds., *Regional Economic Change in Russia* (Cheltenham: Edward Elgar, 2000).

P. Krugman, *Geography and Trade* (Cambridge: MIT Press, 1991).

P. McCann, "Journey and Transactions Frequency: An Alternative Explanation of Rent-Gradient Convexity," *Urban Studies* 32:9 (1995): 1549-1557.

P. McCann, *The Economics of Industrial Location: A Logistics-Costs Approach* (Heidelberg: Springer, 1998).

P. McCann, *Urban and Regional Economics* (Oxford: Oxford University Press, 2001).

P. Romer, "Growth Based on Increasing Returns due to Specialisation," *The American Economic Review* 77:2 (May 1987): 56-62.

P. Romer, "Increasing Returns and Long-Run Growth," *The Journal of Political Economy* 94:5 (October 1986): 1002-1037.

P.E. Graves, "Migration and Climate," *Journal of Regional Science* 20:2 (1980): 227-37.

R. E. Ericson, "The Classical Soviet-Type Economy: Nature of the System and Implications for Reform," *The Journal of Economic Perspectives* 5:4 (1991): 11-27.

R. Pomfret, *Asian Economies in Transition: Reforming Centrally Planned Economies* (Cheltenham: Edward Elgar, 1996).

R. Pomfret, *The Economies of Central Asia* (Princeton, NJ: Princeton University Press, 1995).

R.E. Lucas, "On the Mechanics of Economic Development," *Journal of Monetary Economics* 22 (1988): 3-42.

R.J. Barro and X. Sala-i-Martin, "Convergence across States and regions," *Brookings Papers on Economic Activity* 1 (1991): 107-182.

R.J. Barro and X. Sala-i-Martin, "Convergence", *Journal of Political Economy* 100 (1992): 223-251.

R.M. Solow, "A Contribution to the Theory of Economic Growth," *Quarterly Journal of Economics* 70 (1956): 65-94.

S. Kashikov, *Struktura i rost natsional'nogo dokhoda* (Almaty: Kazakhstan, 1976).

S. Kittiprapas and P. McCann, "Industrial Location Behaviour and Regional Restructuring within the Fifth 'Tiger' Economy: Evidence from the Thai Electronics Industry," *Applied Economics* 31:1 (1999): 35-49.

S. Primbetov, "Tsentral'naia Aziia na puti integratsii," *Al-Pari* 4 (1997): 14-16.

S.S. Artobolevsky, *Regional Policy in Europe* (London: Jessica Kingsley, 1997).

Sovetskii Soiuz – Kazakhstan (Moscow: Mysl',1970).

T.A. Esirkepov, *Privatizatsiia gosudarstvennoi sobstvennosti v Respublike Kazakhstan v usloviiakh perekhoda k rynku* (Almaty: University Turan, 1999).

The Central Statistical Agency of the Soviet Union, *Narodnoe xoziaistvo SSSR v 1970* (Moscow, 1971).

The Central Statistical Agency of the Soviet Union, *Narodnoe xozyajstvo SSSR v 1980* (Moscow, 1981).

U. Bajmuratov, *Natsionalnaya Ekonomicheskaia Sistema,* (Almaty: Galym, 2000).

UNDP, "Central Asia 2010: Prospects for human development," *Regional Bureau for Europe and the CIS*, September 1999

V.A. Adamchuk and B.Y. Dvoskin, *Problemy razvitiia promyshlennykh uzlov SSSR, ispolzuia primer Kazakhstana*, (Moscow: Mysl, 1968).

V.A. Ermakov, *Kazakhstan v sovremennom mire* (Almaty, 2001).

W. Andreff, "Twenty Lessons from the Experience of Privatisation in Transition Economies," in Y. Kalyuzhnova and W. Andreff eds., *Privatisation and Structural Change in Transition Economies* (Houndmills, Basingstoke, Hampshire: Palgrave, 2003), 29-59.

W. Leontief, "The trouble with Cuban socialism," *New York Review of Books* (January 1971): 20.

Y. Kalyuzhnova et al., eds., *Energy in the Caspian Region: Present and Future.* (London: Palgrave, 2002).

Y. Kalyuzhnova, "Kazakhstan. 1999-2000. Tributaire. Du Petrole," *Le Courrier Des Pays De l'Est* 1010 (November-December 2000): 55-67.

Y. Kalyuzhnova, "Privatisation and Structural Reforms: Case study Kazakhstan," in Y. Kalyuzhnova and W. Andreff, eds., *Privatisation and Structural Change in Transition Economies* (Houndmills, Basingstoke, Hampshire: Palgrave Macmillan, 2003), 158-179.

Y. Kalyuzhnova, "Privatisation in Kazakhstan – an Overview," *Economic Trends, Kazakhstan (*TACIS Brussels: April-June 1999).

Y. Kalyuzhnova, *The Kazakhstani Economy: Independence and Transition* (London: Macmillan Press, 1998).

Y. Qian and G. Roland, "Federalism and the Soft Budget Constraint," *The American Economic Review* 88:5 (December 1998): 1143-1162.

Y. Qian, "A Theory of Shortage in Socialist Economies Based on the "Soft Budget Constraint," *The American Economic Review* 84:1 (1994): 145-156.

SOVIET AND POST-SOVIET POLITICS AND SOCIETY

Edited by Dr. Andreas Umland

ISSN 1614-3515

Martin Friessnegg
Das Problem der Medienfreiheit in Russland
seit dem Ende der Sowjetunion
ISBN 3-89821-588-1

Nikolaj Nikiforowitsch Borobow
Führende Persönlichkeiten in Russland vom
12. bis 20. Jhd.: Ein Lexikon
Aus dem Russischen übersetzt und herausgegeben von
Eberhard Schneider
ISBN 3-89821-638-1

Martin Malek, Anna Schor-Tschudnowskaja
Tschetschenien und die Gleichgültigkeit
Europas
Russlands Kriege und die Agonie der Idee der
Menschenrechte
ISBN 3-89821-676-4

Andreas Langenohl
Political Culture and Criticism of Society
Intellectual Articulations in Post-Soviet Russia
ISBN 3-89821-709-4

Thomas Borén
Meeting Places in Transformation
ISBN 3-89821-739-6

Lars Löckner
Sowjetrussland in der Beurteilung der
Emigrantenzeitung 'Rul', 1920-1924
ISBN 3-89821-741-8

Ekaterina Taratuta
The Red Line of Construction
Semantics and Mythology of a Siberian Heliopolis
ISBN 3-89821-742-6

Bernd Kappenberg
Zeichen setzen für Europa
Der Gebrauch europäischer lateinischer Sonderzeichen
in der deutschen Öffentlichkeit
ISBN 3-89821-749-3

*Siegbert Klee, Martin Sandhop, Oxana
Schwajka, Andreas Umland*
Elitenbildung in der Postsowjetischen
Ukraine
ISBN 978-389821-829-0

Quotes from reviews of SPPS volumes:

On vol. 1 – *The Implementation of the ECHR in Russia*: "Full of examples, experiences and valuable observations which could provide the basis for new strategies."
Diana Schmidt, *Неприкосновенный запас*, 2005

On vol. 2 – *Putins Russland*: "Wipperfürth draws attention to little known facts. For instance, the Russians have still more positive feelings towards Germany than to any other non-Slavic country."
Oldag Kaspar, *Süddeutsche Zeitung, 2005*

On vol. 3 – *Die Übernahme internationalen Rechts in die russische Rechtsordnung*: "Hussner's is an interesting, detailed and, at the same time, focused study which deals with all relevant aspects and contains insights into contemporary Russian legal thought."
Herbert Küpper, *Jahrbuch für Ostrecht, 2005*

On vol. 5 – *Квадратные метры, определяющие сознание*: „Meerovich provides a study that will be of considerable value to housing specialists and policy analysts."
Christina Varga-Harris, *Slavic Review, 2006*

On vol. 6 – *New Directions in Russian International Studies*: "A helpful step in the direction of an overdue dialogue between Western and Russian IR scholarly communities."
Diana Schmidt, *Europe-Asia Studies, 2006*

On vol. 8 – *Nation-Building and Minority Politics in Post-Socialist States*: "Galbreath's book is an admirable and craftsmanlike piece of work, and should be read by all specialists interested in the Baltic area."
Andrejs Plakans, *Slavic Review, 2007*

On vol. 9 – *Народы Кавказа в Вооружённых силах СССР*: "In this superb new book, Bezugolnyi skillfully fashions an accurate and candid record of how and why the Soviet Union mobilized and employed the various ethnic groups in the Caucasus region in the Red Army's World War II effort."
David J. Glantz, *Journal of Slavic Military Studies, 2006*

On vol. 10 – *Русское Национальное Единство*: "Pribylovskii's and Likhachev's work is likely to remain the definitive study of the Russian National Unity for a very long time."
Mischa Gabowitsch, *e-Extreme, 2006*

On vol. 13 – *The Politicization of Russian Orthodoxy*: "Mitrofanova's book is a fascinating study which raises important questions about the type of national ideology that will come to predominate in the new Russia."
Zoe Knox, *Europe-Asia Studies, 2006*

On vol. 14 – *Aleksandr Solzhenitsyn and the Modern Russo-Jewish Question*: "Larson has written a well-balanced survey of Solzhenitsyn's writings on Russian-Jewish relations."
Nikolai Butkevich, *e-Extreme, 2006*

On vol. 16 – *Der russische Sonderweg?*: "Luks's remarkable knowledge of the history of this wide territory from the Elbe to the Pacific Ocean and his life experience give his observations a particular sharpness and his judgements an exceptional weight."

Peter Krupnikow, *Mitteilungen aus dem baltischen Leben*, 2006

On vol. 17 – *История «Мёртвой воды»*: "Moroz provides one of the best available surveys of Russian neo-paganism."

Mischa Gabowitsch, *e-Extreme*, 2006

On vol. 18 – *Этническая и религиозная интолерантность в российских СМИ*: "A constructive contribution to a crucial debate about media-endorsed intolerance which has once again flared up in Russia."

Mischa Gabowitsch, *e-Extreme*, 2006

On vol. 25 – *The Ghosts in Our Classroom*: "Freyberg-Inan's well-researched and incisive monograph, balanced and informed about Romanian education in general, should be required reading for those Eurocrats who have shaped Romanian spending priorities since 2000."

Tom Gallagher, *Slavic Review*, 2006

On vol. 26 – *The 2002 Dubrovka and 2004 Beslan Hostage Crises*: "Dunlop's analysis will help to draw Western attention to the plight of those who have suffered by these terrorist acts, and the importance, for all Russians, of uncovering the truth of about what happened."

Amy Knight, *Times Literary Supplement*, 2006

On vol. 29 – *Zivilgesellschaftliche Einflüsse auf die Orange Revolution*: „Strasser's study constitutes an outstanding empirical analysis and well-grounded location of the subject within theory."

Heiko Pleines, *Osteuropa*, 2006

On vol. 34 – *Postsowjetische Feiern*: "Mühlfried's book contains not only a solid ethnographic study, but also points at some problems emerging from Georgia's prevalent understanding of culture."

Godula Kosack, *Anthropos*, 2007

On vol. 35 – *Fascism Past and Present, West and East*: "Committed students will find much of interest in these sometimes barbed exchanges."

Robert Paxton, *Journal of Global History*, 2007

On vol. 37 – *Political Anti-Semitism in Post-Soviet Russia*: "Likhachev's book serves as a reliable compendium and a good starting point for future research on post-Soviet xenophobia and ultra-nationalist politics, with their accompanying anti-Semitism."

Kathleen Mikkelson, *Demokratizatsiya*, 2007

Series Subscription

Please enter my subscription to the series *Soviet and Post-Soviet Politics and Society*, ISSN 1614-3515, as follows:

❏ complete series   OR   ❏ English-language titles
                                         ❏ German-language titles
                                         ❏ Russian-language titles

starting with
❏ volume # 1
❏ volume # ___
   ❏ please also include the following volumes: #___, ___, ___, ___, ___, ___, ___
   ❏ the next volume being published
   ❏ please also include the following volumes: #___, ___, ___, ___, ___, ___, ___

❏ 1 copy per volume   OR   ❏ ___ copies per volume

Subscription within Germany:

You will receive every volume at 1st publication at the regular bookseller's price – incl. s & h and VAT.
Payment:
❏ Please bill me for every volume.
❏ Lastschriftverfahren: Ich/wir ermächtige(n) Sie hiermit widerruflich, den Rechnungsbetrag je Band von meinem/unserem folgendem Konto einzuziehen.

Kontoinhaber: _____Kreditinstitut: _____
Kontonummer: _____Bankleitzahl:_____

International Subscription:

Payment (incl. s & h and VAT) in advance for
❏ 10 volumes/copies (€ 319.80) ❏ 20 volumes/copies (€ 599.80)
❏ 40 volumes/copies (€ 1,099.80)
Please send my books to:

NAME_____DEPARTMENT_____
ADDRESS _____
POST/ZIP CODE_____COUNTRY _____
TELEPHONE _____EMAIL_____

date/signature_____

A hint for librarians in the former Soviet Union: Your academic library might be eligible to receive free-of-cost scholarly literature from Germany via the German Research Foundation. For Russian-language information on this program, see
      http://www.dfg.de/forschungsfoerderung/formulare/download/12_54.pdf.

Please fax to: **0511 / 262 2201 (+49 511 262 2201)**
or mail to: *ibidem*-Verlag, Julius-Leber-Weg 11, D-30457 Hannover,Germany
or send an e-mail: ibidem@ibidem-verlag.de

ibidem-Verlag

Melchiorstr. 15

D-70439 Stuttgart

info@ibidem-verlag.de

www.ibidem-verlag.de
www.ibidem.eu
www.edition-noema.de
www.autorenbetreuung.de

www.ingramcontent.com/pod-product-compliance
Lightning Source LLC
Chambersburg PA
CBHW070545270326
41926CB00013B/2213